Delivering New Homes

Unless Recalled Earlier

DATE DUE

Delivering New Homes

Processes, planners and providers

Matthew Carmona, Sarah Carmona and Nick Gallent

 Routledge
Taylor & Francis Group

LONDON AND NEW YORK

First published 2003 by Routledge
11 New Fetter Lane, London EC4P 4EE

Simultaneously published in the USA and Canada
by Routledge
29 West 35th Street, New York, NY 10001

Routledge is an imprint of the Taylor & Francis Group

© 2003 Matthew Carmona, Sarah Carmona and Nick Gallent

Typeset in Akzidenz Grotesk by Keystroke, Jacaranda Lodge, Wolverhampton
Printed and bound in Great Britain by TJ International Ltd, Padstow, Cornwall

British Library Cataloguing in Publication Data
A catalogue record for this book is available from the British Library

Library of Congress Cataloging in Publication Data
Carmona, Matthew.
    Delivering new homes: processes, planners and providers/
    Matthew Carmona, Sarah Carmona and Nick Gallent.
        p. cm.
    Includes bibliographical references and index.
    ISBN 0–415–27924–0 (hardcover : alk. paper) –
    ISBN 0–415–27925–9 (pbk. : alk. paper)
    1. Housing–England.   2. Housing–Great Britain.
    3. Land use–England–Planning.   I. Carmona, Sarah.   II. Gallent, Nick.
    III. Title.
    HD7334.A3 C37 2003
    333.33′8′0941–dc21   2002152029

ISBN 0–415–27924–0 (hbk)
ISBN 0–415–27925–9 (pbk)

Contents

List of figures

List of tables

Preface

The purpose and scope of this book

The broad purpose of this book is to examine the processes and relationships that underpin the delivery of new homes across the United Kingdom. Its focus, however, is primarily on the land use planning system in England, the way that housing providers engage with that system, and how those processes of engagement are changing or might change in the future.

This analysis of what might be considered best practice draws on research undertaken by the authors in 2000/2001 and published as *Working Together, A Guide for Planners and Housing Providers* (Carmona *et al.*, 2001). The present book significantly extends the remit of the earlier work in an attempt to address fundamental questions about the way new housing is delivered in the UK, both by raising questions about how the system in early 2003 works, and – whilst anticipating changes instigated by the 2003 Planning and Compulsory Purchase Act – proposing solutions in order to move practice forward.

It is clear that the value, purpose and contribution of the planning system is recognised by all involved in the delivery of new homes, but that great frustration continues to exist on all sides about how in detail the constituent processes have been operating. In proposing often evolutionary, and sometimes more radical proposals for change, this book makes a contribution to finding a better way of delivering the new homes that the nation increasingly needs.

The book structure

The book itself has three parts. The first part examines the three key processes – planning, market and social house building – that underpin the delivery of new homes in Britain. Chapter 2 examines the nature of the planning process and focuses on who has a role in the way the system operates. It also considers the motivations and constraints of those who engage with planning, together with the purpose of this system in relation to housebuilding. Chapters 3 and 4 deal with the mechanics of housing delivery, exploring first, the general principles and operation of the private housing development process, and second, the changing mode of delivery for social housing.

In the second part of the book, the processes are brought together to explore the key areas of interaction between planning (mainly local development planning) and the providers of social and market housing. This is done by way of the range of tensions that have consistently dogged those interactions. The six chapters contained in this part mix general discussion with material drawn from a national survey of stakeholder views undertaken in 2000 involving 50 planning authorities, 50 private housebuilders and 50 Registered Social Landlords throughout England. The chapters focus on land, and the way sites are identified and allocated for new housing; on time delays, which are a frequent cause of tension between planners and providers; on the discretionary and political nature of local planning; on design and its growing importance in all development debates; on the extraction of gain from development value; and finally, on the lack of coordination between planning and other areas of the local government remit. Together, these chapters combine to form a complete picture of the relationship shared by planners and housing providers.

Parts One and Two of the book provide a comprehensive analysis of the housing–planning interface, and many of the key debates facing practitioners and policy-makers at the start of the twenty-first century. The book also has a strong practical remit and in Part Three the discussion moves on to explore strategies for building better planner–provider relationships in the future, based on a more effective and efficient planning process.

The third part of the book therefore concentrates on solutions. How can the problems of the current framework and system be minimised, and can clear paths through the minefield of problems discussed in Part Two be plotted? Discussion in this part of the book draws on the *Working Together* research (Carmona *et al.*, 2001), combining problem-solving discussions with analysis drawn from ten detailed case study examples of how planners and providers, locally, have dealt with specific development hurdles. The research here included a series of detailed interviews in each case with the key stakeholders involved in delivering new homes.

Chapter 11 calls for a streamlining of planning and project implementation and a consequent reduction in delay. Chapter 12 considers the degree of inclusivity achieved in current practice, and offers guidance on how different interests might be better represented in local planning. The issue of integrating policy frameworks horizontally and vertically (across tiers of planning and between different areas of policy) is discussed in Chapter 13, whilst Chapter 14 deals with the closely related topic of certainty and transparency within the same frameworks and in the way the various interest groups relate to one another. Many of the issues discussed – and a number of the central messages – re-emerge in Chapter 15. Here, attention turns to the much-discussed issue of how to build a more positive and proactive planning system, one that creates and drives forward visions, rather than merely hampering development to the detriment of residential quality.

The book concludes with a comprehensive look at the way forward (Chapter 16), in which a new – more responsive – agenda and direction for planning in the twenty-first century is advocated. It is suggested that planning must embrace new ways of working if, in partnership with the providers, it is to have any chance of delivering improvements in housing quality and quantity over the next 50 years.

Using the book

Through its structure and detailed discussion, this book builds into a compendium of both planning/housing difficulties and some of their potential solutions. The subject area, however, is vast and no single text can capture every concern from all points of view. The context – physical, economic and political – for housebuilding is constantly changing, nevertheless it is hoped that this book will contribute to an understanding of core concerns and recent developments in the field, while offering some pointers for future discussion.

The book is addressed to several audiences: students of planning, housing, urban studies and related disciplines; seasoned teachers and researchers; and those working in housing or planning practice. Some may wish to gain a better holistic understanding of processes, and are encouraged to follow the structure as laid out. Others may be interested in particular issues, perhaps the land question or planning gain. In these instances, the best strategy might be to begin at the relevant Part Two chapter and then jump to Part Three where the various 'solution' chapters cut across the tensions set out in the previous part. Likewise, the case studies all have fairly broad foci, dealing with a number rather than a single issue or solution, and cross-references in the recommendations try to show how case studies in the separate chapters also relate to solutions discussed elsewhere. Like the solutions, the book aims to separate out key issues for discussion, but readers should never forget that the real benefits can only be gained by a more integrative approach to delivering new homes.

Acknowledgements

We would like to thank all those who took a lead or otherwise assisted with the research.

In the research itself, the authors were assisted by David Joyce and Matthew Clarke.

Staff at the Royal Town Planning Institute – Michael Napier, Joanna Ross and Sarah Lewis – provided the main points of contact with the wider project steering group.

The steering group itself comprised Bob Chalk (Waveney District Council), Yvonne Edgar (Thames Valley Housing Association), David Melling (Wigan Metropolitan Borough Council), Jon Morris (Focus Housing Group), Mike Newton (formally of the House Builders Federation), Steve Ongeri (The Housing Corporation), Barry Simons (freelance housing consultant), Tim Southall (formally of the National Housing Federation) and John Williamson (DETR Planning Directorate).

Financial backing was provided by the RTPI, the Housing Corporation, the HBF, the NHF and the DETR.

It would also have been impossible to progress the research without the help of numerous local authority, housing association and private housebuilder officials who, despite their own hectic schedules, remained ever committed to supporting this work. Thanks are also due to Judith Hillmore (UCL), Gwyn Williams (Manchester University) and Anna Richards (Arup Economics and Planning) and to the anonymous reviewers of the book proposal for their valuable advice.

The authors wish to thank the following for permission to reproduce material: Louis Hellman for cartoons from *Built Environment*, volume 22, number 4, 1996 and from *Building Design* 1995; HMSO for *Public Services Productivity: Meeting the Challenge* (2001) CO2W0001721 HMSO; Sedgemoor District Council for the development concept plan for South Bridgwater; Professor M Ball for our Fig. 3.4 from *Housing Studies*, volume 14, number 1, pp. 9–12, 1992 and David Shenton for his cartoon from *Building Design*, 6 July 2001.

Finally, thanks to Caroline Mallinder and all at Routledge.

Matthew Carmona
Sarah Carmona
Nick Gallent

Part One:
Processes

Following a general introduction in Chapter 1 – which sets out the housing-planning context and looks more widely at the parameters of England's current housing problems – the first part of this book focuses on the three key processes behind the delivery of new housing. The intention is to provide the necessary context for understanding how the planning system works and how development occurs. It also provides some immediate appreciation of how tensions can arise between different groups and particularly between the providers of new homes and those operating the English planning system.

Chapter 2 explores the planning system itself, focusing on current policy and practice but also casting an eye over the changes that may emerge during the next few years on the back of the government's 2001 Planning Green Paper and 2003 Planning Act. Emphasis is placed on the nature of planning, why we plan, and on the mechanics of planning processes and procedures. Discussion extends to the policy context for planning for housing, and to the scope and limitations of the current and future systems.

Chapter 3 looks broadly at the development process, paying particular attention to the nuances of residential development. It examines how the housebuilding industry operates and places this analysis in the context of theoretical models of the development process. In particular the issues of risk and reward and certainty are explored, and how the housebuilding industry has typically reacted to the challenges they face, the particular nature of the speculative house, the housebuilders themselves and the new house buyers they target. The emphasis throughout is on the engagement of the housing development process with the planning system.

Chapter 4 extends the development process overview into the arena of social housing provision. After explaining how housing associations (Registered Social Landlords) have come to occupy centre stage in the delivery of new social housing (provided with capital or land cost subsidy), the chapter relates the way RSLs are funded to the general development processes. It focuses on both the direct provision of housing by RSLs (funded through a mix of private borrowing and grant support), and the way in which social housing development may be part funded through developer's contributions. This second means of delivering new affordable homes is returned to in Chapter 9 which looks more broadly at the issue of extracting 'gain' from market housing development.

These three 'process' chapters build into a comprehensive account of some of the theory and frameworks behind housing development in England (and with some variation in the rest of the UK).

1

Introduction

Delivering new homes

Housing has and always will be important. The quantity, quality and location of new homes are major factors in determining how people live their lives, the opportunities they enjoy and the contribution they can make to a wider society. The way in which new homes are delivered has an impact that extends far beyond the physical environment. New housing in the wrong place may, on occasion, mean the unwanted consumption of greenfield land, but it is equally likely to mean that people are locked out of social networks, are unable to secure employment and, through no fault of their own, contribute to unsustainable living. Poor quality housing – whether poorly planned in the wider sense, or badly designed – has been the hallmark of a commodity culture where housing has sometimes been seen as nothing more than a demand good, to be thrown up wherever the price is right. This does little to enhance quality of life or to meet the aspirations of a population whose needs constantly change.

The tendency in the past has been to focus on the issue of housing quantity; location came in a close second and quality trailed some way behind. In planning-speak, this pecking-order was enshrined in the philosophy of 'predict and provide' (see p. 36), described more recently as a rather blunt numbers game where housing numbers were predicted at the national and regional level and authorities at the local level were required to deliver their allocation in advance of demand. Its replacement by a less-than-clear 'plan, monitor and manage' system anticipated a more local and responsive approach to planning for housing. It also conveniently took the pressure off national government in the act, but relied on an under-resourced and unresponsive local planning system to ensure that the planning and monitoring was actually taking place.

This simple overview of the UK's housing problem suggests that difficulties which have developed – and that remain unresolved – are largely down to planning: if only the planning system could deliver, then a fairer, healthier and happier society would quickly follow. But planning is only one part of the equation. It certainly has a capacity to help or hinder the providers of housing, setting up a strong or weak framework for location decisions, signalling – through development and design control – the type of housing that should be built, and (through site identification and land release) systematically removing the legal constraints to new development. But its culpability for all housing problems is limited. National policy makers, with remits extending beyond land-use planning into the realms of economic strategy, public finance and general housing policy, must share the burden of blame. So too must a housebuilding industry that has traditionally shrugged off social and environmental responsibility and prioritised the pursuit of profit. Blame can also be cast in the directions of the successive national governments who have under-invested in public services and steadily withdrawn from social housing provision, and to the local providers who have pushed for the wrong housing in the wrong places.

If it is the case that the blame for past failures must be shared around, then it seems logical that a solution should be based on all parties (those listed in Table 1.1) striving to improve first, what they do individually, and second, what they do together. This book begins with the premise that housing of the wrong type and quantity is all too frequently built in the wrong location, and at the heart of this problem is the consistent failure of the various interest groups – principally planners and housing providers (the key stakeholders) – to address the problems collectively. In the remaining part of this introduction, the intention is to provide an approximate sketch of Britain's housing failure as it exists at the present time by focusing on the three issues of housing quality, quantity and location, and in so doing offer a statement on some of the problems that planners and housing providers must face.

Table 1.1 Key and other stakeholders

Key Stakeholders

Local Authorities: Can be viewed as 'gatekeepers' and enablers, holding the key to securing planning permission and planning for sufficient housing (market and affordable). They have a duty to release land for all types of new housing, and through their housing departments to monitor and enable the provision of new affordable housing. Authorities comprise officers and members, the former advising the latter on planning and housing matters. Procedural views sometimes clash with political views, resulting in planning delays that can frustrate those seeking planning permission. On occasion, separate departments in authorities (e.g. planning and housing) approach problems from different viewpoints, prioritising social above land-use considerations or vice versa. This can result in interdepartmental tensions.

Private Housebuilders: Operate under market conditions and are driven by the need to make a profit, although they may also take on social concerns. They want to see sufficient land allocated for housing, mainly to service their immediate and future business needs, and they require good market intelligence to limit risk. They also face constraints in the construction industry: for example in the supply of skilled labour and materials. One means of limiting risk is to market tried and tested 'standardised' products. Hence housebuilders are sometimes accused of being unresponsive to local needs and wishes, and of being unwilling to innovate.

Registered Social Landlords: Are the main providers of new social housing across the UK. Ensuring the affordability of their product is their main motivation, though in recent years they have had to adapt to a switch to mixed public-private funding (see Chapter 4). Long-term reductions in public funding (expressed, in part, by lower Social Housing Grant (SHG) rates) have meant increasing reliance on private funds for new schemes. Many see this as a significant threat to affordable housing, as is the scarcity of suitable land for such development – particularly now that local authority land banks have all but disappeared. RSLs increasingly look to the planning process to deliver new, affordable housing (through planning gain).

Table 1.1 continued

Other Stakeholders

The Government: Concerned with balancing conflicting objectives: in particular, meeting the nation's housing needs without compromising important environmental and economic goals.

Landowners: The group with the most to gain from market development of housing. The permission to develop is likely to lead to huge potential profits for the landowner.

Adjacent landowners: Will usually be concerned with the effects of new development on their own property, whether environmental, economic or both.

Private funders: Concerned with low-risk, high-return investments, pushing developers and RSLs towards safer development products.

Public funders: The controllers and awarders of grant support. Concerned with value for money in the use of public funds.

Highways authorities: Mainly concerned with the functionality and safety of the roads and footpaths that they will be asked to adopt. Often, they are accused of creating car-dominated environments.

Police authorities: Concerned with the contribution that built form can make to the reduction of crime, and therefore with 'designing out crime' principles.

Other service providers: Various other service providers will take a keen interest in new residential development, and they will have a role to play in providing basic amenities such as water, sewerage, gas and electricity. Similarly the providers of public transport, open space, leisure and shopping facilities (and many others) will be carefully weighing up the implications of new (and especially larger) developments for their own business strategies.

General public: The requirement for public consultation means that communities, and the general public, get involved in housebuilding. Resident groups, in particular, often succeed in preventing or reshaping developments. The public also has an increasingly powerful effect on the nature of new housebuilding, as environmental concerns become more central to local political agendas.

Homebuyers: Want their investment in a new house to be a good one. Their decision to buy is driven by cost, value for money, functionality and size of home, and location and design.

Tenants: Want to live in a high-quality environment and a stable community, just like owner-occupiers. Need and cost also drive their decisions.

The book aims:

1. To critically examine the way land is developed for housing, and how market and social housing is currently delivered (Part One).
2. To identify the critical junctures at which planners and housing providers come together (sometimes, actual stages in the planning process), and how their different motivations or the constraints under which they operate can negatively impinge on the way housing is delivered (Part Two).
3. Through case study material, to show how better practice can be developed and therefore how housing of the right type and quality can be delivered in the most sustainable locations (Part Three).

4. To separate out what can be achieved under the current system from what can only be delivered following a fundamental overhaul of Britain's planning policy framework. This issue is addressed throughout the book and especially in Chapter 16.

Housing quality, quantity and location

The failure to provide sufficient homes of the right type and in the right locations has been a recurring theme within a range of social science disciplines throughout the twentieth century. The social consequences of poor-quality housing, including its links with health, crime and deprivation have been outlined by countless commentators since Edwin Chadwick's pioneering work of 1842. In recent sociological literature, for example, Somerville and Sprigings (2003) focus attention on the various linkages between housing (quality) and broader social policy, including the relationship between physical and social regeneration. Similarly, the locational mismatches between the supply of and demand for housing have occupied geographers for decades. The nature of the relationship between population movement, births, deaths and patterns of household formation has in particular been the subject of intense academic and political debate at least since the 1950s, with, again by way of example, Holmans (1970, 1987, 1995; Holmans *et al.*, 1998) work on forecasting techniques and the future geography of housing demand across the UK spanning much of this period. Housing studies therefore exist across several different specialisms and within each of these a different focus is prioritised. Sometimes the focus is on housing and social welfare, sometimes on housing and (natural) environmental change. Other studies offer analyses from a purely political or economic perspective, treating dwellings as consumer goods, existing to win votes or absorb demand.

Kemeny (1992) has argued that the compartmentalised way that housing is studied is a consequence of its lying across a number of pure disciplines. He argues that it lacks any natural home, and despite the growth in the number of 'housing studies departments' at British universities, those engaged in the study of housing tend to have a background in a separate discipline: they are economists, political scientists, sociologists or architects. Or, failing that, they hail from one of the hybrid disciplines, for example geography or town planning.

Nevertheless, despite the apparent complexity of the connections between housing, society, the economy and the environment, the importance of housing – across all these disciplines – remains inexorably linked to questions of quality, quantity and location. The basic challenge for the providers of housing, and those who plan its provision, is to ensure that these concerns are given equal attention.

Housing quality

A number of factors influence the quality of a new dwelling; these may relate specifically to the dwelling itself or more broadly to its local setting. Quality is most straightforwardly determined by the utility value enjoyed by its occupant(s) and therefore, to meet the most basic quality threshold, the dwelling must satisfy need. This means that good quality housing is provided with the user in mind and offers a healthy and safe living environment. At one level, it provides basic amenities – water, heat, light, cooking facilities, sewage removal – and at another, it meets the longer-term aspirations or needs of a household: i.e. to grow or to age.

In the past, housing quality was often narrowly defined in terms of a small number of quality measures. These included access to an inside toilet and, in later years, the existence of gas central heating. The physical dimensions of a dwelling were also seen as contributing to quality, and were measured according to 'Parker Morris' standards (Parker Morris, 1961). Hence, the main criteria against which housing quality was judged related to the characteristics, and particularly the internal layout, of the dwelling. Improvements in quality were therefore to be achieved through changes to the Building Regulations and then enforced via planning and building control.

Today, assessments of quality are linked more closely to the different needs of housing occupants. This means, for example, that more detailed assessments of housing needs, undertaken in many instances by local authority housing and planning departments, are concerned less with simple dwelling numbers and more with understanding the profile of housing types required by the cross-section of local households. Authorities are keen that any new housing provided – or converted from existing stock or non-residential buildings – will reflect the particular needs of single person households, of families, of older people or of those with physical or mental disabilities. Moreover, needs are not simply defined in the here and now, but are projected into the future. For example, high-quality housing that meets the needs of families today may not be appropriate for an ageing population that will display a very different demographic profile in 20 years time.

So the definition of quality has become much broader; it is about tailoring housing to changing needs and about ensuring that dwellings retain their utility value as society changes. Dwellings must provide a high quality of accommodation over the long term. This type of thinking on the quality issue is reflected in the concept of lifelong homes (which can be adapted to an occupant's changing circumstances during different life stages) and is part of a wider rationale of creating sustainable communities. In recent years it has become a key part of the household growth debate, with questions focusing on the type of housing required by a society that looks set to be dominated by older and smaller households in the coming years.

The design issue is also becoming critically important as policy moves in the direction of higher density living (see Chapter 8). In this context the issue of quality extends beyond the individual dwelling units to the wider residential environment – its urban design. Thus many of the recent housing needs studies have fixed not only on the issue of individual unit quality, but also on the quality of surrounding open spaces, the look of buildings, the amount of greenery, the layout of roads and walkways, and the way all these factors contribute to the 'feel' of a place (see for example, Karn *et al.*, 1998). Quality in this sense is about creating appealing residential environments where people will want to live.

So what are the consequences of low-quality housing? It is difficult to isolate the quality issue from concerns over the quantity and location of housing supply, as most of the great housing failures of the past have resulted from a combination of these different factors – low-quality housing, sited in out-of-the-way disconnected locations, or housing over-supplied in areas with few job opportunities. For example, the abandonment of houses in the North West and North East of England in recent years has been linked to the low quality of housing provided (Power, 1999), although in that instance the problems of location (in areas of economic decay) and oversupply have probably been the most critical. The consequences and characteristics of low housing quality might include:

At the dwelling unit level:

• Overcrowding – homes unsuited to the present or future size of occupant households. Whilst the proportion of overcrowded households has fallen off nationally in recent years, numerous studies continue to demonstrate that particular sections of society continue to live in homes that are too small. Recent figures show, for example, that black and minority ethnic households are still more likely to endure overcrowding or other housing stresses than their white neighbours (DTLR, 2001b). Using an indicator based on overcrowding, sharing, and children living above the ground floor, some 180,000 black and minority ethnic households in London are estimated to be in housing need (Housing Corporation and London Research Centre, 2000).

• Poor building standards – can take various forms but include problems such as inadequate sound or heat insulation. The neighbourhood disputes arising from noise pollution have been vividly highlighted by Gurney and Hines (1999) and this is an issue of heightening concern in relation to the question of density. On the whole, basic construction problems pre-date the current building regulations and are less prevalent in new homes, but recent research in Austria has revealed that relatively low levels of background noise can raise blood pressure in children and lead to learned helplessness syndrome (Evans *et al.*, 2001), thus emphasising the importance of even detailed design considerations.

• Lack of basic amenities – like the issue of building standards, a lack of basic amenities – private open space, light, air – is less often a problem in new housing but still affects older stock, particularly in many inner city neighbourhoods that escaped the slum-clearance programmes of the mid-twentieth century. It also remains an issue in the light of the higher density agenda.

• Inappropriate internal layout standards – although the problems of poor construction standards and basic amenity provision may be less significant today, the layout and design of new homes remain standardised, and homes can easily be mismatched to local needs. The reduction in householder size (see below), for example through greater numbers of people living by themselves, may not necessarily imply that such households aspire to lower space standards, although assumptions in policy often make this case.

As basic constructional standards have improved, the debate over housing quality has refocused away from internal layout and standards, to neighbourhood design – although the former still remain major concerns.

At the area level, the major concerns revolve around two main groups of issues:

• Urban design – with its increasingly broad agenda relating to the quality and function of the spaces and places between buildings, and the sustainability of the infra-structure that serves them. These issues are discussed at greater length in Chapters 3 and 8: suffice to say here that the failure to deliver good urban design has created the sprawling, road-dominated, unsustainable, disconnected housing estates that characterise perceptions of much new housing development.

• The mix of uses – the inadequate supply of services (public transport, schools, doctors and so forth) and other uses (retail, workplaces, etc.) is another issue linked with quantity and location because all such uses require a threshold of demand to make them viable. It is also the case that poor planning and design can lead to mono-use environments simply because such issues have not been given priority in the delivery of new homes, or because a particular design solution makes their provision impossible.

Quality is a complex concern that to a large degree determines the way people feel about their homes. It is also a game of two halves, in that whilst detailed standards of house construction and basic amenity standards have improved, the battle to deliver good quality urban design and mixed use environments remains unresolved. Quality is an issue that will be returned to throughout this book; arguably it is also an issue to be resolved once decisions have been reached over where to locate housing and in what quantity. That is not to say that it is a secondary consideration, but rather that the process of delivering good quality housing follows on from decisions of quantity and location.

Both the planners and providers of new housing must share a concern for the way that dwellings are built and the way neighbourhoods are formed. They must focus on design at various scales, and ensure that both dwellings and the wider neighbourhoods adequately satisfy needs, and not just those of the current occupants, but also of future generations. Housing quality has much to do with flexibility or the ambivalent nature of the postmodern world (Bauman, 1991). The main challenge for planners and providers is to recognise that needs are changing and will continue to change in the future. Housing that can adapt to these needs – and does not become redundant in ten years time – will have the quality to endure.

Housing quantity

Housing quantity, together with siting decisions, has been the overriding preoccupation of planning for much of the last 100 years, something that has been true for both market and social housing. Governments have been elected to power after making ambitious pledges to increase housing supply, providing 'homes fit for heroes' after the First World War, and more recently, 'Decent homes for all' (DETR, 2000c).

The history of housing provision over the last 50 years has been marked by two processes: the near complete privatisation of the means of production (housing associations aside – see Chapter 4); and the nationalisation of development rights, with public control of development falling into the hands of the local state. The vast majority of all housebuilding in Britain is now undertaken by the private sector, although the processes by which land for new housing is allocated and released are controlled by the public sector through local planning authorities. Housing has therefore become a critical juncture between public and private interests, with the fiercest battles centring on how much housing should be provided, particularly in areas of high demand.

During the last five years much of this debate has focused on the household projections. These are derived from the Government Actuary's Department's (GAD) projections of population change, and are a means of taking natural population increase and converting it to a projection of the growth in household numbers based on forecasts of the types of households likely to form in the next 25 years.

The recent decline in larger family units, and the commensurate increase in the number of people choosing to live alone, means that recent projections (DoE, 1995a; DETR, 1999) have been dominated by single person households. If households are to get smaller, then the absolute number is set to increase. The 1992-based figures, for example, suggested that an additional 4.4 million households would form in England up to 2016. The more recent 1996-based calculations put the overall figure at 3.8 million (to 2021), although this apparent slowing of growth has been refuted by many commentators (Holmans, 2001).

The role of planning in relation to these figures is first to ensure that the gross national figure can be translated into estimates of the need for new housing at the regional level. Strategic housing figures are then derived for the county (strategic) planning authorities or unitary authorities (where no county authority exists) and expressed in the form of required building rates (for keeping pace with projected demand). County figures are next divided among the district planning authorities and it then becomes the respon-sibility of these authorities, along with unitary authorities, to allocate and subsequently release sufficient land for new housing.[1]

This system is not without its critics. Planners frequently deplore this top-down approach (Select Committee on Environment, Transport and Regional Affairs, 1998), arguing that it fails to reflect local reality and is blind to many of the issues that shape demand at the local level. Housebuilders tend to support the process in theory, but often argue that excessive political intervention at the different planning levels means that the system actually releases only politically acceptable rather than sufficient housing sites and cannot, therefore, satisfy current let alone future demand.

Both views have merit. In moving away from a philosophy of 'predict and provide' to one where local agencies have a greater monitoring role, government is accepting that there must be some bottom-up perspective on future housing need, although this acceptance has been tarnished by recent top-level interventions in the projection debate in South East England, suggesting to some that the old system is alive and well (Friends of the Earth, 1997). At the local level, planning decisions are heavily influenced by com-munity pressure which typically opposes much new housing development, for example the planned extension at Stevenage West in Hertfordshire (see p. 72), where opposition has been mobilised around 'CASE' or the 'Campaign Against Stevenage Expansion' (see CASE web site: www.case.org.uk/index.htm for a history of the campaign).

This combination of procedural and political difficulties means that issues of housing quantity are always controversial. An added complication is that in a housebuilding system without a strong public sector presence, some of the housing provided by the private sector must be affordable if a full cross-section of society is to enjoy access to adequate housing. So the potential problems of not providing sufficient new housing can be further exacerbated if an inadequate proportion is affordable – perhaps as much as 30 per cent of new homes (Holmans *et al.*, 1998).

The following is a list of critical concerns noted in recent political and academic debate. Again, these cannot be separated from issues of housing quality or location, although broad volume concerns relating first to overall supply and then to affordable housing can be identified:

- Constraint – not an issue *per se*, but a factor preventing the supply of housing from keeping pace with demand. Constraint can derive from physical conditions (locally), or from a lack of capacity in the construction industry, but is more usually associated with the operation of the planning system. The procedures governing the release and allocation of land are often politically rather than economically driven, and therefore a bottleneck in the supply of land may mean that the system remains unresponsive to demand.
- House prices – if demand outpaces supply, then existing property acquires greater scarcity value and prices rise. With other commodities, this might result in lower demand and therefore automatic correction and a levelling off of prices. But housing is a fundamental need (Ware and Goodin, 1990). Buyers respond to higher prices by borrowing more (if they can) or suffering inadequate housing conditions (if they must). Rising prices are the signal of a buoyant (or an overheating) economy and in

---

[1] Under the provisions of the 2003 Planning and Compulsory Purchase Act, county planning authorities will have a much reduced role in housing allocations in the future (see Chapter 2).

a climate of confidence, interest rates may be cut, reducing the cost of borrowing. This may increase the threshold number of people able to enter the market, particularly if lenders relax borrowing criteria in order to capitalise on a strong market. But those falling below the threshold will find it very difficult to access housing.

- Private renting – many of the problems of housing quantity are typified in London. House price 'to average income ratios have always been much higher in London than elsewhere' (Hamnett, 2001, p. 83), pushing many households into the private rental sector. This sector is larger in London than elsewhere, providing the first port of call for people moving to the city for the first time. Because the cost of buying a home is so prohibitively high in many areas for certain types of household, for example the ubiquitous single 'young professionals' typically on incomes of between £25,000 and £30,000 per annum, the rental sector has over time refocused on this market. The rented housing that remains affordable to the majority of people in this category tends to be of low quality, cramped and expensive (Hamnett, 2001).

- Homelessness – the problem of homelessness is not merely a consequence of a housing shortage. Mental health problems, domestic violence, drug dependency and a whole host of other social problems result in people finding themselves on the streets (Daly, 1996). However, local authorities across the country have a responsibility (in partnership with RSLs) to rehouse those who have sought their assistance, although this task has become increasingly difficult in recent years as the pot of available social housing has dried up. It is often the case, for example, that people seeking help are rehoused back in the same poor quality estates where they are dragged back into the cycle of deprivation and crime that landed them on the streets in the first place.

- The economy – housing supply is linked to the economy at several levels. Insufficient supply (in the right location) is a barrier to labour mobility and therefore to the economic development of particular places: it ties the labour force to the wrong areas, creating unemployment which itself hinders growth. Those factors underpinning constraint (see above) also impinge on the building industry. The size of the industry is governed by the availability of land and its profitability is influenced by the ease with which land can be developed. In general terms, planning constraint affects the entire construction industry, limiting the number of jobs available within this and related sectors and impacting on the national economy. Housebuilding represents a significant slice of the wider industry and therefore housing land, and subsequent unit supply, is critically important (see Chapter 3).

Moving on to affordable housing, the current housing and planning framework dictates that the availability of public finance for social housebuilding is limited and capped. The same framework therefore seeks to extract a contribution from development value for the procurement of affordable housing (see Chapter 9; Bishop Associates, 2001; DTLR, 2002a). Overall supply issues will inevitably dictate the magnitude of the contribution, but so too will the way this (i.e. planning gain) system works.

In respect of affordable housing, two key issues are critical:

- Supply – the recent Spatial Development Strategy (SDS) for London (Greater London Authority, 2001), for example, recognised that the supply of affordable housing in the capital is inadequate. Planning authorities currently negotiate for gain contributions on a site-by-site basis, but it is argued in the SDS that local planning authorities should have a figure of 50 per cent in mind (35 per cent social rented plus 15 per cent shared ownership or some other form of affordable housing) when drawing up Section 106 agreements with developers. If they do not increase this type of planning-based contribution, London's key workers (teachers, nurses, police officers and so forth) will continue to suffer, which, in turn, will decrease the viability of public services. Supply issues are at their most critical in London, but are significant issues in much of the country.

- Type – in the past social rented housing managed by RSLs was seen as the only realistic option. Today, shared ownership is seen as an alternative answer in many more expensive areas. Recent Section 106 agreements, particularly those drawn up in London, also include references to 'subsidised market rents' or housing specially targeted at certain types of worker. Developers are keen to aim the gain contribution at particular sub-markets (especially middle-income groups) and planning authorities, along with their legal departments, seem to feel that this is the right way forward (GLA, 2002a, p. 104).

The quantity issue is critical, and some commentators argue that the right quantity of housing, available in the right locations would circumvent the need for any affordable housing strategy, in other words, the market really could provide. But such a belief ignores the fact that planning serves a whole host of purposes: the public good, environmental protection and existing private interests. It also aims towards sustainable solutions, pricing in the externalities of the development process. A system of housing supply based only on market signals, and unhindered by planning constraint, might go some way towards solving the supply – and therefore affordability – issue, but the price on other fronts is likely to prove too high. Although quantity is a critical issue, so too are quality and location. Planning has a responsibility for juggling all three: like quality, quantity is an issue that will be discussed throughout the book.

Location

The phrase 'location, location, location' has meaning not only for estate agents and home buyers, but for anyone balancing the need to live in an attractive, safe environment, with the imperative to work, send their children to decent schools, shop and be generally mobile. Housing location, alongside quality and quantity issues, is also of paramount importance, and concerns over location are present not only at a personal, but at a strategic level.

Housebuilders generally want to deliver homes in the most profitable locations. In some instances, these just happen to be close to good schools, services, public transport and jobs. But on other occasions, especially when housing is targeted at mobile sections of society, proximity to services may not be the major concern. Unspoilt areas of countryside, for example, will appeal to many potential homebuyers, and where there is a demand, developers inevitably will wish to exploit it. The desire to decentralise – apparent throughout much of the twentieth century – and secure a healthier lifestyle away from cities and their various social problems (Rogers and Power, 2000), coupled with the massive surge in private car ownership since the 1950s, have underpinned this drive to develop new housing on what are now deemed to be unsustainable sites.

Concerns over housing location and quantity have been central to the debate surrounding sustainable development in Britain (Brown and Dühr, 2002). Sustainability, in its simplest form, is about consuming as little as possible in the most benign locations. In housing terms, this means delivering well-designed homes at higher densities, and on brownfield land where feasible. Planning, and particularly strategic planning, has a vital role to play in ensuring that new development follows a set of basic rules. These rules are now set out in the most recent Planning Policy Guidance Note for Housing (PPG3 – DETR, 2000a) and can be explained as a series of 'dos' and 'don'ts'. Do, for example, develop new homes on brownfield sites: this means putting housing in existing towns and cities and not in open countryside or other (perhaps urban) greenspace. Don't repeat the mistakes of the past, which included the development of low-density, standardised housing (Fisk, 1997) on unsuitable, disconnected, out-of-town locations. The central message is that building should occur first within the existing urban footprint, second, and only if necessary, the footprint should be extended (i.e., the so-called urban extensions option; DETR, 1998a), and only finally if no other options are viable, should a new footprint be proposed.

Recent policy emphasis has been placed firmly on land recycling. This means that the location issue is closely bound up with questions of land availability, urban capacity and, because of the problems of developing brownfield sites, land contamination (Syms and Knight, 2000; see also Adams *et al.*, 2002). The last Conservative administration (1992 to 1997) expressed the view that 50 per cent of new housebuilding should occur on recycled land (DoE, 1995a). The incoming Labour government raised this figure to 60 per cent (DETR, 1998a), although the long-term achievability of the target has been questioned in recent years, particularly if taken on a region by region basis (Urban Task Force, 1999). So in planning terms, location decisions are heavily influenced by the environmental imperative. But this has to be balanced with an appreciation of market conditions. Many local authorities in the north of England, for example, have been concerned that housing built on some brownfield sites will not sell and have instead felt impelled to give developers, and their customers, exactly what they want – houses on greenfield sites close to motorway access (DETR, 2000b).

Difficulties such as these have various underlying causes: weak regional economies, inner city decay (equating with crime and bad schools), good road networks but poor public transport infrastructure, and sometimes large-scale contamination problems within and around post-industrial cities. All these factors conspire to make the most sustainable housing locations also the least appealing and therefore the least viable for development interests. Solutions to these difficulties will only be found in the long term; getting the right housing in the right locations is impossible without balanced regional development, investment in public transport, changes in attitudes towards private car use, and the profound regeneration of many inner city areas. So in location terms, and from the point of view of planning, the challenges lie in contributing towards the creation of the conditions under which people will want and need to live in sustainable locations. The rationale and processes behind strategic location decisions are discussed in Chapter 5, which focuses on procedures and practices for site identification and land allocation. In the following summary, some of the effects of badly located housing are considered, drawing on examples of past failures.

• Isolation – a key lesson from the past is that mislocation equates, almost inevitably, with isolation in one form or another. History is littered with instances of well-intentioned planning professionals grasping development opportunities on what seemed like attractive sites, only to find that the projected increase in service levels, jobs or new investment in public transport never materialised. One example is that of Pen Rhys in South Wales (Osmond, 1994), developed on a hillside – 1,200 feet above sea level – in the Rhondda valley in the 1960s, and subsequently judged as one of the most catastrophic failures in public housebuilding in modern times. Those who moved to the site enjoyed reasonable quality housing, but were immediately isolated from jobs, services and their social networks. Many felt that things would improve – that transport would get better and that new investment would bring decent shops and other services – but instead Pen Rhys rapidly became one of Britain's worst sink estates. Such experiences have not been confined to public social housing. In the 1970s, the designation of Wellesbourne (near Stratford-upon-Avon in Warwickshire) as a first tier 'key settlement' (Cloke, 1979, p. 82) resulted in a massive expansion of new housebuilding in the village, tripling its population between 1970 and 2000. Seven hundred and fifty units were provided on just one of the new private estates, with buyers persuaded to move to the area with the promise of good shops and services in due course. Twenty years later the shops arrived, although the estate is still served by only a single bus to Stratford at irregular intervals, and most of those living on in the settlement are utterly car dependent, working in Stratford (7 miles), Birmingham (25 miles) or even London (100 miles).

- Car dependency – Geddes' (1915) ideal of harmonising where people work, live and play remains a primary goal of the planning system. A failure to achieve this harmonisation results in car dependency, with people regularly journeying between home, the job, leisure opportunities and their social contacts. Car dependency is not only about these locational mismatches; it also stems from the emphasis people place on flexible personal mobility. It may be, for example, that public transport can never totally replace the private car, although in many instances it could provide a realistic and perhaps more comfortable alternative. The first step towards achieving this is to ensure that people are able to live close to good transport opportunities, and this means either taking new homes to transport hubs, or bringing those hubs to the new housing. The former approach is frequently easier and less costly, especially when it is part of a strategy of land recycling i.e. providing housing within the existing urban footprint, rather than building on disconnected out-of-town locations (RICS, 2000).

- Work – the issue of connecting work and homes is now one of the most pressing issues facing planners at all levels. The Town and Country Planning Association followed up its 1996 study of housing location (Breheny and Hall, 1996) with a parallel study of the changing geography of employment in 1999 (Breheny, 1999). But creating a spatial fix between where people live and where they work is not easy. Allen *et al.* (2002) have argued that reflexive winners in the new knowledge economy have unpredictable career paths, regularly moving from job to job, or choosing not to work in a fixed location. Countless studies of changing work patterns under the conditions of globalisation (see for instance, Giddens, 1998) have pointed to the ambivalent nature of location decisions. This boils down to a more difficult climate in which to predict where housing will be required in relation to the geography of work.

- Low demand – low demand, and the subsequent abandonment of housing, may not seem relevant to the wider (market) housing debate, but it illustrates what can happen in the worst-case scenarios. Power (1999) has described vividly the problems facing some areas in the north of England where the bottom has dropped out of the social housing market and where homes have, in recent years, changed hands for just a couple of thousand pounds. For example, changing economic fortunes have meant that much of the housing built in parts of Newcastle upon Tyne and east Manchester is simply not needed. Even properties built in the 1980s ended up being demolished less than 20 years later because nobody wanted to live in these areas and it was not practical, economic or safe to do so.

So, in some instances, the real cost of poor location decisions can be measured in human misery. The wrong houses in the wrong locations lock people out of social and economic opportunities. They are unable to access work or enjoy good services, and without jobs, they cannot afford to run cars, are increasingly isolated and find themselves stuck in hopeless situations.

Undoubtedly these are extremes, and for the majority of people living in less than ideal locations, the biggest problem they face is inconvenience marked perhaps by long drives to work, tiredness and a reduction in the quality of their home life. Nevertheless, the processes underpinning these personal costs include excessive car use, the consumption of greenfield land, and the underuse of public services. The mislocation of housing is central to the unsustainable lifestyle of many, and a root cause of real hardship for the few.

The challenge for planners and housing providers

Given the way that housing problems form – through poor quality provision of too few homes in the wrong places – the challenge facing the planning profession, in partnership with providers, is to ensure that every new development reflects need in terms of quality, quantity and location. New housing has to meet not only local need (now and in the future), but must also to address wider strategic concerns. With respect to quality, the homes delivered will need to avoid the pitfalls noted above, and follow sound and enduring design principles. In terms of quantity, too much can be as bad as too little, and supply concerns relate not only to market housing but also to affordable homes and the way these are delivered (increasingly through the planning system). Furthermore, the success or failure of housing schemes will always hinge on location decisions. Even the right housing, put in the wrong location, is doomed to fail in one way or another.

Many of these points may seem straightforward, but they are where the process of delivering new homes begins, and each conceals a myriad of complexities (see Fig. 1.1). This book is about how to achieve quality housing that serves the country's lasting needs, accepting of course that different parts of the UK face a range of different problems (see Table 1.2). It has already been argued that the problems of the past cannot be attributed to the failings of any one sector or agency. More often than not, the provision of too few homes in the wrong locations is a consequence of the way planners, charged with the statutory regulation of land-use change, and housing providers have failed to work together. Their perspectives on problems are often contradictory, as are

1.1 The complex housing provision debate (Hogg, 1996) from Planning, *6 December 1996.*

Table 1.2 Housing challenges: the difference between regions and countries (CIH/LGA Survey of Local Authorities in Goss and Blackaby, 1998)

Urban authorities in the Midlands and the North of England

➤ Hard-to-let local authority and housing association housing
➤ Poor quality stock across tenures
➤ Public/private partnerships – levering in funds for regeneration
➤ Community breakdown/social exclusion

Rural authorities in the Midlands and North of England

➤ Complex housing market
➤ Unemployment
➤ Transport problems

Urban authorities in the South of England

➤ Shortage of land/resources to meet growing need/demand
➤ Improving estate management performance
➤ Poor quality social housing stock
➤ Tackling anti-social behaviour/crime

Rural authorities in the South of England

➤ Reducing resources and growing demand
➤ Shortages of land and high prices of land
➤ Green belt issues
➤ Rural communities/social exclusion/rural poverty
➤ Problems of frail elderly
➤ Transport problems

Urban authorities in Scotland

➤ Poor quality housing across all tenures
➤ Need for regeneration
➤ Surplus council housing in some areas
➤ Community care

Rural authorities in Scotland

➤ Depopulation of villages
➤ Insufficient investment
➤ Community care
➤ Transport problems

Urban authorities in Wales

➤ Poor quality housing across all private tenures
➤ Social exclusion

Rural authorities in Wales

➤ Need for regeneration
➤ Depopulation of villages
➤ Surplus housing in some areas
➤ Poor quality housing across tenures
➤ Transport problems

their motivations. The pressures they each face are poorly or completely misunderstood by the other, and they lack any sign of a shared goal or a common vision.

The challenge therefore facing planners and housing providers at the dawn of the twenty-first century is to work together, and in so doing, develop a shared vision of how to create sustainable communities where concerns of housing quality, quantity and location take equal precedence. These output-related factors appear as overarching concerns throughout the book, although the discussion relates more to the processes inherent in the delivery of new homes.

2

The planning process

The nature and purpose of planning

In this chapter an overview of the planning process is provided, including a discussion of why we plan, the process of planning in the UK, its shortcomings and its role with specific reference to housing. In his book *Urban and Regional Planning*, Peter Hall (1992, p. 9) compares the activity of planning with the challenge of putting a man on the moon. He suggests:

> At first sight this may seem absurd: nothing could be more complex than space travel. But this is to mix up levels of complexity. Space travel presents many technical problems, but there are two features that make it basically simple. First, the objective is clearly understood: there is one aim only, to get men on the moon (or, eventually to Mars or farther). Secondly, the processes involved are nearly all physical: they are subject to laws of physics, which are much better understood, and which appear to be more regular in their application, than laws of human behaviour. . . . [Planning] is inherently more complex. First, the basic objective is not well understood; there is clearly more than one objective, and perhaps dozens. . . . These objectives may not be readily compatible, and may indeed be contradictory. Secondly, most of the processes which need controlling are human processes, which are less well understood and work with much less certainty than laws in the physical sciences.

Thus planning is both multidimensional and multi-objective and concerned with the complex management of change in the built and natural environment. It is this complexity that gives rise to many of the conflicts – and also to many of the challenges – that planners face. The complexity can be seen in a number of contrasting characteristics inherent in the discipline.

Planning is at one and the same time:

- A regulatory process enshrined in a statutory planning system, but also a visionary process through which future visions are developed and implemented for the built and natural environment.

- Both a political arena and a legally defined entity, the former through the operation of the system by democratically accountable local (and national) government, and the latter through the national legislative framework arbitrated through the courts.
- Concerned with protecting both the public and the private interest, in large part through balancing (or reconciling) the objectives of each against the other to optimise outcomes for both.
- A long-term process concerned with defining 10 to 20 year visions for localities, and a short-term process concerned with day-to-day decision-making about development and the management of areas.
- Similarly a large-scale process concerned with urban areas and their regions, and a small-scale process concerned with individual developments and their impacts on localities.
- Concerned with the physical and environmental consequences of development and also with the socio-economic outcomes that development gives rise to.
- Both a generalist discipline concerned with the operation of the statutory process and a discipline concerned with a range of deep specialisms including design, conservation, environmental assessment, sectorial planning (i.e. retail, residential, commercial, etc.), transport, minerals and so forth.
- Defined by a process which is both iterative and cyclical (see below) and analytical and conceptual, but also a product (output)-oriented discipline concerned with the types of places created through successive development episodes.
- A discipline operated through public sector intervention, but also with a large (and increasing) private sector consultant base, working for both private and public sector clients.
- An action-oriented discipline concerned with promoting specific policy and development scenarios and a communicative discipline concerned with negotiating and articulating shared visions with a broad range of stakeholders.

Nevertheless, even within this complexity and the sometimes seemingly contrasting goals it is still possible to identify a set of core characteristics and rationales for planning. One such attempt to define the nature and purpose of planning was undertaken for educational purposes in the UK. The document argues that planning is concerned with 'the way societies plan, design, manage and regulate change in the built and natural environment'. It suggests that planning deals with 'why and how (and with what consequences) societies intervene, shape, organise and change natural and built environments in order to secure an agreed range of social, economic and environmental objectives' (QAAHE, 2002, p. 1). A number of defining principles are outlined, which – suitably adapted – are offered in Table 2.1.

Such 'defining principles' are inevitably idealised aspirations and may not reflect the reality of practice. Nevertheless, they demonstrate the broad and challenging remit of a discipline that extends well beyond the more limited association of planning with the operation of statutory planning processes. Rydin (1998, pp. 350–4), for example, offers a number of rationales for planning, of which three are distinct.

1. Planning is a means of avoiding anarchy and disorder: she argues that there are strong tendencies to disorder in Western economic systems and that the interaction of competitive forces in the marketplace does not automatically lead along the path to the public interest. Instead competition can lead to a mismatch between needs and supply, with, for example, a periodic over- or under-supply of certain goods

Table 2.1 Defining principles of planning (adapted from QAAHE, 2002)

1. Planning is concerned with relationships between society and space.

Planning is about determining the quality of the relationships between people and space. Planners are as much concerned with the impact of their decisions on people and communities and on their quality of life, as they are with the treatment and development of space. Thus the roles, aspirations and powers of politicians, professionals, landowners and developers, organisations and community groups, and other communities of interest, are of critical importance within planning, alongside the importance of an awareness of design, and the physical organisation and sustainability of space.

2. Planning is holistic and integrative.

A key strength of planning is its ability to develop and consider the overview. A key skill of the planner is to synthesise; to recognise the core issues within multifaceted problems; and to be able to propose focused, effective courses of action, and responses to these problems. Planning is as much concerned with managing the whole environment as with the detail of any of its constituent parts.

3. Planning attempts to manage processes of change through deliberate and positive actions.

Planning is a discipline concerned with creating and coordinating action in the environment, and as such requires practitioners to be familiar with a wide range of material, with a view to taking well-informed prescriptive actions in the real world of the built and natural environments. Planners are therefore, first and foremost, creative problem-solvers. Planning prescriptions require an understanding of the balances of power within societies and organisations, and the limitations that these impose upon effective planning action.

4. Planning requires appropriate administrative and legal frameworks for implementing action.

Planning invariably involves societies in developing appropriate administrative organisations and processes to regulate development within legal frameworks related to individual and collective property rights. Knowledge of such frameworks is essential for those wishing to understand planning.

5. Planning involves the allocation of limited resources.

Planning actions often result in changes in the distributions of social, economic and environmental costs and benefits on different individuals and groups within societies. Thus planning requires an evaluation of the likely impacts of decisions, and value judgements about their effects, and how they might be influenced. Planning can be used for oppressive as well as altruistic purposes, and planners need an understanding of the contexts in which each might occur.

6. Planning requires the study, understanding and application of a diverse set of multidisciplinary knowledge.

Planning requires an understanding of the relationships between underlying theory; conceptual thinking and analysis; and policy formulation, evaluation and implementation. It is an activity whose scope and legitimacy is contested, and in which a variety of justifications and views about its purposes and possible outcomes have to be understood, discussed and reviewed.

– perhaps market housing – a complete failure to supply non-market needs – such as social housing – and an over-exploitation of undervalued resources, such as the environment. In this regard planning has a systems maintenance role in ensuring that economic, social and environmental systems continue to operate and do not irreparably break down.

2. Planning has a role in relation to economic and social change in terms of accommodating long-term shifts in structure: the knowledge available to planners about economic, social and physical/environmental systems combined with a future-oriented approach can help to anticipate change and promote new scenarios for the future. Unfortunately, as information is always likely to be imperfect, and mechanisms for intervention crude, the impact of planning will always be limited. Nevertheless, Rydin (1998, p. 351) argues that 'the existence of the planning system represents a strong statement that the worst excesses of a market system need not be tolerated'.

3. Planning has a potential to deal with the distributional impact of change in a demo-cratic and equitable manner: as development inevitably generates environmental and social externalities, planning has a role in regulating and preventing the negative externalities associated with change (for example environmental damage, loss of jobs, or overloading infrastructure), and capturing and even enhancing the positive externalities. Thus planning can – and in the UK was always intended to be – a means of encouraging redistribution in society: 'It can try to redistribute resources through patterns of land use, provision of urban and transport facilities, ensuring access to leisure and beauty spots, and promoting the quality of local environments' (Rydin, 1998, p. 354).

The planning system

The rationales help to illustrate why in a modern society planning represents a necessary state activity, despite not always fulfilling its potential. Indeed, most developed countries at state or local levels operate systems of land use planning precisely because of the speed, impact and intensity of modern-day development. In their commentary on urban England the Urban Task Force[1] (1999, p. 191) agreed, arguing:

> The planning system provides an essential democratic interface for reconciling different interests in land use. We also, however, need to be aware of the limita-tions of the current system as we seek to respond more effectively to current urban planning needs:
>
> 1. The system does not adequately recognise the special needs of urban areas; it is not attuned to the inherent complexity of assembling and bringing forward urban sites for redevelopment;
> 2. The system has become stultified; it generally takes too long to plan and make decisions;
> 3. The system is reactive; it has become too focused on 'controlling' development.

---

[1] Constituted in 1998 to advise the Secretary of State on causes of urban decline in England and to advise on courses of action.

To some degree the problems that the Urban Task Force identified are problems inherent in a planning system that came into existence shortly after the Second World War, and which in its essentials (with the exception of the abolition of development – i.e. betterment – charges) remained the same throughout the remainder of the twentieth century.

The control of land (its effective nationalisation) was in many respects the centrepiece of post-war legislation. Nevertheless, as Cullingworth (1999, p. 1) argues

> The realities of the post-war years rapidly shattered the early dreams. Other issues dominated the political agenda; plans took much time and effort to bring to an operational level, and the resources available were grossly inadequate to implement them. Both public and private investment was held back.

From that date on, he suggests, 'positive' planning was limited and the regulatory regime only worked at first because there was so little activity to regulate. Thus as early as the return of the Conservative government in 1952 the system was viewed as overly restrictive, whilst the delivery of social housing (rather than comprehensive planning) was seen as the grand visionary project of the time. The Ministry was even renamed, from the Ministry of Local Government and Planning, to the Ministry of Housing and Local Government.[2]

Over subsequent decades, and despite the sometimes fundamental reorganisation of other policy areas – health, housing, education, transport, etc. – the accelerating rate of change that the planning process has had to deal with has been handled within essentially the same legislative machinery. Furthermore, as more proactive aspects of the broader public planning remit such as the new towns programme, slum clearance and town centre redevelopment schemes brought with them their own problems (not least their cost) and were steadily abandoned, government increasingly looked to the private sector for vision and development know-how.

Throughout the 1980s, the system of deciding planning applications in the UK came under particular strain as decisions were increasingly overturned at appeal by the Secretary of State in his capacity as final arbiter of planning applications (see p. 25). The practice undermined not only the increased development certainty which any planning system is meant to provide (through consistent and objective decision-making), but also the democratic authority of locally elected councils as planning authorities. The problem was compounded by the unique discretionary system of planning in Britain whereby the development plan remains just one of the material considerations authorities need to weigh in coming to their decisions (Booth in Cullingworth, 1999, p. 31) – see Chapter 7.

In 1991, the Planning and Compensation Act modified the earlier legislation and introduced a plan-led system. This marked a decisive departure from earlier practice and was an attempt to increase the certainty with which planning decisions were made, thereby overcoming what had come to be characterised as an appeal-led system (Purdue, 1994). Guidance issued in Planning Policy Guidance Note 1 (PPG1) (DoE,

---

[2] Subsequently planning became part of the Department of the Environment (1970–1997), the Department of Environment, Transport and the Regions (1997–2001), the Department of Transport, Local Government and the Regions (2001–2002) and (most obscurely and recently) the Office of the Deputy Prime Minister (2002–) (Dewar, 2002a). The frequent changes, and the omission of 'planning' from any of these titles, give some indication of national priorities.

1997a), outlining the general policy and principles by which the planning process operates in England, described the plan-led system as follows:

> The planning system regulates the development and use of land in the public interest. The system as a whole, and the preparation of development plans in particular, is the most effective way of reconciling the demand for development and the protection of the environment. . . . The Government is committed to a plan-led system of development control. This is given statutory force by Section 54A of the 1990 Act. Where an adopted or approved development plan contains relevant policies, section 54A requires that an application for planning permission or an appeal shall be determined in accordance with the plan, unless material considerations indicate otherwise.
>
> (para. 40)

The note went on to outline the objectives of the plan-led system as:

* ensuring rational and consistent decisions;
* achieving greater certainty;
* securing public involvement in shaping local planning policies;
* facilitating quicker planning decisions; and
* reducing the number of misconceived planning applications and appeals.

Nevertheless, 'by the 1990s, despite the rhetoric about the importance of "plans", planning policy had become almost entirely regulatory' (Cullingworth, 1997a), with a policy vacuum around key issues such as population dispersal, transportation, urban design and urban revitalisation. Increasingly from the mid-1990s onwards commentators (including those from the planning profession – see p. 38) began to argue that it was time for a change.

The system's scope and limitations

PPG1 suggests that

> A key role of the planning system is to enable the provision of homes and buildings, investment and jobs in a way which is consistent with the principles of sustainable development. It needs to be positive in promoting competitive-ness while being protective towards the environment and amenity. The policies which underpin the system . . . seek to balance these aims.
>
> (DoE, 1997a, para. 1)

This balance between economic pressures (which are often short term in their objectives and requirements and driven by private interests) and environmental and social objectives (which are more usually long term and driven by public interests) sits at the heart of the planning process. The resolution of economic, environmental and social objectives is broadly what most planning concerns. However, the means at the disposal of planners to make these judgements are relatively limited and boil down to one key power – control over right to develop land (both new development and changes of use).

Although the public sector has much broader powers to plan the social, economic and physical fabric of localities, most lie beyond the statutory planning process. They include:

- transport planning and investment
- economic development and regeneration
- land reclamation
- urban management and maintenance
- environmental standards
- education and training
- health and social services
- social housing provision
- cultural and leisure provision
- police powers
- building control
- tax and fiscal powers (local and national).

Therefore planners and planning authorities do not have the ability to single-handedly deliver on many of their policy goals, because key powers and resources (public and private) lie outside their control. As a consequence, planners are faced with the situation that planning by its nature attempts to meet broad social, economic and environmental goals, but the system only delivers a relatively blunt instrument to achieve these ends. Local planning policy, for example, might plan to revitalise an urban community with new housing, job opportunities and social infrastructure, but if the private sector will not invest in the area, then the plan is likely to come to nothing.

In this regard, planning as constituted in the UK to a large extent depends on demand for development before it can achieve its aims. It also depends on an ability and willing- ness to work alongside and with a wide range of private sector and public sector interests, to negotiate and to coordinate interests and activities to meet agreed ends. Nevertheless, if the demand exists, then control of the right to develop land can be a powerful tool. Indeed it impacts directly or indirectly on all of the areas of public policy outlined above, and on the vast majority of private sector development decisions. It provides no less than the means to spatially orchestrate key public and private sector investments and, in so doing, to meet broad social and environmental objectives using the power to give and (just as importantly) withhold planning permission.

The operation of the planning process

Within the confines of the statutory process, planning in the UK also varies in the style of its operation. Brindley *et al.* (1996), for example, identify six distinct styles of planning in a typology determined by the prevailing attitude to market processes and the relative prosperity of the locality (Table 2.2). Regulative planning has largely reflected the domi- nant approach to planning in the UK inherent in the 1947 Planning Act, in other words the view that through regulation of the right to develop, development activity could be positively directed to meet prescribed ends. Trend planning crudely represents the antithesis of regulative planning and was to some degree advocated by the Thatcher governments of the 1980s. It represents a hands-off process, with planning seen in the main as a means of better facilitating the actions of the market. Popular planning con- versely is directed towards the satisfaction of local community objectives through public participation and direct involvement in the planning process. It combines direct state intervention with an active popular base and has rarely occurred in its true form in the UK.

The major characteristic of leverage planning is the use of public sector finance to stimulate investment in otherwise weak markets as was done in the 1980s, for example,

Table 2.2 A typology of planning styles (Brindley et al., 1996, p. 9)

Perceived nature of urban problems	Attitude to market processes	
	Market-critical: redressing imbalances and inequalities created by the market	Market-led: correcting inefficiencies while supporting market processes
Bouyant area: minor problems and byoyant market	Regulative planning	Trend planning
Marginal area: pockets of urban problems and potential market interest	Popular planning	Leverage planning
Derelict area: comprehensive urban problems and depressed market	Public-investment planning	Private-management planning

through the work of the Urban Development Corporations. Leverage planning is nearly always favoured today over public-investment planning, which, as the name suggests, relies on direct public investment in areas where urban problems are intense and private sector investment is unlikely. Finally, private-management planning relies almost completely on the private sector to turn places around (although usually with big subsidies). It hands over large areas (for example former public housing estates) to private sector management and control (Brindley *et al.*, 1996, pp. 12–25).

Although scope continues to exist for the operation of all these planning styles within the UK system, it is regulative planning (and to a lesser extent leverage planning) that has dominated the statutory process. The lack of direct public sector investment in urban areas (not least in the housing stock), nevertheless continues to be a significant point of criticism amongst commentators and a reason that broad public planning objectives often remain unmet (Urban Task Force, 2000).

Planning in the UK operates at four key levels (see Table 2.3), at national, regional, subregional and local levels (all in turn influenced by supranational planning operating at the European Union level above). The first two levels are dominated by central government, leading to a highly centralised system of planning. Thus in 2002 the Government can drive and influence the process of planning for housing in ten key ways:

1. Through the power to legislate and change the detail, or less frequently the fundamentals, of the whole planning system. In 1991, the plan-led system was introduced in this way; ten years later in 2001, the Planning Green Paper: Planning, Delivering a Fundamental Change represented a prelude to further legislative change.
2. Through the preparation of a detailed national guidance framework (in England through the Planning Policy Guidance Notes – PPGs, and from 2002 through the publication of Planning Policy Statements – PPSs) which authorities are required to take into account in the preparation of their development plans, and in making decisions on planning applications. Advice in new PPGs can even supersede

policies and land allocations in adopted development plans, as PPG3 makes clear: 'Where the planning application related to development of a greenfield site allocated for housing in an adopted local plan or UDP, it should be assessed, and a decision made on the application, in the light of policies set out in this guidance' (DETR, 2000a, para. 38).

3. Through the preparation of regional guidance (in England the Regional Planning Guidance Notes – RPGs, and from 2003 Regional Spatial Strategies – RSSs), after taking advice from regional conferences or chambers of local authorities – although in the future responsibility for the preparation of regional guidance may be moved to directly elected assemblies as it currently is in London (ODPM, 2002f).
4. Through publication of a raft of good practice guidance on a wide range of planning issues, e.g. housing capacity or design.
5. Through the representations of the regional government offices on development plans (strategic and local) during the plan preparation and adoption process.
6. Through the power to call in and/or modify development plans if deemed to depart from national policy.
7. Through the appointment of Plan Inspectors to conduct Public Local Inquiries on all development plans.
8. Through the operation of an appeals process to the Secretary of State on individual planning applications.
9. Through the power to call in individual planning applications and to make final binding determinations of planning permission.
10. Through establishing national indicators of planning performance and inspection regimes of service provision through the Best Value framework (see Chapter 6).

The centralised nature of the system to some extent undermines its democratic accountability, with key decisions made in the name of the Secretary of State far removed from the localities where their consequences are felt. Arguably, however, it also increases the consistency of decisions and reduces the opportunities for local authorities to undermine national objectives or abuse the process.

Nevertheless, planning is justified on the basis that the process is democratic and accountable, with decisions concerning development made by locally elected councillors and not by the uncoordinated actions of private interests. The 1990 Town and Country Planning Act provided for local authorities in their guise as local planning authorities to operate the next two levels of planning action. In two-tier local government areas, County Councils have provided the broad strategic planning framework, with district authorities providing a local framework. In single-tier areas the Unitary Development Plan has been produced by the unitary authority and contains both strategic (Part I) and local (Part II) planning policies. In Scotland and Wales no strategic tier exists, although authorities still produce joint structure plans in partnership with neighbouring authorities.

Under the 1990 Act, local planning authorities are provided with two key powers and responsibilities, the power and responsibility to make development plans and the power and responsibility to control development through issuing planning permissions. Most planning departments within local planning authorities are structured to reflect these basic functions, with forward planning teams responsible for writing and adopting the development plan, and development control sections dealing with planning applications. Typically, councils have established a planning committee through which the plan is

Table 2.3 *Hierarchy of planning policy guidelines (adapted from Carmona et al., 2002)*

Policy hierarchy 2002	Role and utility	Future policy hierarchy
	National guidance	
1. Primary Legislation (planning acts)	Provides the statutory basis for planning and conservation, and therefore also for development control – 1990 Town and Country Planning. 1991 Planning and Compensation. 2003 Planning and Compensation Purchase Acts.	**1. Primary Legislation** (planning acts)
2. Planning Policy Guidance (PPGs)	Sets out and elucidates government policy on key planning matters. Such guidance is a paramount material consideration, but remains general and flexible in nature, requiring interpretation in the light of local circumstances. Guidance is offered on subjects as diverse as green belts, housing, telecommunications, transport, town centres and retail development, enforcing planning control, nature conservation. planning and noise, etc.	**2. Planning Policy Statements (PPSs)**
	Will gradually replace PPGs, and in so doing set out Government policy on planning matters in a more clear, concise and focused manner. Will focus on implementation of national objectives, but will focus on policy, and therefore avoid straying into advice. Will remain the foremost material consideration in writing policy and making planning decisions.	
3. Government Advice Circulars Design Bulletins Good Practice Guides	Gives government advice on more detailed and technical planning concerns such as crime, road layouts or housing design. Such advice is also a material consideration. For example. PPG3: Housing has been supplemented by five good practice guides.	**3. Government Advice** Circulars Design Bulletins Good Practice Guides
	Strategic guidance	
4. Regional Planning Guidance (RPG)	Establishes the broad regional emphasis/priorities on environmental, economic and social concerns and a framework for the production of strategic plans. Regional advice includes broad housing allocations, advice on where that housing should go and targets for affordable housing. Prepared by conferences of local authorities or regional chambers.	**4. Regional Spatial Strategies (RSS)**
	Will have statutory status as the new strategic guidance under which local development frameworks and local transport plans should be prepared. Will be slimmed down from RPGs, but will have statutory status as part of the development plan and local development frameworks will need to be consistent with the relevant RSS. To be prepared by regional assemblies if and when elected.	
5. Structure Plan/ Unitary Development Plan (UDP) Part 1 Policy	Provides strategic advice and a framework to ensure consistent policy across borough/district authorities. County councils produce structure plans, the Mayor for London the Spatial Development Strategy (SDS) and unitary authorities produce unitary development plans (UDPs), the first part of which contain strategic policies. Structure plans outline required housing provision in and across their area.	**5. Subregional strategies**
	Will be prepared in some areas only as part of the RSS, i.e. where administrative boundaries would otherwise prevent proper planning, and will distribute housing to districts. Like RSSs they will provide an early opportunity to establish the quality thresholds for development. Will be prepared by conferences of authorities or regional chambers, and if and when elected by regional assemblies.	
6. Landscape character	Ensures emphasis is given to landscape concerns and helps ensure proper regard is had to natural environment/ecological issues as well as to those concerning the built environment. Such appraisals are of maximum value if able to inform policy (prescriptive rather than descriptive).	**6. Landscape character assessment**
7. County Design Guides	Influential over the years particularly for residential development, i.e. Essex. Cheshire. Kent. Sussex guides. Ensure a consistent approach to design across districts. Tend to focus on county matters such as road hierarchy and broad vernacular, but they provide an opportunity to establish broad urban design principles, e.g. Essex. General at best, and no substitute for district policy.	**7. County Design Guides**

Table 2.3 continued

Authority-wide guidance

8. Community strategy

Provides the opportunity to establish a community vision and aspirations and to coordinate local authority services and actions towards securing more sustainable patterns of development. Local development frameworks are required to assist in the delivery of policies in the community strategy and are prepared by Strategic Local Partnerships, usually (but not necessarily) led by the local authority.

9. Local Plan/ Unitary Development Plan (UDP) Part 2 Policy

Provides the most potent tool in the planning authorities' armoury, benefiting from the "full force of section 54A. Local plans and UDPs (like structure plans) are closely scrutinised by central government to ensure consistency with national and regional planning policy. They cover the full range of planning policy areas and generic policies as well as site-specific policies and proposals.

10. Authority-wide Supplementary Planning Guidance (SPG)

Sits outside of the plan and is therefore not subject to the status and provisions of Section 54A of the 1990 Planning Act. It nevertheless represents an important material consideration in the making of planning decisions. Government guidance advises that all key concerns that form the basis for decision-making should nevertheless be formally adopted in the development plan.

---

8. Community strategy

9. Local Development Framework (LDF) – Core Strategy and Proposals Section

Develops the vision in the community strategy for land use planning and provides a concise statement of policy across all areas of the planning remit, including housing provision and design. The LDF carries the same weight as development plans in a plan-led system and provides a framework for more detailed action plans. Site-specific policies are included in the proposals section.

10. Local Development Framework (LDF) – Authority-wide Guidance

Has the potential to incorporate all previous authority-wide supplementary planning guidance as local development documents (LDDs) within the LDF. Suitable for establishing design principles for particular types of development, or principles for the delivery of affordable housing expanding on the principles in the LDF Core Strategy. LDDs may be formally adopted as development plan documents or not.

Local guides: Can be used to elucidate and disseminate policy advice and to educate applicants, councillors and development controllers. Well suited to single issues such as affordable housing or sustainable development, or to different development types and contexts. They are most often used to develop design policy in the form of local design guides, and to establish expected design standards with illustrated examples of best practice.

Development standards: Largely relate to residential amenity considerations (health and safety concerns) and to residential roads. Such quantitative measures rarely secure good development quality by themselves, and need to be operated flexibly and with skill, alongside other urban form policy to avoid over-regimented solutions.

Development strategies: Give spatial expression to urban design policy, and provide a mechanism through which detailed briefs and frameworks can be generated, e.g. the Birmingham Urban Design Study. A proactive form of guidance, best suited to expressing broad urban design/development issues and planned interventions/investment in the urban fabric. They require an agreed vision of future form.

Landscape strategy: Focuses on managing and enhancing, as well as protecting landscape (urban and rural). Such strategies help integrate natural and built environment concerns, ensuring a more sustainable approach to future development, for example *Cherishing Outdoor Spaces, A Landscape Strategy for Bath.*

Table 2.3 continued

Area or site-specific guidance

11. Area/Site-specific Supplementary Planning Guidance (SPG)		11. Local Development Framework (LDF) – Local Action Plans (and other non-statutory SPG)

Sits outside of the plan and is therefore not subject to the status and provisions of Section 54A of the 1990 Planning Act. It nevertheless represents an important material consideration in the making of planning decisions. Government guidance advises that all key concerns that form the basis for decision-making should be formally adopted in the development plan.

Potentially includes all previous area or site-specific supplementary planning guidance. These are proactive LDDs most likely establishing a design strategy for areas of change, but are also appropriate in areas of conservation. They can also be formally adopted as development plan documents in the LDF or can remain non-statutory.

Area appraisal: Although resource intensive to prepare, area appraisal should form an essential part of the policy writing process, ensuring that proper regard is given to the visual, social, functional and environmental context. It is useful to make appraisal analytical rather than purely descriptive, and to publish it alongside policy as a material consideration. Appraisals include conservation area assessments.

Design codes: Area-related (but not site-specific) urban design codes are usually used to guide the form of comprehensive development over long periods, often alongside a master plan. They can borrow cues from the surrounding context or define a new context, but do not by themselves provide certainty over the eventual urban structure, though developers can adopt them. They also require long-term will to implement, for example the *Guide to Development in Hulme, Manchester*.

Development/design frameworks: Provide a proactive approach to encouraging an appropriate infrastructure and urban form on large, long-term development sites – roads, public transport, landscape and open space, nodes, connections, vistas, etc. They allow flexibility for designers to design within a coordinated controlling framework, and can be used to coordinate individual development briefs.

Master plans: Three-dimensional vision of future form (allowing architectural freedom within limits of defined form). They maximise certainty, but can reduce flexibility if too prescriptive. Their great advantage is their role in articulating a vision and ensuring appropriate relationships are created between built form and public spaces.

Development briefs: Proactive, readily adaptable, resource-efficient guidance, well suited to defining the urban design, development and planning (not architectural) requirements of individual sites. Can be used to aid policy implementation, consultation, marketing and to lever planning gain. In practice they are too often ignored and lack design content, but nevertheless represent a material consideration, and are capable of ensuring the best possible use of land and promoting design quality.

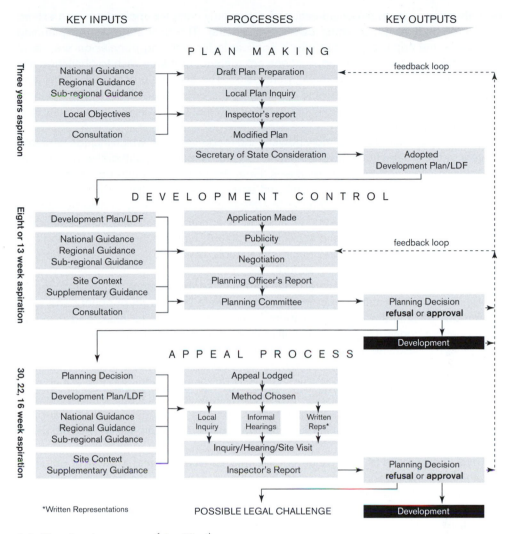

KEY INPUTS   PROCESSES   KEY OUTPUTS

P L A N   M A K I N G

Three years aspiration

National Guidance / Regional Guidance / Sub-regional Guidance	→	Draft Plan Preparation	← feedback loop
Local Objectives		Local Plan Inquiry	
Consultation		Inspector's report	
		Modified Plan	
		Secretary of State Consideration	→ Adopted Development Plan/LDF

D E V E L O P M E N T   C O N T R O L

Eight or 13 week aspiration

Development Plan/LDF		Application Made	
National Guidance / Regional Guidance / Sub-regional Guidance		Publicity	
		Negotiation	← feedback loop
Site Context / Supplementary Guidance		Planning Officer's Report	
Consultation		Planning Committee	→ Planning Decision **refusal** or **approval**
			Development

A P P E A L   P R O C E S S

30, 22, 16 week aspiration

Planning Decision		Appeal Lodged	
Development Plan/LDF		Method Chosen	
National Guidance / Regional Guidance / Sub-regional Guidance		Local Inquiry / Informal Hearings / Written Reps*	
Site Context / Supplementary Guidance		Inquiry/Hearing/Site Visit	
		Inspector's Report	→ Planning Decision **refusal** or **approval**

*Written Representations

POSSIBLE LEGAL CHALLENGE   Development

2.1 The planning process (simplified).

approved and planning decisions are made under the auspices of professional planning staff.

Figure 2.1 offers a highly simplified diagram of the statutory planning process as constituted in the 1990 and 2003 Acts. It indicates the distinct nature of the plan-making and development control processes, and also their interdependent nature, with development control reliant on plan-making to provide a basis for control, and (ideally) the outcomes of the control process feeding back into policy revision and plan review. Nevertheless, the timescales of the two processes are by their nature very different. Thus plan-making is a long-term and highly complex process aimed at establishing a long-term policy framework for development (ten years plus). In England the process of plan adoption has also typically occurred over a period of years (two years up to – in the worst cases – ten years to adopt a plan). By contrast, development control is a relatively short-term process – eight weeks being (until 2002 – see Chapter 6) the Government imposed aspiration for 80 per cent of applications to be determined by authorities – although consideration of particularly complex applications can extend over many months (or in some cases even years). The final stage in the planning process is the appeals process which applicants for planning permission are, as of right, entitled to utilise if their applications are refused, or if they wish to challenge any conditions attached to their planning permission. The appeals process (like local plan inquires) is presided over in England on behalf of the Secretary of State by the Planning Inspectorate, an executive agency of central government (equivalent mechanisms exist elsewhere in the UK).

In addition to their basic statutory powers and responsibilities, which include separate powers in the areas of conservation and enforcement, planning authorities rely on two other key powers and two key processes. First, the power as granted by Section 106 of the 1990 Planning Act to negotiate and agree planning obligations. This 'Planning Gain' is discussed in depth in Chapter 9; suffice to note here that planning obligations allow planning authorities to negotiate financial or actual contributions from developers in the form of related physical and social infrastructure. Typical subjects for planning gain include social housing, transport infrastructure, public open space, public realm improvements, related local facilities, and so forth.

Second, the power to prepare other forms of supplementary planning guidance (SPG). Table 2.3 identifies a range of such guidance in the form of county and local design guides or strategies, development frameworks and master plans and development briefs or codes. The intention of all of these documents has been to elucidate the policy in the development plan for specific areas, types of development or specific sites. Most have a particular focus on design but also consider the wider range of planning and development issues. They are non-statutory documents (although this will change – see p. 32) which constitute material considerations in evaluating planning applications. The weight attached to supplementary planning guidance increases if subject to public consultation and formally adopted by council resolution (DETR, 2000k, paras 3.15–3.18).

Third, the process of negotiation on planning applications and thereby of ensuring that they meet key planning objectives. Negotiation occurs on the basis of key power relationships which are dictated in turn by how badly local authorities need to attract development to their locality, and by how much and how quickly housing providers and other developers need planning permission. A key (negative) power that authorities have is the ability to refuse or delay planning permission, and – even if they intend to grant planning permission eventually – the ability to negotiate on the basis that they might not (in other words the ability to bluff).

Finally, the process of coordinating the actions of others. This reflects the key role of planning: to develop a future vision that foresees how the many investments that collectively create and maintain urban environments can be orchestrated. In this regard planning is potentially – although in reality often not – the natural point of coordination for investment in the built environment. Thus planners are often aware of the range of private sector stakeholders in their locality, and about how their interests can be combined with public and third (voluntary and non-profit) sector activities to ensure that the best outcomes are delivered for all. Coordination extends to investment sources, land resources, grant regimes, development interest, policy frameworks, public sector investments and public involvement, and is discussed in greater depth in Chapter 10.

By all these means the planning process can fulfil the tripartite functions of guidance, incentive and control, outlined in 1992 planning guidance (DoE, 1992b, para. 4.27):

- Guidance, to help people plan the use of their land confidently and sensibly, and to help planning authorities to interpret the public interest wisely and consistently.
- Incentive, in that by allocating land in policy and guidance for particular types of development, local authorities may stimulate that development.
- Control, which ensures that developers cannot ultimately insist for private reasons on a change which would be against the public interest, and that people affected by proposals for change can have their views considered.

Delivering a fundamental change

Perceived inadequacies with the planning system, some of which have been discussed above, and many of which are elucidated at length in Chapters 5 to 10, finally led in December 2001 to proposals for reform in the Green Paper *Planning: Delivering a Fundamental Change* (DTLR, 2001a), taken forward in July 2002 in the Planning Policy Statement: *Sustainable Communities – Delivering Through Planning* (ODPM, 2002a) and the 2003 Act. The decision to reform the planning system was driven to a large degree by business lobbying for a system that is more responsive (read faster and more sympathetic) to business needs (see Fig. 2.2). The CBI (2001), for example, argued in 'Planning for Productivity' that the system was too slow, too uncertain, and offered too much scope for poor decisions (in their terms those that fail to have appropriate regard to economic considerations). Nevertheless, the need for reform had broad support amongst planning (RTPI, 2001a), private and social housing (HBF, 2002b; NHF, 2001a) and amenity interests (CABE, 2001), although interestingly in the run-up to the Green Paper, the Housebuilders' Federation (HBF) were noticeably less ambitious in their aspirations for reform than most other interests, arguing that the existing system required modification but not radical overhaul (see p. 54).

2.2 The driver of reform (Shenton, 2001).

The proposals in the Green Paper responded to a number of perceived weaknesses with the planning system (DTLR, 2001a, pp. 3–5):

- Planning, and in particular the multi-layered hierarchy of adopted plans, is too complex.
- The process is too slow, with plans often out of date before they are adopted.
- Planning is too often negative and seen as a set of rules aimed at stopping development, rather than encouraging high-quality development.
- Policy frameworks often lack clarity and therefore undermine the predictability of the process.
- The system fails to engage the interest of the communities for whom it is operated.
- Planning is not customer focused.

The need for, and value of, the planning system was nevertheless emphasised, as was the philosophy of a plan-led (if still discretionary) system. The DTLR (2001a, p. 2) argued, 'We believe in good planning. The present system, by general consent, does not deliver our objectives. . . . It is time for fundamental change'.

The solution was seen as a system based on a simplified policy hierarchy, including: shorter, better focused plans which can be adopted and revised more quickly; better integration between planning policy and other local strategies; more community involvement in policy preparation; and a system that prioritises higher-quality development (DTLR, 2001a, pp. 5–6). Key provisions of relevance to housing development are outlined in Fig. 2.3, and notably included: a new policy hierarchy with a particular emphasis on proactive local planning and slimmed-down policy frameworks (see Table 2.3); an end to structure plans and planning at the county level; the incorporation of much former supplementary planning guidance into the statutory adopted Local Development Framework (LDF); and a variety of approaches to speed up decision-making. The final

---

Planning Policy

➤ Replacing structure plans, local plans and unitary development plans with continually updated local development frameworks prepared by district and unitary authorities, constituted of a folder of local development documents:

  1. A core strategy setting out the local authority's vision and strategy to be applied in promoting and controlling development throughout the area;
  2. More detailed action plans for smaller local areas of change, such as urban extensions, town centres and neighbourhoods undergoing renewal. Action plans might also be prepared on a topic basis for wider areas;
  3. A proposals section and map showing the areas of change for which action plans are to be prepared, existing designations such as conservation areas, as well as sites for future land uses and developments.

➤ The core strategy would be short and focused in nature, consisting of:

  1. A statement of the framework's role in delivering the long-term vision for the area;
  2. Clear objectives for what the authority is seeking to achieve in terms of the development and improvement of the physical environment of its area, together with a proposed timetable;
  3. A strategy for delivering the objectives and key diagram;

4. A statement of community involvement setting out arrangements for involving the community in the continuing review of the framework, and in significant development control decisions;
5. Criteria-based policies to shape development and deliver the strategy. These would form the basis for development control and be accompanied by a written justification.

➤ Action plans would be reviewed regularly, and would articulate a clear physical vision for their areas and have a strong design emphasis. Action plans would either be statutorily adopted as development plan documents, and through independent testing gain the weight of Section 54A of the 1990 Act, or would remain non-statutory material considerations. They might include:

1. Area master plans – comprehensive plans for a major area of renewal or development covering design, layout and location of new houses and commercial development supported by a detailed implementation programme;
2. Neighbourhood and village plans – setting out how the distinctive character of a neighbourhood, village or parish is to be protected, the location of any new development, the key services and facilities, and the design standards to be applied;
3. Design statements for an area or type of development – setting out the design standards and related performance criteria for an area or type of development;
4. Site development briefs – setting out detailed guidance on how a particular site is to be developed.

Development Control

➤ A number of changes (although much less fundamental) to the system of development control, including proposals to:

1. Introduce a planning checklist to encourage submission of good quality planning applications
2. Tighten targets for determining planning applications
3. Encourage masterplanning to improve the quality of development
4. Replace on a trial basis the system of outline consents with statements of development principles about specified parameters – i.e. provision of affordable housing – and that for a defined period, a detailed application should be worked up
5. Promote better community involvement by offering community groups advice on planning
6. Introduce delivery contracts for planning for major developments
7. Seek tougher enforcement against those who evade planning requirements
8. Promote greater use of mediation for resolving planning disputes
9. Reject the introduction of third-party rights of appeal.

National and Regional Planning

➤ Scrapping strategic planning at the county level and replacing Regional Planning Guidance with Regional Spatial Strategies (RSSs) with statutory status. Subregional planning (where necessary) to be undertaken as part of the RSS process.
➤ Simplification of the national planning policy framework, separating policy from advice.

2.3 Key provisions of the 2001 Planning Green Paper, 2002 Planning Policy Statement and the 2003 Planning and Compulsory Purchase Act.

chapter in this book concludes by returning to the proposals in the Green Paper and subsequent planning act and considers how the key stakeholders discussed throughout this book view the changing planning agenda.

Planning for housing

The challenge to plan for an adequate supply of high-quality housing in the right places and at the right prices/tenures was both the driving force behind the establishment of a planning system in the UK, and one of the main reasons for the reforms. Today, the challenge is driven by a new set of drivers (see Fig. 2.4). Responding to some of these, a new framework for planning for housing was laid out in March 2000 in a revised version of Planning Policy Guidance 3: Housing. The note outlines a range of clear objectives for the planning system (DETR, 2000a, para. 2 – see also Fig. 5.1), requiring planning authorities to:

- plan to meet the housing requirements if the whole community, including those in need of affordable and special needs housing;
- provide wider housing opportunity and choice and a better mix in the size, type and location of housing than is currently available, and seek to create mixed communities;
- provide sufficient housing land but give priority to reusing previously developed land within urban areas, bringing empty homes back into use and converting existing buildings, in preference to the development of greenfield sites;
- create more sustainable patterns of development by building in ways which exploit and deliver accessibility by public transport to jobs, education and health facilities, shopping, leisure and local services;
- make more efficient use of land by reviewing planning policies and standards;
- place the needs of people before ease of traffic movement in designing the layout of residential developments;
- seek to reduce car dependence by facilitating more walking and cycling, by improving linkages by public transport between housing, jobs, local services and local amenity, and by planning for mixed use; and

---

➤ The deterioration of global and local environments and the increasing prominence of the sustainability imperative
➤ The regeneration of declining or underutilised urban assets and the emergence of the urban renaissance agenda in the UK
➤ The opportunities and threats posed by globalisation and new technologies
➤ Changing living patterns and redistributing populations, leading to a continued and sustained demand for new housing
➤ The poor quality of many public and private residential developments in recent decades and their segregated and roads dominated nature
➤ The move away from direct state provision for social housing
➤ The increasing resistance to development from many established communities (the NIMBY – Not In My Back Yard – phenomenon)
➤ Increasing market segmentation, with market resistance to mixing uses and tenures
➤ Increasing demand differentials across regions and subregions, and the separation of demand from where supply is being encouraged.

2.4 Fundamental challenges on planning for housing (Carmona, 2001a, p. 41).

- promote good design in new housing development in order to create attractive, high-quality living environments in which people will choose to live.

The guidance indicated a significant departure from earlier policy which had effectively put the needs of the market and the quantity of new homes ahead of the needs of the environment and qualitative concerns, or indeed the demands of the non-market housing sector. Thus, for example, the infamous 'Circular 22/80: Development Control – Policy and Practice' established the national policy context for the next two decades announcing that:

> There must be an adequate and continuous supply of land, with planning permission, suitable and available for immediate development, and situated where potential house buyers are prepared to live. . . . In the absence of such an identified five year supply there should be a presumption in favour of granting permission for housing except where there are clear planning objections which in the circumstances of the case out-weigh the need to make the land available for housing.

On housing type and tenure it warned that:

> Functional requirements within a development are for the most part a matter for the developers and their customers. [Local authorities] should only regulate the mix of house types when there are specific planning reasons for such control, and in doing so they should take particular account of marketing considerations.
> (DoE, 1980, paras A2 – A3 and A14)

The new guidance in PPG3 pre-empted the publication of an Urban White Paper in 2000 building on the work of the Urban Task Force. The Urban Task Force (1999) had seen the demand for housing in the UK (the infamous 4.4 million new homes by 2021) as an opportunity to reinvigorate England's urban areas rather than as a threat to the countryside. The White Paper – subtitled 'Delivering an Urban Renaissance' – largely accepted the arguments, and shared the vision of creating more socially balanced, environmentally sustainable, mixed-use developments of a high design quality to meet housing needs (DETR, 2000d). It promised a reinvestment in urban areas and the increased use of previously developed land for housing to prevent further urban sprawl.

Reflecting the new policy agenda, PPG3 established a national target of 60 per cent of additional housing to be provided on previously developed – brownfield – land by 2008 (DETR, 2000a, para. 23); a target to be achieved at the same time as sustaining the supply of new land for housing. Methods were to include:

- concentrating most additional housing development within urban areas;
- making more efficient use of land by maximising the reuse of previously developed land and the conversion and reuse of existing buildings;
- assessing the capacity of urban areas to accommodate more housing;
- adopting a sequential approach to the allocation of land for housing development;
- managing the release of housing land; and
- reviewing existing allocations of housing land in plans, and planning permissions when they come up for renewal (DETR, 2000a, para. 21).

These issues and their implications (discussed in greater depth in Chapter 5) accompanied a shift from a system of 'Predict and Provide' for new housing (predict housing growth 20 to 25 years ahead by examining population trends and movements and plan in advance for its delivery) to 'Plan, Monitor and Manage'. The new system was intended to be more sensitive to changes in household growth patterns by annually monitoring trends and reviewing proposed provision targets every five years or sooner. Although subtle, the change reflected a new belief in the value of planning to meet local needs 'based on a clear set of policy objectives' (DETR, 2000a, para. 8). It anticipated a planning process that needs to be more responsive to changing circumstances, and more proactive in changing to meet those needs.

Delivering planning – 2003

This chapter has focused on planning both in an idealised sense, as regards the rationale for planning and what it aims to achieve, and also in a pragmatic sense, as regards the operation and scope of the statutory planning process, and its relation to housing. In an idealised sense, planning is a value-driven activity concerned with 'the management of the competing uses for space; and the making of places that are valued and have identity' (RTPI, 2001a). However, in a pragmatic sense the limitations of the system in the UK (particularly in England) have too often seemed to undermine these objectives, not least the closely defined nature of the statutory process, the undermining of local initiative from a heavily centralised system, and the failure to coordinate the activity of planning with other public sector activities, including housing. To add to the challenge is the increasing complexity and interdependency of urban problems as reflected in the findings of the Urban Task Force (1999).

At the turn of the century, a range of commentators wrote about a crisis in planning and about a need to rethink the purpose and meaning of the discipline, not least the Urban Task Force (see above). In the UK, this situation has manifested itself in a crisis of recruitment to accredited planning degree programmes, a marginalisation of planning activities within local authorities, a lack of investment in planning as a public sector service, and the widespread perception that planning as a discipline is largely technocratic, negative and reactive.

The rhetoric in the professional press echoes to some extent that heard during the last crisis in planning in the late 1970s and 1980s. At that time writers recorded a widespread disillusionment with planning and a recognition that the profession had largely failed to live up to the claims made for it in the post-war world. The 'clean-sweep' mentality in particular was criticised, a feeling that planning had run out of steam was widespread (Brindley *et al.*, 1996, p. 3), and there was a recognition that it had failed to achieve the wholesale modernisation of the built environment that had been promised. The challenge to planning activity that took place in the 1980s and the move away from direct public sector investment in large-scale development effectively led to a retrenchment of the discipline away from its former role as a positive instigator and director of change. Instead it became a profession more narrowly focused on the operation of the statutory planning process – plan-making and development control.

By the end of the 1990s, the new more limited role was again being questioned as planners were increasingly criticised for lacking the vision of their predecessors. Although the predicted death of planning during the Thatcher era never came to pass, its refocusing had to some extent divorced much of the more positive activity in the guise of urban regeneration and direct public development from the statutory process. The result weakened both regeneration activity (undertaken largely by Urban Development Corporations and their like without social or environmental values or accountability) and planning, which more and more operated without vision.

Although planning is credited with a number of conspicuous successes since 1947, not least (many, although not all, would argue) the containment of urban England, in many respects its theoretical potential as envisaged by the pioneers of the planning system remains to be fully realised. Reasons for this failure (or at least underperformance), can be variously postulated and include:

- A fundamental flaw in the basic rationale of planning, which – it could be argued – tries to control highly complex systems with highly simplistic processes. From time to time the whole purpose of planning has been challenged in this way, most famously in the seminal paper from 1969 – 'Non-Plan' (Banham *et al.*, 1969).
- Structural flaws in the operation of planning (in the particular mechanisms and processes of planning) rather than with its rationale. Successive legislation and government guidance concerned with the operation of the system have attempted over the years to refine the system and improve its effectiveness. Criticisms nevertheless persist.
- Unreliable information or its imperfect understanding, which might distort the assumptions on which planning is based, undermining decision-making processes. The tendency to follow trends in policy without research or adequate questioning in relation to context falls into this category, whilst the cyclical favouring of different residential street layout systems (cul-de-sac/modernist/cul-de-sac/perimeter block/ etc.) represents a case-in-point.
- The lack of resources to implement planning effectively and efficiently represents a consistent lament of practitioners, which when taken to extremes undermines all but the most basic operation of the statutory planning process. The lack of resources portrays a further potential problem, the lack of political support at national and local levels for planning.
- A wide range of other forces acting to undermine the outputs of the planning process, inherent in limitations in the scope of the statutory process (see p. 22) and in the limited aspirations of and/or resources available to other stakeholders, for example in their desire to see and deliver better quality environments.

Of course any system that attempts to balance interests and which plays off one set of stakeholders' objectives with another's is likely at times to generate criticism, if for no other reason than it restricts the freedom of different interests to do as they would if no such system existed. In this regard, the value added by planning (although often not adequately celebrated by the profession) must include what is not built as much as in what is. Furthermore, the existence of a planning system in almost every developed society tends to support the value of at least some system of planning, even if imperfect. Indeed, very few interests would argue for no planning, if for no other reason than it guarantees that once a development is made, its value will be maintained as neighbouring developments are controlled. Reflecting broader political movements, a 'third way' in planning has been increasingly promulgated in the UK as the discipline recaptures at least some of its former visionary zeal, a way with a more balanced view about how this might be delivered (through a partnership of public and private interests), and with a greater regard to both the quality of the final development and to the impact of new investment on old.

In 2001 the 'New Vision for Planning' from the Royal Town Planning Institute (RTPI) represented an attempt to develop such an agenda and to redefine the role of planning in the UK. It argued that the new vision 'challenges us to think beyond the scope of statutory systems and to take a broader view of what society needs through planning' (RTPI, 2001b). The New Vision for Planning is built around the core ideas of planning, that is:

- spatial – dealing with the unique needs and characteristics of places
- sustainable – looking at the short-, medium- and long-term issues
- integrative – in terms of the knowledge, objectives and actions involved
- inclusive – recognising the wide range of people involved in planning
- value-driven – concerned with identifying, understanding and mediating conflicting sets of values
- action-oriented – driven by the twin activities of mediating space and making of place.

The vision demonstrates an attempt to question established practice. It argues that 'Whilst the potential of spatial planning is not in doubt, the arrangements for planning in the future will need to be very different from today. Change is required in both the product and process of planning' (RTPI, 2001b). In Part Three, this book goes on to suggest how such a planning process might operate.

3

The private housebuilding process

The development process: risk v. reward

The intention in this chapter is not to discuss in detail the development process, a subject covered in all its complexity elsewhere (Gore and Nicholson, 1991; Healey, 1991, 1992; Adams, 1994; Cadman and Topping, 1998). Instead, drawing on Carmona's (2001b, Chapter 4) earlier more detailed discussion of the private housing development process, this chapter examines the particular nature of the private housebuilding process, and in so doing attempts to clarify why new-build private housing development so often takes the form it does. Before focusing on the particular characteristics of the housebuilding industry, it is appropriate to briefly discuss a few of the more generic characteristics of the private sector development process.

First, the traditional approach to development by the private sector is to look for investment opportunities which have a high probability of financial success: success which can be better guaranteed by reducing financial exposure – and therefore risk – and increasing certainty. For this reason, anything that increases costs (and therefore risk) is generally opposed by developers, for example delay in granting permissions, contributions to infrastructure, or bespoke design solutions. Conversely, anything which increases certainty or drives up reward is generally supported, including development that meets clear market preferences, or which is supported in planning policy.

In a perfect market, an equilibrium is reached in which sites will be secured by that use which can extract the greatest return from the particular set of advantages (i.e. location) that it offers (Harvey, 1996, p. 215). Such neo-classical ideas form the basis of equilibrium models of the development process which emphasise demand and supply in the land and property markets, and which see the price mechanism as the dominant force in the development process. In reality, a whole set of cultural, political and regulatory processes distort the market (including planning), and so conditions of perfect competition rarely exist.

Second, the risk attached to any development opportunity reflects the complexity of the procurement process and the number of uncertainties inherent in that process. Lang (1994, p. 377), for example, has argued that the development process is a particularly complex one, involving a number of key stages, each of which carries its own costs. This notion of the development process as a series of stages characterises the most widely adopted (if simplistic) models of the development process – event-sequence models –

and although the stages vary in their nomenclature and organisation, the sequence roughly moves from the recognition of a development prospect, through feasibility to implementation (Barrett *et al.*, 1978).

Initially the developer is required to scour the existing environment for development opportunities, a process which requires some prediction of what the property market will be in the future. On identifying an opportunity, a feasibility study is required and some early projection of development costs and cash flows in terms of expenses and incomes over time. Next, short-term and long-term financing must be obtained (including any grants), plans finalised and all the relevant permissions obtained from the statutory authorities. After contracting arrangements and costs are sorted out, the project then moves onto site and the execution of the development on-site has to be managed. Finally the completed scheme is marketed and either sold or let and the ongoing process of adaptation and maintenance begins. At any stage the project is vulnerable to a whole series of external and internal risks, not least the whims and fluctuations of the market and the need to ensure cash flow is secure.

Fig. 3.1 presents a simplified model of the stages in the development process and the associated risks at each stage. Thus as financial exposure increases, so does risk and the need to expedite the development by selling the products (in this case the houses) as quickly as possible. In reality this is unlikely to happen at one moment in time, as, depending on the market circumstances, sales (particularly in the housing sector) can be a long drawn-out process. Financial exposure can nevertheless be managed to some extent by, for example, managing the purchase of the land to share the risk with the land owner (see p. 48). Moreover, event-sequence models are inevitably simplifications of the process because stages more often than not occur concurrently. Thus design occurs from feasibility to completion, and marketing usually as soon as on-site development commences (or even before).

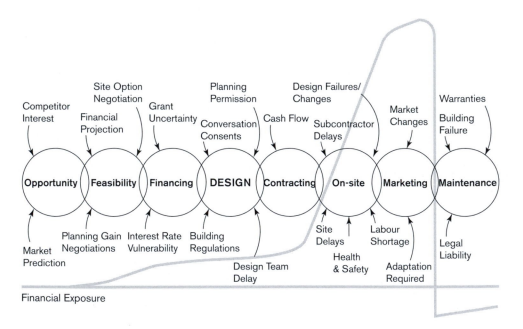

3.1 Risks and the development process.

Agency models complement event-sequence models and help to illustrate the complexity by representing the process as a series of stakeholder relationships, as well as – a third key feature of the development process – the relationship between private and public sector activities. Generally they give a better grasp of the complex development activity itself than event-sequence models as they clearly link stakeholders to events, and emphasise motives in negotiations (see Chapter 1). Ambrose (1986), for example, sees the development process as the product of three key sets of actors: the public sector, the finance industry and the construction industry. The model indicates that the 'production of the built environment results from the control that particular actors exercise over powers and resources and from bargaining and negotiation between actors which enable such powers and resources to be activated' (Adams, 1994, p. 55). The public and a variety of pressure groups and special interests then influence these powers and resources from the outside.

The resources available to different stakeholder groups in turn inform the power relations between groups. These power relations form the basis for a further type of development process model – structure models. Structure models derive from the Marxist tradition and emphasise the way land and property markets are structured through the power relations of capital, labour and land ownership (Boddy, 1981; Harvey, 1985). Although very general in their focus, such models remind us that it is those with resources that in the final analysis have the real power to deliver development, and that these resources include capital, labour and land. Like neo-classical models, however, they underplay the potential of the state to influence the market, for example through planning, and largely ignore state delivery of development, for example of social housing. In reality, therefore, the power relations in the development process are far more complex than structure models suggest, and although developers have considerable power, they are also dependent on the workings of the public sector to meet their objectives.

The various models perhaps come closest to the true nature of the development process if used in combination as a series of interlinked and interacting processes over time, informed by market forces, stakeholder roles and objectives, differential power relationships and public/private relations. Some of these issues are brought together and summarised in Healey's (1992) institutional model of the development process, which emphasises events in the development process, alongside roles in production and consumption (products, outputs and impacts) (see Fig. 3.2).

The model is useful because it places key roles and relationships in their wider market context, and therefore provides a means to understanding and perhaps influencing motivations (also a main objective of this book). The particular roles and relationships between the key actors in the housebuilding process have already been discussed in Chapter 1, from which it was apparent that the key interests of the public and private sectors can be very different, although each is reliant on the other. The structuring of the development process which sets actor against actor is perhaps the single most significant factor in this divergence. Thus Lang (1994, p. 375) has observed that

> The market required to support a potential development consists of the population seeking services and their capacity to pay for them. The question the developer must ask is: 'Is the market large enough to support this development?', while the question the public sector asks is 'How is the public interest to be furthered by this development?'.

Roles in consumption
Material values: production, consumption, investment
Property rights
Guardian of environmental quality

Factors of production
Land
Labour
Capital

Events in the development process, e.g.
Identification of development
Opportunity
Land assembly
Project development
Site clearance
Acquisition of finance
Organisation of construction
Organisation of infrastructure
Marketing/managing the end product

Production/outputs
In building:
Material values
Bundles of property rights
Symbolic/aesthetic values

In the production process:
Profits
Jobs
Demand for related goods/services

Impacts
Wider economic, political, environmental, sociocultural effects

Roles in production
Land: ownership rights, use/development rights
Labour: physical production, supplier organisation
Capital: money, raw materials/machinery

3.2 An institutional model of the development process (Healey, 1992).

The variation in answers to these questions lies at the heart of the conflicts discussed in Part Two of the book, many of which relate to the particular nature of the house-builder's product. In Chapter 16 the different components of the development process models are brought together to suggest (drawing on the research) what an optimum housing delivery process might look like (see Fig. 16.3).

The speculative house

Criticism of the standard product of the housebuilding industry has been persistent. In 1995, in an about-turn in policy, the constant criticisms from professionals, amenity groups and local authorities was given added impetus by the then Secretary of State who came out strongly against the homogenisation of the 'executive cul-de-sac; the zoning madness, and the creeping standardisation' of housing. He declared it 'an insult to our sense of place to offer precisely the same house in Warrington as in Wallingford, Wadebridge or Wolverhampton' (Gummer, 1995, pp. 4–5). In 2001 the then Minister for Planning suggested that little had changed: 'Too many of these housing estates are designed for nowhere but found everywhere. They fail to sustain local services, they waste land and they promote dependency on the car. They easily end up being soulless and dispiriting' (Falconer, 2001).

Against the chorus of criticism of much new housing, housebuilders argue that they know the market and only build what the market wants, and that their houses would

3.3 The speculative house and estate (photo: M. Carmona).

not sell if they were disliked by the public (Davison, 1989; Osborne, 1991; Bateman, 1995). Supporting their view is the fact that for those choosing to move into a new-build speculative residential property, levels of owner satisfaction with their home are likely to be very high (90 per cent plus according to research – Forrest *et al.*, 1997, p. 33). The housebuilders further argue that real improvements in quality cost money, something which purchasers are not willing to pay for (Davison, 1991). The emphasis for most housebuilders (until recently) has therefore remained on the production of 'suburbs' – single-use, single-tenure, car-reliant developments on the edge of existing settlements.

Critiques of such houses (see Fig. 3.3) nevertheless remain vehement, and regularly include (Carmona, 2001b, pp. 89–90):

- context: a failure to respect or respond to urban and landscape context;
- sense of place: a failure to adequately define an identifiable sense of place;
- community: a failure to encourage a sense of community or social diversity;
- urban space: a failure to create coherent urban spaces and visually interesting layouts;
- legibility: a failure to create legible environments;
- connectivity: a failure to create connected, permeable environments;
- movement: a failure to consider the pedestrian experience;
- car dominance: a failure to successfully integrate the needs of the car;
- security: a failure to create secure environments;
- innovation: a failure to deliver architectural quality or innovation;
- flexibility: a failure to create flexible, adaptable houses and environments;
- choice: a failure to offer real variety and choice;
- landscape: a failure to consider landscape (hard and soft) and to integrate open space;
- sustainability: a failure to respond to the sustainable agenda;
- mixing uses: a failure to move beyond the strict zoning philosophy.

With around 170,000 volume-built houses produced each year (Birkbeck, 1999) – dipping to 162,000 in 2001 (Stewart, 2002) – such perceptions inevitably represent generalisations. Nevertheless, the freedom sought by the housebuilders and the indirect conservatism of their outputs is a long-established feature of the speculative market, dating back to well before the twentieth century (Booth, 1982, p. 21). This conservatism – some argue – has only been bucked when the planning process through the production of policy and guidance has forced improvement to the standard product, which more often than not has also released improved market potential (Hamilton, 1976; Hall, 1990). For them, the housebuilding sector is different from most other sectors of the development industry, being characterised by (Black, 1997, p. 81):

- a build and walk away trading ethos – closely linked to the rise in home ownership;
- commitment to a manufacturing, rather than a design or planning process – geared to the production of large numbers of units on a production line principle;
- minimal design input or respect for local consultation or environment (social and physical).

To understand if and why this is so, it is necessary to understand the particular nature of the housebuilding sector in the UK.

The industry

The private house building sector is worth around a third of the entire construction industry (Welsh, 1994, p. 5), with new home sales valued annually at £19 billion, and new private house building contributing 1.2 per cent to GDP (Stewart, 1997). This accounts for 180,000 jobs (HBF, 2002a). Furthermore, for each additional 10,000 new private homes created, 7,000 jobs are provided in the construction industry and 4,600 in the wider economy (Cambridge Econometrics, 1995). Criticism of the planning system from the housebuilders has therefore understandably been consistently persuasive on successive governments.

Because of the capital-intensive nature of the industry, to be amongst the top 50, a housebuilder will typically need to be a public limited company. Most investors in that company will be institutional with a statutory responsibility to their own investors and a loyalty to the company that is only as strong as its performance. For understandable reasons, therefore, concern for design quality, social sustainability and other public objectives feature poorly in most managers priorities, and financial performance and stock market profile feature much more highly (Davison,1987a, pp. 65–7) – 'We are, after all in the business of making money, not houses' commented one national housebuilder (in Leopold and Bishop, 1983, p. 123).

This situation is compounded by the fact that of the 20,000 builders registered with the National House Building Council (NHBC) in 1998, just ten were responsible for over 35 per cent of the combined UK output – 40 housebuilders for 60 per cent (Birkbeck, 1999) – and thus wield great influence and largely set the priorities of the sector. The situation contrasts with that in the 1950s when 90 per cent of private house building was built by local builders; builders with local connections, using local labour and capital, and depending on local knowledge and reputation. By the 1970s most private housing was being built by firms that operated on a regional or national scale, and 'it was possible to buy a Wimpey House in every English county' (Couch, 1986, p. 1). In recent years, local housebuilders have accounted for just 25 per cent of housing output and self-builders for about 7 per cent.

For the housebuilder, the market is often clearly delineated and the industry has on many occasions been accused of concentrating on particular parts of the market to the exclusion of others. For example, most housebuilders have tended to concentrate on the lower end of the market and on starter homes to the exclusion of the upper end. Indeed, research undertaken in the late 1980s found that as house buyers moved up the housing ladder the aspiration was increasingly for an older house and decreasingly for a new home – perhaps explaining the trend (Bishop and Davison, 1989). In providing for this market, research points to the poor standard of provision when compared to international comparisons. Thus the UK has the fourth smallest average floor area per dwelling in Europe (79.7 square metres per dwelling), the second largest average number of rooms (5.0), and the second lowest proportion of flats (19 per cent) in the housing stock (European Commission, 1998). So people are living in small houses with exceptionally small rooms (Stewart, 2002). Furthermore, homes and average plot sizes are getting smaller – 1980s and 1990s housing was 10 per cent smaller than pre-1980s dwellings (DETR, 1998b), indicating the continued decline in provision (on this one indicator only) by the sector.

The subtleties of the housing market contribute to distinguish housebuilding as a specialised sector of the construction industry significantly different from other sectors, with its own trends, requirements and development cycles (Black, 1997, pp. 81–2). Thus although the construction aspect of what the housebuilders do is important, it is only one part of the whole. Their major objective is to 'find land and on it to create market value' (Madden, 1982), a process in many respects more akin to a marketing business than a building business. Therefore in the 1980s and early 1990s many of the companies with wide-ranging unrelated activities that had also maintained a housebuilding division, began to sell out to more specialist companies. Some of these specialist housebuilders were subsequently able to record substantial growth records by either further specialising within the housebuilding market (i.e. McCarthy and Stone – in 1999 the UK's 24th largest housebuilder – grew by specialising in housing for the elderly), or by steadily acquiring other housebuilders (i.e. Beazer Homes – by 1999 the UK's second largest housebuilder) (Davison, 1987a, pp. 63–4).

The trend towards increasing concentration within the industry, and arguably therefore to product homogenisation, can be partly laid at the door of the planning system. This is because the larger companies have been the major beneficiaries of restriction caused by the planning system – when land is scarce and land allocations and permissions are time-consuming and resource-intensive to secure, the companies with the greatest financial resources and technical skills have consistently been able to acquire the best sites (Baron, 1983, p. 19). The need for the public sector to lever any necessary infrastructure costs out of new development also favours increasing concentration, as planning authorities deliberately make larger land allocations in order to ensure delivery (Adam, 1997).

Furthermore, the larger firms have been much more able to raise the vast sums of capital necessary to expand and build more homes through retained earnings, rights issues or extra borrowings. Finally, the increased sophistication of the housebuilding industry favours the large builders, particularly the requirement for more sophisticated marketing techniques and a much wider range of in-house skills to ensure that large developments can be started and sold at acceptable rates. The ubiquitous concentration pressures in the industry continue to undermine even the limited regional variation that exists. Thus, regional differences in the products offered by subsidiary companies are being rationalised away (Hooper and Nicol, 1999, p. 801). The intended consequence of this product branding is the ability for housebuilders to offer the same product solutions nationwide.

Significantly, however, the advantages of the volume builders begin to reduce as sites reduce in size, and as site oncosts[1] begin to increase as a proportion of the final sales value. This makes small housebuilders more competitive on small sites (Baron, 1983, p. 20) and offers one reason why the volume builders have been so hostile to the switch away from large greenfield developments.

Responding to uncertainty

It can be argued that the approach of housebuilders is largely beyond their control, being a by-product of the nature of the housing development and marketing process itself. This is because the characteristics of housing as a product are very different to any other consumer good. Housing 'has first of all a very high capital value' with large amounts of a developer's capital tied up in the purchase of land and materials. Second,

> Its production time is far longer than for most other commodities. Developers are therefore forced to achieve as fast a turnover as possible; delay is extremely costly; and in time of recession, the product cannot be stored against a change in the market without financially disastrous results.
>
> (Booth, 1982, pp. 20–1)

Consequently, it is of the utmost importance to housebuilders that houses are completed and sold as quickly as possible. Hence the heavy reliance on well-tried and tested (marketable) formulae, on conservative approaches to development that avoid complexity (for example responding to local needs), and on the need to gain all relevant approvals as quickly as possible (Beer and Booth, 1981, p. 3).

The result is a standardisation in the products of the housebuilders in order to produce a product that has sold in the past, that can be built quickly and cheaply and that has previously gained the necessary approvals without difficulty. 'In the housing development process, considerations of investment viability, minimising financial risks and maximising potential sales dominate the brief . . . Planning and highways concerns are seen as technical requirements that must be met within the financial parameters' (POS *et al.*, 1998, p. 8). Therefore only in exceptional circumstances will housebuilders be prepared to consider bespoke solutions for individual sites (although with the increasing emphasis on brownfield solutions this is becoming more common). Instead, their standard ranges provide cost-effective living spaces to current construction standards in shells that change little as stylistic treatments come and go and which with their standard plot sizes minimise land take (for the most part narrow fronted, deep plan units with integral garages and low roof pitches). Hence, the volume builders have developed standard portfolios of (in some cases) up to 70 basic house types. Sometimes these have further subtle variations to relate better to regional preferences expressed through the planning process, taking the count up to 150 different models (Anon., 1998a). The emphasis is nearly always on incremental refinements to these ranges and rarely on radical overhauling.

---

[1] The fixed on-site costs that all sites carry regardless of size, i.e. the setting up costs and the running costs of a foreman, site huts, compound, small plant, rates and usually one or more labourers. These costs vary little with volume.

For the housebuilders, standardisation represents a rational response to the risk and uncertainty they constantly face from a range of sources:

- volatility in the market and land costs (in the pattern of demand and confidence of potential purchasers);
- risks of delay between the decision to build and completion;
- changes in the availability of financing for both builder and purchaser; and
- changes in the availability and cost of materials and labour.

These uncertainties are increased because of the long and irreversible nature of the production process (by comparison with other commodities) and because of the difficulties in accommodating substantial changes during the production process. The volume-built speculative house and mono-tenure/use estate is therefore in one respect simply the form of housing that best minimises the special risks associated with housebuilding. In doing this it must also ensure that the housing so produced does not undermine the marketability of the final product – 'the wants of the final user, the purchaser, though perhaps not the first priority, must also not be the last' (Leopold and Bishop, 1983, p. 123).

The standard unit also provides the basic means for housebuilders to monitor and plan spending against a budget by allowing reasonably accurate estimates of cost and production time to be made for any potential site. It furthermore ensures on-site familiarity with the product (leading to better construction standards through repetition), exposes potential defects, and offers the ability to cut costs through economies of scale. In this respect the standard house provides 'a small oasis of certainty where unknowns have been largely eliminated and snags progressively ironed out' (Leopold and Bishop, 1983, p. 123). It also represents to some extent the cumulative experience of the company, and a guarantee – at least from the technical point of view – that a development can proceed at minimum risk. Therefore, as marketing, planning and site variables change from place to place, the house carries with it the major element of continuity from site to site.

Because profits for the housebuilders often remain tight (frequently less than 10 per cent – Adam, 1997), the emphasis tends to be on achieving the least costly solutions. Consequently, housebuilders are often reluctant to instruct any consultant designers until as late as possible (to avoid abortive fees), and pay the designers on a fixed fee per unit basis. The practice puts pressure on designers to limit their time input, and, regardless of context, to maximise house numbers on sites (POS *et al.*, 1998, p. 12) whilst optimising achieved sales prices through a careful balance between density and target market preference. The result is:

- little time available to deliver good design;
- rarely time for site analysis or even site visits;
- few attempts to guard the quality outcomes of the process;
- usually no designer involvement after a development begins;
- a subcontracted production process managed to deliver programme and cost targets rather than to deliver design quality;
- careful linkage of design to marketing objectives to maximise returns.

For these reasons, design is marginalised by the housing procurement process (see Chapter 8). The result is that design costs are usually less than 1 per cent of total unit costs, a minimal percentage given that the expenditure by housebuilders on marketing is typically 3 per cent (Adam, 1997).

Housebuilders and planning

As was argued in Chapter 2, the powers of planning authorities derive directly from one source: control of the valuable commodity *land*. Two opposing views characterise these powers. First, that the planning system improves pure market outcomes because it can generate beneficial externalities that in turn generate higher land prices associated with the higher development values and lower risks through the process of plan making. Second, that the planning system acts as a constraint on the market, producing higher land costs without commensurate benefits, and notably with a less responsive land supply, higher house prices and increased time lags before development.

Undoubtedly reality reflects something of both views and, as research has shown, the best outcomes might be ensured by a balance between certainty brought about by an effective planning process, and avoidance of undue constraint brought about by an adequate supply of land. Without these characteristics, respectively, oversupply or overdevelopment can result. As presently operated, however, housing which is produced is frequently 'neither that which planners aim to produce nor that which a free market would prefer' (Monk and Whitehead, 1999, p. 420). Thus policy can too easily impose a set of increased costs which result in higher land and house prices and a different (less desirable) built product in terms of quantity, quality and mix than is preferred.

Research has shown that supply of new private housing in the UK is very inelastic; in other words, it is unresponsive to increases in demand (Meen 1996; Meen *et al.*, 2001). This has become particularly obvious in recent years, where despite a growing economy, and fast increasing household formation, supply of new homes remained static between 1994 and 2000, and fell in 2001 to the lowest level for twenty years (Stewart, 2002, p. 22). Housebuilders argue that this is not a result of inefficiencies in their industry, which has consistently been criticised for its failure to innovate (Carmona, 2001b, pp. 111–14), but is a direct result of planning constraints.

Because of the scarcity of land for residential development, starts and completions of new houses are kept artificially low (HBF, 2002b, para. 2.2), and owners of housing land expect (and in the case of many public bodies are obliged by law) to secure the best return for their asset. The result is often the suppression of aspects that reduce the land value. Therefore, because poor quality development (overdevelopment with uniform house types on minimum plots that ignores site characteristics and – beyond what sells – local housing requirements) can increase land values, this is often the form proposals take. Such proposals come either from landowners themselves eager to secure outline permission before sale, or from housebuilders, forced by the market cost of the land to maximise their return and so make development viable (POS *et al.*, 1998, p. 12).

Landowners' expectation of value is understandably based on recent market activity and on development patterns that maximise return. Therefore expectations are conceived in a planning vacuum, with – usually – no consideration given to the costs of delivering higher-quality development. Aggravating such expectations are the processes of selling land, where land is sold to the highest bidder based on its residual value.[2] Therefore the

---

[2] Residual value is calculated by estimating the number of units to be built on the land in question, the building costs per unit and hence for the site, infrastructure costs, and allowance for contingencies. The sum of these costs is then deducted from the total estimated selling price of the houses, and the residual is the land value, assuming a constant profit margin.

landowner achieves the highest value for the land, whilst the housebuilder has often had to strategically ignore local authority aspirations to make the bid (POS *et al.*, 1998, p. 14).

The result is developers on low profit margins, who risk their investors going elsewhere for a better return on their capital investment (20 per cent is required but rarely achieved), and who are vulnerable to delay and fluctuation in market value. Effectively they are left to pursue any means available to reduce delay and maximise the value of the land purchased (land which typically absorbs 40–50 per cent of their capital investments in order to maintain a two- to three-year land bank – Baron, 1983, p. 20). Consequently, many housebuilders will go to considerable lengths to persuade authorities that high land values do not permit planning objectives (i.e. planning gain requirements) to be met, and that instead larger units and smaller gardens are required to make development pay (Adam, 1997). Others will reduce the size of their land bank (particularly as land as a proportion of total house cost has dramatically increased – commonly up to 50 per cent in the South East), a practice which represents a risky strategy, and one which leads to further land price inflation and reduces time for design in an effort to maintain outputs (Davison, 1987a, p. 66).

A categorisation of housebuilders based on their approaches to the planning process has been suggested by Short *et al.* (1986, p. 111). Firms can be classified as:

- cautious: restricting their interest to safe sites with existing planning permission;
- naive: often submitting unacceptable planning applications which are refused;
- negotiators: with a high success rate based on a willingness to engage with the planning process and test its limits;
- aggressors: with a tendency to go to appeal instead of negotiating, but also testing the limits of the planning system.

Like most private industries, speculative housebuilding depends for its survival on maintaining cash flow in the short run and profitability in the long run. In practice this means tightly controlling investment in land (see Chapter 5), and once on site, building and

Table 3.1 Perceived importance of site selection criteria by housebuilders (Pacione, 1989)

Criteria in site selection	Ranking of importance
Market factors	1
Planning permission (availability or ease to get)	2
Basic services (existing and ease to supply)	3
Social class of neighbourhood	4
Condition of subsoil	5
Access to schools	5
Site availability	5
Topographic conditions	8
The asking price of the land	8
Size of site	10
Access to city centre	10
Proximity to local shops	10
Physical environmental quality	13
Access to employment	14
Availability of clearance grant	15
Existing ground cover	16

selling as many houses as a volatile market can take as quickly as possible (Leopold and Bishop, 1983, p. 122). The natural tendency has therefore been for most house-builders to act as aggressors, to take the planning system head on and to have recourse to the appeals system to settle the inevitable disputes. It also means the very careful selection of sites, with considerations of marketing, the chances of obtaining planning permission, the social context and the availability of servicing all weighing heavily on housebuilders decisions (see Table 3.1).

In such a context, housebuilders are consistently critical of any regulatory attempts to alter their standard house types. Thus they are dismissive of much supplementary planning guidance, which, although rarely impacting on the all-important standard footprint of house types, frequently imposes additional constraints on elevational design and layout, or additional social requirements, such as the provision of affordable housing. The variability of planning authority approaches in this regard continues to be the greatest bugbear to the industry (Hooper and Nicol, 1999, p. 802).

The buyers of new homes

Hooper (1999, p. 5) has argued that throughout the debates on housing supply in the late 1990s, very little analysis was ever undertaken on consumer choice. Thus, debates have focused on the production of the physical artefact (the house), rather than on the activity of dwelling (the home). So, just as housebuilders have not always been responsive to consumer choice, neither have government or local authorities in their guidance. Consequently, such documents have not always reflected the wishes of the residents whose lives they were designed to improve. For example, the most famous British design guide – the 'Essex Design Guide' of 1973 – was never based on any survey of residents' opinions.

This lack of consultation may have as much to do with the difficulties of successfully measuring residents' attitudes to new housing as to any paternalistic attitudes amongst planners and councillors (i.e. that they know best). This is because the home environment is unlike any other product in a further way, in that it engenders strong personal and emotional reactions that colour residents' impressions of their surroundings (on top of the psychological impact of their financial stake). Studies of residents' attitudes have revealed conflicting findings on the subject (Booth, 1982).

A tendency for residents in post-occupancy studies to remain uncritical of the developments they had bought into (so avoiding running down their investment or implying they had made a mistake) has also been recognised in specific research on residential density and levels of satisfaction. When interviewed, planning officers associated with the identified developments also put uncritical views of house buyers down to 'low expectations, that builders had "re-educated" the public to accept low space standards, and that clever designers were adept at creating the impression of space in higher density schemes' (Farthing and Winter, 1988, pp. 70–71).

In part, attitudes might be explained by the unique attitude of the British towards home ownership, where societal norms pressure individuals and young couples to struggle onto the first rung of the housing ladder at the earliest opportunity. The inevitable result is that purchasers buy for the short term, hoping that what they buy will be a stepping stone to something better – and usually bigger – in the near future. Thus, issues such as space standards (as opposed to number of bedrooms), energy efficiency, and even environmental quality become secondary concerns to the concern to buy and to benefit from the endemic house-price inflation that characterises so much of the country.

By providing features such as the maximum number of bedrooms, the fitted kitchen and the mock Tudorbethan exterior, the development industry is still able to achieve a good selling price for producing a product which is by any international comparison substandard.

(Rudlin and Falk, 1999, p. 115)

Further research has identified seven main factors determining house-buyer decisions:

- price and value
- locality
- estate (urban design)
- house design
- liveability (the house itself)
- features
- construction.

Of these, aspects of liveability and estate (especially the spaciousness in the home and variety in the layout) were rated most highly by residents (Bishop and Davison, 1989, p. 42). In this study of the purchasers of upmarket new homes it was found that new residents generally liked the appearance of their homes, valued the clustering of their homes into identifiable groups, preferred more spacious layouts and were critical if plot sizes were too small and densities too great. Residents also preferred locations on quiet culs-de-sac, tended to be critical of the lack of landscaping and requested more imaginative design, greater privacy and a wider range of layouts and house types (Bishop and Davison, 1989, pp. 42–5, 60). More recent research on housing attitudes for the Government (Hedges and Clemens, 1994, p. 157) also identified a clear preference for detached over semi-detached houses and for semi-detached houses over terraced houses (respectively 93 to 80 to 51 per cent of respondents were willing to entertain living in each).

When examining the reasons for households buying on new-build estates the market pre- and post-1990 further distinguishes motivations. In the late 1980s in a booming market, new houses offered the opportunity to get onto the housing ladder at affordable prices without the need to purchase in the inner city. In the 1990s such properties were amongst the cheapest in the market as builders keen to sell in depressed times offered a variety of attractive incentives to buy. Furthermore, they offer a ready-made environment – more often than not – close to the countryside, where everybody is new (a particular attraction to longer-distance migrants), without the maintenance problems associated with older property or negative perceptions of purchasing in inner-city areas (Forrest *et al.*, 1997, p. 64).

A high-profile study significantly entitled *Kerb Appeal* amounted to a survey of potential customer and non-customer attitudes (819 in all) to new-build residential development, the aim being to uncover the public's views on such housing, and – if possible – the reasons for any prejudices and preferences (Popular Housing Forum, 1998). What was revealed was a widespread disdain for the perceived products of the housebuilding industry, but also some rejection of the emerging professional consensus on how to improve new residential environments. Most obviously, the survey revealed strong support for traditional (suburban) residential development, preferably built at not too high a density, and designed to fit into the already established context.

This confirmed earlier research sponsored by the HBF, this time of 818 new home owners, who – perhaps unsurprisingly given the fact that those surveyed had just made

Table 3.2 New speculative housing – push and pull factors (Mulholland Research Associates Ltd, 1995)

Urban 'push' factors	%	Suburban 'pull' factors	%
Traffic problems/lack of safety	39	Attractiveness of development	57
Busy crowded nature of context	23	Quiet secluded area	46
Levels of crime	20	Good environment for children	30
Poor environment for children	17	Safety from traffic	29
Lack of adequate gardens	17	Good local schools	26
Poor parking facilities	15	Green open environment	21
Lack of privacy	13	Proximity to other families	20
Noisy troublesome neighbours	12	Clean unpolluted environment	19
High levels of pollution	12	Good views of countryside	15
Street disturbances	12	Good privacy	15
Poor standard of schools	8	Secure environment from crime	10

the choice – revealed a strong preference for quiet, leafy areas rather than for urban living (Mulholland Research Associates Ltd, 1995, p. vi). When distinguishing between which factors had pulled them to their current development, environmental factors rated highly in their assessment alongside social factors (see Table 3.2). Thus, the survey revealed a population more than happy to rely on their car to get to any necessary facilities and to get to work (91 per cent took an average journey to work of 15.2 miles, spending over an hour in their car each day). Conversely, the new home owners valued life in a cul-de-sac location, with no dangerous traffic, freedom from pollution and secure back gardens, well separated from any local amenities.

Factors that *Kerb Appeal* revealed were specifically unpopular included mixed-use developments, a sense of urbanity, and living on both lively and cosmopolitan streets or on through-roads. The outcomes represent a significant gap between what many house buyers perceive to be important in a potential residential area and what many theorists and practitioners (and increasing national planning advice) argue is good for them.

Despite derision in the professional press, in the housebuilders' own press the report was largely received as an endorsement of what the industry was delivering, namely suburban, single-use, traditionally styled environments:

> Self-appointed intellectuals and aesthetes don't like the fact the people want to live in 'traditional' looking homes, just as they don't like the fact that everyone watches TV soaps before settling in for the football. But as an industry, house-builders have long argued that their job is to provide the homes that people want – and once again comprehensive research finds that pitched roofs, four windows and a front door in the middle are pretty much what folk require from a new home.
>
> (Roskrow, 1998)

Significantly, however, Hooper (1999, p. 11) observed that after recording in 1996 an increase in the proportion of first-time buyers who preferred a brand new home rather than a second-hand property, the housebuilding sector's own research recorded a decrease in the proportion of people preferring a new dwelling to a second-hand one. This, he suggested, reflected the concern (in both the public and private sectors) for quantity rather than quality in housing provision, whilst increasing incomes in real terms were leading to a steady increase in expectations – expectations often unmet in the new-build sector. In 2001, according to the Industry's own research, this perception began to turn around (HBF, 2002b, para. 6.4).

Delivering market housing – 2003

This chapter has discussed the particular nature of the housebuilding sector and house-building process. A number of the concerns raised are represented in a diagram by Ball (1999), which sums up the unique market contexts faced by the housebuilding industry (see Fig. 3.4). The diagram highlights that the industry operates across a number of key markets (housing, land and the construction markets of labour, materials and plant/equipment), all of which are in turn influenced by external inputs – the customer, public policy (building regulations and planning policy) and subcontractors. Therefore, to be successful, housebuilders need to successfully conceive developments, negotiate each market, and oversee the construction process.

Ball (1999, p. 20) concludes that none of these inputs are conducive to innovation and change. He argues that the housebuilding industry is a classic case of market failure, because it actively militates against innovation. For him, public intervention is the only answer to reduce volatility in new housing markets, lower the focus on land development profits, subsidise innovations in housing production and provide a regulatory regime which is more innovation-friendly.

At the start of the twenty-first century the industry itself has nevertheless been forced to change in part because of the significant tightening of planning policy brought about by the adoption of the urban renaissance agenda through PPG3 (DETR, 2000a) and other guidance (see p. 34). It may be, however, that the innovation that the planning process nationally has itself required is now being stifled by the failures of the process locally to keep up. As the former Head of Planning at the House Builders Federation (2001b, para. 6.6) put it:

> At present, our industry is promoting radical change in the design, construction, layout and location of new homes, within the context of a diminished land supply and severe restrictions on output. This combination is in danger of becoming

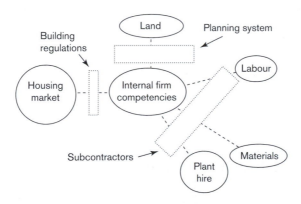

3.4 Housebuilders' market contexts (Ball, 1999).

commercially untenable. It is hard to innovate against a background of increasing commercial risk. This is caused by planning policy that denies the need to maintain housing supply and no longer provides any certainty in establishing the principle of development.

Although the housebuilders support the role and purpose of the plan-led system, they have argued that considerable potential for improvement in the planning process exists without the need for major reform or significant changes in legislation. In a mainly positive agenda (HBF, 2002b) they argue for:

- Action to bring forward brownfield sites (in so doing accepting the inevitability of government policy on this issue) through a presumption in favour of brownfield housing, fast-track decisions and appeals, and moves to restrict planning gain requirements which – they argue – continue to threaten the viability of brownfield development.
- Action to improve the operation of development control, by recognising the importance of the service and resourcing it appropriately, better staff training (particularly in development economics) and prioritisation of key proposals, joint working between authorities and developers, streamlined processes for planning gain, and enforced targets and penalties for performance.
- Action on development plans to restore commercial confidence in the plan-led system by upholding development allocations once made, using plans to introduce government policy, reducing plan preparation timescales to no more than two years and not allowing preparation to hold up development, simplifying the policy hierarchy and reducing repetition of policy.
- Action on government policy to more forcefully promote the need for new housing, reflect economic realism and viability and actual availability of housing land, and to provide greater consistency and clarity.

What is clear is that a failure to provide for the new housing the nation needs may have far-reaching economic impacts, and that housebuilders are increasingly arguing this case in order to influence the national agenda. Research has shown that although the failure to provide new housing does not have a significant immediate effect on the national economy, it does have a significant long-term impact on regional and local urban economies, which in turn add up to a significant indirect impact on the national economy (Meen *et al.*, 2001). One of the most important direct influences is the impact of housing supply on the labour market, and on labour mobility. Thus too few homes to meet the population's needs will lead to labour shortages and drive up wages and labour costs, which in turn affect the competitiveness of local economies – too few larger homes will reduce the availability of managerial and professional employees, and too few affordable homes will reduce the availability of key workers. Too few homes can also provide a barrier to migration within the UK, hindering regional economic convergence (Stewart, 2002, p. 11).

All this leads to higher house prices, higher national interest rates than would otherwise be the case, and to housing market instability (including potential for boom and bust). The result is less housing built as demand is volatile and the certain, stable climate housebuilders need for investment is undermined. Thus the impact of new housing is a cumulative and two-way process – 'the economy influences housing, and housing in turn influences the economy' (Stewart, 2002, p. 9). Planning in turn influences both, but is just one part of the complex development process that housebuilders need to negotiate.

4

The social housing process

A changing role

General development processes affect public and voluntary sector providers in much the same way as private housebuilders. Those delivering social housing do not operate in a vacuum, and in many instances it is impossible to isolate the processes of market provision from social provision, often because the same developer will deal with both types of new housing. This is particularly the case under the planning-led system of provision, where social housing units are procured as part of an agreed gain package.

In this chapter, less emphasis is placed on the issue of planning gain (which is dealt with explicitly in Chapter 9), and the discussion focuses instead on the changing role of the public and voluntary sectors in social housing provision. In particular, the chapter deals with the way current funding mechanisms fit in with the provision of social housing through public–private partnerships (used here as a general term, rather than a specific government-sponsored approach). This chapter considers a number of basic questions:

1. What is the background to public/voluntary housing provision in Britain?
2. Who provided social housing in the past, and who provides it today?
3. How do current funding mechanisms help or hinder Registered Social Landlords (RSLs) engaging with the private sector on market housing schemes?

The focus is initially an historical one, switching in the second section onto the changing nature of the providers and then finally onto the environment within which modern RSLs operate. The main purpose of this chapter is to examine whether the operational context for social housing providers is a positive one, enabling them to work effectively with the private sector.

From state landlordism to voluntary housing

In Britain today, most new social housing – that is, housing made more affordable through the use of some form of grant subsidy – is provided by Registered Social Landlords or, as they were known until very recently, housing associations. A full explanation of what RSLs are and do is given in the third part of this chapter. In the past, the public sector, through local authorities, was the main provider of social, or as it was more commonly known, council housing. Housing associations existed (indeed, they have a

Table 4.1 Housing stock in Great Britain 1981 to 2001 in thousands (DTLR, 2001c, p. 7)

Year	Owner-occupied	Rented privately	Rented from RSL	Rented from Local Authority	All dwellings
1981	12,171	2,340	470	6,115	21,094
1982	12,345	2,322	484	6,110	21,261
1983	12,721	2,310	497	5,929	21,457
1984	13,038	2,300	512	5,812	21,662
1985	13,320	2,267	528	5,744	21,859
1986	13,660	2,205	550	5,655	22,070
1987	14,027	2,139	567	5,558	22,292
1988	14,435	2,077	582	5,432	22,527
1989	14,848	2,069	586	5,239	22,742
1990	15,120	2,128	635	5,055	22,939
1991	15,175	2,177	689	4,959	23,000
1992	15,306	2,264	733	4,879	23,183
1993	15,452	2,330	811	4,759	23,353
1994	15,615	2,394	884	4,634	23,527
1995	15,804	2,438	976	4,496	23,713
1996	16,007	2,446	1,078	4,368	23,898
1997	16,212	2,451	1,136	4,273	24,073
1998	16,448	2,447	1,214	4,141	24,251
1999	16,669	2,427	1,335	3,983	24,414
2000	16,901	2,428	1,463	3,789	24,581
2001	17,146	2,442	1,588	3,558	24,733

long history – see p. 58), but their role in delivering homes was ancillary to that of councils. In terms of direct provision, these traditional roles have been reversed; RSLs now provide and local authorities offer assistance and support. This fact is underscored by figures for RSL and local authority new-build since 1980 which show that as local authority provision of new homes has declined, RSL provision has increased (see Table 4.1, which also shows change in other tenures). It should be noted that the gap between what used to be built and what is built today is ever widening, leading many commentators to argue that the pace of social housing provision is being outstripped by demand (Weaver, 2002).

This metamorphosis of traditional roles has been examined in countless housing texts over the last 20 years, so that today the relationship between the public and voluntary sectors (the RSLs are dubbed voluntary because their board members work without financial reward) can be described as one of 'enabling-providing' (Goodlad, 1993). The change was a consequence of many factors but critical amongst these was Margaret Thatcher's denigration (whilst Prime Minister) of the local state and promotion of a culture of privatism (Cole and Furbey, 1994). She believed that:

> The state, in the form of local authorities, has frequently proved an insensitive, incompetent and corrupt landlord [therefore . . .] as regards the traditional post-war role of government in housing – that is, building, ownership, management and regulation – the state should be withdrawn from these areas just as far as possible.
>
> (Thatcher, 1993)

So rather than managing or building, local authorities were refocused to provide a strategic input. The nature of this input was set out in the 1987 Housing White Paper:

> The future role of local authorities will essentially be a strategic one identifying housing needs and demands, encouraging innovative methods of provision by other bodies to meet such needs, maximising the use of private finance, and encouraging the new interest in the revival of the independent rented sector.
>
> (DoE, 1987, p. 14)

The Housing Act of the following year established a framework that bears close resemblance to that in place today: RSLs provide housing, but fund a significant slice of their activity through private sector borrowing; local housing authorities take a back seat, but play a coordinating role. This means that alliances between different sectors are essential if social housing is to be provided, whilst the responsibility of ensuring that it is provided, and local needs are met, remains with local government.

This then is the current situation, but how did it evolve? Numerous policy texts provide detailed descriptions and analyses of British housing and social policy during the last couple of hundred years (see, for instance, Birchall, 1992; Malpass and Murie, 1999; Balchin and Rhoden, 2001). The intention here is to give only a brief synopsis of policy changes affecting social housing provision over the last 150 years, thereby setting the context for today's policy and illustrating the changing fortunes of the social housing sector.

Pre-1890

The account begins in the mid-nineteenth century, and is linked closely to the processes driving forward urban expansion. The transition from a mainly agrarian society to one based on factory production fuelled nineteenth century urbanisation, and was marked by the concentration of people within new manufacturing towns in the north of England, and in established centres such as London, Birmingham and Bristol (Carter and Lewis, 1990). The consequences of this expansion and concentration are well known. The combination of industrial pollution with the inability of existing services (water supply, sewerage and so on) to cope with rapid growth resulted in squalid and unsanitary living conditions (Berry, 1974). Those with the means to do so fled the inner cities in an initial wave of counter-urbanisation. Those without the means suffered appalling living conditions (see Hall, 2002) and were shoehorned into expensive and overcrowded private lettings. Their plight was famously highlighted in Edwin Chadwick's *Report on the Sanitary Conditions of the Labouring Population of Great Britain'* (1842). In concluding the report, Chadwick made a number of recommendations designed to appeal to private enterprise and the Exchequer. He pointed out that:

1. Poor living conditions frequently led to the early demise of breadwinners, with implications for poor relief;
2. That preventative measures would reduce the cost of the Poor Law;
3. And that more generally, sickness amongst the work force was holding down productivity and profitability.

The case was made, therefore, for some kind of intervention. Factory production resulted in low wages, a concentration of population, and consequent high rents and poor conditions. Intervention was required in order to stave off an early crisis of capitalism.

But the prevailing structure and rationale of local government scuppered any hope of concerted action. The types of problem identified by Chadwick were the sole responsibility of Local Boards, which derived jurisdiction from Local Acts of Parliament. Chadwick believed that the scale of the urban problem necessitated a central response, although this would mean wrestling power from the Local Boards, and running contrary to the spirit of self-determination; a cornerstone of local government for centuries. So although various pieces of legislation were brought forward between 1848 (the Public Health Act) and 1875 (the Cross Act), these all hit the inevitable barrier of local inaction. It was not until the creation of county councils in 1888 and then district councils in 1894 that national government found itself, for the first time, in a position to coordinate and affect the way housing, planning and social concerns were addressed up and down the country. The first legislation with any real teeth, therefore, was the Housing of the Working Classes Act of 1890, which was followed nineteen years later by the Housing, Town Planning Etc. Act 1909.

So despite Chadwick's early work, effective intervention was not possible until the close of the nineteenth century. Local government had to evolve before the state could assume any real control over how people were to be housed. Nevertheless, Chadwick did see some early fruits from his labour, as despite government's hands being tied, there were others ready to take up the challenge laid down by Chadwick and his contemporaries through the early housing association movement.

Accepting Chadwick's economic arguments, leading philanthropists such as Peabody and Guinness recognised the link between the needs of labour and capital, and encouraged property investors to accept lower returns (typically 5 per cent) on new housing schemes, thereby contributing to better housing conditions. Thus what began as the 'five per cent philanthropy' of the 1840s (Carter and Lewis, 1990), became the housing association movement of today. Although not entirely selfless in their actions, this early influence has a direct legacy, and the Guinness and Peabody Trusts remain leading RSLs.

But the importance of these trusts faded against a background of increasing state intervention throughout much of the twentieth century, only to re-emerge in the 1970s and 1980s following the first signs that council housing's golden age was about to come to a close. As noted above, this golden age for public sector housing provision was ushered in by the new system of local government that established the framework for a more pervasive state. The Housing of the Working Classes Act 1890, for example, was built on the foundations laid by the Royal Commission on the Housing of the Working Classes of 1884. This provided the legislative basis for council house building before the First World War, although few houses of this type were built prior to the 1909 Act, and then only 24,000 nationally up until 1914 (Berry, 1974).

Post-1900

In 1919, the Liberals under Lloyd George pledged to build 'homes fit for heroes'. This attempt to woo voters to the Liberal cause paid dividends, and the Liberal-dominated coalition government was able to put in motion a building programme that yielded 213,000 council homes over the next three years, all built under the provisions of the Housing and Town Planning Act 1919. Generous Exchequer subsidies meant a surge in public housebuilding, but were also partially to blame for rising post-war inflation and a near-crisis in a building industry already starved of manpower in the aftermath of the Great War.

These factors put paid to Liberal political ambitions for the time being and the next Conservative government scrapped these open-ended subsidies, opting instead for fixed Exchequer payments available to either private or public providers (Housing Act 1923). Almost inevitably, the first Labour administration repealed this system, replacing it with one that favoured housebuilding by the public sector (Housing Act 1924). A cyclical pattern of subsidy advance and withdrawal continued unabated during the run-up to the Second World War with money (when available) going into both new-build and slum-clearance programmes, with around one million council homes added to the municipal stock between 1923 and 1939. As a consequence, by 1939, 11 per cent of Britain's housing was publicly owned, although almost half of this was destroyed during the war years.

Five years of war resulted in a major housing shortage, and no government was electable unless it demonstrated a firm commitment to council provision. Labour was seen as the natural champion of public housing in 1945, winning the election in spite of Churchill's personal popularity. But disappointed by the achievements of Labour in the following five years, the electorate voted in a Conservative government (with Harold Macmillan as Housing Minister) in 1951. The target of building 300,000 council homes each year was met in 1951/52, and by 1954 a staggering 74 per cent of all new completions were council homes.

This was truly the golden age for council building and was to continue – with a mix of surges and retreats – for the next 15 years. A final 'golden phase' took place between 1964 and 1970 when Labour's Housing Minister, Richard Crossman, pledged to build a further 500,000 homes by the end of the decade. Despite a fall-off in general completions as a result of inflationary pressure after 1967, the Housing Subsidies Act of the same year gave new impetus to the construction of blocks of flats with more than four storeys. Hence the high-water mark of Britain's public housebuilding programme coincided with the promotion of high-rise living. By 1971, 31 per cent of all housing in Britain was public rented. The state, through local authorities, was far and away the dominant provider of social housing.

Post-1970

The final leg of this historical account moves to the present day and to a situation in which public housing is overshadowed by the work of the voluntary sector. Two strands are important: the first concerns the changing fortunes of the public sector itself and the second relates to the arrival of the voluntary sector's own golden age.

The way council housing fell prey to monetarist economic thinking in the 1970s, and then to privatisation in the 1980s, is examined by Cole and Furbey (1994) and is too complex to recount in full here. Nevertheless, changing governmental attitudes as described above to the 'over-pervasive state' in general, and the public sector housing function in particular, was the decisive factor in rolling back government intervention in housing provision. Successive Conservative governments from 1979 onwards pursued a policy of privatisation and safety net welfare provision. This was manifest in the promotion of home ownership, selling off council housing (following the 'right to buy' provisions of the Housing Act 1980) and an emphasis on both private renting, and, where necessary, provision by housing associations.

Turning to the rise of housing associations, the first landmark date was probably 1964, a year which saw the arrival of the Housing Corporation and the creation of the first loan system for cost renting and co-ownership schemes (Ravetz, 2001, p. 200). It was another ten years, however, before the system that was to revolutionise the housing association movement arrived. This came in the form of the Housing Act 1974 which introduced:

1. subsidy for capital works in the form of Housing Association Grant (HAG);
2. public sector loan finance either directly through the Housing Corporation or through local authorities;
3. a revenue deficit grant;
4. a new supervisory role for the Housing Corporation;
5. a public register of associations (only registered associations could take up grant support, something that remains the case today).

The introduction of HAG, and the full funding of capital projects, catapulted housing associations into uncharted territory. It was believed, and had been anticipated by the Cohen Committee of 1971, that associations could replace the public sector as the principal provider of social housing, whilst also dealing with the significant gaps in private rental provision. Hitherto, their focus had been on special rather than general housing needs. By the time Margaret Thatcher had begun her own crusade against the public sector in 1980, the associations had moved to centre ground in the provision of all new social housing.

But whilst the associations retained their privileged position during the first two Thatcher governments, this position was always a precarious one. Even though they were not public agents – in the strictest definition of the term – they were still wholly resourced by the state. This reality did not fit squarely with the prevailing philosophy of privatism, and in the 1987 Housing White Paper there were strong hints that thirteen years of open-ended funding were about to come to an end, with associations being pushed into closer alliances with an enabling local state whose responsibility it would be to innovate and privately fund future social housing.

The change came via the Housing Act 1988, which brought, amongst other things:

1. Housing Action Trusts (HATs), which were a means of channelling resources into public housing estates without recourse to the incumbent local authority;
2. Tenant's Choice, which provided the machinery through which council tenants could opt out of local authority control and transfer their tenancies, en masse, to housing associations;
3. a switch from full capital funding to a form of deficit funding whereby housing associations would resource future housebuilding through a mix of grant support and private borrowing.

Although the 1988 system has now been superseded, this broad strategy of mixing public and private finance has remained intact. Today the system for delivering social housing is spearheaded by associations that draw on public and private support in various forms. Private support can take the form of capital borrowing or the private contribution derived through planning gain (see pp. 63–7).

Registered social landlords

Helen Cope's updated text *Housing Associations* remains the best source of information on RSLs. In it, she describes them as:

diverse, independent, not for profit organisations. The term registered social landlords was introduced in 1996. Originally called 'registered housing associations' (i.e. registered under section 5 of the Housing Associations Act 1985), all registered housing associations became registered social landlords under section 1 of the Housing Act 1996.

(Cope, 1999, p. 1)

RSLs are part of an independent sector (independent from local authorities) that provides affordable housing and 'related services for people on low incomes and in housing need'. They are voluntary (see above) because they provide housing not because of statutory obligation, but because of the 'energy and commitment of lay volunteers who have combined to form an organisation to meet perceived housing needs (Cope, 1999, p. 1). Some of these organisations (which exist in a variety of forms) have been around for more than a hundred years; others are relative newcomers. But all share similar objectives, and are only differentiated by the size, nature and area of operation.

According to Cope (1999, p. 3), there were 2,150 RSLs in England in 1997. More recent Housing Corporation (1999) data put the figure at 2,070, a reduction that may be explained by the ongoing processes of merger and rationalisation that have characterised RSL activity since the late 1980s (in this respect mirroring experiences in the private sector – see Chapter 3). RSLs vary significantly in size; a third manage fewer than six units, while the top 12 per cent together control 90 per cent of the total RSL stock. The size of English RSLs, gauged in terms of the number of units controlled, is shown in Table 4.2. The ten biggest RSLs (in 1999) are shown in Table 4.3, a table in which Guinness and Peabody have kept their positions as two voluntary sector heavyweights.

For the most part, RSLs provide housing for general needs comprising a mix of rental and units for sale. But they also build and manage homes to meet either special needs

Table 4.2 RSLs in England by size in units (1999) (Housing Corporation, 1999)

Size in units	No. of RSLs	% of RSLs	No. of units (1000s)	% of RSL stock
0–5	628	30	0.9	0
6–1000	1,196	58	112.3	10
Over 1000	246	12	1,049.0	90
Total	2,070	100	1,162.2	100

Table 4.3 The ten largest RSLs by stock (1999) (Housing Corporation, 1999)

North British	35,969
Home	25,794
Anchor	23,570
Sanctuary	23,391
Riverside	19,035
London & Quadrant	18,586
Guinness Trust	17,541
William Sutton	15,493
Northern Counties	14,679
Peabody Donation Fund	14,286

Table 4.4 The distribution of RSL stock (1999) by Housing Corporation investment areas (Housing Corporation, 1999)

Investment region	Population share (%)	RSL stock share (%)
London	14.2	21
South East	15.9	18
South West	9.8	11
East Midlands	8.4	5
Eastern	10.7	9
West Midlands	10.9	11
Yorkshire and Humberside	10.3	6
North East	5.4	4
North West	10.3	10
Merseyside	4.0	5
England	100 (47.1m)	100 (1,162k)

or the needs of older people. Some RSLs specialise in this type of provision, whilst others cast their net widely, developing a portfolio of stock tailored to a full range of needs. Many conduct or collaborate in research – often in partnership with local authorities – aimed at assessing the scale and nature of housing need within their operational area.

RSLs provide housing across the breadth of the country. Some, such as the Guinness or William Sutton Trusts listed in Table 4.3, have a national presence. Others are regional agents, or even operate in just one area or town. Their particular geographical interests often reflect the way they were formed, i.e. by local people with a concern for the needs of their home communities. But national coverage is not uniform, and variations reflect Britain's distribution of population, and relative housing problems in particular parts of the country. London and the South-East, for example, have a 30 per cent share of England's population, but almost 40 per cent of total RSL stock, reflecting the difficulties facing households trying to access market housing at a reasonable price within the region. Elsewhere, there is a closer correlation between population and RSL stock percentages, though in the East Midlands and in Yorkshire and Humberside the ratio of stock to population share is much lower: figures are given in Table 4.4.

In the 1980s, housing associations were promoted as the third arm of government's housing strategy, sitting between the public and private sectors. These partner sectors were handed the respective tasks of enabling and delivering new homes, a tripartite relationship that has grown in importance, especially during the 1990s, a period which saw RSLs levered into even closer alliances with private sector interests. This is true in both general terms (with RSLs forced to borrow more from the private sector as capital grant rates have dwindled) and as regards the use of developer contributions to RSLs. Because this book is concerned primarily with these tripartite relationships, the next section deals with the operational procedures that RSLs must now follow when working with developers, receiving a developer contribution, and also (in some instances) utilising capital grant in the form of Social Housing Grant (SHG – HAG's replacement since 1996).

During their long history, much of the existing RSL stock was built up through direct development of new units. After 1988 and the arrival of Large Scale Voluntary Transfers (LSVTs), a great deal of additional stock – 406,727 units in total between 1988 and 2000 from 87 authorities (Wilcox, 2000) – was transferred out of local authority control to either existing or newly created RSLs. In the more recent past, RSLs have found an additional source of new housing, derived from developer contributions, whereby planning authorities negotiate for the inclusion of affordable housing units in market schemes. The strategy is part of the planning gain approach, stemming originally from Section 52 of the Town and Country Planning Act 1971, and now from Section 106 of the updated 1990 Act.

Direct development

The Housing Corporation has an annual capital-spending limit determined by the Treasury. This is known as the Approved Development Programme, or ADP. The ADP breaks down into capital funding (for new rental schemes, repairs, rehabilitation and improvement), home-ownership funding (for mixed-funded ownership schemes or initiatives such as Home-Buy (Balchin and Rhoden, 2001, p. 267)), and revenue funding (for recurrent management costs). ADP allocations have a very specific timetable. On the basis of spending and costs in the previous year, the Housing Corporation submits grant rate and Total Cost Indicator (TCI) proposals (Cope, 1999, p. 153) to the Government in July each year. These TCIs are a critical part of these proposals as they provide an 'estimate of the norm total cost of providing different types of housing in different parts of the country' (Housing Corporation, 2002, para. 2.1). After the submission, a seven-month funding process is set in motion, which involves the following steps:

1. Each of the Corporation regions (see Table 4.4) issues a Regional Policy Statement after consulting with constituent local authorities and RSLs.
2. Following a consultation exercise involving the Housing Corporation and the National Housing Federation (which represents 1,400 RSL members), TCIs and grant rates for the forthcoming year are published in August (by central government).
3. RSLs bid for capital and revenue funding in November.
4. Draft allocations for the regions are produced in December, and these also show approximate allocations for specific RSLs.
5. The allocations should be formalised by February, although the complexities of the sequence mean that there is regular slippage.

Investment across different areas is targeted with the help of a Housing Needs Indicator (HNI). The HNI was developed in 1996/7, the aim being to target resources to those areas with the greatest needs, 'whilst ensuring that where possible housing need elsewhere is still considered' (Cope, 1999, p. 155). The way that the HNI is actually constructed is complex, and frequently controversial. Similarly, the procedure followed by RSLs in bidding for capital and revenue funding is also technically involved. It begins with the Regional Policy Statements that set out spending priorities (in turn, these regional statements reflect a national strategy) for the next year. RSLs bid competitively for grant funding, which is channelled through initiatives that reflect national and regional priorities, for example the Purchase and Repair programme. The Housing Corporation judges bids against a range of criteria, including contribution to community building or regeneration, wider social objectives, affordability and value for money. A recent development in the bidding process also allows joint commissioning, whereby local authorities can link up with preferred partners and forward joint bids to the Housing Corporation. A concern here is what may happen to less 'preferred' associations if this approach becomes more commonplace in the future.

Finally, costs (estimated with the use of TCIs) are set against needs (based on HNI calculations) and these determine grant rates and area-based resources. Given these needs, costs and priorities, RSLs enter the competitive bidding process in an attempt to access capital and revenue funding. Receipt of this funding is a major determinant of the future activity of individual RSLs, not only in terms of new build, but also as regards their ongoing housing commitments.

The funding issue and particularly the timing of grant input is a key concern for RSLs, both in direct development and in those schemes where they are dealing with a private developer contribution. Ensuring that funding cycles match development opportunities as part of the wider development process (see Chapter 3) represents an ongoing problem. All RSL new-build must also comply with the Scheme Development Standards (see Chapter 8) that cover 'the quality of housing, the probity of procurement and compliance and certification' (Cope, 1999, p. 188). In other words, the procedures and products of grant-receiving must comply with rigorous standards set down by the Housing Corporation. Having a track record for high-quality delivery is therefore an asset in securing capital funding through the competitive bidding process.

In the days before TCIs and HNIs, local authorities and then housing associations could enter into capital projects with only the most basic cost estimates to hand, but sure in the knowledge that the Treasury would fully fund the final costs. Today, the situation is very different and RSLs must closely synchronise their grant submissions with the development process, anticipating all costs at key stages, with the burden of any serious cost overruns falling on the RSL. Cope (1999) lists seven key stages in RSL development activity, linking these to the bidding, grant application and grant receipt phases in the yearly funding round.

1. Feasibility: before the capital bidding process begins, RSLs will seek out potential development sites. Once likely sites have been identified, exhaustive feasibility studies are undertaken and these explore the particular strengths and weaknesses of the site in terms of its planning context, any specific physical site issues, general matters of financial viability and likely out-turn rent levels. If the site looks like it might have potential, the RSL will approach its elected valuer and obtain an estimate of the site's market value. Feasibility is measured in terms of this valuation against development potential (i.e. what can be built on the site in terms of mix, density and layout). Critically, grant will only be available on the market value, not the asking price. As this stage draws to a close, the RSL will make a final decision based on a financial model that calculates probable rent levels on the basis of 'costs, interest rates and the likely length of the development process' (Cope, 1999, p. 168). The calculation of costs should, as closely as possible, square with the TCIs set out by the Housing Corporation, and if they do, the scheme should be both financially viable and affordable for prospective tenants or co-owners. If everything looks feasible, the RSL will approach the local planning authority for outline permission, and start detailed negotiations with the vendor. However, an extension of the process because of delay (e.g. planning delay) will reduce the viability of the scheme.
2. Grant confirmation: the RSL now requires grant approval. The *Capital Funding Guide 2002–2003* (Housing Corporation, 2002) outlines this process, which involves a full submission of costs (with a comparison of these against the TCI) along with a breakdown of revenue and capital funding sources (rents are set at this stage). Once the submission arrives at the Housing Corporation, costs are checked against the TCI and those costs qualifying for grant are confirmed (e.g. for acquisition, works costs

and oncosts). The possibility of some moderate cost overruns are permitted within the grant allocation, but Cope (1999) explains that several factors can push costs beyond this buffer zone, bringing severe difficulties for poorly costed schemes:

> Undue delay in progressing the scheme to tender, adverse site conditions, changes in interest rates and high levels of building cost inflation can all produce cost overruns. If at this stage the scheme is already at 130 per cent of TCI there is no scope for funding of overruns through the subsidy system.
>
> (Cope, 1999, p. 169)

3. Acquisition: grant is delivered to the RSL in a series of tranches. The first tranche is claimable on site acquisition.
4. Design: a detailed drawing stage when issues of layout, housing mix (tenures and types) and density must all be resolved.
5. Tender: this stage begins with the selection of contractors and the administration of the tendering process. It ends with the scheme starting on-site and with the RSL claiming its second slice of grant funding.
6. Construction: a contractual agreement is reached with the contractor(s) or developer. The scheme is progressed, and this progress in monitored by the RSL. On completion, a Certificate of Practical Completion is issued, and although the units are not yet ready to let, the RSL claims the final tranche of grant. The units are inspected and if satisfactory, they are officially handed over to the RSL and can now be let.
7. Post-completion: after completion, the RSL will keep a 'retention against contract'. If any construction faults come to light, the retention gives the RSL added leverage, ensuring that these are swiftly rectified. Eventually a Final Certificate is issued and the retention released to the contractor(s) or developer.

For RSLs, the most critical issue in this chain of events is the budgeting. The RSL must ensure that the cost and out-turn rent calculations are accurate if it is to avoid running into financial problems. In particular, it must pay close attention to the TCI, as this provides the benchmark against which the level of available grant funding is gauged.

This broad framework applies equally to developer contribution-based schemes. Although the developer will be obliged to provide free or subsidised land or units, it will share a similar relationship with the RSL, acting to all intents and purposes as a contracted developer (and therefore retaining a 'contractor's profit' on all units it builds). The main difference, however, relates to funding and how this is provided and managed, and the more complex issue of setting grant subsidy against the private sector planning gain contribution.

Planning gain approach

The way in which planning gain in general, and affordable housing in particular, are dealt with on new development sites is the subject of Chapter 9. The question here is how these developer contributions are treated within the framework of RSL activity described above. The responsibility of local planning authorities to allocate sufficient land for housing in their development plans is outlined in PPG3 (DETR, 2000a). This is supplemented by Circular 6/98: *Planning and Affordable Housing* (DETR, 1998c), which states that authorities may, as a condition of granting planning permission, require that a proportion of affordable housing is provided as part of a proposed housing development.

This use of the planning system to procure additional affordable housing has come under close scrutiny in recent years, although the rights and wrongs of the approach are not a subject of discussion here.

In response to the publication of Circular 6/98, the Housing Corporation (1998) issued its own guidance on the treatment of development contributions, outlining how the costs of works arising from Section 106 requirements should be treated in schemes funded through Social Housing Grant. Two scenarios are outlined. The first involves 'an on site contribution in the form of discounted land and/or a contribution to the construction costs', the second is an 'alternative arrangement for delivering an agreed element of affordable housing on a different site' (Housing Corporation, 1998, paras 2.1–2.3).

In the case of developments on a different site, the seven-stage process described above is followed, but any developer contribution (in cash or in kind) is not treated as a public subsidy. Rather, it is subtracted from the calculation of costs and therefore affects the level of capital grant requirement. But this does not mean that the contribution simply replaces SHG. Because these planning gains are seen as being ancillary and additional to normal funding routes, the RSL will be able to use any saved grant allocation on other schemes. In other words 'The basic objective of developer contributions, whether or not the scheme also receives SHG funding, is to provide additional affordable housing, either directly or by reducing the SHG requirement' (Housing Corporation, 1998, para. 2.2).

With on-site contributions, developers will sometimes provide affordable housing directly for sale to an RSL (exactly how this is to be done, and how many units are to be provided, will be written into the Section 106 Agreement). In these instances, the agreed unit price will be set at a level where no SHG will be required. The developer cross-subsidises this discount sale with the profit made from the market housing, although ultimately it is the landowner who has shouldered the subsidy burden by accepting a price for the land fettered by the Section 106 Agreement. So in some instances, these unit contributions from the developer may cut out the need for capital grant funding altogether. Similarly, cash contributions (either directly to the RSL or via a local authority) may be sufficient for the RSL to progress a new scheme without SHG funding.

The whole process is inevitably simplified when capital funding from the Housing Corporation is not required. But often the contribution is combined with SHG and this means that a clear view of the size and nature of the planning gain must be established at a very early stage so that this can be factored into the cost and feasibility appraisals noted above. The clarity and timing of the Section 106 agreement is therefore critical. This is particularly true where the contribution is in the form of discounted land and/or a contribution to construction costs. In this situation, the RSL must feed these contributions into its financial model of the scheme (see p. 64), showing precisely which costs will be footed by the developer and which by the RSL. Only RSL costs will qualify for capital funding.

The process then follows that outlined in the *Capital Funding Guide 2002–2003*. The Housing Corporation will check that the scheme represents value for money, 'allowing for the discount or cash contribution provided by the developer'. The acid test is whether or not the developer contribution has provided additional units, and therefore whether there has been a demonstrable planning gain. Alternatively, the Housing Corporation may accept that the developer contributions can be used to progress schemes that would otherwise fall outside TCI limits. This means that the gain approach can be used to provide affordable housing in more expensive locations. But in the case of 'off-site' contributions, the RSL must be able to demonstrate that the 'payment is not being used to subsidise a high cost scheme where there are opportunities to develop lower cost schemes elsewhere in the same locality' (Housing Corporation, 1998, para. 2.5).

Hence, there is a degree of inbuilt flexibility with the planning gain approach and the detail of exactly what is to be done is a matter for negotiation between the planning authority, the developer and the RSL prior to the signing of a Section 106 Agreement. However, certain general principles remain fixed; these include the principle of additionality (the demonstrable gain), the need to ensure that a clear distinction is made between developer contribution and remaining RSL costs, and the overarching importance of the TCI. These remain the benchmarks against which all grant-receiving developments are judged. But it should also be remembered that RSL activity remains dependent on the funding framework and process described earlier. In most instances, developer contributions, where available, must coordinate with this framework and complement it. This means that Section 106 negotiations, and subsequently the timing of contributions, must synchronise with the capital funding sequence. If they do not, then the RSL will incur overrun costs that do not qualify for capital funding.

Delivering social housing – 2003

Many of the issues raised in this chapter are examined again in Parts Two and Three of this book, with case study examples used to illustrate particular approaches. What has been provided above is essentially a sketch of the changing environment for social housing provision during the last 150 years, and more specifically the current framework for RSL delivery.

Whether or not this current arena is a positive one for social housing provision is a question that is addressed throughout this book, although some interim remarks are perhaps useful at this stage. The discussion so far has revealed how the burden for providing affordable housing has shifted away from local authorities to a voluntary sector comprising about 2,000 registered social landlords (in England). The way in which the social housing programme is funded has also changed: from open-ended subsidy (of local authorities) in the inter-war period, to full grant funding of housing associations after 1974, and then finally to the deficit funding of capital projects after 1988. The current framework, which involves the Housing Corporation coordinating the allocation of SHG, is a revision of this 1988 system.

The system today is based on a competitive bidding process whereby RSLs seek a grant allocation from a centrally approved development programme fund. They are awarded an indicative allocation and then submit claims for capital funding for individual projects. Capital funding is available to meet qualifying costs that must fall within the parameters of agreed TCIs for particular types of housing, built in different parts of the country. In some instances, the need for capital funding can be offset by the use of developer contributions based on Section 106 agreements.

Within this system, local authorities play the role of coordinator, negotiating Section 106's or overseeing the allocation of funding to RSLs (i.e. LASHG, Local Authority Social Housing Growth). Sometimes they also engage in joint commissioning of capital projects with preferred partner RSLs. Whilst the environment for RSLs is not as free and easy as it was between 1974 and 1988, they still retain a great deal of autonomy and because of competitive bidding some are able to draw on generous allocations of funding, although others, inevitably, miss out. The environment for developers is rather more complex, particularly since the advent of planning gain and the 'negotiated corruption' that some commentators feel now precedes all new development (see Campbell *et al.* 2001 for a review of the system).

   Each of the key stakeholders has a different take on the new environment, and almost inevitably, many of those working in the different sectors will regard past conditions as more favourable:

- local authorities had a direct role in social housing delivery;
- planners did not need to negotiate planning gain agreements;
- RSLs received more grant, with less strings attached;
- the private sector was unfettered by gain contributions and generally avoided social housing at all costs.

But does the current system work, and does it deliver the right quantity (of social housing) of the right quality, in the most advantageous locations? On the quantity issue, like housing for sale, it is possible to state categorically that insufficient affordable housing is being provided in Britain today. Numerous reports and studies point to this unavoidable conclusion. But issues of location and quality are less clear cut, and the chapters that now follow will illustrate some of the problems propagated by the current arena, and reveal some of the solutions to hand.

Part Two:
Tensions

Having examined the three key processes underpinning the delivery of new homes in England, the intention in Part Two of this book is to set out key areas of tension. The research indicated that tensions – between planners and housing providers – tend to focus around particular issues or 'events' in the planning process. For that reason, this part of the book is divided into six chapters dealing with the following issues:

- **Land**: with a particular focus on the procedures and practices culminating in land allocations for new housing, Chapter 5 looks generally at the land issue and draws on research findings to show how the way that land is allocated and sites are identified remains a key tension in the development process.
- **Delay**: the various causes of delay are explored in Chapter 6. Of particular concern are the statutory hurdles – public consultation, plan-making and plan review, development control processes – that must be successfully negotiated before developments can proceed. The aim in this chapter is to demonstrate why the planning and hence development processes may sometimes be held back, and to examine national responses to the issue.
- **Discretion**: the unique discretionary and political nature of the British planning system are reviewed in Chapter 7. Of fundamental concern are the critical differences between regulatory and discretionary decision-making, the blurring of distinction between law and policy, and the relationship between salaried planning officers and elected local members. All these issues are examined with a view to explaining how the clarity of decision-making can be sacrificed in the name of local flexibility.
- **Design**: issues of design and density are examined in Chapter 8. The concern here is with approaches to increase design standards whilst ensuring that different groups share a consensus over what exactly constitutes good design and what levels of residential density might be required and accepted in the future. Inconsistency in design standards and disagreements over density are shown to represent separate but related sources of tension in the housing-planning process.
- **Gain**: the extraction of 'planning gain' or 'developers' contributions' from market development – on the back of planning obligations – remains one of the most fiercely debated topics in modern land-use planning. Besides the general rights and wrongs of the system, a more detailed argument usually hinges on the level of contribution that developers should make in order to secure planning permission. Chapter 9

reveals this – and in particular the delivery of affordable homes as gain – to be a highly controversial topic and one at the heart of planner–provider tension. It is also a subject that Government has grappled with via the 2001 Planning Green Paper.

- **Coordination**: a lack of corporate working – at a strategic or development level – remains a key source of conflict within the housing development process and is the subject of Chapter 10. The tension is manifested in a variety of different ways: RSLs feeling that they have not been adequately involved in Section 106 negotiations; developers believing that they should have been, but were not, consulted on policy; and housing departments frustrated by planning 'going it alone' on housing issues. Poor coordination can also result in communities feeling disempowered in the development process, leading to a huge source of local tension as NIMBY attitudes take hold.

These six chapters attempt to capture a flavour of the current tensions inherent in housing development. A review of evidence-based solutions – means to ease these tensions – follows on in the third part of the book.

5

Land

The question of land

Land is the essential ingredient in housing development. Finding it, buying it and unravelling the constraints that may hinder its use are essential prerequisites to delivering new homes. In this chapter, the principal concern is with the way in which land is made available for housing rather than the physical characteristics of the commodity itself; although the chapter would be incomplete without discussion of the current brownfield/greenfield debate.

The central question addressed in this chapter is how is land for new housing identified and subsequently allocated within the framework provided by the planning system? Short *et al.* (1986) argue that 'land search and assembly' is the primary consideration within a four-stage housing development process (Table 5.1). It involves a complex

Table 5.1 *Stages and stakeholders in the housing development process (Short* et al., *1986, p. 39)*

Stages	Stakeholders
Land search and assembly	Landowners
	Estate agencies
	Financial agencies
	Planning agencies
Development design and Planning permission	Architects
	Planning agencies
	Planning authorities
Housing production	Architects
	Subcontractors
	Financial agencies
	Public agencies
Marketing and selling	Estate agencies
	Building societies/banks
	Advertising agencies
	Consumers

interplay between a number of stakeholders, including landowners, estate agents, funders and planners, working in both local authorities and the private sector. Making land available for housing is the end-goal of a process that often involves lengthy political, financial and administrative negotiations.

The elements of this interplay are set out in later sections. An important first point, however, is that the means by which housing sites are identified and then allocated is potentially the most controversial stage of the entire development process. It frequently pits planners against developers, and communities (especially existing homeowners) against absolutely everyone perceived as having an interest in developing a site. This is set against a context in mid-2002 of increasing land values which now account for 37 per cent of the value of an average new-build home (the highest since 1992), whilst FPD Savills' 'Index of greenfield land values' shows a 170 per cent rise since 1993, and casts the blame on restrictive planning policies (Morris, 2002a).

A case that neatly illustrates the controversies is that of Stevenage West, which was mentioned earlier in Chapter 1. The allocation of land for a phased development of up to 5,000 new homes over a period of ten years (to 2011) has made national headlines, with local communities mobilising opposition to the allocation behind CASE: the Campaign Against the Stevenage Expansion. Projections of household growth support the need for this additional housing and Stevenage Borough's own urban capacity study has found no additional brownfield sites able to absorb the growth (Chestertons, 2001). It should be emphasised, however, that the site is a strategic allocation (in the structure plan), so the objective of the Stevenage capacity study was not to find alternatives to Stevenage West, although other greenfield allocations were deleted from the Unitary Development Plan (UDP) as a result of the study. Yet despite the forecast crisis that the area will face if the homes are not built, the opposition remains adamant that any new housing should be located elsewhere.

Some of the conflicts arising from allocation decisions are perhaps unavoidable, as the staunchest of NIMBYs will oppose the majority of development proposals (see the discussion of Basildon, p. 178). But other conflicts – which are potentially avoidable – stem from the procedures by which land is allocated for housing. At a very general level, the way in which regional estimates for new dwellings (and therefore building rates) are converted to land requirements have been labelled crude and unrealistic (Select Committee on Environment, Transport and Regional Affairs, 1998).

The basic argument is that the top-down process of deriving housing requirements from national and then regional estimates of future household growth involves a complex, and sometimes contradictory, series of calculations. In particular, it is impossible to reconcile national estimates with local requirements given the absence of effective strategic planning at the intermediate regional level. Hooper (1996), for example, argues that the regions offer neither methodological nor political coherence when it comes to rationalising government's household projections with local need or capacity. Often snap decisions are made at the regional level for political reasons (a Secretary of State may, at the eleventh hour, downsize or up housing requirements), making it impossible for local authorities to 'sell' the figures to their electorate. This unpredictability explains some of the general conflict surrounding housebuilding.

At a different level, developers commonly accuse local authority planners of having a weak grasp of housing market dynamics. There is a clear argument, for example, for suggesting that land should be allocated not only because of its availability, but also because of its location in an area where there is a reasonable (and potentially profitable) level of demand. Jackson *et al.* (1994) have pointed out that developers are often frustrated by planning's assumption that demand focused in areas of constraint will automatically transfer to areas of availability. This is a rather oversimplified argument, but numerous instances could be cited where poorly located housing (admittedly public housing, as private interests are unlikely to build where their own market appraisals suggest a lack of demand) subsequently suffered the scourge of low demand. Planning authorities frequently find themselves in a precarious situation, juggling the demands of existing communities with the pressures exerted on them by developers and the need to acknowledge changing market conditions. An added complication is the importance of ensuring that land allocations sit comfortably with employment, transport and environmental policies (Hooper, 1996) – in other words, housing land decisions have to reflect joined-up thinking and adhere to the principles of sustainable development.

The implication is that it is the allocation of land that will frequently cause conflict, particularly if greenfield rather than brownfield land is being allocated (see p. 74). Community groups, as in the case of Stevenage, possess a natural propensity to oppose new development that they feel is a threat to their way of life (and property values) and, in response, developers are often heard accusing planners of allocating acceptable rather than sufficient housing sites within development plans. Siting decisions are essentially political, making it difficult on occasion for authorities to 'allocate sufficient land for new housing' (DETR, 2000a); nevertheless, this remains their statutory duty.

For housebuilders, the buying, holding and bringing forward of land for development represents one of the biggest risks they face (see Chapter 3). The extent and nature of this risk depends on the nature of the housebuilder, and particularly on the extent to which they in turn rely on land price inflation for their profitability. For companies that maintain the minimum land bank of two to three years the major source of profit is derived from the construction and sales of houses, and crudely, therefore, profit levels will relate directly to turnover. For others, such as Wimpey Homes whose long-term strategy has been to build up a considerable land bank – including non-designated agricultural land – profit is greatly enhanced by increases in land value (Bramley *et al.*, 1995, p. 93). Because of the nature of their funding, very few RSLs can engage in significant land banking.

Research has indicated that only a fairly small proportion of land is purchased without planning permission, although because it is substantially cheaper, the purchase of 'white land' has the potential to increase profits. Generally, however, only larger developers are able to take such risks, and when they do they are able to use substantial resources to get the land zoned for development. Similarly, the majority of land is purchased for development to begin within three to four years, although for the larger companies sites can be under preparation for 10 to 15 years. Most land is purchased through options, with the payment of 10 per cent of the existing use value of the land a common outlay until outline permission has been secured. At that time, the option is taken up through payment for the land at its new market price less a 10 per cent discount, or payment of the agreed price at the time of purchasing the option. The use of options helps to reduce unnecessary interest payments on sites prior to planning permission being secured, and, in the face of high land values, allows a better land bank to be maintained (Monk, 1991, p. 9).

Because of the vast increases in value available to landowners on the allocation or sale of their land for residential development, some commentators have consistently argued that the only real means to deliver public objectives such as better designed, more sustainable, mixed-use and tenure development, is to tap into this value (Davison, 1991). With little current scope (besides planning obligations – see Chapter 9) for this value to revert to the state through a betterment tax or similar mechanism, the free market in land and its scarcity ensures that most of the profit associated with housing development goes straight back into the pockets of the fortunate few landowners. Harnessing this value and utilising it to pay for public needs represents one great potential of the planning system that in recent years has been neglected.

Brownfield v. greenfield development

Before moving on to look at the mechanics of the land allocation processes, it is important to consider the subject of land recycling. Central government's 1992-based household forecast raised the projected numbers of new households to the now fabled 4.4 million over the 25 year period beginning 1991. At the time the projections raised fundamental questions about the need for new houses versus the desire to protect the environment and contain urban sprawl. The projections fed on existing and widespread perceptions held by many commentators and much of the general public that new housing development is bad, and that such development – particularly on greenfield land – far from enhancing the environment is increasingly destructive (Carmona, 2001b, p. 5).

These attitudes mark something of a paradox, in that research has consistently shown that although anti-urban sentiments remain strong in England and aspirations for a rural (or at least suburban) lifestyle remain keen (URBED *et al.*, 1999, p. 4–6); there is an equally strong desire to protect greenfield land, if necessary by building at higher densities where development does occur (Popular Housing Forum, 1998, p. 58). This latter and strongly held national view has driven much of the subsequent debate following publication of the 1992 household projections. The debate which for the first time in a generation brought planning issues back to centre stage in England, drove successive governments to adopt first a 50 per cent target for brownfield land reuse and then a 60 per cent target (DETR, 1998a). The latter was adopted despite revised (1996-based) household projections that reduced the 25-year projection to 3.8 million (see p. 9).

To meet these objectives as well as the restated target of 60 per cent of the required additional housing on previously developed land (DETR, 2000a, para. 23), PPG3 introduced a sequential approach to the allocation of housing land, with the onus on planning authorities not to release greenfield sites until brownfield, intensification and regeneration options have been explored and exhausted (para. 30). PPG3 also included guidance on the use of urban extensions, residential development in public transport corridors, in village expansions and infills, and in new settlements (paras. 65–75), all of which, before they are allowed, should broadly follow the same sustainable principles used for new housing in urban areas. Figure 5.1 includes a summary of the key policy objectives contained in PPG3.

Much has been written about the brownfield/greenfield debate in recent years, including a full exposition of the virtues of brownfield over greenfield development in Rogers and Power (2000; see also Balchin and Rhoden, 2001). In particular, debates surrounding land recycling have intensified the basic housing land debate during the last few years, with views often becoming polarised. Locating new homes within the existing urban footprint is certainly a laudable aim that can have a number of benefits, the most significant of which are:

- protection of the countryside and greenfield land
- revitalisation of existing urban communities and reduced social polarisation

- reduction in travel distances and more viable public transport opportunities
- recycling of derelict and under-utilised brownfield land
- less public (NIMBY) opposition to development in urban brownfield locations.

Equally, however:

- where the demand for new housing is at its greatest (in much of the South East), the availability of brownfield land is at its lowest;
- much greenfield land both within and especially around existing settlements is of poor quality and might be enhanced through development;

Implementation	Greenfield development
➤ **The end of 'predict and provide' and the formal adoption of 'plan, monitor and manage'.** Regional Planning Guidance housing figures to reflect: 1. The latest household projections 2. The needs of the regional economy 3. The capacity of urban areas to accommodate more housing 4. The environmental implications 5. The capacity of existing or planned infrastructure. ➤ **A 'sequential approach': local authorities to undertake urban capacity studies, and setting a target of 60 per cent of housing on previously developed land by 2008.** The sequential approach places a presumption on developing previously developed sites before greenfields, using the following criteria: 1. Availability of previously developed land 2. Location and accessibility to jobs, shops and services other than by car 3. Capacity of existing and potential infrastructure 4. Ability to build communities 5. Physical and environmental constraints on development. ➤ **Local authorities asked to review all existing land allocations** and applications for the renewal of planning applications in the light of these criteria ➤ **Local authorities required to review existing planning policies** and adjust planning practice.	➤ **Favours urban extensions over new settlements**, suggesting that 'planned extensions to existing urban areas are likely to provide the next most sustainable option after building on appropriate sites with urban areas' (para. 67). New settlements, on the other hand, 'will only infrequently be a viable option due to their scale and the time required to develop them. New settlements will not be acceptable if they will simply function as a dormitory of an existing larger settlement' (para. 72). ➤ **Stronger emphasis on linking housing development with public transport in both urban and rural areas**. It is conceded, however, that 'just because a potential development site is well served by public transport does not of itself mean that it is an appropriate location' (para. 48). ➤ **Establishes a target for development on previously used land and a sequential approach to land allocation** (see Implementation).

Design and density

➤ **Places greater emphasis on improving the quality of new housing development and making more efficient use of land through promoting mixed-use schemes, increasing densities and improving design.** PPG3 states that 'local planning authorities and developers should think imaginatively about designs and layouts which make more efficient use of land without compromising the quality of the environment' (para. 54).

➤ **Supports initiatives such as Village Design Statements (VDS)**, suggesting that shared visions between stakeholders and communities should be developed.

➤ **Poor design should become a critical factor in refusing planning applications**: 'In determining planning applications, local planning authorities should reject poor design particularly where their decisions are supported by clear plan policies and adopted supplementary planning guidance, including village design statements' (para. 63).

➤ **Increase the efficient use of land, by increasing development density**: 'Local planning authorities should avoid the inefficient use of land. New housing development in England is currently built at an average of 25 dwellings per hectare but more than half of new housing is built at less than 20 dwellings per hectare. That represents a level of land take which is historically very high and which can no longer be sustained' (para. 57). Efficiency is to be enhanced by:

1. Reviewing all existing standards for car parking and road layouts
2. Avoiding maximum density standards
3. Avoiding developments of less than 30 dwellings per hectare
4. Encouraging an increase in density to 30–50 dwellings per hectare.

Housing needs

➤ **PPG3 does not replace the DETR Circular on Planning and Affordable Housing (6/98), which remains in force.**

➤ **It promotes mixed communities with a better social mix**, the integration of affordable and market housing, and greater efforts to match house types to housing needs (e.g. responding to the growth in single-person households, or other trends suggested by growth projections).

➤ **Supports indicative estimates of the need for affordable housing in Regional Planning Guidance.**

➤ **Emphasises the importance of adequately assessing local housing needs** and government-issued further guidance on this issue later in 2000.

➤ **Local plans should include a figure for affordable housing which should be required as part of any development**. The failure by a developer to propose sufficient affordable homes 'could justify the refusal of planning permission', and hence PPG3 reiterates affordable housing's status as a material planning consideration.

5.1 Key policy objectives in Planning Policy Guidance Note 3 (2000) (CPRE 2000; DETR 2000a).

- overdeveloping urban areas might lead to congestion and in some places to social tension;
- increasingly the 'easy' brownfield locations are being developed, leaving the more problematic sites for the future;
- demand clearly exists for lower density, suburban development (see Chapter 3).

Therefore, although much of the recent debate has been painted as black and white (or rather brown and green) with some groups intent on halting all greenfield development, for many this polarisation of views is thought to be unhelpful and oversimplifies the debate. The Town and Country Planning Association (TCPA, 2000, p. 5), for example, has argued that 'The current debate about planning and housing is dominated by dogma which places an infinite value on saving greenfields regardless of the social consequences and simply assumes that higher densities will reduce car dependency and congestion'.

Again, this concern can be illustrated by the case of Stevenage West, where opponents of the proposed scheme claim that building over agricultural land amounts to environmental vandalism and is inherently unsustainable. Defenders of the proposal point to the fact that Stevenage West will form an urban extension, linking into existing transport networks. Gains from the development – in the form of various community facilities – and a strategy promoting mixing of uses will also reduce the need to travel, giving the site a degree of self-containment. They also argue that the scheme must go ahead as there are too few land recycling opportunities in either Stevenage itself or neighbouring North Hertfordshire or indeed across Hertfordshire (Hertfordshire County Council, 1998). Hence the site passes the sequential test set out in PPG3 that local authorities should allocate greenfield sites in local development plans only when all recycling opportunities are exhausted.

More broadly, housebuilders are becoming alarmed at the attention being lavished on brownfield land, believing the push to achieve ever greater recycling targets will lead to higher land values and consequent shortages (of profitable sites). The whole debate over recycling is summarised by Hooper (1996) as a stalemate between housing requirement- and environmental capacity-led approaches. Issues of demand or need and capacity are equally important but because some groups prioritise one over the other, conflict becomes inevitable. Breheny and Hall (1996, p. 73) suggest that there needs to be a meeting of minds, with the allocation of different types of land reflecting the nuances of different contexts – 'The scale of required housing development is such that single solutions – infill, urban extensions and new settlements – will not be sufficient in most areas. Some combination of solutions will be required' – and that these must be tailored to regional and local circumstances.

'Planned provision on sustainable development principles [therefore] offers a third way forward which meets environmental conditions without leaving the population seriously under-housed' (TCPA, 2000, p. 4). As part of such a balanced approach to provision, the Town and Country Planning Association (TCPA, 2000, p. 19) has argued for a move away from anti-greenfield dogma, suggesting that

> Well planned, spacious, greenfield development is a positive and desirable part of the national approach to housebuilding. Obsessive protection of all countryside from use for new housing serves neither social nor environmental purposes and is likely to further damage, rather than improve, the cities whose regeneration is so important.

PPG3 (DETR, 2000a) opens with the assertion that the allocation of land for housing is one of the principal duties of planning authorities, and goes on to clearly prioritise brownfield development. Thomas and Ansbro (2000) represent a significant body of opinion when they argue that current policy guidance has an overbearing urban slant, and that if the sequential approach is applied uniformly in all parts of the country, it could often lead to the allocation of land miles from actual housing demand. Others, in particular the Council for Protection of Rural England (CPRE), have taken a consistently hard-line approach on greenfield development. The news, for example, that by 2002 government had reached and exceeded its target for brownfield reuse (60 per cent by 2008) relatively easily and well ahead of schedule (increasing from 56 per cent to 61 per cent between 1997 and 2001) (DTLR, 2002b), persuaded some that the target had not been ambitious enough, and that a higher target of 75 per cent reuse should be set in the future (Schopen and Lindsay, 2002).

The CPRE (2001a) has nevertheless identified what they describe as an inbuilt inertia within the planning system to respond to the new national policy on greenfield development. Thus, based on a survey of 154 local authorities' responses to PPG3 a year after its introduction, the CPRE (2001b, p. 18) found that although 62 per cent aimed to undertake an early review of their plan, only 49 per cent had undertaken a capacity study, 23 per cent reviewed their allocation of employment land, 26 per cent their parking standards, 27 per cent density standards, 39 per cent their greenfield allocations, 19 per cent their design policies, and 47 per cent had given planning permission for housing at below 30 dwellings per hectare. They agued that

> The full benefits of the Government's new planning policies to curb sprawl and promote an urban renaissance are far from being felt on the ground. Inertia, poor communication, weak leadership, a lack of belief in the Government's commitment and a lack of information and staff resources are some of the factors combining to obstruct change.
>
> (CPRE, 2001b, p. 15)

The case of Halton (briefly discussed on p. 81) illustrates an authority that for market reasons has been unable to respond to the agenda in PPG3. A number of reports also reveal the considerable barriers that frustrate more brownfield development, highlighting, in particular, the inadequacies of a range of local urban governance processes (including, but not only, planning) (see Table 5.2 and Chapter 10). The first from the Civic Trust Regeneration Unit (1999) examined 54 potential brownfield housing sites across 11 locations in England and Wales that had been originally examined by the House Builders Federation (HBF) for research in 1986. The research identified the range of barriers that over the 12-year period had acted against bringing forward housing development on the sites, and confirmed the importance of the public sector in an enabling and coordinating role (particularly the new Regional Development Agencies – RDAs).

A second report, this time from the HBF (1999), again highlighted reform of the processes of urban governance – particularly the operation of the planning system – as the primary means to overcome important obstacles. A final report from the TCPA (Breheny and Ross, 1998a) also focused largely on delivering brownfield housing through more effective urban governance processes. Fundamental to the TCPA's argument was the need for more resources to be directed by government towards urban areas, to be complemented by new thinking and innovation by those responsible for tackling past neglect:

Table 5.2 Problems and possibilities for reusing brownfield land

Problems (Civic Trust Regeneration Unit, 1999; HBF, 1999)	*Possibilities* (Civic Trust Regeneration Unit, 1999; Breheny and Ross, 1998a)
➤ a general failure of market mechanisms to see the opportunities presented by the sites – many were developed as social housing; ➤ a preference held by public authorities to work with housing associations rather than private housebuilders when public funding is involved; ➤ a general failure of public landowners and utilities to bring their land forward for development and a general unwillingness of landowners to sell; ➤ contaminated land remains one of the largest problems in bringing brownfield land to the market, while housebuilders remain cautious of such land; ➤ the failure of local authorities to fully embrace their new role as enablers rather than developers of new housing development; ➤ the need for authorities to utilise a more subtle mix of knowledge and skills, including project management, partnership-development and grant brokering, and to combine flexibility and creativity with proactive technical knowledge; ➤ the importance of public gap funding to make sites viable being undermined by the lack of availability, the short-term nature of many regeneration programmes and the complexity of others; ➤ a failure of the public sector to understand market conditions and the importance of location; ➤ an absence of community involvement and a failure to consider the possibilities provided by mixing uses; ➤ the operation of the planning system, particularly out-of-date policy frameworks, unrealistic employment allocations on brownfield land, local opposition, unrealistic planning gain requirements, delay and indecision; ➤ the lack of effective policies for dealing with contaminated land; and ➤ contradictions in the taxation and grant funding regimes.	➤ the need for a regional strategic focus with skills and resources marshalled to assist local authorities and their private partners; ➤ better definition and availability of gap funding requirements; ➤ the need for urban design, project management and development skills to be available to local authorities; ➤ more effective land remediation mechanisms and more effective land assembly powers; ➤ the need for enabling and flexible local authorities; ➤ the nurturing of a partnership culture; ➤ provide a much greater level of financial resources for cities; ➤ move forward plans and policies based on clear visions of the future; ➤ determine the appropriate degree of intensification that will maximise housing growth within urban areas whilst maintaining their attractiveness; ➤ persuade communities and politicians of the virtues of such development through demonstration projects; ➤ link housing to jobs to ensure the long-term viability of regenerated areas; ➤ adopt 'zero-tolerance' approaches to urban management and maintenance; and ➤ bring urban professions together to understand the problems and collectively devise solutions.

The scale of investment and ingenuity has now to move to a different plane – requiring a resource commitment never contemplated by Government before. The potential gains are enormous: the revival of our great cities and towns; major strides towards genuinely sustainable lifestyles; and enhanced protection of the countryside.

(Breheny and Ross, 1998b)

This issue of public resources for gap funding and land remediation is likely to be more critical in the future as viable brownfield sites are increasingly developed, leaving the more costly sites for the future. Equally, a change in culture is required, accepting that sustainable development may not equate to easy development, but will imply that difficult choices need to be made in the future if national urban renaissance objectives are to be delivered. It might also imply that to be socially sustainable, greenfield development may also often be necessary. These are just a few of the broader debates surrounding the housing land issue at the current time; others – taken from a summary of the current PPG3 – are listed in Fig. 5.1. They receive additional attention elsewhere in this book, and particularly in Chapters 2 and 8. This chapter now examines how, in procedural terms, land for new housing is identified and allocated.

Site identification and allocation

There is no discrete split between the procedures of site identification and those of land allocation. Rather, the physical search for future housing land and its subsequent allocation within development plans are parts of a single continuous process that begins with a land availability appraisal and ends with plotting lines on a map. There is a real distinction, however, between public and private roles in the way land is allocated and sometimes developed. This distinction centres on differing views of land availability. For local planning authorities, availability is largely a question of planning status; land either is or is not allocated for housing. For developers, planning status is merely one consideration, and availability is also judged in terms of physical constraints, market conditions and issues of ownership. This means that the identification and allocation of sites will not automatically lead to their development.

Planning authorities find and release land, which in their judgement is developable; but this judgement may not reflect that of the private sector. A critic might argue that planning authorities deal with theory (allocating land according to the latest planning paradigm – sustainability perhaps), whilst housing developers deal with reality, and particularly the reality of the market. But such a criticism would be unfair in many instances, as planners do not find and allocate land in a vacuum, but in partnership with local housing providers, balancing political and environmental considerations with the advice offered by those who will actually deliver new homes.

The legal basis for working in this way was provided by the Local Government, Planning and Land Act 1980, which set local planning authorities the task of making periodic assessments of land available and suitable for development for residential purposes. A follow-up Circular (9/80) not only set out a methodology for conducting Land Availability Studies but also 'urged co-operation between local authorities and housebuilders in establishing the local situation' (Cullingworth and Nadin, 1997, p. 147). Throughout the 1980s, however, the way such studies were undertaken was often viewed as excessively deterministic; i.e. the process of identifying sites remained dominated by a planning-led rather than a market-led philosophy. In particular, whilst the private sector looks for market signals when seeking land for development, planners are less concerned (and able) to read such signals. Moreover, the signals can fluctuate rapidly, whilst planning has had a responsibility to identify and allocate sites on a fixed five-year cycle. Thus, once plans are adopted, the signals may completely change, rendering the allocations redundant. This is a fundamental problem arising from the fact that planning provides a fixed (or in the context of the discretionary British system semi-fixed – see Chapter 7) framework for land release, whilst the market demands flexibility. Development plans are by their nature unresponsive to change during intervening plan periods.

In order to be less deterministic about finding new housing land and more flexible, facilities to review allocations, and to switch between different sites, are provided in recent policy guidance. PPG 3 now makes provision for the reallocation of employment and other land to housing during the lifetime of development plans. Government advice suggests that some authorities may have 'allocations of land for employment and other uses which cannot realistically be taken up in the quantities envisaged over the lifetime of the development plan' (DETR, 2000a, para. 42). Therefore, authorities are called upon to 'review all their non-housing allocations when reviewing their development plan and consider whether some of this land might be better used for housing or mixed use'. This form of flexibility is taken forward into the proposed Local Development Frameworks which keep land allocations under constant review. It is also designed to secure more land recycling on brownfield sites when and where opportunities arise. How local authorities practically identify new land for housing, in more general terms, can be illustrated using the example of one local planning authority in the north of England.

Halton Borough – located on the lower reaches of the River Mersey, some 25 miles from Liverpool – has an abundance of brownfield sites, but very few have been allocated for new housing in the most recent Unitary Development Plan (Halton Borough Council, 1999a). The Borough's forward planning team could have chosen to adhere closely to the advice coming from central government, and allocate hundreds of hectares of land adjacent to the Mersey, but all recent demand appraisals (for instance, Wong and Gallent, 1999) and deliberations with local housebuilders indicated that these sites were unmarketable. The cost of the clean-up operations required to bring the sites into effective residential use would also run into millions of pounds, a cost that in the absence of public subsidy would have to be passed on to homebuyers. Already, housebuilders can only afford to provide new homes in the borough if eventual unit prices are lower than those in neighbouring and more attractive towns, so this extra cost effectively made the sites unviable.

Therefore, developers are working on tight budgets and costs must be kept to a minimum. They need to find marketable sites, which have been identified as greenfield locations (with lower unit construction costs) close to motorway junctions that are attractive to buyers who commute to either Liverpool or Manchester. Hence the least sustainable sites are the only marketable sites in the borough, and the Borough's Land Availability Register for 1999 showed that over the next five years and beyond almost 90 per cent of new homes have been allocated to such sites (Table 5.3).

The site identification procedures used by Halton have therefore been heavily weighted towards marketability, with an input of advice from the private sector. Knowing where sites are vacant – or have a potential for redevelopment – is the simplest part of the task. From a long list of potential sites, Halton, like many local authorities, draws up a shortlist on the basis of individual site appraisals conducted by officers of the local

Table 5.3 Land allocations by type in Halton, 1999 (Halton Borough Council, 1999b)

	Greenfield	Brownfield	Total
No. of dwellings available in more than 5 years (and type per cent)	100.0	0.0	1,090
No. of dwellings available within 5 years (and type per cent)	65.9	34.1	1,197
Area (hectare) (and type per cent)	89.6	10.4	165.77
Total no. of dwellings (and type per cent)	81.5	18.5	2,314

Table 5.4 The scoring of development sites (Halton Borough Council, 1999c)

Criteria	Scoring
Demand and supply criteria	
Marketability	0 to –20
Planning constraints	0 to 5
Access constraints	0 to 5
Infrastructure constraints	0 to 5
Contamination constraints	0 to 5
Ownership constraints	0 to 5
Sustainability criteria	
(i) Urban regeneration	
Urban area	☺ or ☹
Previously developed land	☺ or ☹
Contaminated land	☺ or ☹
(ii) Protecting natural assets	
High-grade agricultural land	☺ or ☹
(iii) Minimising environmental impact	
Sustainable transport (housing)	☺ or ☹
Sustainable transport (employment)	☺ or ☹

authority. These appraisals focus on sites allocated in the previous plan period, potential redevelopment sites, open space sites and unallocated sites. Developable land is rated against a series of scoring criteria, which are more broadly categorised as relating to issues of 'demand and supply' and sustainability (see Table 5.4).

In line with government's drive to make development plans more flexible, the authority also conducts periodic reappraisals of sites allocated for employment use within the existing UDP, checking whether there is any benefit in reallocating these for residential use. The procedure follows a number of key stages:

1. Sites are scored against marketability (with advice from private sector partners) and overall demand and supply scores are calculated following an assessment of site constraints (see Table 5.4). The sites with the lowest scores are considered most likely to come forward for development (a marketability score of –20 is excellent, as are constraint scores of 0).

2. Sites closer to 0 in relation to marketability and with high constraint scores are least likely to come forward for development.
3. The overall sustainability score (denoted by sad or happy faces) for each site is placed next to the marketability/constraint factor.
4. Sites with the lowest indicator scores and the most happy faces (signifying that they are more sustainable) are the ones most likely to be identified as high-potential sites, and subsequently allocated for residential use.
5. But even unsustainable sites will be allocated if they score −20 overall (excellent marketability and no constraints whatsoever). This means a negative assessment against three of the six sustainability measures.

Thus development potential is judged against a site's positive and negative attributes, and high marketability (positive) can outweigh, for example, both existing ownership constraints and the need to protect agricultural land (both negative). In the authority's judgement, ownership constraints can be overcome on a profitable (marketable) site as the developer will have greater flexibility in the price they can offer for the land; and the need to provide new homes can outweigh agricultural considerations. The basic question that the authority is asking, therefore, is whether sites really are available from a developer's point of view. Its interest lies in identifying sites with positive development potential, and not those that fit a particular planning ideal but have little hope of being purchased and developed.

The particular balance placed on various considerations in identifying sites for development is a matter of local judgement, and Halton is perhaps an extreme case because of its particular local circumstances. Considerable research has nevertheless been undertaken on developing appropriate methodologies for more rigorously assessing the availability and potential of brownfield sites (see discussion of capacity studies in Chapter 15). Using local knowledge to find sites, and subsequently appraising them (in both market and planning terms) prior to allocation within a development plan is a logical and standard beginning to the development process and one that is illustrated by the Halton example. The final stage in this process involves formal allocation of sites in the plan before the plan can move through the adoption stages of consultation, revision, deposit, inquiry and final adoption. So even with the best intentions and market intelligence, the final allocation of housing sites within a development plan will lag some way behind the latest market conditions, making constant review and reappraisal the most critical element of the entire process.

In England, *Planning to Deliver: The Managed Release of Housing Sites* (DTLR, 2001d) was published as best practice guidance to supplement PPG3 on the release of sites for residential development. It suggests three possible approaches for releasing sites for development:

- Site release based on set criteria – such as location, which are clearly specified in the plan (only suitable if little greenfield development is anticipated, or where demand for new planning permissions over the plan period is likely to be low).
- Ranking of sites for development – by establishing a preferred order of release, or grouping sites into categories for release.
- Releasing sites over time periods defined within the plan (phasing) – with each time period lasting a specified number of years.

Of the three, the third approach is favoured in the guidance, but all rely on the annual monitoring of site development as a necessary feature of the 'plan, monitor and manage' approach, and to ensure that the sequential approach envisaged in PPG3 is working. The process of monitoring provides the basis for subsequent alterations to the plan, for proactive action to intervene and stimulate appropriate development if allocated sites are not coming forward as anticipated, and – if necessary – to alter the order of site release, preferably based on clear criteria set out in the plan (DTLR, 2001d, pp. 16–17).

Stakeholder views

The general importance attached to the land question by RSLs, private housebuilders and local authority planners was revealed in the survey of stakeholder views (see Fig. 5.2), from which it was obvious that all stakeholders regarded land as a key source of concern. These concerns fall into one of four groups: general attitudes (towards planning's role in the allocation process); the level of coordination between national and local policy; the degree of market and capacity realism behind allocation decisions; and the understanding of development constraints reflected in (national) policy.

General attitudes

It was widely held that with regard to the housing land question, short-term goals often vie with long-term objectives. This was true at the local level, where developers may have a fleeting interest in a site, whilst planners may have longer-term objectives, hoping to pull each new scheme into a wider development strategy. It was also true at the regional level, where a projection of housing demand stretching some way into the future can be re-interpreted locally as simply an immediate opportunity. Local planning authorities are particularly critical of national housing allocations, and suggest that targets are almost invariably blind to local circumstances, reflecting limited understanding of capacity, windfall contributions and/or land conditions. Interestingly, respondents were almost silent

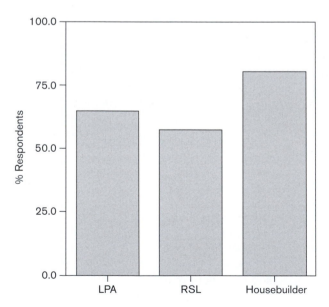

5.2 Views on the significance of land identification and allocation as a source of planner–provider tension (per cent rating as significant).

on the issue of local procedures for allocating housing sites, but in clear agreement that the majority of conflicts stem from central government practice in dealing with land for housing.

Realism

Realism in land allocation represented a critical issue for providers, in particular whether authorities were undertaking objective site appraisals, and allocating brownfield sites with due regard to their marketability. Many believe that authorities have been blinded by government's 60 per cent brownfield target and are consequently less rational in their land allocations. One respondent argued that planning authorities pass over high-demand greenfield sites and allocate only contaminated land where there is little chance of translating an allocation into development. Planners are unable, as one respondent put it, to 'see past the end of the current plan' or accept that simple constraint will not, alone, achieve the goal of sustainability.

But housebuilder frustration is not only levelled at planning professionals: local council members are frequently blamed for misallocation. Constraint policies are seen by housebuilders as the 'obvious but incorrect' political answer to electoral pressure, believing that 'demand transfer simply does not occur: hence current land price hotspots'. But planners offer a contrary view, claiming that just because housebuilders 'shy away' from brownfield sites, that is no reason to hold back on such allocations. They are, according to one authority 'land hungry, and will convert all types of opportunities into sites'.

Coordination

Many respondents saw a lack of coordination between national aspirations and local realities as the major barrier to realising workable, acceptable and sufficient housing land allocations. Key messages in PPG3, for example, were considered impossible to act upon within the context of existing development plans. The sequential approach, the sharper focus on recycling, and a stronger anti-greenfield bent appeared (at least to some survey respondents) to render 'current allocations obsolete'. Authorities believed they faced a stark choice: to stick with existing plans and implement gradual change (but risk having to fight more appeals because of changed national policy) or to abandon their plans and start again in the light of PPG3. North Hertfordshire, for example, chose the latter route after legal advice and faced the uphill struggle of running a development control service without any local policy framework. Other councils opted for gradual change, choosing to defend existing allocations on their merits.

The critical issue here is that of speed. National guidance can (and does) alter relatively quickly, but plans can respond only slowly to the changing political climate. This reality has led to strong criticisms of the development plan system in recent years, but while some commentators welcome the emergence of a new system (see Chapter 2), others feel that national policy is at fault, and urge greater support for the status quo.

The turmoil surrounding plans was less of a concern for housebuilders, who, through the appeals system, hoped to capitalise on this political confusion. They were more concerned about the lack of coordination between development planning and regional policy. As one developer put it: 'availability of land is dealt with on a local authority basis, which does not reflect regional demand. [This] creates an artificial shortfall of land, thereby increasing values'. This link between strategy and implementation was a constant theme through the survey responses, but for a range of differing reasons. Developers hoped for some guarantee that housing figures would translate into profitable allocations; authorities recognised the need to coordinate action across administrative boundaries, thereby ensuring that social and economic problems are not shunted between different areas.

Constraints

All stakeholders pointed to the need for a full debate on the 60 per cent target, to address the issue of low land values and demand. There was, however, a general view that allocation policies should not be prescribed from above, but should be based around local assessments of cost, remediation, regeneration potential, conversion potential, conservation and employment impact. As one RSL put it, 'I have yet to see any serious attempt by any central or local government agency to address [housing] demand. Current application of political targets will, regrettably, hasten social polarisation rather than reduce it'. This is perhaps a one-sided view, borne of particular local experiences, but there was a general disagreement over the extent to which development constraints are factored into regional recycling targets and local allocations.

Two clear conclusions emerge. First, the biggest controversy in the current housing land debate does not stem from local allocation practice, but from the top-down approach to demand calculation taken by central government. There is a belief, shared by planners and housing providers, that the process lacks effective coordination between the different levels, fails to achieve realism (sometimes showing little appreciation of local needs) and is ignorant of local development constraints. Second, all these problems are compounded by the political nature of allocations – centrally, political interference has a huge impact on regional housing figures; and locally, the sufficiency of allocations is commonly sacrificed to NIMBY interests, with members giving little credence to the advice of their officers. These are fairly sweeping statements and do not apply equally everywhere. But the cascading down of housing figures from central government to the regions and eventually to development plans, alongside the discretionary nature of British planning, often makes the process of land allocation for new housing uncertain and prone to controversy.

Finally, whilst this chapter has focused mainly on the process of allocating land for new housing, it needs to be stressed that other issues and problems remain important. A recent inquiry into 'Land for Housing' for the Joseph Rowntree Foundation concluded that 'simply constraining urban development in southern England will not solve the region's housing problems, nor will it solve those of the rest of the country' (Barlow *et al.*, 2002, p. 24). Instead, there needs to be:

- a fuller and more serious debate on the nature of housing demand and need, stemming from the capacity of existing housing to accommodate growth as well as demographic trends;
- movement beyond the narrow greenfield versus brownfield debate, to a discussion that takes into account macroeconomic needs and the sustainability of both urban and rural economies, and the fact that, for economic reasons, greenfield development may be essential;
- discussion about how higher densities can be coupled with good design (see Chapter 8) – increasing housing densities merely to avoid development on greenfield

land may well be incompatible with the housing space needs of the twenty-first century;
- creative thinking on how to deal with high land prices and thereby tackle the affordability crisis facing lower-paid workers in both rural and urban areas.

6

Delay

Delay – an eternal problem

In this chapter the issue of delay is explored, including its causes and attempts both today and in the recent past to grapple with this recurrent problem. The case that planning intervention unduly impacts on the efficient operation of the market has long been a theme of debates surrounding the planning system. Most famously Michael Heseltine (1979) as the first Secretary of State for the Environment under the Thatcher governments complained that 'thousands of jobs every night are locked away in the filing trays of planning departments'. The Circular that followed (22/80) made the unequivocal case that:

> The magnitude of the investment at risk from delay is very large . . . Unnecessary delays in the development control system can result in wasted capital, delayed production, postponed employment, income, rates and taxes, and lower profitability. They can create a poor climate for future investment. Local planning authorities have a clear responsibility to minimise delay.
>
> (DoE, 1980, para. 5)

Underpinning the thinking of the Thatcher years was a notion that 'physical planners were obstructive bureaucrats, all too ready to stifle wealth-creating private enterprise by unnecessary curbs on development' (Ward, 1994, p. 205). Immediately on coming to power, the performance of local planning services began to be measured by the single crude measure of the percentage of planning applications decided within eight weeks (see p. 93). The quarterly publication of these figures ever since has been used as a stick with which the development industry and government can 'beat' the planning system.

Arguably the nadir for planning came in these years with the issuing of the White Paper 'Lifting the Burden'. Planning, along with a number of other areas of government activity, was identified as a barrier to the development of an enterprise culture, and therefore in need of reform. The reforms that followed, however, brought with them their own uncertainty and delay as the downgrading of development plans to material consideration status raised the levels of uncertainty, leading to the lengthy process of planning by appeal (Ward, 1994, p. 212).

The restoration of the plan-led system in the early 1990s (see Chapter 2) was therefore equally a response to uncertainty, this time as an attempt to reduce the number of appeals. It brought with it, however, other forms of delay in the extra time taken to adopt the new development plans because of their increased status and the resulting attempts (often by housebuilders) to influence their preparation. Cronin, for example, observed that following the introduction of Section 54A of the 1990 planning act which effectively ushered in the plan-led system, a tenfold increase in objections to the new plans was not uncommon. 'The consequence of this is extremely long inquires . . . Kingston's borough plan inquiry lasted 10 sitting days in 1988 and the UDP inquiry [1992/3] lasted 55 days spread over 11 months' (Cronin, 1993, p. 16).

Cullingworth and Nadin (2002, p. 150) argue that attempts to streamline the planning process represent a reoccurring theme, although the reasons have differed. In the 1970s the concern was with the huge increase in applications and appeals stemming from the property boom of the period; in the 1980s the concern was with the cost of the planning process and cutting back public expenditure, as well as with abandoning bureaucratic controls; in the 1990s the emphasis was on balancing efficiency with the quality of public services, whilst since 2000 the issue of relieving business from the perceived burden of regulation has increasingly been stressed.

The issue of delay (or more correctly the time taken in planning decision-making) has therefore continued to dominate debates on planning, whilst the history of planning to some extent reflects the fact that as long as there is a planning system there will be a cost in the time taken to make decisions. Furthermore, the more open and publicly accountable (democratic) a system is, the more it is likely to cause delays. On one side of the debate, therefore, it is argued that delays in the planning process impose unacceptable constraints on the operation of the market, with knock-on effects on the overall competitiveness of the economy. On the other, supporters of a more community-based planning process argue that democracy takes longer (Anon., 2001a) and that because the impacts of many developments are likely to be felt for decades to come, it is appropriate to take the time to ensure those decisions are correct in the first place.

These arguments were the subject of a major review of the development control process by George Dobry in 1975. Dobry was concerned with streamlining the development control process, but at the same time with answering the increased calls for public consultation and participation and with clarifying the basis of decision-making (DoE, 1975). He started with a recognition that delay is the price paid for democracy and that if it is thereby possible to deliver better quality, more environmentally sensitive development, it is a price worth paying. His solution was to separate applications into major and minor categories. Simple applications should thus be distinguished early on and dealt with by planning officers according to a compressed timescale, although allowing some time for consultation.

Dobry's approach was therefore to free up the system from the vast majority of relatively straightforward applications and so allow time and resources to concentrate on the more complex major applications. At the time his conclusions were not implemented as a change in government in the same year (Conservative to Labour) brought with it a different agenda. Nevertheless, the process represented the first attempt to grapple with the problem of delay, and to establish a set of positive and practical solutions that clearly echo thinking over 25 years later – see p. 99.

As discussed in Chapter 3, delay can be particularly problematic for private housebuilders in a highly changeable marketplace that requires short lead-in times to ensure that a development is still viable when it is completed. Equally, Housing Corporation (1999) research revealed that schemes often have to reduce the provision of new social housing in order to reduce opposition (and therefore delay) enough to meet funding timetables. For both private housebuilders and RSLs the need to meet such financial targets and deadlines makes the appeals system with all its uncertainty particularly unpalatable, and therefore, within limits, provides an incentive – if not a necessity – to negotiate.

The causes of delay

Research by Bramley *et al.* (1995) in Avon found that delay was perceived to be a particular problem at the detailed planning permission stage, when the unpredictable political intervention of planning committees occurred. However, if local politicians are a cause of major conflict in the housing development process, this is likely to be because they themselves are in a difficult position. On the one hand they administer a planning system that is ultimately pro-growth. However, many represent constituencies where anti-growth remains the dominant opinion of their constituents, and therefore the safest electoral posture (Short *et al.*, 1986).

The problem extends from market to social housing. Thus a survey of housing associations in Devon and Cornwall revealed that RSLs were experiencing increasing problems of members going against officers' advice and being prejudiced against social housing schemes. Members were (understandably) particularly sensitive to local views and often considered proposed social housing schemes to be politically unacceptable (Housing Corporation, 1999).

Bateman (1995) identifies several key factors which are increasing the delay experienced in the housing development process:

- the complexities of the development plan adoption process (which often includes prolonged statutory consultation);
- what he calls the 'obligatory' Section 106 planning gain negotiations;
- the demand by many local authorities for a development brief before negotiation can begin;
- the imposition of an excessive raft of conditions on many proposed developments; and
- the meddling of unqualified planners in design issues.

Bateman (1995) observes that a number of years can now elapse before development of an acceptable site starts on the ground. The Housing Corporation for their part have argued that 'issues related to the planning process have risen to the top of the list of reasons why housing association projects are delayed or lost' (Housing Corporation, 1999, p. 12).

The problem of delay therefore remains serious for providers, with DTLR monitoring in 2001 showing 16 per cent of local planning authorities still having no adopted local or unitary plan some 10 years after introduction of the plan-led system. Furthermore, of those with adopted plans in 2001, 214 were due to reach or pass their original end-date within two years, and almost all of those had not put any proposals forward for their replacement.

Undoubtedly the planning process has become increasingly more complex and difficult to administer. This is particularly so as regards housing development, with more and more expected of the process, not least the delivery of affordable housing and recycling of brownfield sites. Nevertheless, Thomas (1997, pp. 232–3) argues that many causes of delay are simple and out of the hands of planning officers. They include:

- applications submitted incomplete or the slowness of applicants to provide information;
- the time required for adequate consultation;
- the time required to negotiate agreements and conditions;
- the planning committee cycle;
- varying development control workloads reflecting economic conditions;
- developer delays between outline permission and resolution of reserved matters;
- the varying degree of delegation of decisions (from councillors to officers);
- the proportions of applications relating to more sensitive contexts, such as in conservation areas.

In addition, the structuring and inbuilt complexity of both the plan-making and development control processes have been heavily criticised for building delay into the system. Thus in the case of development control, authorities are required to go through a series of complex negotiations and consultations following receipt of a planning application (and ideally before as well), whilst in the plan-making process no fewer than five rounds of consultation (at varying degrees of complexity) have been required (see Table 6.1). Furthermore, once planning permission is given or a site allocated for development in the development plan, there is no guarantee that development will come forward quickly (or indeed at all). Delay of this type can undermine planning objectives and make planning a more uncertain process as future permissions are held back by uncertainty about whether permissions already in the system will be implemented or not. In this regard, delay is likely to be a two-way process, and proposals in the 2001 Planning

Table 6.1 Key stages in development control and plan-making processes (in 2002)

Key stages in development control (usually eight weeks minimum) (adapted from Carmona, 2001b, pp. 159–60)	*Key stages in plan-making (usually two years plus)* (based on Cullingworth and Nadin, 2002; DoE, n.d)
A. Pre-application	A. Pre-plan
➤ offer the means for potential developers to consult the authority about design proposals	➤ survey of plan area
	➤ review existing policy and prepare position papers
➤ if necessary instigate design briefing procedures	
➤ if appropriate instigate collaborative arrangements	B. Pre-deposit
	➤ preparation of consultation draft of development plan
➤ if appropriate instigate participation arrangements	➤ publicise draft plan
	➤ undertake public and statutory consultations
B. Post-application	➤ obtain statement of conformity from strategic authority
➤ application checked, registered and acknowledged	➤ consider objections
➤ publicise application	
➤ consultation procedures (statutory/ non-statutory consultees)	C. Pre-inquiry
➤ visit and appraise the site	➤ revise plan and prepare first deposit draft
➤ review established policy context for the site (national/strategic/district-wide/site-specific)	➤ publicise deposit plan
	➤ undertake public and statutory consultations

Table 6.1 continued

➤ obtain skilled/specialist advice/ information (i.e. on environmental impact assessment, conservation, design)
➤ on the basis of information negotiate alterations
➤ negotiate implementation requirements (phasing, planning gain requirements, reserved matters)
➤ write report and make a reasoned recommendation to committee or decision under delegated powers
➤ hold planning committee to make (or defer) decision
➤ notify applicant of decision and record in the planning register

C. Post-decision1: following a negative decision
➤ where necessary fight any appeal
➤ use the appeal decision to monitor policy and guidance
➤ where necessary fight statutory review in the high court

D. Post decision1: following a positive decision (or an appeal successfully made)
➤ monitor the implementation of all aspects of the project (and if necessary enforce decisions/conditions)
➤ evaluate the final development outcomes on the ground
➤ use the information – where necessary – to revise policy and guidance

➤ consider objections and negotiate with objectors
➤ revise plan and prepare second deposit draft
➤ reconsider statement of conformity
➤ make available for inspection of changes
➤ consider objections on changes

D. Inquiry
➤ inspector appointed by Planning Inspectorate
➤ public local inquiry held (adversarial and informal hearings)
➤ inspector's report prepared
➤ recommendations considered by local planning authority

E. Post-inquiry
➤ draft modifications and reasons prepared
➤ consultation on modifications held
➤ consider objections to modifications
➤ revise plan or hold second public local inquiry
➤ adopt plan by council resolution (if no objection from Secretary of State)
➤ fight possible challenge in the courts
➤ Monitor implementation and begin next review

Green Paper (taken forward in the 2003 Planning and Compulsory Purchase Act) to limit periods of consent from five to three years represent an attempt to address this aspect of the problem (DTLR, 2001a, p. 40).

In one of the few pieces of commissioned research to directly address the issue of planning delay, delay was perceived by housebuilders to be the most severe constraint to production, exceeding issues of market demand and land price (Roger Tym and Partners, 1989, pp. 63–4). The research ranked the causes of such delay as:

• extended negotiations on density and design;
• local authority staffing problems (low numbers and poor calibre of staff) caused by a lack of resources;
• the time taken to negotiate legal agreements;
• planning committees overturning officers' recommendations;
• the appeals process (where initial reasons for refusal were not confined to planning matters;

- statutory consultees, who were too slow in responding to requests for comments;
- inadequate plan coverage, leading to increased confrontation.

Significantly, although delays had increased development costs for 40 per cent of the sample, sales receipts had also increased for 37 per cent of the sites, dramatically reducing any impact on gross profit margins. Importantly, however, the work was undertaken in a buoyant housing market, and the results might not have been replicated if market conditions were flat. Furthermore, despite the negligible impact on profit margins, delay had a considerable effect on cash flow, particularly of smaller companies, whose expansion plans were thereby curtailed (Roger Tym and Partners, 1989, p. 51).

Planning officers interviewed as part of the research agreed that negotiations over design standards were a common cause of delay, although in their view second to staff shortages (Roger Tym and Partners, 1989, p. 63). The housebuilders for their part conceded that the recommended eight-week period for determining most planning applications was too short and, as standard, budgeted for a three- to six-month period to obtain planning permission. On that basis, delays of two to three months were already anticipated, and their financial effects were written off. Their prescriptions to speed up the process included the greater use of pre-application negotiations and consultations with local residents, as well as higher design standards based on a fuller appraisal of context in order to smooth the path once applications were made. The most recent evidence in the form of research commissioned by the Select Committee on ODPM: Housing, Planning, Local Government and the Regions seemed to close down the issue. It concluded 'there is no evidence that planning is a significant explanatory factor for the UK's low productivity compared to its main competitors', but also 'there is almost no evidence regarding the positive effects of planning on the economy' either (Roger Tym and Partners, 2002, paras 3.22–3.23).

Delays caused by the planning system nevertheless represent a cyclical grievance of the housebuilding industry, and in 1996 the HBF went so far as to blame delays in planning permission for slowing down a recovery in the housing market, arguing that 'The DoE has no effective sanction against planning authorities breaking the eight-week rule on applications' (David Coates in Anon., 1996). With the emergence of the plan-led system in the 1990s, such criticisms from housebuilders extended beyond the development control process to the time taken in plan-making, and in so doing emphasised the complexities and interlinked nature of the development and planning processes. In a plan-led context, it is at the plan-making stage – when the land is first allocated – that much of the risk and potential gain for the developer (and if different, the landowner) lies in bringing land forward for development. At that stage delays can be measured in years rather than weeks or months (Bateman, 1995, p. 27).

The cult of measurement

With the flawed eight-week target remaining – until recently – the only benchmark by which the performance of planning authorities was measured, it is perhaps unsurprising that a concern for speed of decision-making has dominated debates on the relative effectiveness of the planning system. This practice has consistently raised debates about the relative balance between speed and quality in planning decision-making.

In 1979 the Department of the Environment began to compile quarterly figures for the number of applications successfully processed within the now infamous eight-week period. It also published figures relating to the number of applications processed inside a thirteen-week period. Throughout the 1980s this target remained the only tangible indicator of the success of the planning process (Day,1996, p. 26). This ensured that local planning authorities prioritised efficient processes within their operation and con-centrated on reducing the time taken to deliver development control decisions. This was in line with the then Conservative government's desire to speed up the development control process and improve its cost effectiveness.

The Audit Commission established by a 1982 act of parliament was charged with ensuring that local authorities had made proper arrangements for securing economy, efficiency and effectiveness (the three Es). To this end, a central tool was the publishing of key statistics about local authorities, outlining their performance for comparative analysis by their customers – the public and business community. These statistics were specified by the Audit Commission for all local authorities in England and Wales and were revised annually. The Commission also encouraged local authorities to begin to develop their own local performance indicators, although, until recently, few did so.

The context of this emphasis on efficiency in local authority planning was the new culture of efficiency and internal markets within local authorities more generally. Central government, for example, introduced Compulsory Competitive Tendering (CCT) in the Local Government Act of 1988, regulation that 'forced local authorities to move a long way very quickly' (Day, 1996, p. 35). Local authorities were required to externalise service delivery, with government taking the view that the private sector could not only provide a higher-quality service, but would do so more cost effectively. The aim was for the local authority to become the enabler of service provision rather than the sole provider.

CCT, and later the introduction of the Citizen's Charter, led to a more customer-oriented approach to service provision at the local level, which sought better value for money. Although planning was never directly subject to CCT and very few planning services were externalised, its impact was nevertheless clear. Planning became more efficient and planning departments were increasingly assessed comparatively. The use of performance indicators to simulate the pressures of an external market and provide a tangible measure of efficiency was a central part of this approach to measuring the performance of local authorities.

The principal manifestation of the new customer focus under the Conservative government was the Citizen's Charter, a central tenet of which were Citizen's Charter Performance Indicators, devised by the Audit Commission in consultation with central and local government. Under the Citizen's Charter, from March 1992 local authorities were required by law to publish performance against a set of indicators. The Citizen's Charter (1992) initiative was organised to reflect six main principles:

1. Setting, monitoring and publication of explicit standards.
2. Information for and openness to the service user and systematic consultation with users.
3. Choice wherever practical, plus regular and systematic consultation with users.
4. Courtesy and helpfulness.
5. Well-publicised and easy-to-use complaints procedures.
6. Value for money.

The move towards a more comprehensive set of performance indicators under the Citizen's Charter was a significant advance in the measurement of local authority activity. The Audit Commission report 'Building in Quality', which focused on the processes of development control, reflected this wider agenda and concluded that alone, the eight-week rule was too crude a measure to assess planning performance (Audit Commission, 1992, p. 3). The report argued that 'speed in processing planning applications need not necessarily be at the expense of quality outcomes', and that 'A more subtle system in which authorities are monitored against time criteria related to the type of application and the need to negotiate could command greater credibility and therefore be a better spur to efficiency' (Audit Commission, 1992, p. 46).

To aid the process it recommended that authorities could monitor their own performance against a broad range of performance indicators – both quantitative and qualitative (see Table 6.2) – although no new national indicators were promoted and few of those suggested related to outcome quality. Nevertheless, the issue of quality had, even if in a limited manner, belatedly entered the vocabulary of performance measurement in local authorities. Day (1996, p. 50) argues that whilst the Citizen's Charter

Table 6.2 Building in quality – suggested performance indicators

A range of suggested measures balanced to assess overall performance and achievements

Quantitative	➤ Volume	– No. of applications – by type
		– % DC time on applications
	➤ Targets	– committee – by type
		– delegated – by type
	➤ Speed	– within 6 weeks
		within 8 weeks
		within extended prescribed period } by type
		within 13 weeks
		– time to register – % in 2 days
		– time for decision – notice – % in 2 days
		– staff – time per application
	➤ Cost	– cost per application
		– fee income per application
		– % recharges
	➤ Service	– response time to letters/telephone
		– cost per application
		– notifications to objectors
Qualitative	➤ Added value	– compliance with policies/guidelines
		– negotiated improvements/permissions
		– approval rates
	➤ Openness	– public notification
		– reports
		– committee procedures
	➤ Achievements	– appeal results
		– local design awards
		– annual development audit
		– compliance with local plan
		– implementation of local plan
		– % solution of contraventions
		– housing targets achieved
		– industrial/commercial floor space permitted
		– listed buildings/green fields saved
		– peer group review
	➤ Service delivery	– number/types of complaints
		– customer surveys

indicators failed to present a full and coherent picture of planning performance and quality, they did have some use in that they allowed local people to analyse and compare service provision and ensure local government became more accountable (although for planning it is likely that few actually took the opportunity).

Thus performance indicators have been criticised on several grounds (Likierman, 1993; Pollitt, 1994; Stewart and Kieron, 1994; RTPI, 1995a):

- the failure to use such indicators to explicitly improve planning outcomes;
- failing to counter the short-term focus – all indicators were collected on an annual basis;
- failing to deal with external events – the indicators did not have built-in mechanisms to deal with uncontrollable external events, although these clearly impacted on an authority's performance;
- lacking realistic targets – only one of the Citizen's Charter Indicators had an associated target and all of the others had no indication of the standards of performance, thus seriously limiting the indicators as a means of improving quality;
- being too numerous to get the public's interest and being too often misinterpreted or misunderstood;
- effecting local politics and restricting local choice because of their centrally determined nature;
- being primarily concerned with communicating performance to the public rather than actively seeking to improve services;
- creating uncertainty over whether the benefits outweighed the costs of data collection and analysis.

This was the position as regards performance indicators in the public sector at the time of the 1997 General Election. The change in political leadership brought with it fresh impetus for both local government and performance indicators. A follow-up report on the success of 'Building in Quality' in 1998 nevertheless revealed that some considerable progress had been made on the faster processing of applications, although nationally authorities were still falling far short of the 80 per cent of applications decided in eight weeks target (achieving about 60 per cent instead). Evidence on better processes and better outcomes from the planning process was less conclusive, although it was concluded that customer care processes had improved and that some extra efforts were being made by about one-third of authorities to review schemes once implemented and that both the percentage of appeals and percentage of appeals granted had fallen, indicating an improvement in performance (Audit Commission, 1998).

Best Value – speed v. quality

From April 2000, the duty of 'Best Value' required local authorities to make continuous improvements in the way they exercise their functions, having regard to a combination of economy, efficiency and effectiveness (Local Government Act 1999 3[1]). The duty of Best Value involves delivering several commitments at the local level, summarised as:

- ensuring that public services are responsive to the needs of citizens, not the convenience of the service providers;
- ensuring that public services are efficient and of a high quality;
- ensuring that policy-making is joined-up and strategic, forward-looking and not reactive to short-term pressures;

- using information technology to tailor services to the needs of users;
- valuing public services and tackling the under-representation of minority groups.

Thus the vision for Best Value is relatively simple, to maintain and improve the efficiency of services, whilst also ensuring that services are of a high quality and respond to the needs of local people. Local authorities are at the forefront of Best Value, a new leadership role that should be evident in a number of ways, through:

- leadership from members by being more visible in, and accountable to, the local community;
- engaging the community and service users in discussions regarding service provision;
- seeking continuous improvement in service delivery and outcomes by developing challenging performance targets, measuring up to the best of other service providers, being innovative and being creative;
- exercising firm budget control.

Community strategy
Such plans should build on the processes that have been developed to produce Local Agenda 21 plans.

Corporate plans
It is envisaged that the community strategy will provide the starting point for the development of a 'corporate plan', which will set out the local authorities' strategic objectives and priorities and how these will be addressed.

Service plans
Service plans are particularly important. They are specific to each local authority service, defining the aims and objectives of these services and outlining how they intend to deliver the aspirations in the corporate plan. Service plans contain performance information, and outline plans for improvement. These can be used to furnish Best Value reviews and the action plan which flows from the review will be included in the following year's service plan.

Best value performance plans (BVPPs)
The annual BVPP is another piece of the government's Best Value framework. It is intended to give practical expression to the strategic objectives by providing a context for the programme of Best Value reviews and by setting out a summary of the local authority's achievements and targets for improvement. BVPPs are the principal means by which an authority can be held to account for the efficiency, effectiveness and economy of its services and plans for the future.

Delivery and implementation plans
Government stresses the importance of interlinked plans to help deliver the modernisation and Best Value commitments.

Performance indicators
Performance indicators are a central tool which can help local authorities to challenge what they do, compare performance, consult and inform stakeholders about performance.

6.1 The Best Value framework (POS, 2000, pp. 1–6; DETR 1998g).

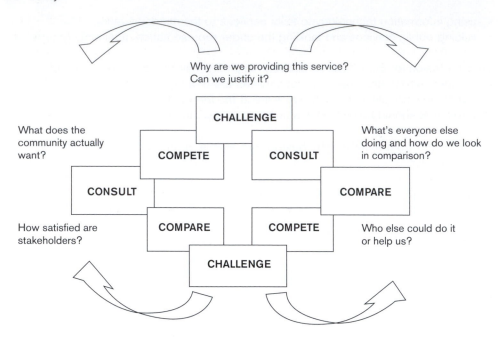

6.2   The interrelation of the four 'C's: a continuous cycle of improvement (Watford Council and Allen, cited in POS, 2000, pp. 1–4).

Best Value is built around a concept of continuous improvement within local authorities, articulated at the local level through a series of strategies, plans and indicators (see Fig. 6.1). Government requires each council to review all of its functions over a maximum five-year period on an ongoing basis in the shape of Best Value Reviews structured around the four 'C's (see Fig. 6.2):

- Challenge: why and how a service is being provided.
- Compare: performance with other local authorities, the private sector and voluntary sector across a range of indicators with a view to matching the top 25 per cent.
- Consult: with local taxpayers, service users, the wider business community and a range of stakeholders in addressing service delivery and the setting of new performance targets.
- Compete: by embracing fair and open competition as a means of securing efficient and effective services.

Performance indicators are also instrumental to the success of Best Value and have a central position in the Best Value framework, alongside Best Value performance plans and service audits undertaken by the Audit Commission. The new approach aims to reflect the outcomes of planning activity rather than just the process. If achieved, this marks a major shift in emphasis from the efficiency-based perspective encompassed in the Citizen's Charter and its predecessors. Thus, the 1999 Local Government Act (section 3[1]) outlines that local authorities must ensure that public services are both efficient and of a 'high quality'. Indeed, the new emphasis on quality is reflected in the identification of quality as one of five dimensions of performance measurement.

The Planning Officer's Society (2000, p. 6/13) nevertheless suggests that measuring quality will be a 'complex task', whilst Rose confirms that in terms of Best Value, 'quality resides in a relatively abstract value-laden world (Rose, 1998, p. 12) and concludes that devising suitable criteria for measuring quality outcomes will be far from easy. Of central importance is the identification of what constitutes desirable outcomes of the planning process and how they can best be measured, particularly given the requirements for measuring performance under Best Value as set out by the Planning Officer's Society (POS, 2000, p. 6/1), to:

* develop a robust framework for collecting, collating and measuring performance information;
* use performance information as a tool to drive improvement;
* compare performance with the top 25 per cent of local planning authorities and the best of other providers in the private and voluntary sectors;
* do not just measure the obvious, but think about service outcomes and develop ways in which they can be measured;
* only collect information which actually says something about the service;
* involve all stakeholders in setting local performance indicators and targets;
* ensure all performance indicators are SMART (Specific, Measurable, Achievable, Realistic and Time-bound);
* use rigorous comparison to help set performance targets;
* set demanding but realistic targets.

So far, like their predecessors, the nationally defined Best Value performance indicators have tended to emphasise process rather than outcomes, although authorities are also encouraged to prepare their own local performance indicators in addition to the national Best Value Performance Indicators (BVPIs). Of the seven Best Value performance Indicators for planning in 2001/2002 (DETR, 2000e), all but one were concerned with process-related issues. Speed and efficiency were still seen as the primary measures of effective planning (BV109 – percentage of applications determined in eight weeks; BV110 – average time taken to determine all applications). Planning cost, per head of population (BV107) and the number of departures from the statutory plan as a percentage of all permissions granted (BV108) were other areas where performance was measured. BV179 measured the percentage of standard searches carried out in 10 working days, whilst a checklist of planning best practice against which authorities are awarded a score (BV112) concentrated exclusively on procedural issues – plan adoption timescales, presence of local indicators and targets, supplementary guidance procedures, pre-application discussions, available charter for development control with targets, percentage of appeals lost, delegation rates, awards of costs etc., one-stop shop availability, and fair access.

The single indicator that gauged planning performance against actual planned outcomes measured the percentage of new homes (including conversions) built on previously developed land (BV106). Finally, a Planning Performance Standard applied to BV109, and to authorities who had not demonstrated that they had determined at least 50 per cent of applications within eight weeks. The standard required that authorities determine at least 65 per cent of applications in eight weeks, or that they be listed as failing the Best Value regime.

For 2002/2003, in order to encourage greater efficiency in the handling of planning applications, BV109 was significantly altered, and departed from the single eight-week standard for the first time, with data collected instead on major commercial, industrial and residential[1] applications determined within 13 weeks, on minor commercial, industrial and residential applications determined within eight weeks and on all other applications determined within eight weeks. The revised BVPI was accompanied by new targets requiring 60 per cent, 65 per cent and 80 per cent respectively of such applications to be made within the specified time frames (lower Performance Standards were set for underperforming authorities). The revised BVPI was accompanied by a new BV (188) on delegation rates to officers, and a target of 90 per cent delegation in order to encourage a greater efficiency in the handling of applications. Finally, BV108, BV110 and BV112 were all dropped, the former two in favour of the revised BV109, and the later indicator because the DTLR argued 'This indicator is very process orientated and not consistent with the longer term objective of a move towards outcome-based indicators' (DTLR, 2002c).

Despite this justification, what becomes clear upon an analysis of the performance indicators used under the Citizen's Charter and Best Value regimes is that the indicators have principally been designed to improve and compare speed and efficiency and communicate process-related performance information to the public. In this regard, the speed of processing planning applications has gradually improved, although the 80 per cent of applications decided in 8 weeks used from 1979 to 2002 as the primary measure of planning performance has never come close to being met (reaching 65 per cent in 2001/2002 – ODPM, 2002b). There has also never been a real desire to use performance indicators to explicitly improve the quality of planning outcomes, or even the operation of local planning services beyond matters of efficiency, the one indicator that attempted this – BV112 – being dropped within 24 months of its introduction. Quality was beyond the limited scope of the Citizen's Charter initiative, and remains an illusive goal for Best Value. To some extent the rationale has been that if the planning process was of a high quality, then this in turn would result in quality outcomes and development. This simple causal relationship has often been questioned and remains unproven.

Furthermore, measurement has focused almost exclusively on the development control side of the planning service. This has remained the case despite the excessive timescales for plan-making in many authorities, and the significance of the plan in establishing key land-use allocations and therefore the viability of development proposals. Announcements in the Sustainable Communities Planning Policy Statement (ODPM, 2002b, para. 73) suggested for the first time that indicators for both plan-making and the quality of planning as the outcome of the system would be measured in the future.

Stakeholder views

The survey of stakeholders revealed a particular discrepancy between stakeholders' views on the issue of delay, with almost 100 per cent of private housebuilders rating delay as a serious problem, compared with about half of RSLs, and, significantly, only a quarter of planners (see Fig. 6.3). Most developers (although not all) viewed the planning system negatively and as a source of frustration, reserving particular derision for councillors as over-politicised and determined to extract all they could from developers. One developer commented 'The planning system is becoming too democratic, and planning

---

[1] Residential applications were not initially included under the revised rules, although Chief Planning Officers were subsequently informed of a change of heart by the DTLR (Anon., 2001b).

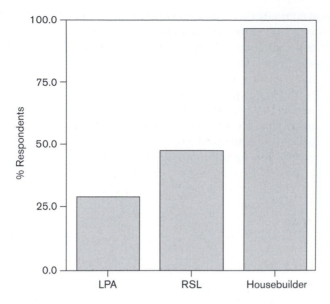

6.3 Views on the significance of delay as a source of planner–provider tension (% rating as significant).

committees appear less informed or aware of their legal responsibilities'; another commented 'Following the publication of PPG3, local plans are no longer relevant, therefore the planning system is in limbo, exacerbating delays and causing frustration'; and a third argued 'As planning requirements become more complex and long-winded, uncertainty and delay is leading to a more drawn-out and risky development process'.

Respondents, particularly planners, emphasised the 'constraints' that lie at the heart of planning delay. These fell into three categories:

- Resource constraints: delays can increase in line with the arrival of new pressures facing planning authorities; these include development brief requirements, capacity studies, and the widening of planning's role, including a stronger focus on sustainability, brownfield reuse and design.
- Policy constraints: these can include out-of-date plans or policy contradictions (mentioned by developers), the uncertainty surrounding pre-PPG3 allocations and the rapidity of the changing national policy context in an age of modernisation.
- Process constraints: shortcomings in critical relationships are also a source of delay. Between the planning authority and developers, this can be a result of protracted or badly handled negotiations, whilst the relationship that local planning shares with the region (e.g., the Government Regional Offices) can lead to policy uncertainty as delays at regional level are passed down the line. In addition, the standard procedural problems already discussed persist: delays in plan adoption, inefficient or over-elaborate working procedures, and the need to demonstrate accountability.

At national level the issue of the lack of resources for planning services was finally recognised in the run-up to the 2001 Planning Green Paper through a DTLR-commissioned survey on resources and planning (see Chapter 11). The results revealed a widespread under-resourcing of planning services, which had increasingly come to be seen as the

Cinderella of local authority services, with underpaid and demoralised staff struggling to meet deadlines in understaffed departments. The survey concluded that planning is grossly underfunded compared with just five years previously, and in need of an injection of cash that a modest rise in application fees would not cover (Dewar, 2001a).

Furthermore, as pressure increases to meet national performance targets with reduced resources and increased numbers of applications, priorities too easily become distorted. Thus it seems that in some authorities early refusal of applications without due consideration is common in order to meet the eight-week target, as is a lack of urgency once the eight-week deadline has past (Dewar, 2001b, p. 14). Significantly, the research revealed that authorities that spend more money, on average, determining applications and/or have fewer cases per officer are more likely to determine cases within eight weeks, and will be subject to less appeals on their decisions. The authors argued, therefore, that extra resources at local authority level could result in a net saving to the public purse as appeal costs are reduced (DTLR, 2002d, p. 71).

Other key events blamed by stakeholders for planning delay included:

- Agreements: the time taken in their negotiation and drafting, often adding three to four months to the planning process.
- Decision-making: developers often believe that officers appear incapable of making decisions. This can be a result of corporate caution or a lack of corporate or individual understanding. Planners for their part believe that if developers (or RSLs) are aware of the policy context (i.e. the need for affordable housing), then much delay will be avoided.
- Local conflict: the politics centring on local community groups – and hence local councillors – is frequently a source of delay, particularly around land allocations.

Research on the delivery of affordable housing through the planning system, for example, focused on the delays caused by agreeing Section 106 planning obligations (see Chapter 9). The research confirmed that confusion at the local level is leading to protracted negotiations, legal wrangling and delay, which holds up the supply of affordable homes. It argued that 'Without clear policies, the granting of planning permission "subject to a section 106 agreement" proves to be the granting of little more than the right to enter into lengthy and costly legal wrangling' (Bishop Associates, 2001, p. 28).

As the survey of stakeholder views and other work indicates, the tension caused by planning delay shows little sign of abating and developers confirmed that the result of delay was greater uncertainty, cash-flow problems (including funding problems for RSLs), and knock-on effects on land and house prices. Furthermore, it appears that some of the problems discussed above have already been magnified in the wake of revised PPG3, for example, the need for all local planning authorities to undertake urban capacity studies to establish how much additional housing can be accommodated within urban areas. Thus in an interview for *Planning* magazine (4 August 2000), Jim Dunning, team leader of planning policy and information in Wokingham District Council, suggested that the new guidance may well delay development by three years whilst the urban capacity studies are carried out.

Delay is often seen as the root cause of risk and uncertainty. It is a cause of tension in itself, and also the product of other tensions between the different stakeholders in the development process. The frustration which many developers feel is summed up in the following comment made by one developer: '. . . surely it cannot be beyond the wit of man, or even the Secretary of State, to do something to reduce these delays'. In this regard, it matters little how speed is measured, and when the clock starts ticking; what is important is the overall time taken for decision-making – from land identification to land allocation, and from pre-application to decision (for large housing schemes often a matter of many years) – and the predictability of that process; in other words, knowing in advance how long it will take.

Many of the proposals in the 2001 Planning Green Paper were aimed at delivering faster and more predictable planning outcomes. The proposals aimed to impact on applications for new housing in a number of key ways, although some were subsequently dropped in the follow-up Planning Policy Statement (ODPM, 2002b):

- faster policy making, adoption and revision processes, including removal of two-tier approaches to planning (see Chapter 2)
- allowing statutory consultees to charge developers directly for their advice if given within 21 days (subsequently dropped)
- encouraging pre-application discussions and allowing authorities to charge for them
- ensuring higher-quality applications are received that can be considered without delay, by issuing a user-friendly checklist
- introducing faster development control processes, including more delegation of decisions to officers, and the new Best Value targets
- reviewing the possibility of integrating different consent regimes (i.e. planning and conservation) into one
- reducing the complexity of planning gain negotiations (see Chapter 9)
- reducing the time taken to determine applications called in to the Secretary of State by setting strict targets
- reducing the period in which applicants are allowed to appeal a decision from six to three months
- through the introduction of time-limiting planning consents
- speeding up the appeals process by giving Inspectors dual jurisdiction over non-determined cases for a determined period after the initial eight weeks
- through the introduction of delivery contracts for major applications between authorities and developers.

Only time will tell what impact the proposals have on this seemingly eternal source of conflict. Significantly, the explanatory notes to the Planning and Compulsory Purchase Bill explicitly identified that 'The purpose of the Planning and Compulsory Purchase Bill is to speed up the planning system' (House of Commons, 2002, para. 4). The statement suggests that for the government, the issue of speed remains of paramount concern.

7

Discretion

Politics and planning

The infiltration of politics into any planning system is inevitable. Planning, because of its nature and purpose, has faced constant challenges to its legitimacy over the years. It is hemmed in by an array of interest groups, which, to varying degrees, are pro- or anti-market control. Tewdwr-Jones (1999, p. 244) has argued that the British planning system has undergone 'a transition from the Thatcherite market-dominated period of the 1980s to a system that attempts to take a more balanced approach in recognition of the environmental agenda'.

This shift in focus has brought with it profound changes in context for British housebuilding. The politics of the 1980s were very much pro-development: the post-Conservative 1990s have not been anti-development, but the political conditions under which land use decisions are reached now hang on a finer balance between economic necessity, social good, and environmental imperative; although the changes proposed in the 2001 Planning Green Paper were widely criticised for pandering to economic interests (Select Committee on Transport, Local Government and the Regions, 2002).

In the early 1980s, the Department of the Environment's first circular on 'Land for Housing' (DoE, 1984) contained one simple message: planning authorities have a statutory duty to allocate sufficient land for new housing. By the late 1990s, planning guidance was attempting to juggle this primary duty with various other considerations, particularly the extraction of developers' contributions (i.e., the public good – see Chapter 9) and adherence to the principle of sustainable development (notably the environmental imperative). The latter has been expressed in the form of land recycling (the sequential test), the mixing of uses and so on. All this means that deliberations over many planning applications are frequently many times more complex than was the case ten or fifteen years previously; and, some would argue, that as a consequence they are less certain as well. This is despite the much greater quantities of government advice available to inform local decision-making and to coordinate local practice.

But the uncertainty that housebuilders face is not only a consequence of increasing planning complexity, it can also be argued that the infiltration of politics into British planning, (compared to other planning systems) is especially pronounced. Arguably, it is the political nature of local planning, combined with the growing complexity of the land-use agenda, that has affected the delivery of new homes. The term 'political' is used here to refer to the way planning authorities operate, and to the significant power wielded by elected councillors within these authorities. Central to this power is the concept of discretion, a cornerstone of the British planning system.

Regulatory v. discretionary systems

Different planning systems across the world usually fall into one of two discrete types: regulatory (often based on zoning systems) or discretionary. Others may display particular characteristics of both and are then described as hybrid. The Canadian provinces, for example, have regulatory systems, but some also have discretionary zones, earning them the hybrid label. The same is true in Hong Kong (Booth, 1996), while many systems in the US exhibit zoning systems alongside separate and discretionary design review panels. Regulatory systems are based on fixed legal frameworks and administrative decision-making, discretionary systems draw a distinction between law and policy, and are based on guiding plans and political decision-making.

Reade (1987) describes the division in terms of a continuum from pure rule of law to pure administrative discretion. In the former, there is a plan and accompanying regulations, and there is a clear divide between what is allowed and what is not. Thus although a high level of expertise is required to put the system in place and to monitor its relative success, it does not require a high level of expertise amongst those charged with administering the controls – 'all that is required is that they can read the plan and regulations, and explain them, and they have the power of enforcement' (Reade, 1987, p. 11). Pure administrative discretion, on the other hand, describes a system where there is no obligation to provide a policy framework and each case is determined on its merits. Such a system would require considerable expertise to operate it day to day and puts significant power in the hands of those charged with its administration, but may not be particularly accountable as there is no obligation to follow a predetermined policy direction, if one exists at all.

Reade argues that no actual land use planning system exists at either end of the spectrum, but most exist somewhere in between, with the British system further towards the administrative end than most comparable Western countries. This, he suggests, goes some way to explaining why planners in the UK are so well organised into a profession because

> The members of a profession clearly cannot be seen to be merely enforcing clearly stated regulations, in the way minor officials do. On the contrary, they must appear to be resolving complex matters, in ways which demand highly developed capacities of expertise and judgment.
>
> (Reade, 1987, p. 12)

Recent work by Gallent and Kim (2001) has compared the regulatory approach taken in South Korea with the discretionary system operating in the UK. In Korea, master plans are drawn up by central government. These have fixed legal standing and will dictate the type of development that is to be allowed in every part of the country. National zoning is extremely broad, governing the development status of metropolitan and non-metropolitan regions. At a secondary level, another tier of fixed zoning identifies development types and status across the regions. Development may proceed if schemes are in line with the law governing development within a particular zone, and also follow the building code that is also set out by national government. The decision to allow a development to proceed is therefore made by local administrators, who merely follow legal procedure and who exist, essentially, to police the development process. The system is therefore a legal system based on administrative decision-making by local bureaucrats, which offers much in the way of certainty, but little flexibility. The system is there to establish rights (to develop) and to create certainty and offers no distinction between law and policy guidance.

Discretionary systems, on the other hand, are shaped by a desire to achieve a flexible response to future development (Booth, 1995, p. 103). In Britain, for example, successive governments of all political persuasions have held the view that it is impossible to predict all circumstances and appropriate policy responses in advance, and that therefore fixed and legally binding plans are undesirable. As all private development rights were nationalised in the 1947 Town and Country Planning Act, preservation of the right to develop is not an issue. Thus central government develops a statutory basis for the planning system through Acts of Parliament, which provide the system's legal framework. Local planning authorities then use this framework as a basis for establishing plans, but these plans are based on an indirect interpretation of the legal framework, drawing on the government's planning policy guidance, issued and periodically updated since 1988, and on planning orders setting out different development types. Although there are legal rulings to be adhered to, government policy is not fixed within any legal framework and therefore represents just one – albeit the most important – material consideration that the authority must take into account when drawing up plans and making planning decisions.

Other considerations include appraisals of local conditions (physical, economic and social) or the weight of local support or objection to the draft contents of a proposed development plan. Thus unlike Korea's legal (or 'prescriptive' – Harris, 1995) plans, development plans in Britain merely offer an indication of the type of development that might be permitted in a particular place, and because development rights are nationalised, those wishing to develop land must obtain permission to do so. This permission rests with the state and for planning purposes the state is represented at the local level by planning authorities. So authorities develop a policy framework and then judge planning applications against this and other material considerations such as local need (in the case of affordable housing) or the weight of local objection (in the case of controversial development). Salaried officers advise on the merits of incoming applications, again judging these against all material considerations, but it is the local councillors (members) who have the power to decide an application, and to establish policy. However because there are various factors to be taken into account before reaching a decision, their powers are – to some extent – discretionary.

The system is – as a consequence – based on political decision-making and on a non-legal framework open to interpretation and even to be overridden (if justified). Referring to the discretionary system of planning in Britain, Booth (in Cullingworth, 1999, p. 31) has commented that:

> Seen from without, the British system is distinctly odd. For where it might be supposed that planning is primarily about removing future uncertainty over the form and location of development, the British system appears to introduce deliberately a blurring of the relationship between policy and implementation.

Thus the plan was (and remains) only an indication of the future pattern of development, as the legislation (Section 70 of the 1990 Town and Country Planning Act, in direct succession to Section 14 of the 1947 Act) grants decision-makers wide discretion. The development plan is therefore just one of the material considerations authorities need to weigh and balance in coming to their decisions.

Table 7.1 illustrates the potential pros and cons of discretionary planning systems and their alternative, the regulatory or zoning systems that are found in much of Europe and the United States. For Booth (in Cullingworth, 1999, pp. 42–3) a number of benefits and disbenefits of discretionary systems are clear. On the positive side, discretionary planning allows responses to development proposals to reflect the circumstances that exist at any one time, without having to revise entire policy frameworks if circumstances change. Flexibility is therefore achieved, and decisions on development can continue to be made in the absence of an up-to-date (or indeed any) policy framework, without necessarily any loss in rigour. In the UK, the discretionary system has also been under-pinned by a successful system of resolving disputes in the form of the public inquiry, which although not always successful (or at least speedy) for large projects of national significance, has been very successful at the small and intermediate project scales. On the negative side, discretion in the UK has created what Booth terms a 'pathological' uncertainty for developers, an overemphasis on the efficiency rather than the quality in the process, and inconsistency in decision-making based on values that are not always fully articulated.

For their part, although zoning systems offer on the face of it greater certainty and less delay in decision-making because provisions in the plan are binding upon the decision-maker and confer a right upon the landowner, studies of zoning in the US and Europe have revealed that decision-makers are 'constantly kicking at the limits that the

Table 7.1 The pros and cons of discretionary, regulatory and plan-led planning systems

	Pros	*Cons*
Discretionary systems	Flexible decision-making Speedier plan-making Responsive to individual circumstances Responsive to community representations Potential for negotiation	Uncertain decision-making Slower planning applications Inconsistent decision-making Arbitrary decision-making Potential for conflict in decision-making
Regulatory (zoning) systems	Certain decision-making Faster planning applications Consistent decision-making Objective decision-making Avoidance of conflict in decision-making	Inflexible decision-making Slower plan-making Unresponsive to individual circumstances Unresponsive to community representations Little potential for negotiation
Plan-led discretionary systems	Some flexibility Reasonably certain decision-making Responsive to individual circumstances Responsive to community representations Some potential for negotiation More consistent decision-making More objective decision-making	Some inflexibility Some uncertainty Slower planning applications Slower plan-making Potential for conflict in decision-making Some inconsistency Some arbitrariness

systems themselves impose' (Booth in Cullingworth, 1999, p. 43). Thus decision-makers regularly find means and mechanisms to circumvent the constraints of such systems and to give themselves an element of discretion. In parts of the US, however, some commentators have rued this loss of certainty, arguing that the unique circumstances rule (for instance) has created 'crazy-quilt patterns of ad hoc zoning' (Reynolds, 1999, p. 127). Booth concludes:

> Regulatory and discretionary systems of planning do not exist as independent phenomena to be changed at will by planners. They are creatures of the constitution and cultures which gave rise to them. The significant strengths of discretionary and regulatory systems carry with them weaknesses, which have to be resolved within the context of the system itself. It is in resolving those weaknesses that the real test of any planning system lies.

Plan-led discretion

The move to a plan-led system in Britain (see Chapter 2) effectively gave primacy to plan policy in the making of planning decisions; however, the system remained a discretionary one as the plan is just one of a range of material considerations (including central government planning policy) that authorities need to consider. The change nevertheless was widely believed to have introduced a presumption in favour of development in accordance with the development plan. Thus the planning system in England and Wales (and elsewhere in the UK) became what can be described as a plan-led discretionary system, with (to some degree) many of the advantages of both regulatory and discretionary systems, but also (to some degree) many of the disadvantages (see Table 7.1).

In particular, although the system offers (in theory) a greater degree of certainty and consistency in decision-making, whilst retaining a degree of flexibility, it also retains a degree of inconsistency, uncertainty and arbitrariness. This is because the retention of discretion in any form potentially brings with it these qualities. The system has also retained its potential for conflict and delay in decisions over planning applications, and has greatly increased the delays associated with plan-making, as the status of development plans – and therefore attempts to influence what goes in to them by all stakeholders (developers, special interest groups, local communities, landowners, etc.) – has increased (see Chapter 6). It might be argued that the system now encompasses both the best and the worst of discretionary and regulatory processes. Cronin (1993), for example, reflecting on the early experience of the plan-led system, argued that certainty remained elusive for three reasons:

- Although the primacy given to the plan aims to increase certainty, the flexibility required by central government in the wording of constituent policies in the plan makes this very difficult to achieve.
- Judgements are still required in balancing different policies against each other to make decisions, as policies rarely lead in the same direction.
- Frequent changes in national policy (e.g. new PPGs) or in local circumstances (e.g. lower than anticipated housebuilding rates) can give inspectors reason to override the development plan.

She argues, nevertheless, that:

Certainty is always going to be elusive in a planning system which is not based on conformity with a set of technical criteria, or a zoning plan. Indeed, too great a degree of certainty would stifle creativity. We appear to be heading for a pragmatic compromise between the primacy of development plans and planning by appeal, balanced rather more in favour of the development plan than has been the case in recent years.

(Cronin, 1993, p. 17)

On the third of Cronin's reasons, case law has determined that although the introduction of the plan-led system greatly increased the importance of the development plan, much still turns on the government's attitude as to when it is permissible to depart from the plan. Thus PPG1, for example, argues that particular policies of the plan may be 'superseded by more recent planning policy guidance issued by the Government' (DoE, 1997a, para. 54). Tewdwr-Jones (2002, p. 100) even suggests that the pre-eminence of government advice raises legitimate questions about whether in fact a plan-led system was ever created at all, since local policies will very quickly become out of date as government guidance moves on. In this context, the plan-led label afforded to local planning might be better described as plan-led providing there is consistency with central government policies.

The dominant role played by central government in British planning has already been described in Chapter 2, a feature of British planning that the introduction of the plan-led system reinforced through an increase in the government's monitoring role of local planning and through a host of other mechanisms. One implication is that in light of their increased status, the government has increasingly insisted on a watering down of policy expression in local plans in order to retain their flexibility through the insertion of words such as 'normally', 'will encourage' and 'will consider' in policy. These replace more forceful forms of expression such as 'will require' or 'presumptions against' certain forms of development. This is despite the provisions of Section 54A of the 1990 Act (see Chapter 2) which already allows for considerable flexibility by allowing other material considerations to be considered alongside the plan (Punter and Carmona, 1997, p. 110).

Another implication is that the lack of certainty is increasingly an outcome of planning at both national and local levels because discretion continues to exist at both levels. Purdue (1994), for example, has observed that development plans are being applied more inflexibly, and that these decisions are being upheld on appeal, but equally that policies are still being overturned at national level on the grounds that material considerations indicate otherwise. He concludes that 'there is still considerable flexibility in the system and that while policies in the plan do now have a higher status, they will not be slavishly applied where there are strong reasons for coming to a contrary decision' (Purdue, 1994, pp. 406–7). This, he argues, fits in with the way Section 54A has been interpreted by the courts. It distinguishes British planning as in essence still discretionary.

Political decisions at the national level also chop and change as Secretaries of State and Ministers of Planning come and go, both posts having seen a succession of short-term occupants in recent years. Thus political decisions on housing numbers, call-ins, planning policy, and sometimes the whole philosophy of the planning system (i.e. the market-led philosophy of Nicholas Ridley, followed soon after by the 'local choice' philosophy of Chris Patten) have changed as successive politicians have tried to stamp their own agenda on the process. The inevitable consequence is increased uncertainty, with little time for new processes to bed-down and be refined before new changes come along.

Discretionary decision-making

Thomas (1997, p. 9) argues that although discretion in British planning is constrained by national policy, and by development plan policy determined locally, planners use discretion in development control to:

- cope with the uniqueness of every application for planning permission;
- select the factors taken into account in decision making;
- frame the terms of the decision.

Equally, authorities have discretion (within limits, e.g. the need to be land-use based) about what to include in their plans and over what other forms of supplementary planning guidance they choose to produce (design guides, development briefs, etc.). Booth (1996), who has written most extensively about the discretionary nature of planning, provides a sketch of the purpose and parameters of discretionary decision-making, taking care to emphasise the essential link between discretion and fixed rules:

> Discretion may be necessary to free decision-makers from the inflexibility of rules; rules will be necessary to ensure that discretion is not merely a matter of personal whim that leads to injustice and reduces the possibility of redress. Discretion and rules are not merely opposites; they are interdependent.
>
> (Booth, 1996, p. 110)

He goes on to summarise the various facets of the discretionary system. Some of the general points made by Booth (1996), and in earlier literature, are noted below and related to the perceived difficulties of getting the 'right' decision from the planning system in relation to new housing development:

1. Discretion is rarely absolute but operates within defined limits. These limits are set by policy, by the accountability of politicians, by law, and by other considerations such as financial constraint. All of these should add up to a degree of certainty for those submitting planning applications – at the very least, a certainty that decision-making outside established limits will result in recourse to the appeals system or the Secretary of State, if applications are called in. But establishing where discretion stops and rules take over is not easy: the appeals system itself is uncertain, based on complex case law and precedent, and both planning inspectors and the Secretary of State have freedom to interpret law and policy. So from the housing providers' perspective, limits are often unclear and the pendulum more regularly swings in favour of uncertainty than certainty.
2. 'Discretionary power is a direct reflection of power relationships within society as a whole' (Adler and Asquith, 1981 in Booth, 1996, p. 111), or rather who discretionary power favours is determined by the wider political climate. In the 1980s, the pro-development philosophy of the Thatcher governments meant a bias towards business and development interests. Less-defined policy guidance belied a more liberal planning framework in which limits were far less of a hindrance to discretionary power, whilst this power itself reflected a culture of leniency towards development and a

distrust of intervention. Because more recently the balance of power has swung in favour of a bigger state, and emphasises social responsibility over personal freedom, the limits are a little tighter and the way discretion is used mirrors this changing social (and environmental) emphasis. Therefore, whilst in the post-war period decisions were more likely to reflect corporate pro-development interests, today those with an environmental agenda wield greater influence.

3. Discretion takes two distinct forms. It also exists at different levels (see 1 above), but by 'forms', Booth is referring to the discretion that stems from interpretation (of rules and regulations) as distinct from that which derives direct legitimacy from a higher body (i.e., the explicit conferment of discretionary power, such as from parliament). Members of the Planning Inspectorate, for example, are assigned the power of interpretation based on personal experience, although these powers have defined legal limits. Planning officers making delegated decisions or advising on planning issues, on the other hand, have discretion, but because this discretion is subject to local political control and subsequent challenge through appeal, it is less absolute. The implication for providers is that there is often greater scope and opportunity to challenge planning authorities, and the advice of individual officers, than central agencies or appointees.

Because the limits to discretion are often unclear (oscillating in a grey area between policy and law), and because the central influence of business interests has waned (at least as compared to the 1980s), the ease with which development can be progressed is now far more dependent on local political priorities. At the same time, a different power relationship between development and environmental/local interests, reflected in local politics, may result in a more combative relationship between authorities and housing providers. In many instances, acceptance of this difficult relationship may mean that recourse to the appeals system becomes an integral part of the planning process, with housebuilder challenges exploiting the form that local discretion often takes (see 3 above). In practice, open and possibly idiosyncratic interpretation of a constantly shifting framework acts to reduce clarity of decision-making and possibly gives housing providers the grounds for appeal.

Discretion and local politics

The rather simplified view of different planning systems provided earlier, along with the discussion of the nature of discretion, serves to highlight the political power that exists at the grass roots of the British planning system. Kitchen (1997, p. 10) argues that:

> One of the reasons why elected members have such an important part to play in the British planning system is that this widespread process of the exercise of discretion is very often ultimately a political act; it is about what values or aspirations or interests to emphasise, acting on behalf of the community as a whole.

One critical point here is that some councillors – unlike planning officers – are likely to be less concerned with the technical merits of an application and much more concerned with its acceptance amongst local voters. A study of the role of elected members in plan-making and development control, for example, revealed that councillors see their main job as representing the people of their ward, and in this context serving the public

➤ Ward representative
➤ Member of a political party
➤ Member of the leadership of a political party, in particular a member of the leadership of the majority group on the council
➤ Chair or Deputy Chair of the Planning Committee
➤ Member of the Planning Committee
➤ Member of another committee whose work impinges on the work of the Planning Committee
➤ Member of the council, particularly in the wider sense of its role as representative of the city
➤ Protagonist of individual policies or views, often working in partnership on these matters with relevant interest groups
➤ Individual in their own right, with their own interests and particular behaviour patterns, and with their own personal ambitions

7.1 The nine roles of councillors as they impact upon the planning process (Kitchen, 1997, p. 41).

interest (RTPI, 1997, p. 8). Here therefore lies the source of much controversy, for while planning authorities may argue that decisions are made to serve the public interest, even apparent deviation away from policy, or away from the advice of officers, may be viewed as parochialism. Housebuilders, for example, may believe that the anti-development fervour within some councils exists merely because particular councillors are either pandering to NIMBY attitudes (see p. 178), or hold certain political prejudices.

Kitchen (1997, pp. 40–1) argues that such a view of councillors oversimplifies both their roles and motivations. He identifies nine roles that councillors play (see Fig. 7.1) – roles that often conflict with each other, and in relation to which individual councillors either have to resolve or act as chameleons in different settings. Thus individual councillors can often adopt a wide range of perspectives on the planning process when seeking to influence or use it. Fundamentally, however, they tend to be people who are both highly knowledgeable about the local communities in which they live, and care passionately about them. 'At its best, the combination of these perspectives and concerns and the professional knowledge and skill of staff can be both powerful and effective, and the two in partnership represent the positive face of local government' (Kitchen, 1997, p. 58).

Nevertheless, the degree of leeway that members have to interpret policy one way or another, or to accept/ignore officer advice on particular applications, remains an issue central to the tension between housebuilders and planners. Delafons (2000, p. 35) has suggested that NIMBY attitudes, which find expression in the political deadlock in many planning authorities, are at the heart of a burgeoning crisis in housing supply in South East England. He argues that development proposals that broadly adhere to established strategies and policy objectives are being delayed or thrown out by voter-sensitive councils, although these same developments often re-emerge, ad hoc, after successful appeals.

The risk is that future development will not be based on mutually agreed principles, arrived at sensibly by housing providers and planning authorities in partnership, but on a combative relationship between elected members and an ever-more aggressive private sector. In 2000, there were 6,300 major residential planning applications in England and a further 44,400 minor applications; 84 per cent and 76 per cent were granted respectively, but, nearly 12,000 were refused and nearly half of the applicants took their case to appeal (DETR, 2000f).[1] The 2001 Planning Green Paper recognised that many appeals are unnecessary, and might be avoided if developers and planners spent more time dealing with the inevitable sticking points earlier in the process via pre-application negotiations (DTLR, 2001a, p. 31). This trend has huge implications for the supply of new homes and for the degree to which new housebuilding meets strategic objectives, especially if the appeals system (through the Planning Inspectorate) rather than local planning is directing many key development decisions.

So local political discretion can be problematic as members attempt to balance local community pressure with the need for new housing. They do this at two levels: at the strategic level, when land is first allocated for development; and again at the development level, when actual proposals are brought forward. At both levels the system operates to balance competing interests, and to provide both certainty (of supply) and the flexibility to respond to changing market conditions and local needs. The system allows for a comparison to be made of the different material considerations at stake, but, importantly, only the local community can vote, and as a result have a strong hold over local decision-makers, even though their interests may not be the same as either national or regional interests, or the interests of those with inadequate housing provision. In this regard the RTPI research on elected members revealed that:

> Decisions taken against officer advice are common, although the average number of such decisions compared to the total number of applications received is very low. . . . members recognise that they have wide local and political responsibilities and face strong local pressures.
>
> (RTPI, 1997, p. 10)

The discussion above has scratched the surface of these debates, and there is much more that can be said on the issue of discretion, on the accountability of decision-makers in British local authorities, on democracy, or on the relationship between officers and elected members. Indeed, it is not only members who act with discretion, but also officers when offering advice to members, or when dealing with delegated matters. Booth (1996, p. 149) concludes his book on certainty and discretion with a useful series of points that reflect on the appropriate limits of discretion, however it is operated:

- systems for controlling development need to recognise that absolute certainty is unobtainable, but they should be able to define the limits of certainty;
- entirely open-ended systems of control nevertheless depend on standards and criteria that may not be fully articulated;
- negotiation and bargaining are an essential part of the development control process and will take place no matter how rigid the framework is within which the decisions are made;
- development control systems need to ensure that the parameters of such negotiation are clear and the processes not obscured;
- the presence of discretionary decision-making of whatever kind is inevitable in development control;

[1] The appeals figure here is an estimate based on all appeals, as the official data do not break down into development type.

- both the basis on which decisions are taken and the process by which they are taken need to be reasonably accessible for users of the system;
- mechanisms of ensuring the accountability of decision-making need to offer the possibility of debating the appropriateness of decisions.

Interestingly Booth concludes that both developers and local authorities favour a flexible approach to decision-making, the former because it is through negotiation with authorities that they can maximise the profitability of their schemes, and the latter because negotiation is also the primary source of their power to deliver the public interest, something that is difficult within an overly rigid decision-making structure. For both, however, this needs to exist within clearly defined limits that balance short-term flexibility with long-term certainty – 'flexibility is by no means an unalloyed blessing, even to its beneficiaries' (Booth, 1996, p. 144).

Stakeholder views

The other 'tensions' chapters in Part 2 of this book deal in the main with more tangible events within the housing development process – with, for instance, planning gain, or issues of land assembly. Alongside these events, the discretionary and political nature of planning was identified as a significant source of tension for both private housebuilders and RSLs, although it barely registered as a source of concern amongst planners (see Fig. 7.2). In particular, critics of the present system pointed to two areas of difficulty stemming from discretion: first, ad hoc approaches to development planning; and second, clear inconsistencies between different levels of planning sometimes resulting from deviation outside the plan-led system.

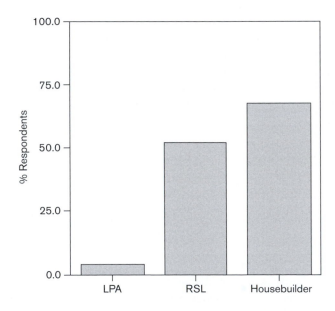

7.2 Views on the significance of the discretionary nature of planning as a source of planner–provider tension (% rating as significant).

Ad hoc approaches

The problem is that without the clear limits discussed above, the system simply becomes too ad hoc, reducing both certainty and clarity for housebuilders (and other development interests). Thus the housing providers surveyed gave a fairly damning appraisal of the way local planning deals with new housing proposals. Political interventions, for example, were viewed as inevitably negative, turning against new housing development. The result, they argued, is that housebuilders often anticipate significant planning constraints, so rather than trying to engage positively with authorities, they attempt to push through the easiest and cheapest developments, so saving money on design, which they believe will need to be spent on fighting an appeal further down the line. Even away from the politics, planning processes generally are seen as negative – out-of-date plans, and obstructive development control sections that stack the odds against 'good development' as providers see it. The 'no' culture of planning committees and the fact that, as one housebuilder put it, 'politicians are now praised for what they can prevent rather than for what they can achieve' means that planning is not only reactionary, but always reacts in a negative way.

Some constructive relationships were identified in the survey, although it is often the case that particular authorities will build up a reputation as being either pro (anything goes) or anti (almost all) development – a reputation that planning officers sometimes acknowledge. Although there is some debate over the actual level of influence enjoyed by local communities and objectors, one authority was unequivocal in stating that there is 'frequent and vociferous input into the political process', reducing the planning system's capacity to work positively. Indeed, there is now a belief amongst some that 'most new housing schemes fall victim to the NIMBY syndrome, regardless of location and design quality' (Anon., 2001c, p. 1).

Of course a positive system is not invariably pro-development; rather, it seeks a balance between competing interests to reach the optimum solution in the light of local circumstances. This was the conclusion of a number of less apologetic local authority respondents who pointed to the key strengths (flexibility, the factoring in of local knowledge, and local accountability) of a system that can respond to the diversity of local contexts. So in the end, the tension is based around polarised views about the relative merits of discretion. On the one hand, some developers see discretion in the form of political interference as a constant barrier to sensible development; but on the other, planning officers view administrative and political leeway as the only route to achieving balance and flexibility.

Inconsistency

A problem was also identified by respondents with the various lateral and vertical inconsistencies between different levels of planning and different planning authorities. These stem from the discretion that exists at all levels of the planning process (discussed on pp. 108–10). It is often the case, for example, that local, regional and national considerations push planning bodies in different directions, resulting in the inconsistencies that many local respondents believed were the product of an overtly and excessively political process.

The starkest contrasts commonly exist between the regions and local authorities. At the regional level a key message is often that a particular building rate is critical if people are to be adequately housed and if regional economic priorities are to be met. But locally, these rates are balanced against other priorities and downsized, so levels of new build that developers thought would be allowed are rejected. Locally, the boundary of discretion is currently fixed by the contents of structure plans, but even here, discrepancies can creep in as local authorities interpret structure plan requirements rather than taking them at face value. Thus, like a game of Chinese whispers, what is seen is a series of lateral shifts as policy cascades down the hierarchy, with housing providers confused by the often contradictory policy signals sent out at different levels.

At the heart of this problem (if it is seen as such) is the leeway to interpret not only evidence within an authority's own area of jurisdiction, but also the advice, research (including the projections), policy and so forth coming from above. On the one hand, this might be welcomed, as policy is often viewed as excessively top-down and there is a need to translate strategic thinking into practical action, tailored to local circumstances. But on the other hand, it was argued by some respondents that national policy advisors are best placed to understand the overall shape of future housing demand, and therefore that growth projections and subsequent building rates should be given greater legal standing.

It can be argued that the local political process (and discretion) has contributed to a volatility in Britain's housing market, decreasing certainty for developers, and hence affecting the steady supply of new homes (Bramley and Watkins, 1996). At a macro level, Booth's (1996) 'balance of power' argument might be used to explain how different political priorities have a huge impact on new housing supply, accentuating or countering natural economic cycles marked by either rising or falling prices. At a more localised scale, political priorities have a comparable effect on the market, with community-driven constraint resulting in house price peaks rather than demand transfer (see Chapter 5). Again, the argument goes that without local political intervention, and with a dominant and global view of the market, these peaks and troughs might be avoided, or a national strategy could counter and smooth acute variations. The market view, for instance, would mean providing considerably more homes in South East England, thereby absorbing demand. More homes would also be built in the countryside, offsetting the housing affordability crisis caused by lower rural wages and an exodus of city dwellers to attractive villages.

Of course, this market view skirts around the issue of environmental capacity and ignores competing priorities. So the unavoidable fact is that the broad priorities of national government must be meshed with different regional and local objectives. This means allowing discretion at the local level. The key issue for the majority of respondents in the survey was to ensure consistency in this exercise of power (rather than to deny it) by more clearly defining the boundaries of local (and regional) discretion. This means having up-to-date development plans, development briefs and other supplementary planning guidance, as the basis for decision-making.

The quantity, quality and location of new homes are not the products of a wholly predetermined, prescriptive process. They also represent political outcomes, or a compromise (or preferably consensus) between different competing interests. Some observers would argue that this compromise negates the advantages of planning or results in a lack of eventual vision and poor quality products. Others maintain that tying the bureaucracy of planning with political discretion is the only means of reaching flexible solutions while achieving democratic accountability. A few of the arguments and counter-arguments were noted above. These are often circular, revealing entrenched positions and a deep-seated mistrust of local democracy or of development interests.

Although changes introduced in the 2003 Planning and Compulsory Purchase Act aim to speed up the process of planning, and ensure up-to-date policy frameworks are in place across the country, they may conversely also increase local discretion, and undermine the certainty currently afforded to developers and local communities by development plans. This is because the relatively short timescale for preparing local development frameworks (three years: ODPM, 2002c, para. 29) and the expectation that they will be more regularly reviewed and updated might undermine the creation and delivery of a long-term vision and the certainty that brings. This effective increase in local discretion might undermine the careful balance that the plan-led system has offered (although not always delivered) since 1991.

8

Design

Quality v. quantity

In Chapter 6 the issue of quality versus quantity was discussed in the context of delay and systems of measuring the effectiveness of the planning process. The issue highlights a persistent pressure for those charged with the delivery of new homes – to what extent does a concern for delivering high-quality homes undermine the objective of delivering more homes, faster? Thus planning authorities are under tremendous pressure to meet the housing targets established for their areas; housebuilders are under pressure to turn their capital around more quickly by building and selling homes faster; and housing associations and housing departments within local authorities are concerned to meet often chronic housing needs locally and a widespread under-provision of housing in their sector. All these pressures can all too easily act to undermine the delivery of higher-quality more sustainable development, as short-term priorities focus on the quantity of houses rather than their quality.

The Urban Task Force was constituted in 1999 by the Deputy Prime Minister in part to grapple with this problem – how to deliver the huge projections in household numbers whilst avoiding sprawl and environmentally destructive development? The solution was found in the deceptively simple notion that with the pressure to build 3.8 million new homes also came an opportunity: the opportunity to regenerate England's urban areas. These had suffered a widespread decline, with people, businesses and retail/entertainment facilities deserting urban areas as a result of decentralising planning policy, social trends, and a general dis-investment in urban areas since the 1970s. Fundamental to delivering an urban renaissance was the requirement that regeneration should be design-led and deliver new housing at higher (more urban) densities.

This chapter first explores the tension of design quality in housing and the nature of private housebuilder and RSL responses to that concern. It then examines public sector policy on design, before exploring the related tension of density. This issue (along with the mixing of uses) is of fundamental importance to the delivery of a sustainable urban renaissance, but requires a new set of design responses in order to meet the challenge.

Design and private housing

The Urban Task Force placed the need to improve urban quality at the centre of their vision for securing an urban renaissance. They argued:

A commitment to quality and creativity in the way in which we design buildings, public spaces and transport networks will form the basis for the sustainable city of the future. We will need to rekindle a strong national interest in design and architecture, so that both the public and the professional work together in the provision of a high quality urban environment.

(Urban Task Force, 1999, p. 39)

Indeed, the Urban Task Force report was widely interpreted as supporting a design-led approach to urban regeneration. It accepts, however, that achieving urban quality encompasses activities ranging from the mundane, such as the removal of graffiti, to major interventions, including the masterplanning of large new residential areas. The report argues that the poor quality of the urban environment has contributed significantly to the exodus from English towns and cities and that to redress the balance a culture of quality needs to infuse public sector activity as well as urban culture. In this respect design is seen as a process as well as a product, as a creative problem-solving activity that determines the quality of the built environment.

The Urban Task Force, like government planning guidance (see pp. 125–7), promoted the value of design briefs, master plans and other planning policy tools for advancing such public sector design aspirations. Unfortunately, recent comprehensive analysis of design policy and guidance relating specifically to the residential environment revealed that although 95 per cent of planning authorities in England (county and district/unitary) possess at least some form of residential design policy or guidance, practice varies greatly from reliance on individual policy or guidance mechanisms based on very general 'mother-hood' aspirations, implemented through rigid and unsophisticated planning standards, to the sophisticated use of the full range of design guidance instruments in hierarchy (Carmona, 2001b). It also revealed that public sector attempts to influence the design of residential development on the whole remain unsophisticated, under-resourced and ineffective. Furthermore, as discussed in Chapter 3, despite the high levels of satisfaction recorded by many amongst the actual purchasers of new-build homes, at the beginning of the century the critiques of such homes remain fairly consistent and vehement.

Research has shown that for the private sector buildability (particularly familiarity with products and techniques) is a key factor in the development and viability of house types – 'the natural outcome of crucial operational requirements such as the need to be able to bid quickly for land ripe for development, to develop sites of whatever size in relatively small batches, [and] to operate with local subcontractors' (Leopold and Bishop, 1983, p. 119). Buildability encompasses the designing out of fussy or awkward work and irregularities, encouraging design solutions that enable as much work as possible to be completed by one man or a gang without interruption, the incorporation of prefabricated components, and arranging layouts to produce simple plan forms for easy access during construction.

At the same time, for marketing purposes and to distinguish their products from their social housing equivalents, housebuilders have to emphasise the individual (as distinct from the collective). The resulting design solution reflects these inherent tensions – the combination of standardised, stable house plans with flexible market-sensitive elevations and trimmings:

The compromise between the long-term stability of the production process and the more volatile demands of the market. A wide range of elevations and, to a lesser extent, finishing materials, combine with minor distinctions in layout and landscaping to confer individuality on a house which, in all other respects, may duplicate its neighbours exactly.

(Leopold and Bishop, 1983, p. 128)

In this context, commentators have observed that choice in architectural terms is largely illusory, as internal domestic space arrangements are standardised and repeated ad infinitum (Hanson, 1999). Individuality then becomes largely a process of 'façadism' where the standard housing envelope is able to accommodate a range of different elevational treatments to enhance the kerb appeal of the front elevation and help attract customers to the house.

Adam has characterised this process as 'maximisation of unit amenity', or maximising the unit price to drive up returns to the developer. He argues 'Housing layout based on highways regulations and maximisation of unit amenity is a geometric discipline not a design discipline. The appearance of housing as a group and, therefore, the creation of a place is not considered in this process' (Adam, 1997). Thus poor design practice is actually seen as increasing the profitability of development, by concentrating on the individual house at the expense of the whole development, while the public sector frequently adds to the problem by adopting road design and space between dwelling standards that make the delivery of good urban design all but impossible (POS *et al.*, 1998).

Nevertheless, the relationship between the house and the development layout is increasing in significance, both to improve marketing and to accommodate what is perceived to be the more detailed requirements of planning authorities (Hooper and Nicol, 1999, p. 801). The results rarely deliver successful urban design, however, as standard house types reject traditional building forms (wide frontage, narrow span, high roof pitches), making it difficult to string buildings together to create interesting enclosed street scenes with buildings that turn corners and define focal points. Furthermore, the target markets identified by developers and the perceived preferences for purchasers to live in single-use estates surrounded by people of similar social backgrounds, make it difficult to achieve variety – '. . . this poses particular problems in seeking to re-create the complexity and variety of the traditional street scene or in promoting mixed use developments. Market-led designs tend to encourage uniformity, and many are dominated by large detached dwellings' (POS *et al.*, 1998, p. 10).

For these reasons, few volume builders have developed house types that lend themselves to urban developments, and whole ranges of new house designs are being required to respond to the increasing emphasis on brownfield land. Alternatively, the suburban types will be brought (with minor alterations) into the cities – the usual response so far (Carmona, 2001b, pp. 89–96).

Although the volume builders rarely make houses to measure, most standard house types have evolved over many years. In this regard they are refined pieces of design, carefully costed, acknowledging the limited skills of the labour force and meeting the aspirations of the market (Davison, 1987b, p. 62). The larger housebuilders, for example, engage in significant market research when developing their product ranges (both inside and out). Wimpey's recent house ranges – 'Celebration' and 'Optima' – were developed after consulting 40,000 existing homeowners. Thus, Wimpey detected in their buyers a demand for traditional houses with character and that 'People do not want anything too modern until they actually step through the door' (Roskrow, 1997, p. 32).

To maintain and develop the range and to respond to trends in the market, most developers employ (usually small) teams of in-house designers, farming house design work out to local architects only when faced with particular local problems (Lyall, 1985,

p. 30). Conversely, layout work – applying the standard types to individual sites – is usually contracted to specialist housing layout designers. The in-house designer's input is usually passive, translating technical, operational and marketing feedback into updated unit designs, but seldom visiting the site or appraising design outcomes to inform future developments (Leopold and Bishop, 1983, p. 137).

Thus the typical design approach of the private housebuilder is determined by:

- buildability – standardisation, speed and cost minimisation
- maximisation of unit amenity – kerb appeal, not places, communities and environments
- market research – products, sales and marketing
- public policy and regulations – meeting the minimum (not sustainable) standards.

Design and social housing

Private housebuilders have consistently detected a desire by many of their customers to distinguish their homes from their public sector equivalents, while historically developers found that they could proclaim owner-occupation by adopting styles that local authority architects would never condone (Barrett and Phillips, 1993, p. 137). In part, the desire of housebuilders to distinguish their products from those in the social housing sector reflects the somewhat chequered history of much social housing, with, in particular, many of the experimental design solutions of the 1960s and 1970s failing within a decade of their completion.

Despite these experiences, the imperative to make limited public sector grant money go as far as possible has in recent years all too often continued to result in the delivery of a substandard product and poor social conditions. The influential report *Building for Communities*, for example, led to considerable debate when it was published in 1993 by accusing housing associations of building overly large estates in order to reduce management costs, which quickly became expensive sink estates that trapped residents on welfare (Page, 1993). Similarly Karn and Sheridan's (1994) work on space in new homes revealed a general lowering of space and amenity standards in the early 1990s in new housing association housing, as associations attempted to compete for a slice of reducing Housing Corporation funds which were allocated on the basis of unit costs (the assumption being that reduced unit cost, rather than better quality, equated to better value for money).

Although they noted that the lowest standards in private housing compared unfavourably with those at the lower end of housing association provision, they concluded that:

> The housing association movement has always tried to provide good design, personal management and small scale developments that will avoid the stigmatisation that attached itself to council housing. Yet ironically, without greater government support for good housing standards, the movement is now in danger of providing 'poor homes for poor people'. It is obviously a difficult time to argue for quality of housing not quantity, because the very low public sector construction of the last fifteen years has led to severe rental housing shortages and high rates of homelessness. However, we should have learnt our lessons from the 1960s, that being panicked into a 'numbers are everything', 'minimum cost per unit' approach is disastrous in the longer term.
>
> (Karn and Sheridan, 1994, p. 100)

The gradual acceptance of these arguments in the latter part of the 1990s led to an increasing concern for housing quality and to a series of initiatives designed to ensure its delivery. Particularly important amongst these was the development of the Housing Corporation's (2000) *Scheme Development Standards* (first published in 1993) under which grants would be allocated, and which encompassed a range of very detailed design standards covering the external environment, internal environment, accessibility, safety and security, energy efficiency and environmental sustainability, and maintenance, durability and adaptability. In effect, the approach represented a return to an updated version of the 1961 Parker Morris standards that had been abandoned in 1980 by Michael Heseltine when Secretary of State for Environment, but which until then had guaranteed at least basic space standards and amenities for tenants. The Scheme Development Standards include essential items and recommended items, the former being required for RSLs to secure Housing Corporation funding, and the latter as best practice guidance.

In 1998 this approach was supplemented with the publication of a very detailed set of good practice standards from the National Housing Federation (1998) covering design process requirements, external and internal design standards, costs in use and accessibility; and in 1999 by a series of *Housing Quality Indicators* (HQIs) from the DETR and Housing Corporation (1999). HQIs provide a methodology for assessing the quality of new (or existing) housing schemes, to build into the procedure of assessing possible projects for public funding. By this means it is hoped that quality will become an explicit component of the assessment process alongside price.

The aim, however, is not to establish minimum standards, but to provide a means to compare different schemes for the same site against a fixed brief. They also provide a means for designers, RSLs and developers to evaluate their designs at all stages during the design process and post-completion in order to monitor their achievement of good quality, and (if necessary) to make design adjustments. The system allows an assessment of quality to be made on the basis of three main categories, location, design and performance, which break down further into ten 'Quality Indicators' (see Fig. 8.1).

Schemes are scored against a wide range of sub-criteria in each category and a percentage calculated overall and for each indicator, which is weighted according to the users' objectives. Thus a single number provides a headline score for each scheme, although the emphasis is on quality profiles that show the strengths and weaknesses of schemes. In this respect the concept of a range of quality is adopted for each aspect, including far more subjective aspects such as aesthetics. 'The final choice of indicators reflects a compromise between the importance of the issue to quality, practicality of use and the information available' (DETR and Housing Corporation, 1999, p. 3), and in time will be published as a series of headline HQI benchmarks to assist in delivering better design quality across the sector.

The significance of the Development Standards and HQIs does not necessarily lie in their value as approaches to ensure the delivery of high-quality housing – that will always require a good designer and an enlightened client – but in revealing that quality is now more explicitly recognised alongside the cost of provision in allocating public funding to social housing schemes, thereby establishing a baseline below which funds will not be allocated. The result, along with a continued use of architects in the sector, a willingness to confront more challenging sites, and the historic interest of the Housing Association movement in design, has led in recent years to the establishment of a stronger design tradition in the social housing sector to that in the private sector. The continual dominance of housing associations in the annual Housing Design Awards confirms this

Scoring:

HQIs work by scoring a series of questions (over 350) divided between the ten indicators. The results are then transferred to a scoring spreadsheet that calculates the final scores according to the weighting system applied by the user and built into the spreadsheet. Each indicator receives one-tenth of the final score on the basis that all are equally important and a low score in any one will jeopardise the overall quality of the scheme.

Quality indicators	Example one	Example two
1 **Location**	Many good features, some poor	Many good features, none poor
2 **Site – layout and landscaping**	A few missing qualities in all areas	A few missing qualities in all areas
3 **Site – open space**	Some opportunities missed	Flats without private open space
4 **Site – routes and movement**	Some opportunities missed	Some opportunities missed
5 **Unit – size**	Basic size only	A little above basic size
6 **Unit – layout**	A few 'plus' features for most units	Includes most 'plus' features for most units
7 **Unit – noise, light and services**	A few missed opportunities	Many good features
8 **Unit – accessibility**	Not particularly good	Most units very good
9 **Unit – energy and sustainability**	SAP* rating OK, BREEAM† omitted	SAP rating OK, basic BREEAM rating
10 **Performance in use**	Adaptability not very good	Houses more adaptable than flats
HQI score	**58 per cent**	**72 per cent**

* SAP: Standard assessment procedure; The SAP rating is a whole number between 1 (very bad) and 100 (very good) which indicates the cost of providing energy heat, light and domestic hot water per m^2 of floor space.
† BREEAM: British Research Establishment Environmental Assessment Methodology.

8.1 Housing quality indicators (HQIs) – worked examples (DETR and Housing Corporation, 1999, pp. 23–4).

observation (Jones, 2000). Some housing associations have been particularly innovative in this regard, for example the Guinness Trust Group's (n.d.) attempt to raise the quality of their housing with their own in-house design guide, or the sponsorship of prefabrication and sustainable housing exemplars by the Peabody Trust (see Fig. 8. 2).

Nevertheless, as in the housing for sale market, although the very best design in the sector is outstanding, such schemes remain the tip of the iceberg. An RIBA report published in 1999, for example, revealed a sector determined to screw architects down to minimum fee levels, and cutting corners to do so, whilst projects consistently emphasised cost before quality in the procurement process, leading too often to poor quality schemes (Wright, 1999). Design approaches in the social housing sector have therefore been determined by:

- innovation in design – not always successfully, but more so in recent years
- cost controls – which in the past have taken a minimum cost per unit approach
- funding guidelines – including recently, development standards and indicators

8.2 Peabody Trust, Bed-Zed housing, Hackbridge. © *Raf Makda/VIEW*

- bespoke design solutions – within the limits of funding cycles, priorities and deadlines.

Developing policy

In national planning policy, a comparison of statements on housing design from 1980 and 2000 reveals a sea change in approach. Thus, Circular 22/80 warned:

> Local authorities may need to control aspects of the design of housing estates where these have an impact on neighbouring development or agricultural land, for example access or overshadowing. But functional requirements within a development are for the most part a matter for the developers and their customers.
>
> (DoE, 1980, para. 14)

This cautious, restrictive and largely negative advice can be contrasted with recent more forthright ministerial statements on housing design. Speaking in 2001 the then Planning Minister argued that:

> Across the county identikit estates, often sold as executive homes, have mushroomed. They make no architectural reference to their region. Too many of these housing estates are designed for nowhere but are found everywhere. They fail to sustain local services, they waste land and they produce dependency on the car. They easily end up being soulless and dispiriting.
>
> (Lord Falconer in DETR, 2001)

This change of tack in government policy had been presaged by the 'Quality in Town and Country Initiative' from 1994 onwards and the revised guidance on design and the planning system in PPG1 (DoE, 1997a). The latter identified design as a theme that underpins the planning system (para. 3), and stressed: the need for good design everywhere (not just in environmentally sensitive locations); the importance of design in delivering sustainable development, economic investment and public acceptance of new development (para. 15); the overriding significance of urban design as the basis for design decision-making; and the need to respond to what is locally distinctive in particular contexts (paras 14 and 19). Nevertheless, it was not until the post-1997 Labour government began to promote the cause of better design that it became apparent that the pursuit of quality represented more than a passing fad. Since then, the concern has been extended specifically to private sector residential development through the publication of a number of significant documents.

The first was the revision to the official government guidance on the design of residential roads and footpaths – *Design Bulletin 32* (DoE and DoT, 1992) – published as *Places, Streets and Movement* (DETR, 1998d) in the form of a companion guide to the original guidance. The decision to revise this guidance was made in order to address the dominant critique of residential design, that new developments are dominated by roads and parking standards. Illustrations in the new guide reveal a sense of its primary inspirations – the 'Urban Villages' movement in the UK and neo-traditional (new urbanist) design generally. Indeed, the design philosophy promoted is essentially one of working with context, promoting pedestrian friendly environments, returning to traditional perimeter block systems, and – where possible – mixing uses. Furthermore, most of the examples in the guide illustrate housing of relatively high density.

Launching the guide, the Minister argued: 'We need to ensure that to build is to enhance and that local authorities, planners, highways engineers and developers consider the needs of all users, not just car users, in the design of new development' (Raynsford, 1998). The philosophy is boiled down into a series of questions:

1. Have the main characteristics of the locality been fully understood and taken into account?
2. Has a framework for development been drawn up and agreed?
3. Does the framework design aim to create a distinctive place through the density and layout of buildings and spaces?
4. Has every effort been made to introduce or retain mixed use?
5. Do streets and spaces contribute to making a high-quality public realm?
6. Does the framework provide for all forms of travel including walking, cycling and public transport?
7. Has full account been taken of the need to create places which will be safe and well cared for?

When published, a range of headlines across the national press portended 'the end of the road' for the suburban cul-de-sac. In reality the guidance was nowhere near as equivocal. It did, however, emphasise the need to design spaces first and the roads thereafter, and favoured traditional connected road systems, rather than the 'branch and twig' hierarchical road systems that dominated residential layouts throughout the 1980s and 1990s.

PPG3: Housing (DETR, 2000a) took the approach forward, reflecting the new emphasis on design up-front in the statement of government objectives, where local authorities are advised to 'promote good design in new housing developments in order to create attractive, high-quality living environments in which people will choose to live' (para. 2). Looking back at the 1992 version of PPG3 that it replaced, the impression given in the 1992 policy is one of lip-service to design, whilst the free hand extended to the housebuilders throughout the 1980s received a further lease of life. Conversely, the 2000 version of PPG3 makes no mention of marketing needs as a driver of design solutions and places no obvious limits on the design aspirations of authorities (except to avoid low-density, mono-use development). Instead, the note outlines a wide-ranging design agenda.

The design advice covers five main areas, the first being an overarching objective to encourage environmentally and socially sustainable communities by decisively breaking away from single-use, socially zoned residential ghettos. Mixed developments are seen as the answer – mixed uses, mixed tenures, mixed housing types and sizes, and socially mixed communities (see p. 133). For example, the notion of community receives an endorsement in the guidance. This objective is to be pursued through design and layout and the allocation of space around development, but also through better accessibility by public transport and an explicit link between housing design and delivery of the urban renaissance agenda.

The second area, the new emphasis on urban design, marks a decisive shift away from the former guidance and an acceptance that urban design exists in predominantly residential areas as well as in more urban contexts. Although far from comprehensive, the advice encompasses townscape, social usage, urban form and functional conceptualisations of urban design, and briefly addresses many of the perceived problems with contemporary residential development. The third area – landscape design – recognises the perceptually significant role of landscaping and open space in living environments and encourages the greening of developments to promote quality, enhance drainage and increase biodiversity. The landscape setting of new development receives a mention as a legitimate issue for local authority concern, as does the need to provide and retain public open space within easy reach of new housing.

Architectural design – the fourth area of concern – marks a further departure from the hands-off approaches of the past. Thus, local building traditions and materials are specifically recognised as legitimate contextual considerations (previously considered matters of detail) and more energy-efficient housing designs (and layouts) are promoted. New building technologies are also promoted as means to deliver acceptable building forms more efficiently.

The final area relates to housing design and the planning process, advice which largely repeats that given in PPG1 that applicants should demonstrate how they have taken the need for good design and layout into account and that authorities should review applications in the light of clear plan policies and adopted supplementary design guidance, including design briefs. Consequently, authorities are encouraged to review their existing design standards in favour of more flexible policy mechanisms that aim to reduce land-take. In preparing their guidance, authorities are also encouraged to 'develop a shared vision with their local communities of the types of residential environments they wish to see in their area' (para. 55) – a departure that recognises the importance of the human as well as physical context for new residential development.

This agenda is laid out most comprehensively in two further documents – *By Design, Urban Design in the Planning System* (DETR and CABE, 2000) and *Better Places to Live, By Design* (DTLR and CABE, 2001). The former makes the case for better design and the role of the planning system in helping to realise it; it outlines a series of urban

Table 8.1 Objectives of urban design (DETR and CABE, 2000)

Objective	Reason
Character	To promote character in townscape and landscape by responding to and reinforcing locally distinctive patterns of development and culture.
Continuity and enclosure	To promote the continuity of street frontages and the enclosure of space by development which clearly defines private and public areas.
Quality of the public realm	To promote public spaces and routes that are attractive, safe, uncluttered and work effectively for all in society, including disabled and elderly people.
Ease of movement	To promote accessibility and local permeability by making places that connect with each other and are easy to move through, putting people before traffic and integrating land uses and transport.
Legibility	To promote legibility through development that provides recognisable routes, intersections and landmarks to help people find their way around.
Adaptability	To promote adaptability through development that can respond to changing social, technological and economic conditions.
Diversity	To promote diversity and choice through a mix of compatible developments and uses that work together to create viable places that respond to local needs.

The objectives are interpreted through eight aspects of urban form: (1) Layout: urban structure, (2) Layout: urban grain, (3) Landscape, (4) Density and mix, (5) Scale: height, (6) Scale: massing, (7) Appearance: details, (8) Appearance: materials.

design objectives (see Table 8.1), explores a policy toolkit to help articulate these – development plans, urban design frameworks, development briefs, design guides and development control – and discusses a range of complementary processes as a means to deliver the toolkit and urban design objectives. The latter focuses specifically on housing, and as a companion guide to PPG3, further articulates a general approach to, and principles for, residential design.

The question of density

The linking of better design with the delivery of wider social, economic and environmental benefits represents a key tenet of the urban renaissance agenda. While definitions of urban renaissance vary, essential elements always seem to include: a network of public spaces that feel safe and overlooked at all times; relatively compact and dense new housing that makes alternatives to the private car viable and that is sustainable in environmental terms; a diversity of activities that encourages street life and creates memorable places; and a balance of population that avoids social exclusion and that encourages economic development. Key issues in delivering an urban renaissance therefore include the delivery of a mix of uses and of higher-density development (intensification).

Despite some arguments to the contrary (see Jenks *et al.*, 1996), the Urban Task Force made a clear case for compact cities, with the significant proviso that they should be well designed and well connected. The Task Force argued that density standards (including residential density, parking standards and overlooking distances) have too often been used in an overly simplistic way to protect basic residential amenity, but in so doing have undermined the design quality of new residential environments. In fact – it was argued – density has very little to do with residential amenity, as well-designed environments guarantee basic sunlight, daylight and privacy requirements across a range of densities. Consequently, 'there can be no hard and fast rules for establishing "ideal" density levels' (Urban Task Force, 1999, p. 63), and guidance – where it is given – should be flexible and directed by local circumstances. Nevertheless, the Urban Task Force recommended that clear guidance on density is desirable and should adopt the principle of 'pyramids of intensity' – allowing densities to rise around transport hubs and in town centres.

PPG3 argues that 'Land is a finite resource', and that 'Urban land and buildings can often be significantly underused' (DETR, 2000a, para. 24). In order to establish how much housing can be accommodated in urban areas, authorities are advised to undertake urban capacity studies. However, a *Review of Urban Capacity Studies* by Llewelyn-Davies (1996) for the UK Round Table on Sustainable Development found that many authorities were reluctant to change their old perceptions about housing densities, design or parking. These constraints, it was suggested, were based on perceived consumer preferences that often remained untested. The researchers therefore advised that capacity studies should adopt assumptions of higher densities, lower car parking provision and less generous road layouts before calculating housing capacity. Such work should also require authorities to take a broader view on prospects for urban renewal, revitalisation and intensification, and make a reassessment of traditional policies on urban design and perceptions of consumer preferences.

Work for Friends of the Earth specifically focused on increasing urban capacity (URBED, 1998). The research revealed that the major barriers to unlocking the capacity of urban areas lay primarily not in the physical capacity of urban areas to take more development, but in the attitudes of people to living in urban areas, the resulting attitudes of developers (not wanting to build there), and in the attitudes of those responsible for taking the decisions on capacity primarily through the planning process. The report argued for more creative searches for capacity and that significant numbers of new homes could come from:

1. recycled land;
2. the redevelopment of council estates;
3. the redevelopment of car parks;
4. the conversion of empty commercial space;
5. living over the shop;
6. the subdivision of existing housing;
7. the intensification of existing housing areas; and
8. the better use of existing housing stock, i.e. bringing empty properties back into use.

Work on housing attitudes has nevertheless consistently reflected some of the difficulties inherent in building to higher densities, a clear preference for detached over semi-detached houses and for semi-detached over terraced houses for example – Hedges and Clemens (1994, p. 157) recorded respectively 93, 80 and 51 per cent of respondents willing to entertain living in each. In addition, Roger Tym and Partners

(1999, p. 40) observed that although households were reducing in size, because households were also getting wealthier, needs and aspirations for space remained the same. Therefore housebuilders questioned the viability of building smaller homes at higher densities. They noted:

> We found evidence from both local authorities and house builders that there is a market for an alternative product, built to higher density in urban areas. What is not clear is how big the market is, or whether it reflects consumer preference or consumer resources (i.e. whether the main constraint is affordability). Neither do we know whether consumer preferences would be modified if the supply of quality high density urban residential development were strengthened.
>
> (Roger Tym and Partners, 1999, p. 66)

On housebuilders' preferences, the work revealed a strong preference to build larger (family) units on suburban and greenfield sites and a general resistance to tackling urban sites – perceived to be less safe locations to build with less certain markets and ground conditions. Nevertheless, all the housebuilders interviewed accepted the need to adapt their products to evolving planning regimes and market demands and all had done so to a greater or lesser degree (Roger Tym and Partners, 1999, pp. 28, 45).

More recent future scenarios work, aiming to project women's preferences forward to 2020 revealed a concern that homes being built in 2002 are likely to be too small and are already failing to meet the requirements of modern society for more flexible living spaces (Andrews *et al.*, 2002). The study revealed that women in particular want their homes to be large enough to allow for changing household dynamics, and that many developers are currently building homes which are too small to meet these aspirations. The report also argues that the individual house should not be seen as the multifunctional space for living, working and healthcare envisaged by some experts, but that services should be clustered in neighbourhood hubs to provide a support network for changing patterns of life. To some degree the work revealed a potential conflict between the smaller units required to build the higher densities required in government policy and needed to support the sort of social infrastructure envisaged in the scenarios, and the aspirations of many consumers for larger, more flexible living spaces.

Changing well-established consumer (and therefore market) attitudes to urban living represented a considerable concern of the Urban Task Force, which commissioned work on the issue (URBED *et al.*, 1999). The work revealed that because where individuals live is based on a relative balance between urban and suburban aspirations, there is scope to tap into any urban aspirations to tip the balance more firmly in favour of urban areas. This task – the researchers argued – will potentially be easier because most people already carry many existing positive attitudes towards urban lifestyles and some discontent about suburban areas. The report concluded:

> Despite a century of urban decline, there remains – or at least has been rekindled – a desire for urban living in the hearts of many British people. While people value what might be called the suburban characteristics of peace and quiet, space, safety and greenery they also miss urban characteristics such as convenience, diversity, life and variety. Many people have returned to live in urban areas over the last ten years and our work suggests there are many more who could be persuaded to do so.
>
> (URBED *et al.*, 1999, p. 39)

8.3 Housing at Poundbury, Dorchester (photo: M. Carmona).

In a more recent Gallup survey, it was not the density of housing that respondents considered important, but the context in which it was built. Thus 73 per cent would consider living in high-density housing in a village or rural setting, 63 per cent on the edge of a town, 52 per cent in mixed commercial and residential areas, but only 28 per cent in a city centre (although young people were notably more positive about urban living). The researchers noted that the Prince of Wales seems to be offering people what they say they really want in his 'controversial Poundbury development on the outskirts of Dorchester . . . high quality, modern housing in traditional architectural styles, in a traditional, high density English village setting' (Strutt & Parker, 2001, p. 2 – see Fig. 8.3). This model has close parallels with the 'Urban Villages' ('New Urbanism') model now being reflected in government guidance (see p. 134).

A final poll of over 1,000 people examining housing preferences revealed a rather different and, in the light of intensification objectives, disturbing pattern of preferences (CABE, 2002). When interviewed about where they would most like to live and offered a choice of house types, the highest percentage – 30 per cent – chose a bungalow and 29 per cent a traditional village house. Modern high-density apartments proved very unpopular (2 per cent), as did modern terraced social housing (1 per cent) and any form of council housing or high rise (0 per cent). Nineteen-thirties semi-detached properties were favoured by 6 per cent, modern semi-detached houses by 14 per cent and Victorian terraces by 16 per cent. The last indicated that if well designed and seemingly 'built to last' (56 per cent regarded this factor to be important), then higher-density housing was favoured by some, but remained a minority preference.

Raising densities

Preferences therefore contrast with national policy in PPG3, which advises that authorities should avoid low-density development of less than 20–25 dwellings per hectare (DPH). Instead, they should encourage housing development that makes more efficient use of land (between 30 and 50 DPH net) without compromising the quality of the environment. This range is broadly supported by the influential Town and Country Planning Association (2000) based on the Garden City experience. The government's guide – *Planning for Sustainable Development* – also supported this general push towards higher densities on the grounds that higher-density building will reduce pressure on undeveloped land. It warned, however, that increasing density is neither a quick nor a sure means of reducing travel needs. Thus, because the existing urban stock changes only slowly, dramatic results should not be expected (DETR, 1998e, p. 37).

Furthermore, developments at increasingly high densities show diminishing returns in land saved. Thus research for the DETR (1998f, pp. 5–7) on the use of density in the planning system revealed that real land economy gains are significant when densities are increased from current predominant densities of between 20–25 DPH to 35–40 DPH, in other words from low to medium densities. Above these levels land-use gains diminish sharply, although the ability to support public amenities and transport facilities continues to improve. The research argued that density measures are not a good means to influence design quality and amenity, but have value in influencing travel demand and land-take.

More focused work on achieving Sustainable Residential Quality (SRQ) has been undertaken by Llewelyn-Davies (1998a, 2000) to examine the potential of design-led approaches to getting more housing in existing urban areas. The work concluded that imaginative design, new ways of thinking about planning and transport and better urban management can help get more housing potential out of towns and cities; and can do it in a way that improves the urban environment and makes patterns of living more sustainable. In particular, it was argued that new thinking about planning standards and policies and assumptions constraining potential are required, for example on:

- parking standards
- overlooking
- density
- conversions
- open space
- industrial land and site
- market constraints.

Research initially in the North West and London and subsequently in the South East (Llewelyn-Davies, 1998b) revealed that much of the extra capacity of urban areas lies not in the already built-up and homogeneous residential areas, but in the 'shatter zones' around the town and district centres and in other interface areas between employment and housing. The work exploring design-led solutions to raising capacities revealed that:

- an average of 40 per cent of sites are given over to cars and car parking, which can be dramatically reduced by better design and reducing standards;
- good design can overcome the impact of standard road geometries in creating unusable spaces and undevelopable corners;

- in and around town centres abandoning suburban standards in favour of more urban solutions driven by townscape rather than density controls raises both the quantity and quality of new homes;
- the majority of the identified capacity utilised small gap sites and underused land, rather than derelict and contaminated land with high remediation costs;
- design-led, relaxed standards approaches can often raise site capacities by 50 per cent, and if car parking is removed altogether by up to 100 per cent.

PPG3 supports much of the SRQ approach, in particular confirming 'local authority requirements for car parking, especially off-street car parking, are also a significant determinant of the amount of land required for new housing' (DETR, 2000a, para. 59). The note warns that standards are often far too high and that an average provision of over 1.5 off-street car parking spaces per house would be unlikely to reflect government objectives for securing sustainable residential environments. In addition, authorities are advised to revise their parking standards to allow for significantly lower levels of off-street parking provision for developments in highly accessible locations, or where users are likely to require a reduced parking provision – for example students or the elderly.

For their part, RSLs have generally been more willing to embrace the higher densities agenda than private housebuilders. Research by the London Housing Federation (2002), for example, examining schemes with densities of between 81 and 455 units per hectare, concluded that higher densities could deliver considerable benefits – not least in meeting the capital's significant housing shortfall and continuously overheating housing market. They argued, however, that although building at higher densities did not necessarily imply building high, it did imply higher construction costs (up to 10 per cent higher), because savings in reduced land costs were soon surpassed by the need for more robust materials because of the higher wear and tear that such buildings were subject to. Providing amenity space, security, landscaping and the implications of building in difficult-to-access urban areas can also add extra costs. The report identified four prerequisites for successful high-density developments:

1. An accessible location – good transport links and within easy reach of jobs, shops, schools and other local amenities
2. Low occupancy levels and child densities – child density levels at no more than 25 per cent of total residents and provision of spare bedrooms and bedspaces
3. Effective management and maintenance – by residential caretakers, estate agreements and strong community networks
4. Good housing design – through good security, sound insulation, dwelling sizes, open space quality, privacy, quality building materials and contextual fit.

Nevertheless, despite government claiming to have reached and exceeded its target for brownfield reuse (see Chapter 5), national targets for increasing densities have remained stubbornly difficult to meet. Thus statistics on land use change in England (DTLR, 2002b) revealed that in 2001 average densities of just 25 DPH were achieved, well short of the 30–50 aspiration. The figures prompted the Deputy Prime Minister to announce that schemes involving densities of fewer than 30 homes per hectare would be called in (Winkley, 2002a). The issuing of Circular 01/02 by the government (ODPM, 2002h) gave effect to the announcement, although only in the South East and London.

Mixing uses and tenures

Clearly the argument for increasing densities remains to be won, and will be fundamental to achieving another of the overarching themes of the planning system as defined in PPG1 (DoE, 1997a, para. 3) – the delivery of mixed-use development. The potential to mix uses occurs on a number of different scales from the scale of the neighbourhood, to the urban block, to the street, to the individual building, and offers the potential for proximity of the home environment to shops, work and to social, educational and leisure facilities. The Urban Task Force argued that good design offers people the opportunity to live near to those services which they require on a regular basis and therefore that the concept of rigid land-use zoning is becoming increasingly outdated:

> Many activities can – with careful design and good urban management – live harmoniously side by side. Except for certain industries or activities that attract very high traffic volumes or create noise at unsociable hours, most businesses and services can coexist with housing.
>
> (Urban Task Force, 1999, p. 64)

PPG1 (DoE, 1997a, paras 10–11) advocates a more flexible approach to changes in the mix of uses in buildings, and for defining flexible mixed-use areas in development plans. It adds that planning conditions, obligations and briefs should be used to help secure delivery and that rigid planning standards should be avoided.

The Urban Task Force also argued that mixing household tenures and income groups is important to help sustain neighbourhood services and to avoid problems of poverty concentration and exclusion. In particular, the report notes that in parts of London and the South East shortages in affordable housing are particularly severe and that planning obligations – the usual means to encourage a better mix of market and affordable housing – are proving ineffective with developers either buying themselves out of obligations or physically separating social housing in site layouts. Greater use of shared-equity schemes and briefs that insist on a better mix of housing types are therefore promoted (Urban Task Force, 1999, pp. 65–7, 204–5).

Research from DEMOS (1999) has tested the extent to which mixing tenures can help to foster more inclusive societies. The work concluded that although mixing tenures can have advantages (and rarely has disadvantages), a more fine-grained mixing is required (street by street rather than in different zones) to achieve any significant cross-tenure mixing. Furthermore, the warm rhetoric often used about such communities as vibrant, balanced and inclusive is frequently not matched by the reality. Nevertheless, guidance in PPG3 supports the principle of mixing tenures and argues that 'The government . . . does not accept that different types of housing and tenures make bad neighbours' (DETR, 2000a, para. 10).

Unfortunately, surveys of consumer attitudes continue to reveal less enlightened views amongst many owner occupiers and a belief that different types of housing should be segregated. Evidence from a consumer survey on attitudes to PPG3, for example, revealed a strong desire for segregation on price, social class and even by age, the subtext being that quality of life and property values would suffer from proximity to low-cost and social housing. 'The majority of people preferred to live near communities of people like themselves' (Mulholland and Associates, 2000, p. 16). Attitudes on mixing uses from the survey of 6,404 adults were considerably more positive, with most people wishing to see a mix of local amenities close to their homes – a convenience store, some specialist shops, a post office, health services, a pub and a cash point.

Urban villages have been extensively promoted – not least in PPG1 – as a means to deliver higher density, mixed use and tenure development. Increasingly a steady stream of urban village proposals have been announced as developers have realised the market potential of the concept and as English Partnerships has teamed up with the Urban Villages Forum to help ensure their delivery. In the US, the New Urbanism movement has been particularly influential in arguing for a move away from more expansive suburban style developments and back towards neo-traditional housing layouts including:

- mixed land uses
- mixed housing types
- plenty of public space
- pedestrian-oriented design, and
- interconnected street networks.

Significantly, rigorous quantitative research on New Urbanist developments in the US demonstrated that houses in such developments return on average an 11 per cent premium over identical houses in surrounding communities (Eppi and Tu, 1999) – a major incentive for housebuilders to deliver better design. A poll conducted by CABE (2002) on housing preferences also revealed a widespread perception amongst the public (72 per cent of those interviewed) that well-designed houses increase in value quicker than average, with only a minority (9 per cent) disagreeing with the statement. Unfortunately, work examining recent attempts at developing such sustainable communities in the UK concluded that many are urban villages in name only, and adopt few of the sustainable and design principles that underpin the concept (DETR, 2000g).

Stakeholder views

The survey of stakeholder views revealed design and density to be serious concerns of planners, with about half of respondents rating these issues to be amongst their most significant worries (see Figs 8.4 and 8.5). In both cases RSLs were less concerned than planners (about 10 per cent less) about these issues and housebuilders were more concerned (about 10 per cent more), with comments accepting that a change in approach to design was required in the light of PPG3, but that 'developers should not be punished for 30 years of adhering to Council Highway standards'.

Design tensions focused around a number of core areas:

- Economic concerns: there was a suggestion that design guidance places new burdens on a developer, increasing uncertainty when requirements are not explicit, and sometimes directly increasing costs. However, there was also a contrary view: that good design increases marketability and addresses the problem of standardisation.
- Skills and understanding: planners were sometimes decried as the weak link in the push for greater design awareness and implementation. But each of the key stakeholders seems to be of the view that the other core groups lack the know-how to take forward the new design agenda. In this regard there is an acknowledgement that there must be a locally available skills base to ensure contextually responsive development and consistent advice. The inappropriate standards-driven approaches of most highways authorities were a particular source of complaint amongst developers and planners, representing an area where greater skills and understanding is urgently required.

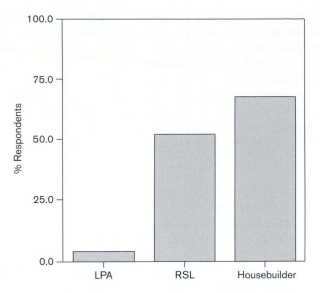

8.4 Views on the significance of design as a source of planner–provider tension (per cent rating as significant).

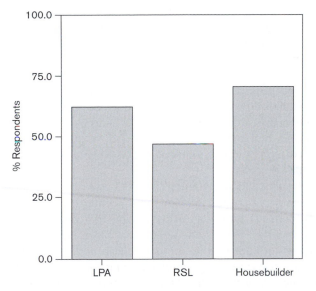

8.5 Views on the significance of density as a source of planner–provider tension (per cent rating as significant).

- Commitment to quality/standards: all the stakeholders were ready to concede that good design is central to good housing and are willing to address it. But these acknowledgements were quickly qualified with references to the conflicts and con-straints that push stakeholders away from the ideal situation. Some developers still supported a 'we know the market and build what the market wants' philosophy, although most accepted that change was required, and that this would require radical change from current practice – both their own and that of authorities.

- Conflicts and constraints: parking standards are a big part of the current design debate and all the key stakeholders indicated that what they feel is achievable is constrained by perceptions of what customers want. But design, from the point of view of developers and RSLs, is constrained by a planning system that restricts innovation and adopts inflexible standards (for example on space between dwellings). But here lies a contradiction. Planning is lambasted for its discretionary nature and lack of any strategic vision (see Chapter 7), but also for its lack of local flexibility. Furthermore, housing providers pointed to the need for planning innovation, but also argued that design innovation may be controversial, leading to local objection and delay.

The issue of urban design skills (or a general lack of them) has been a recurring theme of debates on delivering better quality design. Recognition of the cross-disciplinary need to address the concern led to the setting up of the Urban Design Skills Working Group (2001) by the government, and the adoption of a long-term agenda to address the problem from education in schools, to universities to continuing professional development. The issue is particularly important if higher-density development is to be built without – as one RSL respondent put it – a 'move towards building the "slums" of tomorrow', but the agenda is clearly long term.

Although the key stakeholders recognised the various benefits of well-designed high-quality and high-density development, they also recognised that density remains a thorny political issue. The view was that the public has been conditioned to appreciate the merits of spacious, low-density development and hence perceives attempts to increase densities as 'town cramming'.

This translated into the following key findings:

- Attitudes: with the pursuit of higher densities, it was feared that design would become a greater sticking point, and given that it will be less easy to segregate market and affordable housing, a question mark would hang over the marketability of such schemes. Providers and planners also continued to argue that there are negative misconceptions of high densities, with opposition emanating from local residents and their political representatives.
- Interpretation of policy: whilst guidance in PPG3 was sometimes described as 'too prescriptive', there was also a suggestion that it is being interpreted in different ways. With regard to density, there was a perception that planning committees fail to understand exactly what PPG3 is attempting to achieve. Nevertheless, both planners and housebuilders recognised that a more flexible and sophisticated approach to density is required, acknowledging that higher densities will often, but not always, be the solution.
- Context: tensions revolving around density are therefore as much to do with local contexts as anything else. There was a belief that the issue is not being debated in the context of local market conditions or regional physical and economic differences. Density requirements can, for example, conflict with local character and with the need to provide adequate car parking space in rural areas. In short, developers (and planning authorities) are wary of a zealous promotion of higher-density development in areas where they believe that it simply will not work.

Table 8.2 Principles for housing design quality (Carmona, 2001b, pp. 141–2)

Issue	Principle
Context	The need to adequately respond to established urban design, landscape and architectural context and to what is distinctive about the site and its surroundings
Sense of place	The need to establish sense of place in new developments and, where appropriate, in their constituent parts
Community	The need through design to encourage the creation of a sense of community through the integration of physical and social foci and a well-used public realm
Urban space	The need to establish a coherent network and hierarchy of well-defined individual urban spaces and a visually interesting townscape layout
Legibility	The need to create legible, easily navigable environments
Connectivity	The related need to create well-connected permeable layouts which are fully integrated into their surrounding environment
Movement	The need to create a pedestrian-friendly public realm designed for walking, for child play activities and to encourage social intercourse
Car dominance	The need to adequately cater for vehicular access, but to reduce the dominance of cars in the design of urban space by designing for reduced vehicle speeds and reduced parking standards
Security	The need to create well-used, well-surveilled streets and spaces
Innovation	The need to build to last through high-quality materials and detailing and, where appropriate, through innovation in architectural design
Flexibility	The need to build spaces and buildings that are resilient and adaptable and which can be flexibly used and, in the case of houses, extended if required
Choice	The need to offer variety and choice in building sizes, types and tenures
Landscape	The need to fully integrate and positively address public open space, to invest in high-quality hard and soft landscaping (including trees) and to provide ample opportunity for private landscape display
Sustainability	The need to respond to the sustainability agenda by conserving land and material resources, integrating energy-efficient technologies, designing for ecological diversity, and for less car travel and greater use of public transport
Mixing uses	The need to move beyond strict zoning by designing developments with all appropriate facilities and services, and by mixing housing with other uses when appropriate and feasible
Functionality	The need to create buildings and environments which function successfully, allowing for sun, light and fresh air penetration, reduction and exclusion of noise and pollution, for economy in use (and in purchase), for good accessibility and for appropriate maintenance and servicing as required
Homeliness	The need to create buildings and environments which offer peace of mind through privacy and individuality, which are safe and secure, which carry for their users a sense and meaning of home, and which offer reasonable scope for personalisation

The views of stakeholders confirm that the issue of design quality, and the related concern to increase densities still represent sources of tension, although a learning process is underway on all sides. Karn and Sheridan (1994, p. 1) remind us of an important distinction between the physical and perceived environment, and that 'if a residential environment is going to provide homes not "units of accommodation", it needs to satisfy not just people's physical requirements, but also support their chosen lifestyle and help them express their individual and group identity'. Seen in this way, the concept of quality housing becomes much more than the simplistic provision of minimum physical and functional standards that too often prevail in the public sector, and more than the minimum marketable or rentable standards that equally prevail in the private or social housing sectors.

Indeed, recent work has suggested that the achievement of quality housing design depends on understanding and addressing a wide range of overlapping considerations (see Table 8.2). It argues that:

> If the range of principles seem complex, then in reality they represent the tip of the iceberg, reflecting in turn the great complexity of residential design and the difficulty in balancing the numerous – often conflicting – design requirements to secure high quality residential environments.
>
> (Carmona, 2001b, p. 142)

If nothing else, they underline the futility of public sector attempts to effectively control residential design with only generalised aspirations or rigid standards in policy or guidance, and the inability of housing providers to deliver good quality design without a view to the wider physical and social environment being created.

9

Gain

The purpose of planning gain

The levering of planning gains or contributions from the development process has been one of the most aggressively debated topics in British planning during the last 30 years. For some, it represents the best way of harnessing the economic power of development for social gain. For others, it is little more than negotiated corruption (see Healey *et al.*, 1993 for a discussion of attitudes), a mechanism by which planning permission can be sold to the highest bidder, or a strategy enabling central government to shirk its responsibility for meeting social needs. In this chapter, the intended purpose of planning gain is examined, before focusing on three specific topics, namely

- How gain, in general, is being used at the present time, drawing on recent studies;
- The use of gain to procure affordable housing within market housing schemes – this is assigned particular attention given the overall purpose of the book;
- Some continuing problems and controversies which envelop the present system, drawing on the survey analysis.

Planning gain is one possible – and in the context of new housing increasingly probable – consequence of land development. Under the present system, gain is derived from the obligation or condition placed on a developer to perform a specified action in association with a particular development. The power to impose such obligations/conditions was conferred on planning authorities through the Town and Country Planning Act of 1932 (see Cherry, 1974, pp. 90–1), although planning agreements (the basis of conditions) were rarely used until the 1970s. The terms themselves are fairly misleading, and what precisely is meant by conditions, obligations and agreements is set out in Table 9.1.

What is understood today as planning gain (i.e. an action or physical contribution that is judged to be beneficial – usually to the local community) began life as a mechanism to assist in the management of the development process, and hence avoid particular difficulties. For example, local planning authorities as a matter of course (and of requirement since 1968) impose conditions on new development permissions, indicating that these permissions will lapse if no works commence within three years (five years prior to the 2003 Planning and Compulsory Purchase Act). This strategy is designed

Table 9.1 Conditions, obligations and agreements

Conditions	Actions required from a developer as a condition of being granted planning permission for a particular development. These are used on all development sites and may be a means of regularising the development process.
Obligations	Sometimes dubbed 'super-conditions', these are more common in larger development schemes. Here, local planning authorities reach a voluntary *agreement* with a developer, often obliging the developer to make infrastructure contributions as part of a development gain package.
Agreements	Whilst planning conditions may be generic (i.e., permission time limits since 1968 or parking standard conditions), obligations are a matter of negotiation. Agreements between developers and planning authorities form the basis of ensuring that obligations are met. Today, these are framed under Section 106 of the Town and Country Planning Act 1990.

to avoid land hoarding and means that authorities can release land in a coordinated way rather than running the risk of having a backlog of permissions suddenly unleashed on the local land market. Other similar management conditions include those relating to development phasing – ensuring that large projects are completed in sections so as to minimise disruption to nearby residents. In the case of large-scale housing development, phasing is an essential strategy allowing the developer to sell units whilst the development is still ongoing. The process allows developers to derive income gradually in order to fund the remainder of the project. Other conditions may relate to design, density, building height, development screening, car-parking standards and so forth. Again, these have been a feature of the planning system for some years, and for the most part, they remain uncontroversial. Thus housing providers generally accept the need to abide by certain development standards and practices. Controversy may arise, however, if conditions are viewed as unreasonable.

Government attempted to divert conflicts over conditions in 1985 by issuing Circular 1/85 'The Use of Conditions in Planning Permissions'. Conditions must have legal precedent and 'should not be imposed unless they are both necessary and effective, and do not place unjustifiable burdens on applicants'. They should also be 'necessary, relevant to planning, relevant to the development to be permitted, enforceable, precise, and reasonable in all other respects' (DoE, 1985: superseded by DoE, 1995b, para. 2). However, the arrival of so-called super-conditions or obligations paved the way for planning authorities to demand much more from the development process. Section 52 of the Town and Country Planning Act 1971 ushered in a new era in which relatively minor conditions were to be transformed into sometimes significant requirements. Thus within a few years of the 1971 Act, the term 'planning gain' had arrived and was being fiercely debated. Cullingworth and Nadin (2002) note that gain took on two meanings. The first – 'facilities which are an integral part of a development' – derived from the accepted need to manage development. But the second – '"benefits" having little or no relationship to the development and which the local authority require as the price of planning permission' – was a product of the added impetus given to conditions through the 1971 Act.

A great deal more is said on this issue in the next two sections, but as a starting point, a three-part typology of gains can be identified:

- Those that smooth the development process (i.e. management gains);
- Those that contribute directly to a development (i.e. the facilities required – roads, pavements, drainage and so forth – to ensure development of the right quality); and
- Those that contribute indirectly to community goals (i.e. through infrastructure and services).

Whether gain should encompass such a broad remit is once more an issue of considerable debate and one that is returned to later in this chapter, particularly in the light of the 2001 Planning Green Paper.

The use of planning gain

Some of the most recent work on planning gain has been undertaken by Campbell *et al.* (1999a; 1999b; 1999c; 2001). Their 2001 study, published by the RICS Foundation, provides a detailed appraisal of the current use of planning obligations (Section 106 Agreements) on the back of a general survey of planning authorities in England and Wales, twelve local case studies and the negotiations surrounding two separate developments. Their concern is with the way that 'planning obligations have become a vehicle through which development-related infrastructure and service provision may be funded' (Campbell *et al.*, 2001, p. 2).

Today, local planning authorities enter into agreements under the provisions of Section 106 of the Town and Country Planning Act 1990, the successor to the 1971 Act. But a common misnomer in relation to obligations is that they are widely used and affect the majority of new development. This, however, is far from the truth. In the immediate run-up to 1990, only 0.5 per cent of planning decisions were accompanied by planning agreements (Grimley JR Eve, 1992 in Campbell *et al.*, 2001). The figure slowly rose during the 1990s and, according to the work by Campbell *et al.*, had reached 1.5 per cent by the year ending June 1998. Survey data from the 1998 study (Campbell *et al.*, 1999b) is given in Table 9.2 and this reveals a number of distinct patterns. First, obligations are far more prevalent on major developments, particularly residential developments, of which more than a quarter were accompanied by an obligation. Second, it is far more common for a permission to have an attached obligation in the South than in the North; moreover, 'the average cost of the obligations associated with a development in the North is £148,370, while in the South the figure is £753,830' (Campbell *et al.*, 1999b, p. 5). This difference reflects both underlying development costs and the greater extent of planning gain likely to be extracted from a development in the south of the country.

This of course is a very general picture based on national analysis. At the local level, planning authorities have been far more enthusiastic about the use of planning obligations since the clarification of their purpose contained in Circular 1/97 (DoE, 1997b). This did for obligations what Circular 1/85 had done for conditions twelve years earlier, enhancing clarity and giving this particular planning tool far greater momentum. Within a year, 85 per cent of authorities had policies within their local plans relating to the use of obligations. Furthermore, 75.6 per cent had subject-specific policies, and 37.8 per cent policies that related to specific sites (Campbell *et al.*, 2001, p. 5).

Some authorities began clearly specifying the level of gain expected from particular development types. For example, the Royal Borough of Windsor and Maidenhead now requires 28 primary school places for every 100 houses built (Campbell *et al.*, 2001, p. 6). In the 2001 Stevenage UDP, the 'informal scale of charges' comprises a series of chapter references linking the size of residential development with school, community,

Table 9.2 Planning obligations and planning permissions for the year ending June 1998 (Campbell et al., 2001)

Analysed by	Proportion of permissions with obligations by scale of development (%)		
	Major	Minor	All
Type of Development			
Residential	25.8	3.5	7.1
Retail	18.9	1.5	2.7
Offices	31.1	1.3	2.6
Industry	5.6	0.6	1.4
Other			0.7
Region			
North	14.8	1.5	1.4
South	22.9	1.9	1.6
All Development	17.6	1.7	1.5

health and highways contributions, and in each case the scale of the likely charge is alluded to but not stipulated (Stevenage Borough Council, 2001). Sometimes these requirements are clarified through different forms of supplementary planning guidance, although excessively rigid or prescriptive guidance can cause difficulties as the extraction of gain is supposed to be an outcome of negotiations between the planning authority and developer based on what different sites can bear. This reality often renders scales of charges meaningless or unworkable to all but the local planning team, who may find it useful to set themselves a benchmark against which to judge the success of subsequent negotiations, or as a starting point for discussions. But again, the planning system seeks a balance between certainty and flexibility, so although it may be useful to define expectations, these often have to be compromised. At the Stevenage West site in Hertfordshire (see Chapter 5), expectations have constantly shifted, in part because of the presence of two alternative planning applications (for 5,000 or 3,600 residential units), revealing that the gains from planning are always far from certain.

A number of points follow from this discussion so far. First, the extraction of gain is a significant and increasingly important aspect of many larger residential developments. Second, it is normal for policies relating to the use of obligations to refer specifically to the procurement of affordable housing. This was a policy rationale for 78 per cent of authorities in 1998 (Campbell et al., 1999b) and 89 per cent by 2001 (Crook et al., 2001). Third, obligations have largely been negotiated on a case-by-case, site-specific basis, often with little transparency or accountability. Finally, planning obligations and planning gain are here to stay, despite frequent criticisms that planning policy, in relation to the extraction of gain, is far from clear.

In order to address this latter concern, the 2001 Planning Green Paper (or at least its daughter document Planning Obligations – Delivering a Fundamental Change – DTLR, 2001f) contained proposals for a radical overhaul of the system of planning gain based on four key principles:

- Government stated its belief in the need to regularise the current system and make the clear purpose of planning obligations the 'delivery of sustainable development'.

- This should be achieved through a system of published standardised tariffs set by local authorities for different types of development through the plan-making process.
- The system of tariffs should contribute to meeting a range of social objectives including the delivery of affordable housing.
- 'Negotiated agreements should only supplement or substitute for the tariff where these are clearly justified to deliver, for example, site-specific requirements' (DTLR, 2001a, para. 1.12).

The goal was therefore to enhance transparency by creating a system where the suspicion that planning permissions are bought and sold is removed, whilst retaining and reinforcing the principle that the planning system should be used to extract developer contributions towards wider social goals. Furthermore, although the proposed changes envisaged a system based in part on standard tariffs, the need for negotiation on a case-specific basis also remained intact, further reinforcing the discretionary nature of the British planning process discussed in Chapter 7. Following consultation, the proposed system of tariffs was not taken forward by government, who favoured instead working within the existing legislative framework to streamline the system and make it more transparent and predictable (ODPM, 2002a, para. 53). In the next section, the recent use of planning gain to procure affordable housing is examined in greater detail.

Planning and affordable housing

As discussed above, the increased capacity for local planning authorities to lever wider social gains from new permissions was only gradually realised during the 1970s (Jowell, 1977) and then expanded during the 1980s and 1990s. Initially this capacity was treated with scepticism by the planning profession, with many of those in practice feeling uneasy about linking planning permissions to infrastructure contributions including new housing (Gallent, 2000, p. 128). Indeed, the fiercest critics of this system argued that planning gain was 'both an unconstitutional tax and a form of negotiated bribery corrupting the planning system' (Healey *et al.*, 1993, p. 5).

Much of the negative sentiment at this time was not primarily a direct consequence of the strategy itself, but of the lack of clear instruction offered by government about how the system should be used. During the 1970s and 1980s and prior to the arrival of the system of Planning Policy Guidance notes (PPGs), a lack of guidance and a reliance on local interpretation of primary legislation was a major problem across the planning remit. In the case of planning gain, government had set in motion an extremely contentious mechanism with little in the way of practical guidance. It moved to remedy this situation in 1983 by issuing Circular 22/83 'Town and Country Planning Act 1971: Planning Gain' (DoE, 1983). Gain, of whatever type and including housing, would henceforth have to be so closely related to a proposed scheme that a development 'ought not to be permitted without it' (Barlow *et al.*, 1994, p. 3). By the mid-1980s, some 20 structure plans contained policies indicating that local authorities might, in particular circumstances, require low-cost housing in new housing schemes as a part of a negotiated package of planning gain (Bishop and Hooper, 1991).

Despite this general clarification, nothing in housing-planning guidance mentioned the use of gain in providing new housing for community need. Circular 15/84 'Land for Housing' (DoE, 1984) stuck to the traditional line that planning, in relation to house-building, was solely concerned with the sufficient and predictable release of land. Even when the first PPG on housing was issued four years later, the use of Section 52

Table 9.3 Planning and affordable housing (since 1989)

General approach	The negotiation of contributions from developers of affordable housing within market housing schemes, usually on the basis of Section 106 (Town and Country Planning Act 1990) Agreements. Under this more 'general approach', affordable housing is treated as a planning gain and usually specified as a requirement within the Section 106 (before 1990, Section 52 agreements, derived from the Town and Country Planning Act 1971 served a similar purpose). The inclusion of affordable housing is an obligation negotiated with the developer. It is common for the developer to build affordable homes (a specified number or proportion) and then sell them at discount to a Registered Social Landlord (RSL) (Whitehead, 2002). The government believes that RSLs are best placed to ensure than such units remain for the use of low-income groups in perpetuity. This gain/obligation approach means that social housing is at least sometimes provided as part of a mixed tenure development and may be funded through planning gain, private sector borrowing and/or public subsidy. Gain – generated at the expense of development value – often replaces some, or all, of the public subsidy.
Exceptions approach	The granting of planning permissions for housing on land not allocated for that particular use within the development plan. The initiative aims to reduce land value and therefore housing unit costs though a mechanism whereby land can be purchased at below full development value. This approach is only to be taken in rural areas, and is to be used for the procurement of a small number of units within or adjacent to existing settlements. It is hoped that landowners can be encouraged to sell land at a price nearer agricultural than full development value if this housing is to be occupied only by people with a local connection and demonstrable need. However, the approach only works where an authority has a clear and up-to-date development plan, which is rigidly applied in development control. Most research has shown that where there is uncertainty over a planning authority development strategy or its intentions for a particular site are unclear, owners may be less inclined to release land for exception schemes perhaps in the hope that one day it may be earmarked for market housing and able to command significant value.

received just passing reference in the penultimate paragraph and then only with regard to infrastructure related to new housing schemes (DoE, 1988, para. 32). Much uncertainty remained, therefore, about the appropriate use of Section 52 as a means of delivering affordable homes, and it was immediately clear within the planning profession that government had failed to address this fundamental concern.

Perhaps spurred on by this realisation, government quickly moved to revise PPG3, coming up with a redraft by October 1989 (DoE, 1989). The new document contained five extra paragraphs (paras 25–30) on the subject of low-cost housing for local needs, suggesting that the availability of such housing should be a material consideration in the deciding of future planning applications, and this consideration might lead to a requirement from housing developers to include low-cost housing in market schemes, or the granting of planning exceptions in the countryside (see Table 9.3). However, a number of problems persisted. First, what exactly was 'low-cost housing'? How much evidence would be required by a planning authority to support its inclusion in market schemes? And was a draft document to be taken as official policy?

The first two questions have puzzled developers and local authorities alike ever since the redraft of PPG3 was issued in 1989. The final issue, however, was resolved in 1991 when the government finally published a Circular 7/91 on 'Planning and Affordable Housing' in which support for the policy seemed unequivocal: 'a community's need for affordable housing is a material consideration which may properly be taken into account in formulating local plan policies' (DoE, 1991, para. 1).

In the same year, the government also sought to clarify developers' responsibilities (and the public sector's power) with regard to the general levying of planning gain. DoE Circular 16/91 carried forward the guidelines offered in Circular 22/83, expanding on the rationale for planning agreements and highlighting the duty of developers to return some of the profit to the community through some form of 'betterment' (Healey *et al.*, 1993, p. 6). Both this general gain advice and more specific guidance on affordable housing followed on from the revamped Town and Country Planning Act (1990), which replaced the old Section 52 agreements with Section 106. So, by the end of 1991 a general framework was finally in place (see Table 9.3) and this was bolstered by the arrival of a fully revised PPG3 in the following year (DoE, 1992a).

Critics nevertheless argued that the new framework was full of holes, lacking any real potency – a framework that sought a roundabout means of delivering affordable homes when what was really required was direct and generous public sector investment in new homes. Bishop and Hooper (1991, p. 36), for example, said of the general approach that: 'manipulation of the planning system will never be a substitute for an appropriate level of public subsidy'. Particular vitriol was reserved for the exceptions approach, with Hutton (1991, p. 305) claiming that it 'unfairly advantage[d] those on low incomes who, by good fortune, live in rural areas'.

The suggestion that planning will never replace appropriate subsidy is frequently made, and has proven correct over the last ten years. Gain mechanisms provide an inherently uncertain amount of affordable housing and have only a minor impact relative to the overall level of actual housing need. This reality has remained unaltered during the successive amendments of the policy framework since 1992, but it is only recently that an accurate attempt has been made to put a figure to the actual number of affordable homes delivered through the planning system (Crook *et al.*, 2001 – see Table 9.4). Affordable housing procured in this way should therefore be seen as additional to that which needs be delivered through more conventional means, i.e. through grant subsidy allocated to Registered Social Landlords as part of the Housing Corporation's Approved Development Programme (see Chapter 4).

Nevertheless, government has sought to enhance the efficacy of the strategy since 1992, with the aim of upping its potential contribution to overall supply. Such moves are

Table 9.4 Affordable housing secured by the planning system each year 1992–2000 (Crook et al., 2001)

	Total	*Urban*	*Rural*
Total dwellings completed	179,043	134,858	44,185
No. of affordable units completed	2,926	1,911	1,015
No. of rural exception units completed	991	126	865
Total affordable dwellings	**3,917**	**2,037**	**1,880**
Percentage of affordable units against total dwellings	2.19	1.51	4.25
Commuted sums received	£10,868,323	£10,763,323	£105,000

based on a recognition that both the general and exceptions approach have delivered countless local success stories, bringing social housing and a wider mix of tenures to housing schemes and communities that might otherwise have been dominated by expensive market housing. One of the final actions of the Major government, for example, was to issue a new Circular on 'Planning and Affordable Housing' (DoE, 1996a) that sought to clarify a number of issues. For example, Circular 13/96 aimed to clarify the power and responsibilities of those agencies charged with delivering affordable housing through the planning system. It provided more elaborate descriptions of specific concerns – such as the assessment of need, the use of conditions and the involvement or non-involvement of RSLs (see Chapter 4) in Section 106 schemes. New steps were also taken to spell out key concepts, including the concept of affordable housing which had continued to mean all things to all people. However, these moves to give the policy greater clarity were overshadowed by the introduction, via Circular 13/96, of development thresholds, below which it would be 'inappropriate to seek any affordable housing', different thresholds set for different places: 25 units in inner London, 40 outside London, and 25 in rural areas.

This apparent on-site interference, and move to a more prescriptive policy, met with huge opposition. It was argued, for example, that the economics of developing a particular site should dictate the appropriateness of seeking planning gain, and not Whitehall bureaucrats who could not possibly predict the full spectrum of conditions under which housing developments occur. Clarity was desired, but not clarity at the cost of local flexibility.

In response to the backlash, another revision to the guidance was inevitable and it came, under the new Labour administration, two years later in the form of Circular 6/98 (DETR, 1998c). Prior to the release of the Circular, the DETR dispatched a redraft of 13/96 with an accompanying letter in which it was conceded that the Conservative thresholds were 'too high' (DETR, 1997) and would be lowered. But for many, this in itself was not enough (Anon., 1998b, p. 3). They argued that established policy should be clear (understood and interpreted by all parties in the same way), but should not unduly constrain or dictate what happens at the level of individual sites. The presentation of the approach within Circular 6/98 remained largely unchanged and followed the two strands set out in Table 9.3. The policy was also unaffected by the arrival of a new PPG3 in March 2000.

Current approaches to gain and social housing

The principle of delivering affordable homes through planning obligations nevertheless retains strong support, although a major criticism persists that government guidance continues to confuse local planning authorities, developers and RSLs who have to implement the system. This support, qualified with concern, was recently expressed by the Royal Institution of Chartered Surveyors (2001):

> Thriving communities are based on mixed neighbourhoods offering a choice of housing for a wide range of households, including those on low incomes. In development areas the provision of affordable housing, often through the use of Section 106 agreements . . . is an important part of government housing policy. But confusion at local level is leading to protracted negotiations, legal wrangling and delay, which hold up the supply of affordable homes.

This was the central message contained in a further report into planning and affordable housing sponsored by the RICS and the Housing Corporation (Bishop Associates, 2001). The report focused on the general approach, on the use of SHG subsidy in gain schemes, and on the negotiation of Section 106 schemes. The study team posed a number of basic questions: Which authorities are adopting the approach? How are they justifying its adoption? How do they identify appropriate sites? When might it be more advantageous to request off-site gain contributions? What is the current relationship between gain and public sector subsidy? And how easy is it to achieve the desired outcome through Section 106 negotiations? These are all very topical issues and the results of the study show very broadly the current state of play between housing providers and local planning.

They found, for example, that most authorities in England (95 per cent: a figure that differs from the 89 per cent figure arrived at by Crook *et al.*, 2001) have developed an affordable housing policy within their local plan – an indication to developers of their intention to seek this kind of gain from planning permissions. They also found that successful schemes are always well justified, often using income data demonstrating the inability of certain households to compete for homes in the open market. However, strong evidence of need often remains patchy, giving the entire approach a less robust platform. Instead, sites appropriate to Section 106 schemes are usually identified by planning authorities based on their size or with reference to the government's prescribed thresholds (see above).

The researchers confirmed that acceptance of commuted sums in lieu of on-site contributions has rapidly become a major bone of contention, and nearly half of authorities have accepted housing contributions off-site, or money – ostensibly in exchange for planning permission – which can then be used for housing or other social gains elsewhere. The problem with this approach is that the entire affordable housing strategy can potentially be thrown into disrepute and fail to deliver mixed communities, with developments ending up entirely owner-occupied and social housing being concentrated in areas of lower land value. Indeed, if this strategy became the norm, then the provisions of Circular 6/98 would simply deliver another route towards residential and social segregation.

A major concern tackled by the Bishop study (Bishop Associates, 2001) was the relationship between the implicit private subsidy generated through planning gain and the use of public funding of RSL schemes. Planning requirements always affect site value because the value of a site subject to a Section 106 contribution will reflect the reduced profit attainable from housing development. Thus land values are effectively suppressed by gain policies, which means that a landowner – and to some extent the developer – foot the cost of an implicit subsidy. The landowner is obliged to accept a lower price for his/her land, although this may not fully reflect the total reduction in profit margin to the developer as market values change whilst a scheme is on-site. Effectively the landowner pays a hidden subsidy and the developer incurs an opportunity cost.

The question posed by Bishop was whether this implicit subsidy/cost can or should completely replace public subsidy for social housing. Currently, SHG can be used to cover 56 per cent of RSL development costs, the remainder being met through borrowing. The question therefore is what proportion of the 56 per cent can/should be covered by planning gain. Bishop found that some authorities were capping the gain contribution, meaning that RSLs used a three-part mix of SHG, borrowing and gain to fund schemes. The case of Doncaster Metropolitan Borough Council fell into this category, where the authority capped gain contribution at 15 per cent of total cost. But in

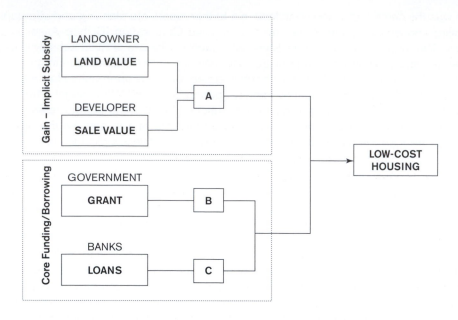

Notes:
The balance between A, B and C will vary from one scheme to another. Some authorities may see
A (gain) as a replacement for B (public subsidy via SHG). There will always be some element of C
(private sector borrowing). Most schemes mix A, B and C, though the total value of A is not always
clear.

9.1 Implicit subsidy and explicit funding.

Tower Hamlets, the expectation was that gain should be used to entirely replace the
public sector contribution. What this means in practice is that developers provide rented
units to RSLs in Tower Hamlets at a discount equivalent to the replaced SHG (i.e. at
44 per cent – 100 minus 56 per cent of cost). Such an arrangement is rare and it is
more common to find the extent of gain determined on a site-by-site basis and varying
greatly in level and form. The Bishop study demonstrates the mix of funding sources
employed in Section 106 schemes, a mix that is summarised in Fig. 9.1.

These are the broad concerns regarding the general approach to delivering affordable
housing through the planning system. A great deal more could be said on this and also
on the exceptions approach mentioned earlier, although these topics have received
extensive coverage elsewhere: see Gallent (2000), Gallent and Bell (2000), Bishop
Associates (2001) and Crook *et al.* (2001). One final point that should be made, however, is that many observers maintain that there are better ways to secure affordable
housing, both through the planning system and through general subsidy and taxation.

It was noted earlier that planning makes an uncertain contribution towards the national
supply of affordable homes, and a more predictable and constant supply might be
generated from an 'affordable housing' tax levied from development (i.e. in the form of a
standardised commuted sum, which many councils are already using – see Table 9.4
above for national totals). Alternatively, there might be greater reliance on core funding
if government were able to dedicate additional funds from the public purse over the
long term. But such suggestions ignore the more specific purposes of planning and
affordable housing, to secure mixed communities and provide an additional supply
of low-cost housing over and above that which can be provided through core funding.

This issue of additionality is crucial. Where planning gain is able to replace – at least an element – of public funding, then this funding should be available for other schemes elsewhere. Therefore this approach, if used effectively, supplements rather than replaces society's wider commitment to assisting low-income groups.

Stakeholder views

The extraction of planning gain from the development process has always been a controversial issue. For some, the bartering process underpinning gain gnaws at the foundations and integrity of the planning system. The procurement of affordable housing has been viewed with particular suspicion, and some have argued that it is inappropriate to control house price and tenure through land-use mechanisms. It has also been said that it is not the moral responsibility of private interests to meet social needs other than through general taxation obligations. But society has changed and there is a growing acceptance of the need to achieve social goals through a broader range of mechanisms. This philosophical shift from state to wider social responsibility has brought with it a readiness to embrace new ways of achieving the same goals.

However, an acceptance that planning gain and the delivery of affordable housing through planning are here to stay does not mean that those operating or working within the current system believe that everything is operating as it should. The different stakeholders rated the negotiation of gain generally – and affordable housing more specifically – as significant sources of tension in the delivery of new homes (see Figs 9.2 and 9.3). Unsurprisingly, RSLs were most concerned about the issue of delivering housing through the planning process; indeed, almost all RSL respondents expressed considerable disquiet about the engagement of the planning process with the issue of delivering affordable housing. Planners were far less concerned, with private housebuilders somewhere in between. Planners and private housebuilders showed almost identical

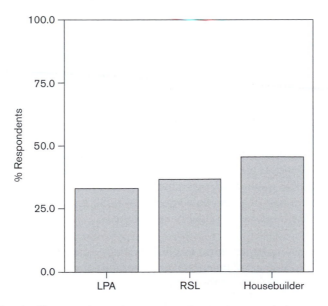

9.2 Views on the significance of planning agreements as a source of planner–provider tension (per cent rating as significant).

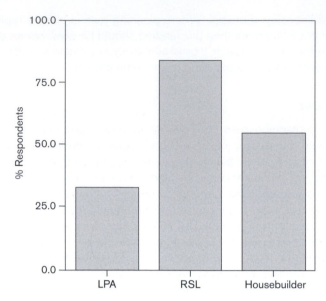

9.3 Views on the significance of affordable housing as a source of planner–provider tension (per cent rating as significant).

levels of concern over general issues of gain as respectively they did for affordable housing, while RSLs were noticeably less concerned, perhaps reflecting their less frequent engagement with such negotiations, beyond those associated specifically with affordable housing.

The survey pointed to a range of key and persistent concerns which have been collapsed into three topic areas in the following analysis.

Expectations and conflict

Planning gain has an enormous propensity to provoke conflict, and it seems that the battle lines are not only drawn between developers and local authorities. Within authorities, for example, the aspirations of forward planning sometimes sit uneasily with what development control believe is attainable from particular schemes. The research suggested that more often than not, those with an apparently inflated expectation of what might be extracted from a development win the day, turning aspirations into unrealistic wish-lists. One developer rather poetically compared housebuilders with the 'golden goose', asking who would build homes – either market or affordable – once the goose was slain (Section 106 presumably being the cause of death)? Disagreement over what can and should form part of a gain package is inevitable and the survey revealed some of the depth of current feeling amongst housebuilders:

> Local authorities make [hitherto] viable schemes – particularly on brownfield sites – unviable because of unrealistic and onerous planning gain requirements. They have no appreciation of the economics of site development.

> Planning gain is now subsidising a lack of government investment in schools, highways and housing.

Most local authority planners see agreements as punishments rather than solving specific development-related issues. One result is the continued request for planning gain on 'struggling' brownfield sites. Attend a 'Section 106 seminar' and watch the local authorities outmatching each other in size of gain packages.

Many of those working in local government attribute conflict over gain to the 'no-can-do' mentality of developers who will 'naturally' wish to maximise profits and reduce opportunity costs. They in turn balk at the suggestions that their own expectations are inflated. Others, however, are more circumspect and argue that tensions are an inevitable product of the contrasting motives and objectives of the public and private sectors. These respondents argued that a meeting of minds is possible, especially if policy is clarified and different groups get together early enough to sort out areas of disagreement. For their part, a number of RSLs called for more national guidance to clarify the use of agreements. They argued that it is often the case that the RSLs have no input into the early form and content of Section 106 agreements, even though further down the line they are expected to manage the new housing units.

Levels of extracted gain

How much gain is generated and in what form is perhaps the central concern affecting all development sites, but this issue seems to be of particular importance on brownfield sites where many respondents suggested that gain requirements should be more closely regulated and prevented from becoming an unwarranted hindrance to development.

A key threat identified by housebuilders was the 'lack of appreciation' of development economics displayed by some planning authorities and, perhaps more critically, by their political masters. Here a Catch 22 was observed. Thus on the one hand, developers often deride planners for not understanding commercial reality, but on the other, planners are unable to make informed decisions over the contents of a Section 106 if they are excluded from the financial negotiations between landowner and developer. Without such an open book, the planning authority is only guessing at what gain might be deliverable from a particular site. In practice this means that authorities will often go for what they believe to be the maximum possible gain and work backwards, if necessary, from that point. Likewise, developers will conceal commercially sensitive information and seek to make only modest concessions to the planning authority. So the two parties begin their negotiations at opposite ends of a very broad spectrum and only slowly and painfully work towards a compromise.

This strategy lies behind much of the conflict centring on gain. To overcome the problem, one authority argued for 'more open discussions between all parties particularly on land value, housing development cost and infrastructure needs', although another conceded that 'developers are very unlikely to share financial information'.

Dealing with uncertainty

Uncertainty exists at two levels. First, there is the uncertainty that derives from inconsistent policy application, and second, the uncertainty that has been a long-standing feature of the entire gain approach. The critical issues tend to relate to the clarity and scope of policies established by the planning authority and the procedures and protocols followed during Section 106 negotiations. The process of negotiation was commonly held to be 'ad hoc and uncertain', not least when more than one local authority department (usually planning and housing) were involved.

This highlights the concerns that many respondents shared over the apparent absence of corporate working within local authorities (see Chapter 10). This is a particular problem with affordable housing, where housing departments may have a clear view of the contribution that planning could make to realising their housing strategy, but either do not share this view with their planning colleagues or are ignored. It is not uncommon, for example, for developers to be told different things by different departments regarding the type of affordable housing that they may be asked to provide. Alternatively, they end up providing types of unit unsuited to local need.

One RSL argued strongly that planning departments are being asked to 'lead on too many fronts' with an inevitable over-stretching of resources. But at the same time, local policy prioritises the need for flexibility, encouraging officers to negotiate on a site-by-site basis. This strategy has both an up and a down side. On the down side, planning resources are further stretched. On the up side, it implies the flexibility (if uncertainty) that is necessary to take into account the particular conditions that apply on different sites. Collectively, the response agreed that greater consistency in establishing charges locally would be beneficial, perhaps supporting the tariffs system suggested in the 2001 Planning Green Paper.

The added complication with affordable housing is the uncertainty over the willingness of developers to make this type of contribution on-site. This is in part due to the complexity of the system affecting all Section 106 obligations and also – in relation to affordable housing – perceived problems with the mixing of different tenures on a single site. Developers have always been uncertain and wary of the impact that affordable units will have on the marketability of other units. In the past, this has led them to tuck away those units to be transferred to a housing association in the least advantageous corner of the site (DEMOS, 1999). More recently, they have pushed for the more extensive use of commuted sums, arguing that – particularly on high-value sites – these sums will enable a local authority to build a great deal more affordable homes elsewhere. Many authorities have judged the use of this strategy a success, but it remains to be seen how far this de facto linkage fee has diluted on-site planning gain. The extent to which changes to the system of planning obligations proposed in 2001 may also reduce on-site contributions is another interesting topic for future examination.

What is significant is that the actual level of contribution secured through planning gain over the period 1999 to 2000 was limited to fewer than 4,000 units (2.19 per cent of total build) nationally. So the strategy remains contentious and uncertain and, at the same time, fairly ineffective in national terms. The delivery is not helped by the complexity of delivery mechanisms. Some authorities simply accept commuted sums, others get developers to build homes and then transfer them with discount to RSLs. Sometimes the planning gain element is mixed with grant funding, on other occasions it is used to completely replace SHG. Elsewhere, affordable units are actually built by the RSL on land transferred at less than market value from the developer. Exactly how units become affordable and this process of changing hands is possibly one of the most under-studied aspects of the planning and affordable housing debate and one which, like obligations and gain in general, is likely to become increasingly important and contentious over the next few years.

10

Coordination

Local government

Local government has existed in some form in the UK since Anglo-Saxon times, although the relationship between national and local government has not always been an easy one. Thus local government has sometimes been seen (and even on occasions viewed itself) as an alternative and opposing power base, as a source of inconsistency in practice, and frequently as a profligate and inefficient drain on resources. Such views have always been balanced, however, by the obvious potential of local government to more easily respond to the needs and priorities of local populations, deliver national objectives at the local level, and extend the democratic mandate and responsibility downwards (Wilson and Game, 1994, pp. 30–1).

In recent times, however, control of local government has become increasingly centralised, and it is important to note that local government is wholly subservient to national government, which remains sovereign. Thus national government has the power to disperse or retain power as it sees fit. Nowhere has this been more apparent than in the areas of planning and housing, where despite devolving considerable responsibility to the local level, central government had always retained the whip-hand (see Chapters 2 and 4). The financing of local government (and therefore also local tax raising) has also increasingly been tightly controlled from the centre, a trend established by the Conservative administrations of the 1980s and 1990s and continued by subsequent Labour administrations.

Elcock (1994) argues that local authorities have three main functions: 'the provision of services for citizens; the management of their resources of money, land and people; and planning to reduce uncertainty about the future'. The traditional pattern of administration and decision-making of these various activities has been a series of departments, each answering directly and in isolation to a separate committee of councillors, and relating their work (only occasionally) to other departments in the authority (see Table 10.1). Increasingly, however, these traditional forms of local government management have come to be regarded as inadequate because:

- They fail to deliver coordinated responses to issues of concern, including to policy development or the use of resources.
- They fail to adequately address the needs of the users of the services.

Table 10.1 Traditional (hierarchical) management structures in local authorities (Wilson and Game, 1994, p. 73)

Departments	*Committees*
Local authorities are ORGANISED into DEPARTMENTS.	Local authorities are GOVERNED BY councillors OR elected members, who meet regularly and publicly in FULL COUNCIL to take authoritative decisions for their local area.
These departments are staffed by APPOINTED OFFICERS and OTHER EMPLOYEES – administrative, professional, technical and clerical staff, manual workers – who legally are the PAID SERVANTS of the elected council.	Most councils DELEGATE MUCH OF THEIR WORK to COMMITTEES AND SUB-COMMITTEES of councillors which concentrate on a particular area of the council's work and are responsible for determining the council's policy in that area.
These officers and staff IMPLEMENT COUNCIL POLICY as determined by its councillors, and run the authority on a day-to-day basis.	
Departments can be divided into SERVICE DEPARTMENTS, which provide a service directly to the public, and CENTRAL or CO-ORDINATING DEPARTMENTS, which provide a service for the authority as a whole.	Each committee will have a CHAIR(PERSON), who chairs its meetings, speaks and acts on its behalf, and liases with relevant officers.
Each department has a CHIEF OFFICER, usually a professional specialist in the work of the department and responsible for it to a committee and its chair.	Council meetings are presided over by the MAYOR or CHAIR(PERSON) OF THE COUNCIL, elected annually by and from all members of the council.
Most authorities have a CHIEF EXECUTIVE, the head of the council's paid service, responsible for coordinating the operation and policy of the council, usually through a CHIEF OFFICERS' MANAGEMENT TEAM.	The LEADER OF THE COUNCIL, its key political figure, is generally the elected leader of the majority or largest party group on the council.
	Most authorities have a coordinating POLICY (AND RESOURCES) COMMITTEE of mainly senior councillors, usually chaired by the leader.

A council's POLICY is the outcome of the formal and informal interaction between elected councillors and their appointed officers.

Councils have considerable discretion over their internal organisation; no two councils, therefore, will have precisely the same departmental and committee structures.

- New approaches to public sector management increasingly stress the new values of economy, efficiency and effectiveness – the 'three Es' (see Fig. 10.1) – which local government has not always delivered.

The consequence of the pressures for change, particularly through the 1980s, has been an increasing diversity in the management arrangements of individual authorities, and generally a strengthening of the central executive in authorities in order to better coordinate activities and resources. These trends began in the 1970s, when a series of

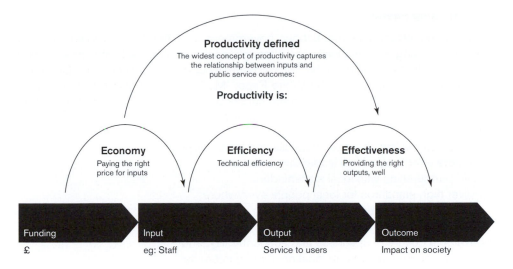

Productivity defined
The widest concept of productivity captures
the relationship between inputs and
public service outcomes:

Productivity is:

Economy
Paying the right
price for inputs

Efficiency
Technical efficiency

Effectiveness
Providing the right
outputs, well

| Funding | Input | Output | Outcome |
| £ | eg: Staff | Service to users | Impact on society |

*10.1 The three Es (*Public Services Productivity: Meeting the Challenge, *Public Services Productivity Panel, 2001, p. 4).*

reports to individual authorities recommended a variety of approaches to deliver a more 'corporate management' style (Elcock, 1994, pp. 266–79). Approaches included:

* establishment of policy committees and resource subcommittees responsible for the overall coordination of policy, as well as the management of resources;
* appointing a Chief Executive Officer to head a management team of chief officers and so coordinate management and policy advice;
* streamlining committee structures to increase coordination and reduce the number of committees and their tendency to become preoccupied with matters of detail;
* fewer departments in order to streamline activities and coordinate compatible service areas;
* development of central policy and research units in order to coordinate departmental policies through corporate planning and to innovate new policy directions free of the pressures of day-to-day statutory responsibilities.

Despite the changes, local government has continued to be criticised – not least by central government – whilst interest in local government elections has plummeted. Recently, ministers have argued that:

> Too often within a council the members and officers take the paternalistic view that it is for them to decide what services are to be provided, on the basis of what suits the council as a service provider. The interests of the public come a poor second place. The culture is still one where more spending and more taxes are seen as the simple solution rather than exploring how to get more out of the available resources.
>
> (DETR, 1998g, para. 1.10)

A modernising agenda

Following the election of the Labour government in 1997 the approach to local government changed dramatically, and although resources remained tight, the simplistic pressure to externalise services through Compulsory Competitive Tendering (CCT) was abandoned. Correspondingly, the White Paper 'Modern Local Government, In Touch with the People' (DETR, 1998g) and the subsequent Local Government Act of 1999 supported change within local government in order to:

- strengthen the links between councils and local people;
- promote effective political leadership and vision;
- build partnerships with local stakeholders;
- deliver high standards for local people everywhere;
- promote and share best practice;
- tackle failure;
- develop a culture of openness and accountability; and
- become more responsive to local needs and interests.

The 1998 White Paper argued: 'A modern council – or authority – which puts people first will seek to provide services which bear comparison with the best. Not just the best that other authorities provide, but with the best that is on offer from both the public and private sectors' (DETR 1998g). Moreover, in order to reinvigorate the local political process, directly elected mayors and cabinet government structures were advocated, not least to move towards more joined-up and effective local government.

The 2001 White Paper 'Strong Local Leadership – Quality Public Services' reinforced the trend by aiming to return greater independence to local government (at least to those that performed well). The paper outlined a new streamlined approach to Best Value (see Chapter 6) 'to enable authorities to use it as an opportunity for radical challenge rather than a bureaucratic process' (DTLR, 2001e, p. 34), so justifying the overall reduction in national performance indicators proposed for 2002/2003 from 123 indicators to 95 (in planning from seven to five). At the same time authorities were to be subjected to Comprehensive Performance Assessments and classified as high-performing, striving, coasting and poor-performing, with extra freedoms granted to high-performing authorities, and powers removed from those seen to be failing. The carrot-and-stick approach envisaged a new partnership between central and local government based on authorities themselves (within limits) taking greater responsibility for their actions.

Nevertheless, changing the structures and approaches of local government is likely to be a long and difficult challenge. This is because delivering change – as opposed to defining the desired outputs – depends on changing the processes (public and private) that actually deliver change, processes which are often subject to long and established modes of working and considerable in-built inertia. Thus, when examining the Urban Task Force report (1999), for example, it soon becomes clear that almost all of the 100 plus recommendations concern the processes rather than the products of change.

Urban governance

In his famous essay 'A City is Not a Tree', Christopher Alexander (1965) postulated on the ordering structures of successful cities. The answer, he suggested, can be found in complexity, where separate elements of the city interact with each other in a complex series of overlapping relationships rather than in neat orderly structures imposed by the human mind. This, he argued, reflects the complex and exciting variety found in traditional towns, whilst the excessively logical, highly zoned neatness found in many planned towns never allows the natural, proper and necessary overlaps to be created.

This notion of a complex interwoven web of urban relationships, responsibilities and processes underpinning the adaptation and change of cities is a powerful one. The Urban Task Force argued that:

> In a well-governed city, urban living and civic pride go hand in hand. Excellence in urban management is expected, but also rewarded, and anti-social behaviour is minimised. Research and innovation are encouraged, and the responsibilities of government are consistently reviewed in response to changing circumstances. Most importantly, the well-governed city must establish a clear vision, where all policies and programmes contribute to high quality urban development. . . . It is a city which is therefore characterised by strong political leadership, a proactive approach to spatial planning, effective management, and commitment to improve its skills-base.
>
> (Urban Task Force, 1999, pp. 43–4)

At the heart of such a city the Urban Task Force envisaged a planning system which is strategic, flexible and accountable, in which the planning process is regarded as a positive means for guiding change and delivering regeneration objectives, rather than the reactive, negative process it is often perceived to be. However, the governance processes that influence the delivery and management of housing areas extend far beyond land-use planning.

The main processes of governance might be broadly divided into ten key areas (see Table 10.2), although none of these exist in isolation and each is intimately tied to and dependent upon all the others to meet its objectives (broadly defined). Each nevertheless exists within its own legislative framework(s) and operates through its own bureaucratic regime. Consequently, the activities of the public sector are too often criticised as being compartmentalised and uncoordinated, while key cross-policy concerns such as urban sustainability or urban design are left to fall through the gaps between individual responsibilities.

Key amongst the recommendations of the Urban Task Force (1999, p. 307), therefore, was the need to achieve joined-up approaches in government – 'to agree common objectives, to monitor joint achievements and to evaluate success'. This might be important between the different departments operating at national and local government levels, between national and local government tiers, between the different tiers of local government in two-tier areas, and between all these tiers and the key urban regeneration agencies established by government. If, for example, the interests of the ten key areas of urban governance are considered against key tenets of the broad urban renaissance agenda (Carmona, 2001a, p. 182), then the overlapping interests are clearly seen and the case for coordination becomes obvious (see Table 10.2). Discussion in Chapter 5 revealed the importance of appropriate urban governance in delivering just one key strategic housing objective – the redevelopment of brownfield land.

Table 10.2 Governance responsibilities and interests (adapted from Carmona, 2001a, p. 30)

National government (major) departmental responsibilities EP = English Partnerships EH = English Heritage		Key local government (usual) departmental responsibilities CC = county level DC = district level	Urban governance processes (excluding fiscal processes)	Network of influence	Key urban renaissance aspirational tenets from government policy
ODPM		Housing (CC)	Housing policy		Sustainable transport
DfT		Highways (CC)	Transport planning		Intensification
DfT/ODPM		Highways (CC), Environmental services (DC).Recreation (DC)	Urban management		Mixing-uses
ODPM	(EP)	Economic development (CC and DC)	Urban regeneration		Vitality and viability
ODPM	(EP)	Land reclamation	Land reclamation		Access to services
ODPM		Planning (CC and DC)	Land use planning		Management
DCMS	(EH)	Planning (DC)	Built environment conservation		Design
DfES		Education (CC)	Skills, education and employment		People and cars
Dept of Health Dept of Social Security		Social services (CC)	Health, leisure and social services		Cleaning up
Home Office		Police authority (CC)	Crime prevention		Vision

Note: DCMS – Department for Culture, Media and Sport
DfES – Department for Education and Skills
DfT – Department for Transport
ODPM – Office of the Deputy Prime Minister

The joining-up agenda

Clearly the success of efforts to deliver more sustainable housing (alongside all the other objectives in the wider urban agenda) will depend on the linkages between the processes – on filling the gaps, forming the partnerships (public to private and public to public), demonstrating the commitment and vision and on joining-up all the efforts. Rudlin and Falk (1999, pp. 252–9), for example, conclude their book *Building the 21st Century Home* by postulating on what makes for successful regeneration processes, a list that applies equally well to planning for housing. They conclude that stakeholders should:

- devise a shared vision – to change attitudes and ensure coherent, integrated outcomes;
- establish the impetus for change – the people who want change and an overwhelming reason for change;
- promote a balance of projects – using the right tool for the job;
- have the guts to innovate – being prepared to take risks and go against the tide;
- aim to generate enough yield – there needs to be an adequate payoff for investors;
- organise for concerted action – building management capacity and partnerships to use the funds effectively;
- monitor results – delivering, evaluating and learning from lasting improvements on the ground;
- resource the process – without necessary funds (public and private) all efforts are doomed to failure.

The first of these is of key importance in complex local authorities and requires a move away from the established sectorial approach to local governance. In Wycombe District Council (1999), for example, there has been a strong emphasis on joined-up thinking in both projects and committees. Thus key development projects will often be driven by joint teams from development control, urban design, housing, transport (county), and environmental health. The approach is aided by the matrix structuring of the authority and a vision based on four strategic priorities ranging across traditional professional remits – a caring community, a healthy environment, a thriving economy, and value for money. Thus, planning and housing relate to all four objectives, each of which is driven by a committee with cross-departmental membership. For example, there is no formal planning committee, only an environment committee (and delegated planning panel), which considers planning issues as well as other environmental concerns. Similarly, the corporate objectives for housing at Wycombe are fully integrated with planning concerns (see Fig. 10.2), while the housing chapter in the local plan is coordinated with the Corporate Housing Strategy prepared by the Housing Department.

In Purbeck, in an attempt to move away from sectorial thinking, the development plan has been restructured using a number of cross-cutting themes to organise policy. Hence, for example, the traditional Built Environment and Natural Environment chapters are now replaced by an 'Ensuring Quality of Life' chapter, which addresses the need to encourage social interaction and enhance the quality of people's surroundings. The plan also has chapters dealing with 'Conserving natural and cultural assets', 'Avoiding hazards', and 'Meeting economic and social needs' (Purbeck District Council, 1999).

Guidance in PPG3 (DETR, 2000a, para. 13) confirms the government's intention that local planning authorities should work jointly with housing departments to evaluate and

Aim:
Within environmental constraints, to give priority to local housing needs

Objectives:
➤ Providing sufficient affordable housing to meet identified local needs in the long term
➤ Promoting sustainable and self-sufficient communities through housing initiatives
➤ Optimising the use of housing stock in respect of condition, occupancy and 'lifetime' homes principles
➤ Ensuring the provision of an adequate and appropriate range of accommodation types to meet identified local needs
➤ Identifying sites to meet the structure plan allocation for new homes for all housing needs
➤ Identifying and acquiring, where necessary, sites suitable for development to maintain the affordable housing building programme
➤ Promoting the best use of urban land and buildings to meet local housing needs.

10.2 Wycombe District Council (1999) housing objectives.

meet the range of local housing needs. However, as recently as 1994 a review of planning for affordable housing revealed that although close liaison between housing and planning departments was a feature of many authorities, in others tensions remained, with local councillors actively challenging the need for affordable housing provision and the role of planning in its delivery. The work nevertheless concluded that 'Close liaison between planning and housing departments in local authorities is essential for the development of clear policy and the assessment of housing needs' (Barlow *et al.*, 1994, pp. 49–50). Crucially this also allows the coordination of policy documents, in particular the development plan, housing strategy and investment programme.

More recent advice from the Chartered Institute of Housing and the Local Government Association has warned that 'It is important not to under-estimate the difficulties in corporate working. Some new structures have not worked as intended', and there are additional difficulties of coordination in areas where district and county councils split responsibilities. There are also new tensions to be managed between operational and strategic management, and between cultures of different professional groups. Thus the skills that managers have acquired through years of local government work may not equip them for the roles and functions of the future. Nevertheless, these changes may also 'create new opportunities to break down the barriers between departments, and to find new ways to do things' (Goss and Blackaby, 1998, p. 12). Unfortunately, the work revealed that whilst a considerable shift has taken place towards cross-departmental working, for example linking housing and community care agendas, its scope and effectiveness varied widely, with joint working between housing and planning identified as a particular area of weakness. The problem leads to housing strategies being developed with little reference to information about housing capacity or private market provision, and development plans and development control decisions being formulated without due consideration to social housing objectives (Goss and Blackaby, 1998, p. 45).

The report argues that it is essential that planning, economic development and land-use policies are integrated with the housing strategy and vice versa. In this regard the priorities of individual services such as housing and planning should constitute the corporate priorities of the authority (not be added as another layer on top), whilst plans and strategies should be fully integrated across departments. The London borough of Hillingdon offers an example where the maximisation of affordable social housing forms a borough-wide corporate objective. This objective filters into the policies and working practices of the housing and planning departments, with a dedicated team in the planning department to deal with affordable housing applications (or those which should contain affordable housing), procedures to fast-track planning applications, and a determination amongst planning officers to come to terms with the needs of landowners, developers, RSLs and fellow officers in the housing department (Goss and Blackaby, 1998, p. 47).

Research on corporate working practices in Wales revealed that success typically depends on satisfactory consultation between departments, often built on the back of informal liaison based on personal relationships. These informal relationships on the whole were considered effective in the mainly small rural authorities surveyed, although the strict separation of committee structures and their often very different aspirations undermined a corporate response to problems, particularly the bunker mentality of councillors (Tewdwr-Jones *et al.*, 1998, p. 87). Solutions proffered included setting up joint subcommittees or housing strategy committees for housing and planning including elected members and senior officers, establishing policy and resources committees with a broad remit to resolve strategic issues, additional training for members on overlap issues, and coordination of development plan and housing strategy timetables to coordinate consultation activities. Generally these two documents – development plans and housing strategies – were not as well coordinated as might be expected, with housing departments in particular unsatisfied with the limited role they played in site allocation for housing, or indeed as consultees on planning applications. In Wales the desire for corporate working and a more integrated planning/housing relationship was strong, although actual practice rarely delivered on the good intentions.

Community strategies

Since October 2000 local authorities in England have been required to produce community strategies as a means to address (amongst other concerns) better corporate working (DETR, 2000h, para. 10), specifically to:

- deliver the economic, social and environmental well-being of communities;
- allow local communities to articulate their aspirations, needs and priorities;
- coordinate the action of the council, and of the public, private, voluntary and community organisations that operate locally;
- focus and shape existing and future activity of those organisations so that they effectively meet community needs and aspirations; and
- contribute to the achievement of sustainable development both locally and more widely.

Community strategies are particularly significant because they are largely about joining-up the broadest range of contributions to the future of a local authority area, involving the broadest range of stakeholders to construct a vision. They are also about linking and delivering the range of related policy frameworks, including planning policy and housing strategies. Thus the 2003 Planning and Compulsory Purchase Act placed a duty on local authorities to have regard to the local community strategy when preparing their local development documents (Section 18).

Early evidence has indicated that community strategies most commonly cover cross-cutting concerns such as community safety, health improvement, improving the environment, economic investment, tackling social exclusion, and development; and that the experience is helping to join up programmes and increase partnership working (Local Government Association, 2001). In Salford, the authority has pre-empted government advice, and has had a community strategy in place for over ten years. During that time the strategy has evolved to become the key departure point for policy-making within the city. In 2001 a new Community Plan was published establishing the policy direction for the city for the next five years. The UDP, which was adopted in 1995, is now being rolled forward and will build on the broad vision outlined in the Community Plan. To ensure this happens, nine area plans are being prepared to respond to the views of the nine area community committees involved in drawing up the Community Plan. These area plans will have the status of supplementary planning guidance and will provide the detailed context for the UDP.

Salford's vision is to

> Create a city where people choose to live and work. We aim to improve the quality of life of all our citizens by creating an economically prosperous city with a buoyant and competitive economy; creating and maintaining strong, safe, healthy and sustainable communities where all citizens can participate to the fullest extent in decisions which affect their communities; providing a better education for all, to enable children and young people to thrive and fulfil their potential; creating a city that is good to live in by providing quality homes and a clean and healthy environment.
>
> (RTPI Think Tank on Modernising Local Government, 2001, p. 27)

Seven cross-cutting themes are established to deliver the vision, with the UDP and housing strategies having the key roles in creating 'a city that's good to live in'. Planning, housing and community development therefore go hand in hand.

The London Borough of Camden's community strategy – 'Our Camden Our Future' – establishes a vision to address the huge inequalities in the borough, in part by harnessing the equally huge opportunities. Six key aims are identified:

• a place with stronger communities
• a safer place
• a healthier place
• an economically successful place
• an attractive and environmentally friendly place
• a place with excellent services.

Against each aim are listed the key plans and strategies for their implementation, with, for example, the UDP identified as the key delivery mechanism for an attractive and environmentally friendly place. Both Camden and Salford have gone through a process of partnership creation and consultation to develop their community strategies. In both cases, in order to monitor the implementation of the strategies over time, a range of specific targets have been established under each key strategic theme (96 in Camden and 55 in Salford). Each authority aims to produce annual action plans to set out new targets and identify how they will be met. Camden's first action plan systematically describes each target and identifies:

- When the target will be met.
- Who will take the lead in that process.
- Who else will be involved.
- What actions will be required to meet the target.
- What resources will be required to achieve the target.
- How progress will be monitored.
- How success will be demonstrated.

Partnership approaches

Approaches like those at Wycombe, Purbeck, Salford and Camden are important because they attempt to organise local government around issues and objectives, rather than on the basis of organisational convenience, traditional sectors or professional loyalties. They also attempt to monitor the delivery of complex cross-cutting themes. They therefore have the potential to join-up internal working arrangements and the provision of services. More integrated means of working, however, are far from the norm. The Social Exclusion Unit (2000, p. 75), for example, in its 'National Strategy for Neighbourhood Renewal' found that there is a lack of joined-up thinking across all levels of government, at national, regional, local and neighbourhood levels, ensuring that both policy frameworks and the delivery of initiatives remain uncoordinated and compromised. They argue that partnership working is required: between services, such as housing, planning, education, the police, etc. (often within the same organisations); between levels of government, such as central, regional, subregional (county), local (district or borough) and neighbourhood; between providers and customers; and between sectors, institutions and communities, including the public, private, voluntary and community sectors.

The idea of partnerships across all these levels features heavily in 'third way' approaches to urban governance and most authorities already participate in a wide variety of partnership activities (both internally and externally to the authority). Research by Newchurch and Co. (1999) identifies nine key components to such partnership approaches:

- Partnership is a process where two or more parties cooperate and work together.
- A partnership process brings together and uses the partners' resources more economically, efficiently and effectively.
- Partnerships are a means of achieving outputs and outcomes that are important in relation to the needs of the local community.
- Partners develop a commitment to an agenda for joint or coordinated action.
- The partnership process involves planning each partner's contribution, what is expected of them and how they will benefit.
- The partnership process involves the formulation of effective leadership of the joint or coordinated action being taken.
- A partnership process must involve decision-making processes which respect the needs of all the partners.
- A partnership process includes setting out specific goals and evaluating the success of the partnership's action against them.
- The partnership process provides for an assessment of the partnership's function – not merely whether the agreed goals are being achieved, but if the partnership's work is still relevant to evolving community needs and priorities.

Follow-up work (Newchurch and Co., 2000) revealed that although the costs of partner-ship working can be significant (particularly during initiation) and can often create barriers to the formation of partnerships, once established, partnerships bring significant benefits in terms of better networking, joint thinking and vision-making, access to shared information, access to funding, and more focused and therefore effective service delivery. The work revealed a number of characteristics of successful partnerships:

- Partnership organisation attributes:
  1. commitment, honesty and trust
  2. an understanding of different partners' limitations and culture
  3. a willingness to share advantages and disadvantages.

- Partnership roles and objectives:
  1. a clear set-up, purpose and evaluation process
  2. a win-win situation with benefits for all partners
  3. identification of self-interest/aims for each partner.

- Partner representative skills:
  1. a good leader and decision-maker
  2. partners enthusiastic about the objectives/cause of the partnership
  3. professional, efficient, innovative and open-minded partners.

Increasingly a range of innovative approaches to inter-agency working have been adopted by local authorities in an attempt to break down traditional, monolithic local government models. Nevertheless, substantial barriers to effective collaboration remain, including vested interests, short-term thinking, problems of maintaining accountability, the sheer complexity of many tasks, and divergent professional and organisational cultures (Hambleton *et al.*, 1996a).

The instigation of Local Strategic Partnerships (LSPs) represents one solution promoted in the Urban White Paper *Our Towns and Cities: The Future*. LSPs aim to bring together the local authority, all service providers, local businesses and community groups to:

- develop the Community Strategy as a long-term vision for the whole plan area (see above);
- agree priorities for action and monitor delivery;
- undertake joint analysis and action; and
- coordinate the work of more local or specific partnerships.

Thus LSPs are not meant to simply replicate existing partnership structures, they aim to rationalise and coordinate existing activities (DETR, 2000d, p. 34), and are encouraged across local authority boundaries. Research on LSPs in the field of urban regeneration confirms that they help to raise the profile of policy and projects and extend the scope of joint working; although the process of building the necessary trust between partners can be very lengthy. Fundamentally it also requires a willingness on all sides to question established practices (including budgetary priorities) and a strong vision of what the partnership can achieve (Russell, 2001). Key questions for such partnerships are presented in Fig. 10.3, whilst the responsibility to produce the Community Strategy presents a potentially powerful focus for their efforts that will also deliver lasting influence on the full range of local authority activities.

Stage 1: Clarifying the purpose of the partnership

➤ Why have it?
➤ What added value can it bring?

Stage 2: Examining the internal and external operational environment

➤ What are the local needs and opportunities?
➤ What are the relevant policy developments and trends?
➤ What is the partnership able to deliver collectively and via its members?

Stage 3: Agreeing a vision and making strategic choices

➤ What should the vision be?
➤ Whose vision should it be?
➤ What are the main routes for arriving at it?
➤ How will we know we are going in the right direction?

Stage 4: Translating the strategy into an action plan

➤ What activities will take place under each strategic objective?
➤ Who will be responsible for planning?
➤ Who will be responsible for delivery?
➤ What targets and milestones should be met?
➤ Who will monitor and evaluate?
➤ What steps are individual organisations taking to build their capacity for partnership and joint working?

Stage 5: Squaring the circle

➤ What will the accountability mechanisms be?
➤ How will the partnership review its activities to inform its future policy?
➤ How will it review its partnership structures and mechanisms to ensure they remain appropriate?
➤ How will good practice lessons be disseminated?

10.3 Key questions for strategic partnerships (Russell, 2001).

At the construction end of the housing development process partnering has also been increasingly stressed both for private housebuilders and in the social housing sector as part of the 'Rethinking Construction' agenda inspired by Sir John Egan's 1998 report (DETR, 1998h). It is seen as a means to enter into long-term relationships with suppliers (including designers and contractors) in order to question established working relationships and reduce conflict and inefficiency. Housing Corporation funding streams, for example, are now tied to compliance audits, to examine (amongst other issues) how RSLs are addressing the Egan agenda, particularly the role of client organisations in forming partnerships for quality-based solutions and continuous improvement (Housing Corporation, 2000, pp. 2–3). The agenda goes beyond construction, however, with partnering supported anywhere where a service is offered as a means of improving coordination and trust (Drury, 2000). In one form or another, therefore, partnerships are supported to smooth the delivery of strategic through to detailed policy objectives and to engender greater cross-disciplinary understanding.

Education and community involvement

In the UK, the need for greater cross-disciplinary awareness and training represented a key outcome of a national consultation exercise held on how to improve the 'Quality of Town and Country'. The clear support in the consultation exercise for improved training in matters of environmental awareness and design for a wide range of interest groups, including local politicians, all-built environment professionals, developers, community groups and particularly children, was of particular interest as a cross-disciplinary perception (DoE, 1996b, pp. 12–14). More recently the dearth of a wide range of skills in the development professions was recognised by the Urban Task Force (1999, pp. 157–67), which argued for a greater emphasis on cross-disciplinary skills and an end to the heavily compartmentalised development industry where individuals specialised in their own area and therefore failed to gain a broader understanding of other disciplines and the wider process. Particular gaps were identified in:

- design
- project management
- proactive planning
- community involvement
- urban management
- development finance and project appraisal
- infrastructure development
- land assembly.

Furthermore, the Task Force identified that the skills deficit existed right across the range of professions involved in delivering new development and contributed to the bunker mentality of the development industry and the ongoing failure to work together. In the area of planning, the 2001 Planning Green Paper argued that the planning profession in particular was suffering from a shortage of properly qualified planners, and needed to be made more attractive to appeal to the calibre of people required to deliver the reforming agenda. The lack of expertise amongst elected members was also singled out for action (DTLR, 2001a, paras 6.38–6.40). On the development side, the Egan agenda (see p. 165), with its goal of modernising construction, initiated a process of rethinking the skills base of housing providers under the auspices of the newly created Housing Forum.

A further important, if often forgotten, set of stakeholders to whom the whole development process largely remains a mystery, but to whom fully inclusive partnerships should logically extend, is the wider community. Today planning-related issues (including the provision and location of new homes) are rarely out of the headlines and represent significant concerns at the local political level. Parfect and Power (1997, pp. 119–20) argue that

> In order that informed debate and intelligent consideration take place on such issues, it is of course necessary that participants have some clear awareness or grasp of the criteria and processes involved in resolving the issues. . . . This applies to all participants – public as well as professional, lay as well as expert.

Nevertheless, for most lay participants, awareness of the built environment is derived from personal experience (most often in an oppositional role) and from the media, rather than from formal education.

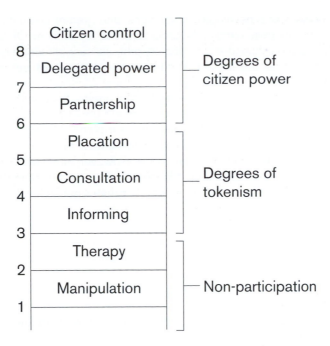

10.4 Arnstein's ladder of citizen participation.

Involving end-users and local populations in the development process nevertheless offers an effective means to pursue wider design awareness and educational goals. Again, the cross-disciplinary 'Quality in Town and Country' consultation exercise clearly indicated a developing industry-wide concern to involve local communities more fully in the development decision-making processes (DoE, 1996b, pp. 8–10). Unfortunately, this commitment in theory is less frequently translated into practice – at least beyond statutory minimum requirements. In that respect there is a significant difference between consultation and actual participation.

In 1969 Sherry Arnstein developed her still valuable and much quoted ladder of citizen participation to illustrate eight possible levels of citizen involvement (see Fig. 10.4). She argued that

> The idea of citizen participation is a little like eating spinach: no one is against it in principle because it is good for you. Participation of the governed in their government is, in theory, the cornerstone of democracy – a revered idea that is vigorously applauded by virtually everyone. The applause is reduced to polite handclaps, however, when this principle is advocated by the have-not[s] . . . And when the have-nots define participation as redistribution of power.
>
> (Arnstein, 1969, p. 216)

In this respect the provision of housing is no different to any other area of public policy – the more power you shift to local populations, the less power resides in the hands of those financing, developing, designing and politically sanctioning the project. This is a trade-off that society makes, and a trade-off that balances revised power relationships against: the potential for early resolution of conflicts; collaborative and supportive arrangements leading to more sustainable outcomes; added value through more considered policies and development solutions; and greater commitment to final outcomes through broader ownership of the processes that led to them. Of course, even the most well-meaning and exhaustive participatory process cannot resolve clashes over fundamental values, and so the impact of participation should not be exaggerated (Christie *et al.*, 2002, p. 4).

The further processes move up Arnstein's ladder, the greater the transfer of power to citizens. In the UK, planning authorities are required by statute to consult local residents and interest groups both when preparing development plans and when considering planning applications. They are also encouraged to consult the same groups when preparing supplementary forms of planning guidance. However, more fundamental forms of participation are not required by statute, the result being that most efforts remain at the level of tokenism. Nevertheless, where it occurs, greater public involvement in the development of policy can help – in theory – to:

- develop and refine designs and policies and fully explore alternatives;
- ensure that the gap between professional and lay perceptions is minimised and build trust between the different parties;
- build consensus about appropriate levels of intervention and prescription;
- give extra weight to policies and guidance in an area which is frequently challenged;
- ensure that amenity interests and design professionals are working towards mutually agreed goals;
- develop a sense of local ownership for policy, guidance and development solutions;
- build community capacity and enthusiasm to ensure that the community has an ongoing influence in their area;
- spread knowledge and awareness of professional and planning objectives;
- tap into local sources of knowledge and expertise;
- speed up post-participation decision-making.

Such arguments influenced the preparation of the 2001 Planning Green Paper, which envisaged a more concerted attempt to involve communities in the preparation of planning policy – Local Development Frameworks – and in making development control decisions. Under Section 17 of the 2003 Act, authorities will be required to prepare a Statement of Community Involvement as part of the LDF 'setting out how the community should be involved in both the continuing review of the Framework and in commenting on significant planning applications' (DTLR, 2001a, p. 17). In the case of large developments, compliance with the terms of the statement would then become a material consideration in order to encourage developers and communities to work together to plan developments, while the statement would provide 'a benchmark for applicants for planning permission about what is expected of them'. In the case of planning policy, the move to local action plans is intended to stir community interest in planning their localities through – preferably – direct community participation. The provisions, however, sit uneasily beside the major thrust of the Planning Act, to speed up both plan-making and development control processes. Nevertheless, if community involvement happens early enough in the policy writing and development processes, it may confirm a major thesis of this book, that by positively planning earlier in the process, time and conflict can be saved further down the line. Community engagement will nevertheless need to be more fundamental than is currently often the case.

Although more fundamental forms of participation take many different forms, they can be broadly conceptualised as top-down or bottom-up approaches. Top-down approaches tend to be instigated by public authorities and/or developers, usually as a means to gauge public opinion and gain public support for proposals. Frequently, therefore, development options or policy proposals will already be prepared as the focus for an arranged participation exercise. The danger of such approaches is that the agenda may already be largely set, leading to the manipulation of local opinion, rather than to genuine participation. On the positive front, such approaches may offer an effective use of resources by using professional expertise to mobilise, coordinate and interpret community opinions. Bottom-up approaches are instigated and led from grass-roots level, usually reacting to some perceived opportunity or threat. Such exercises can offer highly effective means to influence political decision-making processes, but suffer from their time-consuming nature (for all parties involved), because of the commitment required to build up expertise, and from the frequent failure to link aspirations clearly to economic resources. Ideally, whatever approach is adopted, the aim either over the short or longer term should be to develop a mutually advantageous partnership between public, private and community interests, whilst avoiding the dangers of 'consultation overload' (Christie *et al.*, 2002, p. 10) – a rare experience in a minority of long-term development/ regeneration projects when opportunities for participation have become too numerous.

A number of publications now categorise the wide array of participation approaches as a means to encourage the better choice of technique. Recent examples include 'Participation Works!' from the New Economics Foundation (1998) and 'Involving Local Communities in Urban Design' from the Urban Design Group (1998). Together these reports identify 78 separate techniques, many of which have their origin in the US, where community-based participation is long established, and both widespread and well organised at grass-roots level (see Fig. 10.5).

The best known techniques are 'Planning for Real', 'Action Planning,' and 'Design Assistance Teams' (Carmona *et al.*, 2002). Planning for real utilises large-scale 3D models to encourage non-confrontational community involvement in identifying and

Act Create Experience (ACE); Action planning; Activity mapping; Adaptable model; Appreciative inquiry; Architecture centre; Architecture week; Awareness-raising day; Beo; Best-fit slide rule; Briefing workshop; Broad-based organisation; Capacity-building workshop; Choices method; Citizen advocacy; Citizens juries; Community appraisals; Community design centre; Community indicators; Community plan; Community planning forum; Community projects fund; Community site management plans; Community strategic planning; Consensus building; Design assistance team; Design day; Design game; Design workshop; Development trust; Elevation montage; Enspirited envisioning; Environment shop; Finding home – visualising our future by making maps; Fish bowl; Forum; From vision to action; Future search conference; Guided visualisation; Imagine!; Interactive display; Issues, aims, expectations, challenges and dialogues in a day; Local sustainability model; Mobile planning unit; Mock-up; Neighbourhood planning office; Open design competition; Open house event; Open space workshop; Parish maps; Participatory appraisal; Participatory building appraisal; Participatory strategic planning; Participatory theatre; Planning aid; Planning day; Planning for real; Planning weekend; Process planning session; Real-time strategic change; Resource centre; Roadshow; Round-table workshops; Social audit; Street stall; Table scheme display; TalkWorks; Task force; Team syntegrity; Time dollars; Topic workshop; Trail; Urban design game; Urban design soapbox; Urban design studio; Urban studies centre; Visual simulation; Web site

10.5 Approaches to participation in the built environment.

solving their own problems. Participants are then encouraged to make suggestions by filling out suggestion cards and attaching these to the model, the outcomes of which can be pursued in detail at follow-up group meetings. Action planning events are collaborative events, structured to enable different sections of local communities to work with independent specialists from a variety of disciplines to produce proposals for action. Events are usually staged over several days and involve processes of briefing from key stakeholders, analysing the physical context, workshops and brainstorming sessions, synthesis and presentation of proposals, and finally reporting back and publication of the results. Design or urban design assistance teams (UDATs) are a variation on action planning where multidisciplinary teams from outside an area 'parachute in' to facilitate an event, thus helping the local community to devise recommendations for action. Introduced by the American Institute of Architects in 1967, UDATs have developed in the US into a sophisticated means of empowering local communities to develop solutions to design problems.

Unfortunately, despite the availability of ready-made techniques, a number of important constraints undermine the effectiveness of many participatory experiences (Christie *et al.*, 2002, pp. 26–8):

- Hard-to-reach groups and non-joiners will always be difficult to involve, and may require different techniques to committed stakeholders.
- The 'usual suspects' can easily come to dominate the process.
- The 'community' is rarely a unified voice, and may well contain many tensions beyond those between locals and developers.
- Conflicts with the local democratic decision-making processes can undermine the participatory process.
- Participatory processes can be undermined or ignored when they fail to support key private objectives.
- The fact that agreement and consensus will not always be possible.

All these represent difficult dilemmas that different processes will to a greater or lesser extent address. The number of different approaches available offers some indication of the extra effort required to move beyond token consultation procedures, but also of the widespread belief in the value of that effort. It also indicates that participation will likely as not require the development of an approach unique to the circumstances of the locality, as a means to best utilise available resources and to fully engage the diversity of local interests (Carmona *et al.*, 2002).

The experience of active participation in the regeneration of Caterham Barracks in Kent illustrates some of the benefits (Cadell *et al.*, 2000). John Thompson and Partners, working for Linden Homes (n.d.), undertook a Community Planning weekend in February 1998. While community planning had been done before in the UK, this was the first time it had been initiated and led by a private developer. It was held on a Friday for professionals, including a bus tour of the surrounding area, and on Saturday for local people, with over 1,000 people attending. People were invited to tell the consultants about their community – its problems, and their dreams and solutions. The approach was deliberately non-confrontational, with special workshops to ensure that young people were involved right from the start, and the use of Post-it Notes to enable all to participate and record issues and possible actions.

Many people who turned up to the planning weekend believed that the decision had already been made: that the site would be allocated for executive housing of little benefit to the established community. Some were even confrontational and demanded to see the plans. When the developer explained that they had no plans, and that the whole process was about creating a vision, the community were surprised, but also pleased and enthusiastic about being involved. The wish list from the planning weekend was vast. The developer responded that the community could have all of their requirements on the site, but that this would require the building of more than the 110 houses proposed in the local authority's development brief. The result was a planning application for a wide range of community facilities, business accommodation, and a total of 348 new homes (26 per cent affordable). One of the main lessons was that it is difficult to have too much public consultation (there were five significant exercises and each time they raised people's understanding and knowledge), and that through engagement with the community a win-win outcome was possible. The experience also revealed the great benefits of coordinating and combining public sector, private sector and community efforts to create, agree and deliver successful new housing development.

Stakeholder views

The survey of stakeholder views focused on corporate working. The term is normally applied to the way in which different groups or departments within the same local authority coordinate their various roles. But this definition can be extended to encompass the way in which public–private partnerships operate or the degree of liaison between neighbouring authorities or different tiers of government. The research began with the narrower definition, but quickly respondents turned to focus on the broader concerns. All are seen to impact on the way stakeholders are able to work together and on the nature/depth of the tensions that can arise.

The survey revealed corporate working to be one of only two areas (the other being the provision of affordable housing) where RSLs were more concerned than private housebuilders about the issue (see Fig. 10.6). In this case almost three-quarters of RSLs

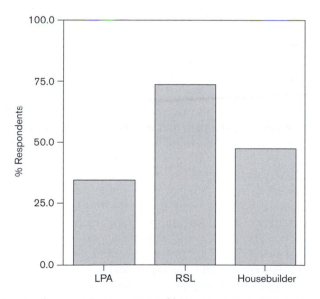

10.6 Views on the significance of corporate working as a source of planner–provider tension (per cent rating as significant).

considered poor corporate strategy and working practices to be a problem, as against half of developers, and 35 per cent of planners, the vast majority of whom praised inter-departmental liaison in their authorities. The finding was significant because it directly reflects the frustration of many RSLs with the seeming inability of planning departments and housing departments in local authorities to work constructively together. One RSL commented 'A local authority that acts corporately – planning, housing, highways, environmental, leisure – is unique indeed!'

Views nevertheless revealed that the frustration around the lack of coordination extends beyond working relationships between housing and planning departments. Developers, for example, were particularly frustrated about the lack of coordination between planning and highways authorities, and in local authority marketed sites about the lack of coordination between planning and estates departments. One developer even commented that tinkering with departmental structures in local authorities was rather like re-arranging the deckchairs on the *Titanic*, with delay and inconsistencies getting successively worse with new management regimes. Tensions focused around a number of core areas:

- Coordination and integration: the degree to which different activities are coordinated/integrated can be a cause of frustration if different departments, sectors, or adjacent authorities fail to pull in the same direction. Providers, for example, complained that confusion often arises out of the publication of contradictory development plans, housing strategies, community strategies and local need assessments. The problems can also infiltrate the consultation process, with highways, legal departments, police and fire services all approached too late in the day.
- The impact of non-coordination: a failure to pull in the same direction seems to have a number of knock-on effects: inconsistency lengthens the negotiation process, as does uncoordinated internal consultation; confusion results in a lack of direction, *ad hoc* responses and therefore ad hoc policies; a lack of coordination means that plans quickly become out of date; a lack of integration can lead to bad planning decisions; and this particular way of working accentuates all the other tensions, particularly those centring on design, density, planning agreements, and affordable housing.
- Commitment: the capacity to work corporately was viewed by many respondents as a personal trait. Some people can work as part of a team and recognise that they are cogs in a much larger machine. Others cannot and do not. Corporate working, it seems, can be less about policy and mechanics, and more to do with people.
- Resource constraints: local authorities in particular were keen to point out that setting up the systems, sharing information, and allocating sufficient time to such activities all placed added burdens on the dwindling resources of local government.

Nevertheless, the stakeholder views to some degree reflected the nature of many local authorities that are going through a radical modernisation agenda, but having to cope with considerable in-built resistance to change from both officers and councillors. Although a widespread acceptance exists that better coordinated and integrated services will in the long run also deliver resource efficiencies, there is at the same time an acute awareness that no additional funds exist to establish either Community Strategies or Local Strategic Partnerships. At the same time with so much of the joining-up agenda reliant on heavy up-front investment to establish new systems and approaches to working, the lack of human and financial resources have been identified as key barriers to change (Local Government Association, 2001, p. 6).

The question of resources was discussed in Chapter 6. What seems absolutely fundamental is that without extra funds it is becoming increasingly difficult for authorities to deliver the 'value adding' activities that the modernising agenda demands. Increasingly authorities have therefore had to retreat to their core statutory responsibilities which further undermines collaborative and integrative efforts and frustrates key users. The experience at Caterham (see p. 170) (and elsewhere) shows that the private sector can play a part in relieving these pressures by taking responsibility for some of the more proactive activities necessary to deliver consensus. However, these examples have tended to remain few and far between, and whilst encouraging increased community involvement, especially in large schemes, the Planning Green Paper explicitly rejected a duty requiring applicants instead of authorities to undertake effective consultation as part of the planning application process (DTLR, 2001a, p. 43). Therefore if the greater coordination of activities required to provide better services and outcomes is to be more consistently delivered across the country as the legislation demands, then extra resources – financial, manpower and skills – will need to be forthcoming as well.

Part Three:
Solutions

In the previous six chapters, an overview of the key points of tension in housing delivery have been discussed as they relate to the planning process operated in England. Although the system will change in the coming years, the tensions experienced in the recent past are likely to remain for the foreseeable future, in large part because they remain inexorably linked to critical relationships in the planning process which will not change, to the discretionary nature of the British planning process, and to fundamental facets of human nature. Thus although certain operational parameters might shift, tensions will always remain as long as public and private interests are reconciled through a planning process.

In the third and final part of this book, the focus shifts to how these tensions can be ameliorated, and sometimes overcome, by identifying different ways of working that embody principles which will remain relevant irrespective of policy shift. The structure of Part Three is based on the analysis of existing research, stakeholder views, and case study experiences that together suggested five headline routes forward:

1. The pursuit of more efficient and effective implementation processes that continually strive to deliver more timely policy frameworks and decisions, and which are responsive to the pressures on those operating within the marketplace or with other funding constraints.
2. Engaging with the full range of stakeholders in a meaningful way, encompassing the principle of all parties signing-up to and 'owning' the process.
3. The coordination of roles, processes, mechanisms and outcomes, through integrated working practices that encourage inter-stakeholder awareness and therefore greater realism.
4. The promotion of more certain and transparent policies and development processes through sharing information and objectives.
5. A planning process that drives change rather than follows it, through vision, proactive interventions when required, and through establishing a positive policy framework well in advance of development.

Chapters 11 to 15 each draw on two local case studies to show how planning authorities and housing providers have grappled with the key tensions to address each of the five routes. Thus:

Chapter 11, Streamlined implementation, draws on case studies from Birmingham and Torbay that provide examples of particular project management processes, protocols and local understandings that together help to streamline the planning process. It shows, for example, in the case of Birmingham how certain types of residential developments may be subject to fast-tracking.

Chapter 12, Inclusive planning and decision-making, draws on recent experience in Cambridge, where an active Development Control Forum and planning workshops have resulted in a more inclusive planning process and the empowerment of groups who might otherwise have been shut out of decision-making. The chapter also examines the use of Village Design Statements in Stratford-on-Avon and the participation in their development that has been facilitated by the local planning authority.

Chapter 13, Integrated and realistic working practices, shows how different agencies may work together more effectively and also how policy may be better attuned to local circumstance. The chapter draws on examples from Braintree and Brent, the former focusing on the operation of a partnership approach to housing development, the latter on the authority's strategy for collecting data, particularly as regards housing capacity, and how this is used in delivering new homes.

Chapter 14, Certainty and transparency, draws on examples of more open project management and coordination employed in South Lakeland and also an open accounting process that was developed in Sedgemoor. Discussion focuses on how levels of trust between housing providers and planners might be raised and the benefits this brings to housing developments.

Chapter 15, Positive and proactive planning, gathers together a number of overarching themes and, using two examples of innovative local policy, shows how planning can drive forward a more positive and proactive development process. The chapter pulls together examples from Newcastle and the London borough of Hammersmith and Fulham.

The five 'solutions' chapters in Part Three lead into a final analysis of the way new homes are delivered in the context of the British planning system, and how, beyond the confines of the prevailing processes of planning more and better homes might be delivered. Chapter 16 concludes by examining the changing planning context in England, by drawing on responses to the 2001 Planning Green Paper.

11

Streamlined implementation

A wicked problem

The delivery of new housing might be termed a 'wicked' problem. For those without decent affordable housing, the ramifications impact on every aspect of their life and represent an overriding concern. Conversely, for those able to afford good quality housing (for purchase or rent) the problem of delivering more homes for others who can not, will typically not feature very high in their priorities. According to Stephens (2001), the British housing model is becoming increasingly polarised, most obviously between the owner-occupied sector and the rest.

In recent years, because at any one time many more people are adequately or well housed (even though they might aspire to a move up the ladder of provision) than those who are poorly housed, politically the issue of housing provision has remained a low priority. Increasingly, the issue of housing provision only makes its way onto the national (and press) agenda when proposals for new development fire up the passion of local resistance. The situation today stands in sharp contrast to the post-war period and the following decades when housing provision (particularly by the state) was amongst the top political objectives of successive governments of both political persuasions.

It can be argued that home owners in particular, who have greatly increased as a percentage of total householders as a direct result of the 'right to buy' policies introduced in the 1980s – now 67 per cent in England and Wales (Boyfield, 2001, p. 77) – have a number of in-built incentives to resist new housing development:

- Much of the UK has been characterised by a highly inflationary housing market (particularly in the South East) to such an extent that the shortage of new homes guarantees high and increasing prices, which (on paper at least) greatly increases the asset value of homeowners, and makes them feel more wealthy. In this regard, the fewer homes that are built, the greater the demand, and the more inflationary the housing market.
- New homes which are built on greenfield sites, either within established urban areas (on playing fields and other open space) or around urban areas (on the urban fringe), inevitably impact (or are perceived to impact) on the amenity enjoyed by existing residents, so giving rise to the classic NIMBY (not in my back yard) resistance to development.

• The provision of new social housing by definition implies housing that is rented at below market rate, and is thereby effectively subsidised through general taxation. Some might argue that this smacks of the 'nanny state', and that these resources could go into other areas of public spending or back to those who contributed them in the first place. Furthermore, many homeowners resist the building of social housing near them, believing the occupants to be potentially troublesome neighbours, or simply and irrationally 'not like us'.

Freudenberg and Pastor (1992) identify three major explanations for the anti-development attitudes that underlie much public debate in new housing development:

1. A paternalistic view that identifies an aversion towards new housing development as a result of irrational and ignorant citizens who do not understand the real impact and implications of development.
2. An aversion towards new housing as a result of rational self-interest, perhaps for all or some of the reasons listed above, but most likely because of a perceived threat to the amenities (and therefore property values) of established residents.
3. The reasonable aversion towards new housing development resulting from prudent citizens who may be more aware of the possible risk associated with new development than the professional planners whom they distrust.

Research by Savage (2001) on local attitudes to new homes graphically illustrates how local resistance to new homes can build and slow the process of site allocation and construction. His research examining the motivations of objectors to the Dry Street development in Basildon (Essex) revealed that on allocation of the site for future housing need in the Basildon local plan, residents were quickly able to marshal their forces and develop a convincing case why the site should not be developed. Arguments included:

• the high rate of development in the area (they had already done their bit to meet housing need);
• that new development would overload the natural capacity of the area, particularly its facilities and amenities (which were perceived to be inelastic to the change in demand);
• that the natural environmental assets of the area would be destroyed;
• that new development would import new people into the area, and not address local needs;
• that if any development was required (objectors conceded that a small amount probably was), this should be much less than the scale of development proposed;
• that the poor design of most contemporary housing development would merely be repeated at Dry Street;
• that the decision-making (site selection) processes were not open and accountable, with little public involvement;
• that development was required but not here (the classic NIMBY case).

What was clear was that in the majority of cases the arguments were rational and well thought through, that they were not (on the whole) motivated by self-interest (even if individual objectors were), but by a broader public interest, with most objectors going out of their way to avoid being labelled NIMBYs. What was also apparent was the profound opposition of the residents to the prevailing 'Decide, Announce, Defend' (DAD) approach used in Basildon (and elsewhere) leading to a spiral of distrust between planners and objectors, with the council seemingly preferring to leave debates to the Public Inquiry in the belief that they would win (Savage, 2001).

Thus, the increasingly organised (and often frustrated) resistance to new development from: an alliance of self-interested and publicly motivated local objectors, environmental groups (most vociferously the Council for the Protection of Rural England – CPRE, 2001c), and anti-development protestors; the low political importance of new housing (nationally and often locally); and the changes to planning policy (discussed in Chapter 2) effectively reducing greenfield development options in favour of more complex and time-consuming brownfield sites was by 2002 dramatically impacting on housing completions. The increasingly forceful pronouncements of the House Builders' Federation make the case. Launching the survey 'Building a Crisis' (HBF, 2002c), in which a range of housing demand and supply statistics were analysed (see Fig. 11.1), spokesman Pierre Williams argued:

> These figures now prove that Britain no longer has enough housing to provide every family with a home. Is it any wonder that house prices have spiralled when as a nation we seem unwilling to provide ourselves with something as fundamental as a roof over our heads? The stark reality is that a 30 year campaign by the anti-housebuilding lobby coupled with a collapse of public investment in housing has resulted in a society unable to house itself. Far from 'concreting over the countryside', urban expansion takes up just one per cent of England's land area every 50 years. . . . The Government has a key objective of 'giving everyone the opportunity of a decent home', but this is being destroyed by opposition at local level. Effective reform of the planning system offers a one-off chance to tackle NIMBYism for the benefit of the whole nation. It must not be missed or the economic and social consequences will be severe.

➤ In 1981, 4.1 per cent more dwellings than households were available; by 2000 this had reduced to 0.2 per cent

➤ By 2001 it is likely that households overtook homes available

➤ By 2000, London had 4.2 per cent fewer homes than households

➤ By 2000, the South East had 1.4 per cent fewer homes than households

➤ 2001 represented a 77-year low in new homes completed

➤ In 2001 162,000 new homes were completed, and 220,000 new households formed

➤ From 1981 to 2000 household growth averaged 193,000 per year, whereas housing stock expanded by around 162,000 units per year, a gap of 31,000 per year

➤ From 1996 to 2000 household growth averaged 196,500, 22 per cent higher than official projected growth figures on which regional housing allocations are made

➤ In 1996, 7.5 per cent of homes were deemed unfit for habitation and 14.2 per cent in poor condition

➤ Britain invests less in new housing as a percentage of GDP (3.3 per cent) than any other major industrialised nation

➤ Britain's housing stock is the second oldest in the European Union

➤ If recent demolition rates are maintained, it will be 1500 years before current newly built homes reach their turn for demolition

➤ Completions by local authorities are down to almost zero, and by RSLs to 20,000 per year

---

11.1 Housing supply statistics in England (Stewart, 2002).

For the housebuilder, new allocations of land and planning permissions for housing cannot come soon enough, although their record of producing less than high quality housing in the past (see Chapter 3) and their obvious economic interest in building more homes might undermine the force of their arguments. Illustrating the characteristically polarised nature of these debates, the former Secretary of State for the Environment John Gummer (2002) criticised the HBF for its ceaseless determination to return to the 'greenfield suburban estate model to which it is so committed'. The CPRE spokesman Henry Oliver also denounced the figures in 'Building a Crisis' as scare mongering, arguing that households do not necessarily translate into homes, and that the acute need is for affordable housing (especially in the South East), something that developers are unwilling to provide (Dewar, 2002b).

Nevertheless, despite this unwillingness, an increasing range of have-nots in the housing arena confirm the need for more housing – first-time buyers, migrants from the north to the south, key workers in expensive areas, and the many families unable to trade-up to a larger home (NHF, 2001b). A report from the Centre of Economic and Business Research (2002), for example, even predicted average house prices in the UK soaring to more than £300,000 by 2020 as a direct consequence of low levels of housebuilding brought on by planning constraints.

In all parts of the country a huge task exists to upgrade the general housing stock. In London and the south east, and a number of other 'hot spots' – Leeds, York, Chester, etc. – the housing shortage is turning into a housing crisis with potentially profound effects. So how might more homes of a higher quality be brought forward more quickly?

Streamlining in planning

Streamlining implies the pursuit of more efficient and effective implementation processes that continually strive to deliver more timely policy frameworks and decisions, and which are responsive to the pressures on those operating within the marketplace or with other funding constraints.

As discussed in Chapter 6, delay has been consistently the most frequent and serious cause of tension between housing providers (particularly private housebuilders) and planners, although the research indicated that RSLs are less concerned with speed than their private sector counterparts. As with so much of the relationship between housing providers and planners, tension is the result of contrasting motives and interests:

- the market imperative of housebuilding versus the public interest of planning;
- the relatively short-term interest of much housebuilding (at least in the houses once built) versus the long-term interest of planning; and
- the site-specific interest of housebuilding versus the area and settlement-wide interest of planning.

For the housebuilder operating in the private sector it is important to seize the opportunity when it arises in an often-volatile market. This is because, as was argued in Chapter 3, like most private industries, speculative housebuilding depends on maintaining cash flow in the short run and profitability in the long run – a difficult and risky business. In reality this implies limiting financial exposure and turning around capital as efficiently as possible in order to maximise investment returns (see Chapter 3). Delay is potentially an immense source of frustration that can increase risk and represent the difference between profit and loss. Indeed, in 'Building a Crisis', the planning system is denounced as the single most significant factor in slowing down the delivery of new homes and the reason behind the dramatic decline in completions. The report argues that the planning system is the primary cause of private housing under-supply, and that deliberate restraint policies in southern England, and in prosperous areas elsewhere, do not allow house building to respond to demographic and economic pressures. For RSLs, funding is an equally uncertain business and the need to secure public and private sources of finance ensures that unnecessary delay can jeopardise funding.

For the planner, the time taken to reach a decision is governed by three major factors:

1. the process to be followed to reach any planning decision, including the need for consultation, design review and negotiation (including of planning obligations) on applications;
2. the changing policy context at a national level, which has resulted in the almost complete (and sometimes dramatic) revision of the PPG series since the mid-1990s, and a process to start again with PPSs (ODPM, 2002b, paras 18–19 – see Table 2.3); and
3. the resources available locally for the purpose of planning, about which DTLR-commissioned research on the 'Resourcing of Local Planning Authorities' (DTLR, 2002d, p. 9) reveals a significant decline in the resources going to planning authorities since 1996; a period in which the performance of planning authorities has also generally worsened.

Many of the key factors determining the length of time it takes to plan – and subsequently implement – are therefore out of the direct control of planning officers. Instead they are determined by statute, by the impact of central government advice and by the decisions of local councillors for whom planning is just one of an often conflicting range of policy responsibilities needing to be resourced. The frequent result is a planning process with a fire-fighting mentality, keeping up with the day-to-day run-of-the-mill applications but struggling to deal as efficiently with the more complex planning applications and with the long-term activity of plan-making. Significantly, the research on planning resources confirmed the switch away from proactive and longer-term work to development control and reactive work, and a lack of resources for enforcement, development plans and conservation matters; it also revealed that upon adoption of the plan, authorities quickly wind down staff resources on the policy side (DTLR, 2002d, pp. 8–9).

Delay is therefore possible in both plan-making and development control. In the case of policy, since the adoption of a plan-led system and the increase in status of the plan, key decisions concerning the allocation of land are now made far earlier in the planning process and are very difficult to change once adopted as policy. Therefore, as Savage's (2001) research in Basildon illustrated (see p. 178), public, community and private stakeholders are now more willing to spend considerable time and effort influencing the allocation of land up front. The inevitable result is a much longer plan adoption process.

Nevertheless, the British planning system is still discretionary, with each application considered on its merits. Therefore as the complexities of applications are increasing (DTLR, 2002d, p. 10) through, for example, the use of planning agreements, affordable housing requirements, the greater complexities associated with brownfield redevelopments, a more vocal public and increased consultation requirements, and the demand for better designed developments, the whole process of development control is also taking longer. The outcome is more time devoted to the process, including greater resources from the private sector (and hence increased risk). The response from government has been a partial realisation that the infamous eight-week development control target has become unrealistic (see Chapter 6), and the instigation of the new eight- and thirteen-week targets from 2002.

The case studies

The case studies demonstrate two alternative approaches to streamlining the development control process. The Birmingham case illustrates:

- An acknowledgement of the difficulties within the process and proactive attitudes towards evolving new methods.
- A regular and established system of user-review to enable ongoing monitoring of performance and to identify and test potential new approaches.
- Streamlining and management of the planning process and accountability of actions.
- A charter that clearly establishes required roles and responsibilities, which all parties sign up to.
- Efficient management of resources to encourage investment and development.
- Active monitoring and forecasting of development activity and potential development activity, enabling appropriate resource-management.

Over time in partnership with a local developer, Torbay have developed an approach that illustrates:

- Investment up front at the pre-application stage in building a relationship between the local planning authority and the developer.
- Decision-making undertaken cooperatively between the parties to deliver a win:win relationship for all.
- An authority providing appropriate constructive and proactive guidance and avoiding negative and reactive approaches where possible.
- A cross-party willingness to understand all aspirations and constraints, and a willingness to adapt and compromise.
- An ongoing relationship of openness and trust built up over the course of many planning applications.

CASE STUDY: Birmingham – accelerating development

During the late 1990s, Birmingham City Council had been proactively engaged in identifying new approaches to different parts of the planning process to enable more clarity and a streamlined and inclusive process. A raft of measures had been introduced to respond to the needs of applicants in the planning process and to foster a more positive climate for development within the city. Many of the initiatives seek to smooth and streamline the process where possible, whilst increasing the involvement of those engaged in it in order to shape the approach to planning and development within the city.

It had previously been felt that the council were hindering development, tying up investors' capital, and consequently discouraging private investment within the city. The initiatives were established because the authority was concerned that they were losing investment (particularly major developments) to other authorities in the region, in part because they were not sufficiently responsive to applicants' needs.

The primary aim was therefore to attract investment by making things easier for investors whilst still maintaining quality within developments and ensuring that the process was inclusive. Several initiatives were instigated to improve forward resource management and implementation of the process.

A charter for development

In late 2000, Birmingham City Council launched its 'Charter for Development', the mission statement of which was 'Building a Better Birmingham'. The Charter effectively spearheaded a move to ensure a more efficient, high-quality process through enlisting the support of the different stakeholders: the City Council, the community and the development industry. It acknowledged that the quality of the process is determined directly by the level of commitment and responsibility of each party.

The Charter therefore set out the City Council's roles and responsibilities and established the actions the authority would require of applicants/developers. A key part of the Charter is the protocol for major development projects implemented through the Accelerated Development Programme.

Accelerated Development Programme

The Accelerated Development Programme is a joint initiative of the different development departments of the City Council – Economic Development, Transportation, Planning and Architecture, and Leisure and Culture. This interdepartmental coordination was driven at the highest level in the council (by the Chief Officers' Group), as a joint initiative to facilitate greater development certainty over time.

Following a conference organised by the authority and attended by representatives of the development industry, it was decided that the City Council would pilot a fast-track system for major development within the planning process. The Development Control Committee ratified the proposal, and a series of consultation events were undertaken with key private sector interests, including workshops focusing on particular issues.

Subsequently, a working group nominated by the Chief Officers and comprising two representatives from each of the interprofessional (Transportation, Economic Development, Planning and Architecture) development teams responsible for different areas of the city produced the Charter. The working group met and discussed the main strands of the approach which were then developed into a first draft by one of the lead officers. This first draft was subsequently shaped and refined by the working group as a whole and approved for industry consultation by the Chief Officers' Group.

Implementation of the programme

In addition to the three main development teams within the Development Control section, a major development team, operating citywide, was established to implement the accelerated development programme. This is coordinated by one of the lead officers responsible for developing and framing the initiative and Charter.

The major development team has six dedicated officers as well as support from the area development control teams. This additional involvement of the area development control officers offers a degree of resource-flexibility within project programming and also helps ensure that the area teams are not left with the smaller (and perceived to be less interesting) applications – initially a major concern amongst officers.

The initiative is limited to the planning process, but is intended to represent a joined-up approach to development across the council. In some cases the Economic Development team may be the first point of contact, or sites may be identified through strategic infrastructure work via the Transportation team, which also has dedicated officers to deal with major development projects.

The accelerated development programme took a year to develop and establish, and since November 2000 has gathered momentum. It is not perceived as a quick-fix solution and it is anticipated that the process will evolve in the light of ongoing feedback. The council nevertheless anticipates that if it is successful some of the key principles could be extended as a model to some of its other statutory responsibilities. It is therefore seen as a move towards adopting a wider 'one-stop shop' approach.

Stakeholder responsibilities

For each potential application a project champion is appointed within the council to drive the application forward and provide the main point of contact. Pre-application discussions are encouraged, and a development team is established as each major project comes forward. All timescales and milestones are agreed up front and linked to the developer's timetable. These are then coordinated between council departments and the applicant, with each party made aware of the process, including their detailed roles and responsibilities which all parties are required to sign up to (see Table 11.1). Thus the council undertakes to action specific tasks at certain times and to give feedback on progress, whilst in return the applicant undertakes to provide any necessary information by specific times. Where amendments to the proposal are required in response to, for example, feedback from the statutory consultations, the applicants are notified immediately to enable amendments to be made quickly.

The Charter also provides a framework for dealing with Section 106 and 278 agreements, and ensures that the council clarifies its position where it holds land or property impacting upon the application. Finally, it defines which developments are appropriate for inclusion on the accelerated development programme; which are usually developments of major strategic significance in terms of regeneration and investment, or with wide corporate involvement; and which are eligible for large-scale time-limited public funding.

Major development list

To enhance the smooth running of the accelerated programme, all appropriate major developments are anticipated prior to application stage through means of the major development list. The list is regularly updated on the basis of enquiries, giving an accurate compilation of potential developments or sites in the pipeline. The list has several stages or categories of project, enabling a site/development to be tracked and anticipated throughout the process: initial discussion (prior to pre-application, when the proposal is likely to be confidential); pre-application (when the proposal is likely to be implemented); and finally an application category for those projects which have officially entered the process.

As soon as a development is mooted (for example a developer may be interested, or an enquiry may be received from land/property owners) it gets flagged up on the list, enabling the planning authority to anticipate when the project is likely to come on-stream. The major development list and specific projects are both discussed at the Chief Officers' Group, to which

Table 11.1 Responsibilities under the Charter (Birmingham City Council, 2000)

The City Council will:	*In return the developer should:*
➤ Set a programme for each major development project in conjunction with the developer. ➤ Nominate a project coordinator for each major development project. ➤ Identify the issues and information required in connection with the planning application or any other process at an early stage. ➤ Set out the requirements for consultation and participation as soon as possible. ➤ Tell the developer at an early stage what its aspirations are for Section 106 obligations (including affordable housing), and Section 278 agreements and land value (where the City Council has land ownership). ➤ Chair project team meetings. ➤ Keep its actions under review during the process and provide feedback to the developer through the project team, in order that amendments and revisions can be made. ➤ Make sure that the developer gets a coordinated view from all council officers involved in the development process. ➤ Work with developers to secure occupiers and ensure that the appropriate agencies are brought on board to establish effective recruitment and training packages.	➤ Agree to a programme to get the project on site, including all aspects of the planning process and key milestones. ➤ Provide a completed high-quality planning application submission, including all necessary plans, illustrative material and supporting statements, e.g. environmental and transport impact assessments. ➤ Respond within the mutually agreed timescales to further requests for information and/or amendments. ➤ Agree and contribute to consultation and participation, which may involve public meetings and/or exhibitions. ➤ Attend project team meetings. ➤ Build adequate time into their project for discussion and review to take place. ➤ Keep the City Council informed at all stages of the project. ➤ Cooperate with the City Council and others in creating jobs for Birmingham people through the development project. ➤ Help to publicise the 'Building a Better Birmingham' mission statement on site boards and literature. ➤ Work with the City Council and other agencies to ensure that linkages are made between local people and new employment and training opportunities.

the lead officer from the Major Development Team is invited to give the team a feel for the development activity in the city.

The establishment and maintenance of a list of future and potential development within the city contributes to a streamlined process by allowing the workloads of all of the different development departments (and officers within each department) to be planned with a reasonable level of certainty over the short and medium term. Previously, the development control department had to rely on guesswork to estimate what the future workload would be, a strategy that sometimes led to mismanagement and poor resource control. The initiative impacts on resource allocation right across the authority, and therefore on the processing of all applications – both small and large.

User fora

As the accelerated development programme was focused primarily on the functional interface between the City Council and applicants for major development, the wider community were not consulted on the initiative. Another initiative, however, proved invaluable to gauge industry opinion of the programme – the involvement of the council's user fora. The user fora provide a platform for ongoing feedback and review with representatives of the local development community, and can be used as a means to identify, test and discuss new initiatives. Thus the Planning and Architecture User Forum was consulted on the final draft of the Accelerated Development Programme and Charter for Development.

The Planning and Architecture User Forum (set up in the mid-1990s) is made up of agents, architects and surveyors with whom the council usually have significant contact. The Economic Development team also has a forum made up of agents, surveyors, property agents, and the biggest property owners and landowners. Each user forum usually meet every three months, at which the participants are invited to discuss any relevant issues.

Typically, the Accelerated Development Programme is referred back to the two user fora twice a year for feedback, in line with the council's Best Value processes. This emphasis on industry feedback and support has been an important factor within Birmingham, ensuring that the industry feels a sense of ownership of the initiative and that the initiative is, in turn, responsive to the diverse range of user needs.

Discussion

The Birmingham approach is helping to foster better working relationships between the City Council and developers, and, as a consequence of implementing the Accelerated Development Programme, the local authority is aiming to become more efficient at managing internal workloads. They argue, for example, that as workloads increase, delay and inefficiency lead to increasing numbers of complaints, which tie up resources even further. Instead, by treating the problem at source by improving resource allocation, the cycle can be halted. In addition, developers gain from a better service and increased certainty. Planners, for example, were sometimes unwilling to give a developer bad news early on, the preferred option being to let the bad news surface as a refusal. This practice has now changed.

There are costs involved in the process on both sides. For example, a greater degree of trust and openness is required, which is sometimes difficult to broker. The principle of joint working and establishing a positive dialogue with applicants and agents relies on the commitment of both parties, consequently a two-way dialogue is crucial.

It was acknowledged by the City Council that the 'one organisation' approach (coordinated corporate working within the council) should lead to better understanding internally, although there was still potential for a greater understanding of the development industry. Nevertheless, the Accelerated Development Programme has been well received, precisely because the council publicly approached and consulted the development industry prior to and also during the implementation of the programme.

Initiatives such as the Accelerated Development Programme, the user fora and the major development list have to be politically supported if they are to succeed. Such initiatives initially often make increased demands on resources, even though over time they lead to greater efficiency. At Birmingham the resource requirement was not considered a great problem, in part because the under-resourcing of development control had already been acknowledged (as part of the Best Value review process) and the authority was committed to addressing the issue.

In essence the approach provides a means to determine and agree what actions or outcomes should occur at specific points in the process. In this respect, the pre-application phase is proving crucial. For housing, however, the authority has found that the nature of funding can be a serious constraint to effective pre-application dialogue. They argue that RSLs in particular frequently have preconceived schemes ('in their bottom drawers') as responses to the Housing Corporation funding regimes. This practice encourages inflexibility during the process.

One of the primary concerns with the approach is that the Chief Officers are the main arbiters of what will be fast-tracked. Consequently, the initial criteria for which sites are selected for the Accelerated Development Programme were geared more towards major commercial schemes than residential developments. The principles of the approach could nevertheless be used for any type of application. There is also a perception amongst developers and landowners that non-fast-tracked applications will receive a second-class service. Anticipating that this might increase rather than reduce tension, the City Council have agreed to move towards implementing fast-tracking principles across the board with all applications, although this will have major resource implications.

In this regard it was also recognised that efficient use of resources needs to occur across all types of applications, regardless of size. This highlights a critical conflict in a system with finite and limited resources: how to achieve key city-wide development objectives through the encouragement and facilitation of major development, without sacrificing smaller projects.

CASE STUDY: Torbay – investing up front

Midas Homes are a proactive developer that operates primarily within the South West, developing houses for sale on their own developments, and working in partnership with social housing organisations and local authorities to provide social housing. Based in Newton Abbott, Devon, they complete approximately 600 houses annually of which 300 are social housing.

Midas have established an approach to development that involves the local planning authority at an early stage in the decision-making process, and seeks to engage openly in negotiations, involving the local authority as part of the team. Marina Quay, for example, was built by Midas Homes in the late 1990s and is situated on the waterfront at Brixham in Devon, on the site of a former shipyard. The development comprises 80 townhouses and flats (all market housing) and a medical practice, and responded to Torbay's policy of building more densely on brownfield land, so safeguarding the limited supply of greenfield sites, and minimal and precious green belt. On its completion the development won the local design award.

In the 1980s, there was a move to make Brixham a centre for the America's Cup. A planning consent for development at the Brixham Marina site was obtained, but the original developer went bankrupt before the development could be started. Midas Homes became interested in the site in the 1990s, and approached the local planning authority for initial discussions prior to undertaking a feasibility study and acquiring the land. The local authority were keen to encourage appropriate development on the site as a number of developers had shown interest in the intervening period but without any applications coming forward. The site had therefore lain vacant for some considerable time.

Establishing and maintaining channels of communication

Midas Homes has an internal policy to approach the local planning authority early in the process for pre-application discussion, establishing the aspirations of both parties at an early stage. The added benefit has been that they have never had to waste the time and resources required to appeal a planning refusal. The local planning authority at Torbay are also keen to establish discussion early, and have found that investing time at an early stage avoids delays later in the process. Although it is normally the local authority's policy to produce development briefs for strategic sites, in this instance there was no development brief in place for the Brixham Marina site due to the existence of prior planning consents obtained by previous owners. Consequently, these early discussions between the developer and the local authority were important, enabling the design of the scheme to proceed on an appropriate basis.

The initial discussions between the developer and the assigned planning officer covered issues such as roads, access, street scene, building blocks, materials, height, density and feasibility issues. Density was a particularly important aspect of the discussions. The original planning consent granted in the 1980s was at a relatively low density (64 dwellings were proposed), and it was decided early to increase this figure in response to changing national policy and guidance (advocating increased residential densities). The decision also improved the overall financial viability of the development, and gave the developer the confidence to invest in some initial proposals and sketch ideas that in turn formed the basis for subsequent discussion and negotiation.

Further meetings were held to resolve density, height and accommodation issues, at which stage the conservation officer became involved with regard to detailed design. The only major omission from these early negotiations was landscaping concerns. Thus by the time landscaping was addressed by the local authority, the developer had run out of money and had to reduce the scope of landscaping work. The authority intends to address these important concerns earlier in future development negotiations.

Negotiation and design

The authority recognises that detailed design issues can cause problems during development negotiations, especially within the context of conservation requirements, and that these can have a major financial impact upon development viability. In particular, the requirement for high-quality materials and contextually appropriate (rather than standardised) design solutions can often create difficulty when trying to reach agreement where commercial issues conflict with broader environmental aspirations.

In the Brixham Marina case, as there was no development brief in place, site-specific design guidance was undertaken on the hoof through ongoing discussions between the developer and the conservation officer from the local planning authority. The aspirations of the local authority were established early on and open negotiations were undertaken to determine what was achievable. Clear development-specific guidance was given in the form of drawing and sketching during the meetings to describe and illustrate the different elements and local authority requirements. The developer found this technique particularly useful, in contrast to more common practice where no clear constructive advice is given and applicants are forced to undertake abortive redesigns many times. This cooperative method of design (alongside a level of commercial honesty on the part of the developer) enabled the objectives of both parties to be fulfilled, although the success of this type of approach rests heavily on the skills-base of both parties.

Nevertheless, despite the positive experience at Brixham Marina, the local authority and the developer retain contrasting views about the most appropriate forms of design guidance. Torbay District Council do not issue design guides (design guidance is included within the local plan), although site-specific design briefs are issued as appropriate. Midas Homes, on the other hand, suggests that design guides can be very useful, especially within the context of development inside conservation areas, as they believe design briefs can be too restrictive. This contrast in attitudes perhaps illustrates the different motives of the two parties. A developer may favour the 'kit of parts' route to achieving appropriate development (with overall flexibility), whereas a local authority may favour more strategic control and a more contextual and individual approach to each development site. This contrast is universal, and demonstrates the fine balance required between design freedom, control, appropriateness and quality.

Discussion

This cooperative working relationship between the parties has been established over a period of time over the course of a number of projects. In essence, this history has established a certain credibility for the developer in Torbay. Thus Midas Homes feel that where they have an established relationship with a local authority, they are less likely to encounter adversarial attitudes or cynicism and associated delay to their developments. This in turn enables discussions to be open and frank, which facilitates a willingness to adapt and compromise. A high level of mutual respect seems to be held by the individuals within Midas Homes and the local planning authority in Torbay and both parties acknowledge the skills and knowledge that the other brings to the process.

Midas Homes have found that this approach enables a smooth process and a reduced determination period, where the local authority reciprocates their positive attitude. The approach at Torbay has been largely informal, although the developer suggests that there could be potential benefits in formalising the approach as part of a Charter Mark or Quality Assurance system. Unfortunately, where they have tried to initiate similar approaches with other local authorities, they have usually found that the commitment to a cooperative, relationship-building approach is lacking and consequently the process becomes lengthy and difficult.

Midas Homes also identify the particular constraints they encounter where there is a lack of consistency in approach across the different departments within a local authority, and cite the common occurrence that a local authority legal team may require several months to catch up in drafting Section 106 agreements. This, they argue, is often down to an uncoordinated approach to negotiation or a lack of involvement of the legal team in the earlier stages of a project.

For the approach illustrated at Torbay to work, both parties must be committed to the objectives, and able to assign adequate skilled resources to the process. There is potentially a difficult transition to make in refocusing (frequently overstretched) local authority resources up front in the process to the pre-application stage, although having done so, fewer resources should be required at a later stage, reducing the determination period and potentially the number of appeals.

The process undertaken for the development at Brixham Marina is a good example of cross-party commitment and willingness to cooperate, although the development itself has perhaps failed to achieve all of the local authority's objectives. There is no affordable housing provision on site, for example, as the local authority took a sympathetic view to the cost implications of the conservation requirements, particularly for high-quality materials, reflecting the prominent location of the development on the marina. In this respect it is important to retain sight of key policy and local objectives whilst engaging in negotiation. Potential conflicts can occur when the local planning authority is keen to encourage development on a particular site and consequently there may be a danger of compromising some fundamental aspects in return for achieving development. It can be argued, of course, that making these fine judgements and balancing different policy objectives represents the essential art of development control.

Recommendations

Throughout the following chapters, the need for a greater understanding of the constraints impacting on the key stakeholders in the process is stressed. Understanding is also needed both as regards the reasons why delay can be so costly to housebuilders and RSLs, and why planning as a process takes the time it does to reach the right decisions.

The recent history of British planning is punctuated by attempts to reduce the inevitable charge of inefficiency and delay and to speed up both ends of the planning process, particularly through setting targets (see Chapter 6). Such headline targets only tell part of the story, however, as they do not reflect the quality of decisions being made, the relative size of applications (at least until 2002), the type of authority (particularly the balance between householder and non-householder, and conservation and non-conservation applications received) or the extent to which outcomes are positive in terms of an approved planning permission. It is likely, for example, that most housing providers would prefer to wait a little longer for a permission, rather than receive a refusal because a deadline had been reached that required them to either reapply or appeal, causing further delay. (The available evidence suggests that the requirement for faster applications results in higher refusal rates, and that because of the cost implications of refusals, applicants are more satisfied with longer decision-making timescales that result in an approval – DTLR, 2002d, p. 12.) Furthermore, it is likely that most authorities would prefer to negotiate a little longer on more complex applications to ensure that the outcome better meets their policy objectives.

Needless to say, however, quality and speed in decision-making are not mutually exclusive, and continual improvement in each should be an aim of any modern planning service. It is an explicit aim, for example, of the Best Value regime introduced in the 1999 Local Government Act – delivering planning services as efficiently and effectively as possible, whilst still maintaining open and transparent standards that strive for quality.

The need for continual improvement in the efficiency of plan-making and development control is therefore both a Best Value responsibility and an objective that recognises the constraints faced by other key stakeholders in the development process. Indeed it represents an overarching recommendation that goes hand in hand with delivering both better quality outcomes (better housing) and increased public accountability. It involves a process of continual questioning – how can this task be undertaken more effectively? It also requires that housing providers play their part, coming to authorities early with proposals rather than waiting until development or funding deadlines are critical and hoping for planning permission without a hitch. It is therefore also a two-way process, with each party playing their part to ensure that the other has the information required to make informed and therefore speedy and reliable decisions. Four key approaches emerged from the research:

Fast-tracking processes

A number of the case studies had developed fast-tracking procedures that ranged in both the formality with which they were adopted, and the extent they were used. Fast-tracking arrangements can be one-off processes for particular high-profile schemes where circumstances demand a streamlined approach, such as at Newcastle (see Chapter 15). Alternatively they might be permanent arrangements directed towards particular types of development, such as new housing, for which there is a local need. The need for more affordable housing at Hammersmith and Fulham (see Chapter 15) or to attract major investments at Birmingham provide examples of the latter type. Their introduction can also be seen as opportunities to radically review established planning procedures, or as opportunities to build upon and refine existing processes. Key characteristics of such processes include:

* clear lines of communication to cut through the sometimes baffling corporate complexity faced by housing providers;
* dedicated project officers to drive and champion proposals or one-stop-shop arrangements as at Birmingham;
* preferably a single point of contact with a clear understanding of commercial realities and with the ability to make decisions (or with direct access to those who can);
* a process that offers a greater degree of certainty to housing providers, keeping them informed and involved as their application commences; and
* a process with all its key stages well documented and resourced.

The danger to be avoided is the perception that unless applied across the board, fast-tracking arrangements generate a two-tier planning process potentially leading to resentment that other projects receive a second-rate service. Therefore careful justification of the arrangements is also required, and preferably a commitment to spread best practice across the planning service as resources allow.

Securing adequate resources

The lack of resources (particularly manpower) is perhaps the fundamental problem facing many authorities and the reason for many delays throughout the planning process. In some respects, planning is always likely to face a squeeze on resources when competing with other high-spending and high-profile departments such as education and social services. Nevertheless, the lack of resources may also have much to do with the failure of planning departments to clearly and consistently demonstrate the value added by their existence. The danger comes when the squeeze on resources causes problems to spiral out of control as processes become more reactive. This can lead to further delay as more time is spent dealing with problems that might otherwise have been anticipated and dealt with earlier in the process. In Birmingham, the realisation that the service had been under-resourced led to a reinvestment that enabled the introduction of a fast-tracking system and a major development list. The latter helps the department anticipate future workload and therefore work more efficiently. In Newcastle the housebuilders themselves resourced the project management required to fast-track the development. It illustrates that a two-way process is possible with housing providers providing expertise and resources themselves in exchange for a streamlined service.

The picture nationally is not so rosy. The *Resourcing of Local Planning Authorities* report (DTLR, 2002d), commissioned as a feed into the 2002 national government Comprehensive Spending Review, revealed a huge gap in resourcing for planning which was impacting across planning services, and particularly on plan-making, from where resources were consistently switched in order to maintain development control throughput and meet national targets. More efficient (let alone effective) planning services are unlikely ever to be delivered without adequate resourcing, nevertheless the work revealed:

- a gross under-spending on planning services across the country;
- that at the same time development control workloads had increased by 26 per cent since 1996;
- that applications needing Section 106 agreements were unlikely to be delivered in eight or even thirteen weeks;
- that planning officer staff morale was very low and recruitment was very difficult because of increasing workloads and low salaries (analysis undertaken by *Planning* magazine has revealed that planning is amongst the worst-paid professions, and that planners should themselves be classified as key workers for housing need purposes – Morris, 2002b);
- that an increase of 27 per cent was required in development control staff in order to restore applications per staff member back to 1996 levels;
- that to achieve 1996/97 levels of gross expenditure on planning, 2000/01 levels; would have to rise by 37 per cent for district and unitary authorities, and by 23 per cent for counties.

Pre-application discussions

With increased resources, more time and effort can be spent up front in the planning process in the positive activity of establishing and updating policy frameworks – not least in ensuring that an up-to-date policy framework is in place. Such work, including the preparation of development briefs, design/planning guidance and the undertaking of capacity studies, are discussed in their own right in Chapter 15. Nevertheless, it is important to note here the significant impact that such early investments can have in streamlining the planning process by offering certainty and clarity in a policy framework to which applicants can respond. This finding is confirmed in a published review of good practice in pre-application enquiries which revealed a very high commitment to pre-application discussions in both the private and public sectors, to save time at the formal applications stage, to steer schemes to acceptable forms, and to achieve a 'steady growth in the degree of certainty for proposals' (Taussik and McHugh, 1997, p. 25). On the downside, resource problems seem to undermine the ability of local authorities to always provide comprehensive pre-application advice, and problems remain with the consistency of the advice and later decision-making processes – a problem compounded by the frequently vague nature of development proposals at the early stage. The research recommended a range of measures to enhance the pre-application process (see Fig. 11.2), whilst the Government is actively considering how to levy a charge for pre-application work (ODPM, 2002b, para. 85).

In Hammersmith and Fulham (see Chapter 15) and Torbay, the use of pre-application discussions provided one means to engage early with housing providers and to clarify

➤ All authorities should have a customer care policy and provide training for all staff to ensure that policy is realised. Such training should include negotiating techniques for professional staff

➤ Pre-application discussions should be mentioned in any planning charters, with authorities clarifying that they welcome such discussions

➤ Customer satisfaction surveys should be undertaken on an annual basis

➤ The availability of pre-application discussions should be widely publicised

➤ Authorities should undertake to arrange pre-application meetings as early as possible after an enquiry

➤ Applicants should be encouraged to submit material prior to the meeting

➤ Records should be maintained of pre-application meetings, which should be circulated to appropriate senior officers when applications come forward

➤ Officers should attempt to eliminate inconsistencies in pre-application advice, but should make it clear (perhaps in a charter) that they cannot commit their members to a particular point of view

➤ Officers should be of a level of seniority commensurate with the proposal, and wherever possible the same officer should deal with the subsequent application

➤ If members are approached at an early stage, applicants should be conscious of the clear dividing line which makes lobbying unacceptable

➤ Authorities should coordinate all necessary internal and external advice

➤ Supplementary planning guidance is an effective means of reducing the need for pre-application discussions

11.2 Pre-application enquiries – good practice (Taussik and McHugh, 1997).

objectives and aspirations before any abortive work has been undertaken. In Torbay, pre-application discussions were particularly welcomed by the authority to clarify their design requirements for particular sites. Equally local developer Midas Homes had been able to avoid ever going to appeal on an application. This has been achieved by being willing to engage early and meaningfully to establish both their own requirements and those of the authority. During the research the extension of the principle to pre-plan-making discussions was also highlighted. Such discussions were viewed as a valuable opportunity for housing providers to engage in the plan-making process early on, and in so doing, helped to build understanding and trust.

Protocols and timetables

Most streamlining initiatives are in themselves dependent on a further range of initiatives – the writing of and signing-up to protocols and concordats. At the national scale a range of concordats have recently been signed such as the 'Planning Concordat' between the Local Government Association (LGA) and DETR (1999), or 'The Planning User's Concordat' between the LGA (2000) and the business and voluntary sectors (see Fig. 11.3).

At the local level, the success of any streamlined processes will also be dependent on the writing down of the process for all to see, and on the ownership of that process by operators and users alike. In Brent (see Chapter 13), the use of protocols has been embraced as a means of systemising both the internal/external working relationships of the planning department with local RSLs, and, separately, the internal (to the local authority) working practices between the planning and housing departments. In both cases key tasks are written down and given time allocations in a two-way process in

➤ Up-to-date development plans are essential if the planning system is to deliver speedy processing of planning applications, certainty for developers and the security that local environmental assets will be protected and enhanced

➤ Effective management of the complex plan-making process is critical and adequate staffing and resources, including a timetable, need to be committed throughout the process

➤ A timetable for the development plan process should be published and adhered to

➤ Early and effective involvement of the business and voluntary sectors in plan preparation can help to reduce delay later on, particularly during the public inquiry

➤ Organisations considering applying for planning permission should contact the relevant authority at an early stage for preliminary advice, including advice on any likely planning agreement

➤ Pre-application advice should be sought on the basis of a project brief that clearly establishes key planning requirements – transport, environmental impact, etc.

➤ For more complex applications a pre-application presentation to the planning committee and pre-application consultations with the community might be appropriate and save time later

➤ More complex applications will take longer than eight weeks to process, but it is good practice for the authority and applicant to agree a timetable for the application, including major milestone dates – submission date, date for submission of further details, date for end of statutory and public consultation period, date for committee decision, deadline for resolving outstanding matters such as planning obligations or conditions

➤ The timetable should be widely publicised and modified only on agreement between the authority and applicant

➤ Authorities should clearly establish their requirements for information required for different types of planning applications, and applicants should follow the guidance to avoid delay

➤ The authority should appoint a named case officer of appropriate seniority to handle the complexity of the application

➤ Efficient planning processes are those which allow a reasonable time for views to be expressed without unduly prolonging the processing of the application

➤ The delegation of decisions to officers should be used wherever possible to speed up decision-making

➤ Planning obligations should be progressed to draft agreement stage in parallel with the pre-application and consultation phases of planning applications with an agreed timetable for completion

➤ Appeals should be avoided wherever possible and planning permissions implemented in good faith

11.3 The Planning User's Concordat, key streamlining agreements.

which both sides agree to supply information at the right time in order to expedite the application. In Birmingham, the accelerated development programme is also formalised in their charter. The establishment of key deadlines, critical paths and objectives early enough in the process is the key to success with such initiatives.

The route to streamlined implementation

Other approaches to streamlining are listed in Fig. 11.4. Fundamental to all of the approaches discussed above are the needs to:

➤ **Increase delegation of decisions to officers** – although recent research has revealed that this does not always equate to a faster service, and in particular that no correlation can be found between national planning statistics on rates of delegated decisions and those on rates of determination (Manns, 2000).

➤ **Clear guidance to councillors/committees** – on their roles and responsibilities, and on the dangers of ignoring officer advice.

➤ **Streamlining planning obligations** – start negotiating early in the process or preferably in advance of development activity, with clear requirements set out in the development plan or development briefs.

➤ **Pre-application consultations and community involvement** – to gauge community feeling early and to avoid political backlashes later.

➤ **Avoid planning appeals** – by negotiating early and earnestly and by being willing to address those issues that can cause delay, for example better design or delivery of planning gain.

➤ **Avoid enforcement** – implement planning permissions, conditions and agreements honestly and in good faith.

➤ **Selective updating** – by avoiding the temptation to review the whole plan each time new government advice is released and instead only selectively updating those parts directly affected.

➤ **Streamline the statutory consultee process** – by working with statutory consultees to encourage quicker responses and perhaps even drawing up mutually agreed protocols.

11.4 Other approaches to streamline implementation.

- understand the pressures each party is under;
- continually question established processes and procedures and the opportunities they present for more efficient planning;
- remember that quality (well-designed, sustainable development) is the non-negotiable output and undue haste should never be allowed to compromise that objective;
- engage early and earnestly in negotiations;
- establish the critical path that involves all key stakeholders at the right time to optimise their contribution and avoid delay (there is little point, for example, striving for an eight-week planning decision if the planning agreement takes a further two months to be agreed because the legal team were not involved early on); and
- wherever appropriate, to write down processes and agreements and sign end-users up to common objectives.

Finally, it is worth making six simple observations emanating from the case study experiences:

- Streamlining does not necessarily mean throwing the baby out with the bath water. It is important to start from established practices and procedures, from tried and tested processes, and to think from first principles how they can be improved.
- Attitudes and perceptions will take time to change. A new process is unlikely to solve problems overnight (or necessarily work as intended immediately), or to change external perceptions of a service which will often have been built up over many years.
- Any change requires investment and innovative thinking up front, but that should never provide an excuse not to change in the first place.

- Applicants have just as much responsibility to ensure a streamlined process as planning authorities, in particular by being flexible and willing to negotiate.
- It is important to bring the Government Regional Offices and other regional agencies on board early as regards major plan allocations or new policy approaches, to avoid delays later in the process.
- Planning processes are only part of the equation; highways, funding agencies (including of urban regeneration and social housing) and the community also need to be brought on board early.

12

Inclusive planning and decision-making

Planning – behind closed doors

It is an unfortunate fact that in the recent past, the British planning system has become (either rightly or wrongly) associated with deals made behind closed doors (Figure 12.1). Thus a widely held perception exists that developers can 'buy' planning permissions, and that local communities – who must live with (and in) the places planners and developers create – have been shut out of much of the process.

Although it is unlikely that the worst extremes of such practices ever accounted for more than a very small minority of planning permissions, some of these criticisms were borne out by Lees' (1993) study of malpractice in perhaps the worst case – North Cornwall District Council – which inspired the Committee on Standards in Public Life (The Nolan Committee) (1997) to include a chapter on planning in their third report. Although planning was not considered to be a major problem area, the Nolan Committee

12.1 The democratic planning process? (Louis Hellman, 1995).

➤ Members and officers should avoid indicating the likely decision on an application or otherwise committing the authority during contact with applicants and objectors.
➤ There should be opportunities for applicants and objectors, and other interested parties such as parish councils, to make presentations to the planning committee.
➤ All applications considered by the planning committee should be subject to full, written reports from officers and incorporate firm recommendations.
➤ The reasons given by the planning committee for refusing or granting planning permission should be fully minuted, especially where these are contrary to officer advice or the local plan.
➤ Councillors and planning officers should make oral declarations at planning committee of significant contact with applicants and objectors, in addition to the usual disclosure of pecuniary and non-pecuniary interests.
➤ No members should be appointed to the planning committee without having agreed to undertake a period of training in planning procedures as specified by the authority.

12.2 Code of best practice in planning procedures (Committee on Standards in Public Life, 1997, p. 75).

nevertheless recommended a greater degree of openness in the planning process, and that councillors should undergo training to acquaint themselves with the complexities of the procedural and legal judgements needing to be made (see Fig. 12.2).

Nolan commented that part of the problem lay in the change of perception the public had about the planning system. Whereas when the system was first established in 1947 it had significant public support to drive forward a reconstruction, today the system is largely seen as a means to prevent change and protect amenities, and promotion of development leads quickly to public disillusionment and to pressure on local politicians.

Participation and openness in planning was never an original intention of the planning system as conceived in 1947; indeed, the early view of planning and planners was the rather paternalistic one that professionals know best and should be trusted to deliver what is best for their communities. That is not to say that no public involvement in planning took place; Yvonne Rydin (in Cullingworth, 1999, p. 184), for example, argues that a degree of liaison was a consistent thread of those early years. Nevertheless, it was not until the 1960s that pressure started to build for more systematic involvement in decision-making and a more open process; although interestingly the main impetus for change came from central government, rather than from grass-roots activity, as a means to devolve more planning work down to local government, whilst maintaining support for planning decisions (Rydin, in Cullingworth, 1999, p. 185). Thus more inclusive decision-making was originally intended as a means to cope with potential opposition, whereas experience has shown that the mechanisms provided in fact act to more effectively channel it.

The report of the (Skeffington) Committee on Public Participation in Planning (1969) was perhaps the breakthrough for a more inclusive planning process, although its ambitious programme for participation at all stages of the planning process was greatly watered down in the subsequent legislation. Skeffington had called for community fora and the appointment of community development officers to act as constant conduits of people's views and to stimulate discussion, whilst the public were to be actively involved in plan-making from survey to adoption. The reality was a regime of limited publicity and consultation (in effect merely the right to comment) on development plans and planning decisions. This tokenist (p. 167) approach to involvement has remained unchanged, perhaps accounting for some of the public frustration with a planning system which, through the Skeffington proposals, was supposed to transform into a smoother, less contentious process.

Of course, the procedures of local democracy – voting in or out those sitting or who might sit on local planning committees – should guarantee a degree of popular input into planning. Counter-intuitively, however, as real public participation effectively equates to a movement of power towards communities and away from their representatives, there remains a tension between representative democracy and approaches that offer direct citizen power. Typically, today, all stakeholders – local, economic and other interests, as well as a range of statutory consultees (i.e. English Heritage in the case of development affecting conservation interests) – have the chance to participate in (or at least to be consulted on) decision-making at both the strategic and development levels at a number of key stages.

During preparation of the development plan all key stakeholders have the right to make representations as successive drafts are produced, and to appear in person or submit evidence to the public local inquiry. During the processing of a planning application, stakeholders are entitled to submit representations during the decision-making process, and, at the discretion of the planning committee, to speak at the committee meeting. Thus, both policy-based and development-related consultation is facilitated through statutory and discretionary publicity procedures, with nearly all authorities going beyond statutory minimum requirements in this regard (Spawforth, 1995); although actual hands-on involvement remains the exception rather than the rule. As a consequence, representations received on development plans remain very low (typically less than 5 per cent of the population within a plan area), and representations on planning applications are largely restricted to those on whom they negatively impact.

Therefore, despite countless attempts to raise the levels of public involvement that have been catalogued and evaluated throughout the last 40 years (see, for example, Levin and Donnison, 1969; Johnson, 1984; Planning Officers Society, 1998; Salter and Bird, 2002), the standard forms of involvement in planning have proven to be woefully inadequate. Moreover, in the early twenty-first century, participation in the wider political process is at an all-time low (although how this should be interpreted is subject to fierce debate – Pattie and Johnston, 2001), and it has long been accepted that only the most vociferous and articulate take part in the formal planning process at all (Lowndes *et al.*, 1998; Baeten, 2001). In this context, in bringing forward their proposals for local development frameworks (ODPM, 2002c, para. 30) the government has argued that

> Effective public engagement must be at the heart of development plans. We want to empower local people to feel that they can participate in a system that is really interested in their views. We want to change the culture of planning from one of objecting, to one of constructive participation.

The solution was a statutory requirement that local development frameworks should include a 'Statement of Community Involvement', setting out:

- the arrangements and standards to be achieved in involving the community in the continuing review of all parts of the local development framework and in significant development control decisions

- the standards for good practice in engaging those with an interest in a proposed development
- simple clear guidelines that will enable the community to know with confidence when and how it will be consulted, by the developer at pre-application stage and by the local authority in relation to planning applications
- a benchmark for applicants for planning permission about what is expected of them.

At the same time 'Planning for Real' (see p, 213 and Chapter 10) was promoted alongside other community-based planning techniques to more fully involve the community in the preparation of action plans. Help was also provided for individuals and community groups to develop planning advocacy skills through putting financial assistance for 'Planning Aid' on a statutory footing, but the case for third-party rights of appeal that had been forcefully promoted by a coalition of amenity groups to increase transparency, probity and accountability (Green Balance, 2002) was firmly rejected as contrary to a democratically accountable system. The Green Paper also had little to say about the practical means of sharing responsibility – across the full range of stakeholders.

Inclusive planning

Inclusive planning and decision-making implies engaging with the full range of stake-holders in a meaningful way encompassing the principle of all parties signing-up to and owning the process.

The need to foster a sense of ownership in both the process and outcomes of plan-ning, and hence avoid a situation where interested parties including local communities feel they have no control over what happens in their localities seems fundamental, yet so far this is an area that the planning system has paid little more than lip-service to. Most likely – as is clearly the case as regards third-party rights of appeal (where parties other than the applicant are entitled to appeal a planning decision) – this is because the resource and time implications of doing otherwise could be substantial. The Confederation of British Industry, for example, largely couches its opposition to third-party rights of appeal on the basis that 'The knock-on effects . . . could have a negative impact on business and economic growth' (Winkley, 2002b). Changes in the 2003 Planning and Compulsory Purchase Act do not promise to significantly increase the degree of third-party engagement across the planning process.

Rydin (in Cullingworth, 1999, pp. 195–6) argues that there has been repeated evidence of dissatisfaction with the way in which participation has been delivered, particularly when planning is measured against an ideal of community empowerment and direct community involvement in decision-making. She observes that there is frequent mistrust of planners and a widespread cynicism about participation that it is primarily a means to divert, frustrate or manipulate opinion, but also that there is amongst planners a genuine desire to engage the public and other stakeholders and to develop policies and take decisions that command widespread support. Rydin warns that there are two reasons for suggesting caution in extending the notion of community participation too far. First, because it is notoriously difficult to engage the public in planning decision-making, and so participation is always likely to be skewed to those who have a grievance and to those who are already active in local issues. Thus, for many housing develop-ments, the small number of people that are directly affected in a negative manner by a development (i.e. because their view of open space is destroyed) will tend to be much more vocal than the much larger number who are affected in an indirect positive manner (i.e. because increased housing supply will help to stabilise house prices and support local facilities). Second (and related to the first reason), because planning is a form of collective decision-making which affects far wider economic, environmental and social interests that need to be balanced with, but not ignored in the face of, local interests. Thus public interest and decisions made through public participation are not necessarily the same thing.

The planning system nevertheless remains the interface between the key parties in the development process, and the means through which development is publicly endorsed. It is therefore important that the interests and needs of all of the parties – including the wider community – are acknowledged. But many tensions within the planning process are experienced due to the gulf between the motives and under-standing of the different parties, including the wider community. There is, for example, a widespread perception that many of the principles and elements of current planning policy are not accepted or understood by the wider community, including the council members. The issue of density (discussed in Chapter 8) is one such example. Conversely, there is also a view that many policies and proposals are not realistic or responsive to the local context. This adds to conflict and delay (see Chapter 6) and exacerbates an often already combative relationship between the local community, the elected members, planners and the providers of new housing.

An inclusive process can potentially foster a more cooperative approach, and need not be too costly in time if engagement is early and sincere. Establishing an early dialogue, for example, can potentially overcome contentious issues before attitudes become entrenched (Christie *et al.*, 2002, p. 35). It can also provide an opportunity for each organisation and individual to understand the motives of the other parties, and gain a better understanding of the planning/housebuilding processes described in Chapters 2 to 4. There can, however, be costs to this approach. The actual process can require increased (and differently skilled) resources, and if involvement and inclusion is to be meaningful then a level of compromise (or at least an attempt to reconcile ideas) is to an extent inevitable. Consequently, a willingness to adapt is required. Furthermore, more inclusive planning processes do not guarantee to deliver win-win benefits for all sides on all occasions, although they should at least clarify issues, explore the scope for consensus and open up possibilities for new ideas (Christie *et al.*, 2002, p. 28).

Inclusive decision-making may also require additional time during the initial stages, although potentially this is balanced later by the benefits of having a smoother process overall (saving time by avoiding classic NIMBY responses to development proposals) leading to improved outcomes that all parties sign up to. Some techniques for partic-ipation are discussed in Chapter 10, others extending across key stakeholders, as well as to the public at large, are considered in the context of two local case studies below.

The case studies

The case studies illustrate two different approaches to inclusive planning and decision-making. The Stratford-on-Avon case demonstrates:

- The value of exploring new initiatives in response to specific problems.
- The importance of resourcing the planning process and allocating dedicated officers to initiatives where appropriate.

- The need to produce comprehensive and inclusive design guidance to create consistency and transparency.
- The critical importance of community participation as a means of shaping and formulating guidance of all types.
- A carefully developed corporate working strategy between departments involving an intermediate officer role.
- Intervention to overcome inequalities in land markets to increase the quantity and quality of affordable housing.

In Cambridge, a suite of initiatives has been developed and applied to a recent medium-sized development. The case study outlines:

- The importance of not simply ignoring problems in the process, but dealing with these directly by bringing different parties together (i.e. through a development control forum).
- The value of a strong community, willing and able to shape development opportunities, becoming an active partner rather than a passive victim in the process.
- The need to identify development potential at the earliest possible stage and instigate early consultation.
- This should involve considering different aspirations for sites through public consultation and articulating these aspirations in a shared vision, usually in the form of a design-led development brief.

CASE STUDY: Stratford-on-Avon – design and enabling

The Midlands district of Stratford-on-Avon is primarily rural in nature and encompasses several small market towns and the larger and historic Stratford-upon-Avon. Within recent years there has been increasing pressure upon the housing market within the district. As house prices have steadily risen in neighbouring Oxfordshire (to the south), there has been an influx of people opting to live in Warwickshire and this has led in turn to a dramatic increase in development pressure. In the village of Long Compton, for example, in 1997 two new dwellings were built, whilst in the following year 50 applications were received.

In response to the increasing demands, the approach taken by the local authority aims to improve the delivery and quality of both market and affordable housing through increasing the involvement of the different stakeholders, increasing the levels of certainty within the process, and improving corporate working practices, skills and knowledge within the local authority. The authority has actively resourced a number of different initiatives, including the appointment of dedicated officers.

Design guidance

The publication in 1994 of the discussion document *Quality in Town and Country* by the Department of the Environment (1994) represented a culture shift towards acknowledging the importance of design (see Chapter 8). In response to this new emphasis at national level, Stratford-on-Avon (with cross-party support) introduced several new initiatives at the local level. As a first step, the post of Design Officer was created to coordinate and prepare design guidance and to become involved with negotiating better design on individual sites. By 2001, Stratford-on-Avon was in the process of establishing a full suite of design guidance, from district-wide design guides to Town Design Statements (scaled up versions of VDSs) to Village Design Statements (VDSs).

The aim of the guidance was to clarify the aspirations of the local authority in this crucial area, thereby increasing transparency and certainty. To achieve this, the local authority acknowledged at an early stage the benefits of close consultation and where possible direct stakeholder involvement in the formulation of the guidance, thus ensuring that the finished guidance is realistic and workable, and broadly accepted by all key stakeholders.

Confirming this view, local developers are generally very positive about the design guidance, arguing that such guidance (especially on specific sites) is valuable as long as it is not too prescriptive. In this respect the design guidance offers developers clarity about what can be achieved on particular sites, for example, on the volume of development and its quality in terms of materials and finishes. The approach has developed to such an extent that where design guidance is not in place, developers suggest that they are at a disadvantage as they are unaware of the aspirations of the local authority, and hence of any cost implications that may be incurred.

The District Design Guide (completed in 2000) aims to set out issues and principles rather than present design solutions, and as such the emphasis is broadly educational rather than didactic. The context of Stratford-on-Avon plays a primary role within the guidance, and the district is divided into different character areas, with the characteristics of each outlined and discussed. The guide first identifies key principles, including quality and design of the public realm, character and identity, sustainability, density, size standards, highway design and design character and innovation, and moves on to consider detailed issues working through the hierarchy of built form, from chapters on settlements, streets, highways, open spaces and plot series, to chapters on plots, buildings, design and materials.

This structure evolved through a process of detailed and wide-ranging consultation with key stakeholder groups both locally and nationally (including academics and other authorities). Thus in total 500 copies were sent out for consultation, with local developers involved at an early stage in the formulation of the design guidance and playing an influential role in its development. This has in turn fostered a strong local approval of the guidance, which contributes to positive attitudes in the way that both parties (housing providers and local authority officers) engage in the subsequent negotiation process.

Village Design Statements

As part of the new national emphasis on design in the mid-/late 1990s, the Countryside Commission (now the Countryside Agency) developed a methodology for Village Design Statements (Countryside Commission, 1996a, 1996b). Stratford-on-Avon was involved in a pilot of this approach, with the Countryside Agency funding three Village Design Statements and a Project Officer to manage and enable the process.

The emphasis of Village Design Statements is on the community, with the village community producing a design appraisal and guidance themselves, with support from the local authority. This helps to foster a good working relationship between communities and their planning authority, increasing local knowledge of the planning system and offering an opportunity for the community to influence future policy. The aim of the document itself is to manage change, as opposed to blocking or controlling change. Thus VDSs identify and describe the distinctive character of a village and its surroundings at three levels: the landscape setting, the shape of the settlement, and the nature of the buildings themselves. Building upon these elements, design principles based upon the distinctive local character of the settlement are identified and illustrated. In Stratford-on-Avon (the only authority to have a dedicated VDS officer), the VDS Project Officer plays a key role in the process, making the link between the communities and the policy.

In the village of Long Compton, for example, the first meeting was held in December 1997, after the local authority suggested to the Parish Council that they might wish to undertake a VDS. The Parish Council formed a committee that included a number of village residents that had high levels of relevant knowledge, including an architect/developer, a graphic designer, a builder and a CPRE representative. The VDS Officer provided support including the VDS kit (which contains a series of profiles and steps to follow), and helped to steer the process. A questionnaire was sent to every house in the village, and after responses were received a workshop was organised. This had a fairly good response, with 30–40 attending, although these were noticeably the residents that regularly involved themselves in village affairs. The working group then produced a draft VDS which was circulated to all of the residents in the village, and after feedback was received the document was finalised and issued.

The VDS was a useful exercise to go through, as the villagers felt themselves to be increasingly under pressure of development, and the VDS represented a means for the community to gain a level of control over the process. Initially the VDS was viewed as a means of controlling or blocking development, and there were still vestiges of this attitude remaining once the VDS was completed. This was reflected in the attitudes of some local residents who measured the success of the VDS by whether it had been used as a reason for refusal at appeal.

The Countryside Agency has been keen to extend the principles of the approach to larger settlements, a potential that has also been acknowledged by Stratford-on-Avon. The local authority is therefore now in the process of supplementing the existing hierarchy of guidance with an additional tier – Town Design Statements – that in essence represent scaled-up versions of VDSs.

Improving knowledge and understanding

Officers suggest that the production of design guidance in all its forms is only responsible for '5 per cent of the success of the final outcome'. They argue instead that knowledge, understanding and implementation are the critical success factors that impact upon the quality of resulting decisions and developments, and that these factors follow the production of the guidance. Local developers felt that design advice from the authority is still to some degree at the whim of the authority's urban designers and conservation architects/officers, who frequently contradict each other. To avoid this confusion and prioritise implementation of the key design principles in the guidance, the Design Officer at Stratford-on-Avon has conducted CPD (Continuing Professional Development) sessions within Development Control to present and discuss the guidance. These sessions have also been undertaken for a wider audience to help bring developers and applicants on board by explaining the approach being adopted on design.

The Design Officer also presents specific design issues (relating to particular applications) to the planning committee members as a means of raising awareness and starting discussion. Involvement in the application process usually starts during pre- or mid-application discussions with case officers, following which the Design Officer produces a separate report for the committee. This involvement has been welcomed by the local developers, who feel that it contributes significantly towards the removal of resistance to development per se and also to resistance based around key areas of tension, for example on questions of density.

Development Enabling Officer

On another key area of tension – the delivery of affordable housing – a number of initiatives have been launched. The principal concern of most local authorities has been with meeting day-to-day housing needs, and this has led to a neglect of strategic links between housing and planning. Consequently, some housing providers feel obliged to undertake the role of facilitator, bringing the different local authority departments together. One initiative undertaken at Stratford-on-Avon that seeks to improve working practices within the planning and housing departments, and improve the way that RSLs engage with the planning process, is the establishment of the post of Development and Enabling Officer (which was in place throughout the 1990s). The officer is based jointly within both departments (planning and housing), which aids corporate working and enables the coordination of efforts.

In 2000, the Development and Enabling Officer in Stratford-on-Avon was from a planning background. This was identified as beneficial by local RSLs, as Enabling Officers (where they exist) in other authorities usually have housing backgrounds, resulting in a more housing-focused rather than planning approach to liaison. It was felt that this is detrimental when a key role of the Development and Enabling Officer is to chaperone RSLs through the planning process and ensure that their voice is heard within strategic consultation.

Preferred partner RSLs

The system of preferred partner RSLs is a further method used in Stratford-on-Avon to achieve certainty and consistency within the provision of affordable housing. Since Stratford-on-Avon's entire housing stock was transferred to the South Warwickshire Housing Association in 1997, the capital receipts have been used to fund partnership schemes in social housing. The partnership agreement was signed in 1997 with eight partner RSLs on a five-yearly renewal cycle, and is effectively a working document that sets out overall objectives in terms of the number of houses to be supplied over the five-year period, and what the RSLs undertake to do in terms of working with Stratford as a housing authority.

A more formal means of directing developers (within particular Section 106 obligations) towards preferred RSLs is being explored. As a means of nominating specific partner RSLs for developers it would potentially remove the competitive process of using several RSLs bidding for land against each other, and consequently increasing the cost of the land to the successful RSL. Thus the process would be simplified in tandem with reducing unnecessary costs for the RSLs involved. The objective is to enable an increasing emphasis to be placed on the quality and design of the affordable housing units themselves, rather than on the procurement processes.

Clarity and certainty within policy

Stratford-on-Avon also has an established Section 106 agreement which, coupled with clear and well-established local plan policies, further distinguishes practice in the district. Because the resulting processes are very robust, departures are rarely allowed and the whole process is enthusiastically endorsed by local RSLs. In the local plan, for example, the local authority identifies housing needs and the extent, type and quality of housing, enabling the developer to design specifically for the site, and conferring a welcome level of certainty on the process.

The Section 106 agreements address the issue of land values for affordable housing plots, and if agreement on values is not achieved, then the land has to be referred to the district surveyor. In late 2000, this was in the region of £5,000 for an un-serviced plot and £7,500 for a fully serviced plot. An unwritten understanding exists that the cost of land to the RSL will be in line with the district surveyor's valuation of the land, otherwise the local authority will not support grant funding for the housing (i.e. if the land value has been inflated). As this essentially removes competitive market forces, there is consequently no negotiation required on the affordable housing land element, reducing unnecessary delay and further simplifying the process. The Section 106 affordable housing obligation is simply viewed as another quantifiable cost within the process, and is effectively passed back to the landowner via reduced land values.

Discussion

As an authority, Stratford-on-Avon District Council is willing to think beyond current and accepted practice. They view themselves as a pioneering authority, piloting initiatives that are unique within the country. Thus, for instance, the local authority has a positive view about the impact of the guidance it produces, even though there are mixed views amongst some local housing providers. Some suggest that the initiatives offer certainty and consistency, whilst others hold the view that the guidance at Stratford is inflexible, and still offers opportunities for conflicting interpretations. The local authority acknowledges this potential conflict, and as a result is strongly emphasising the importance of education to overcome inconsistency in implementation and the hijacking of negotiations by council members with political or NIMBY concerns.

In this respect there is also an acceptance that local communities need to gain knowledge and engage more positively with processes of change. From the residents' point of view, it would seem that they were generally content with the level of consultation that was undertaken in the district, via their parish councils and initiatives like the VDSs. However, although the VDS approach represents the embodiment of enhanced community participation, there remains the potential for VDSs to become somewhat unrealistic wish-lists, or the defence mechanisms of a community who see the VDS as a means of preventing rather than managing change. In essence, without education, understanding and consistency, the consultation process could potentially foster frustration and increase barriers between the local authority and community.

Stratford-on-Avon are keen to increase the supply of affordable housing and to this end have introduced several initiatives, including the appointment of the enabling officer, who successfully serves to bridge gaps between local authority departments and to champion the cause of local RSLs. The introduction of preferred partner status for RSLs is also gradually increasing affordable housing output, although this type of approach carries with it distinct risks. It may, for example, be seen as preferential treatment (even as a restrictive practice), leading to uneven distributions of development activity. Some developers, for example, argued that problems have occurred in other authorities where Section 106 provision has been directed towards particular RSLs as a result of close personal links with particular officers.

The local authority was also seeking to encourage RSLs to take more of a lead as developers themselves, rather than relying on private developers to drive the process with Section 106 subsidies. For example, a new initiative that Stratford-on-Avon are introducing is to circulate their urban capacity studies to RSLs prior to wider release, enabling RSLs to act as lead developer, effectively cherry-picking the prime sites. In this way, it was hoped that schemes could be made to suit the needs of local communities and RSLs rather than the profit-driven aspirations of private housebuilders. However, this type of approach can also be seen as a restrictive practice. This conflict in interest between enhancing the function of RSLs at the expense of the private sector represents a common theme running across approaches in many authorities, and perhaps reflects a more fundamental conflict within the system.

CASE STUDY: Cambridge – inclusive approaches to development

Several initiatives have been developed by Cambridge City Council in order to ensure that development is of a high standard and responds to the local context and to the views and wishes of the range of different stakeholders involved, including the local community. The authority has found that this inclusive approach to development control has dramatically improved the output of the planning process and has significantly reduced objections and consequently delay. The attitude of the applicants to this initiative varies, although officers suggest that initial negative perceptions are gradually eroded as the benefits emerge within each proposal. The local residents within Cambridge are very positive about the approach as it reflects a formal platform where specific concerns can be addressed and also serves to promote better (and ongoing) relationships between the community, the local planning authority, and developers who are active in the area. The approach includes pre-application discussions, planning briefs, public meetings and a development control forum.

The City of Cambridge, with a population of 120,000, is predominantly urban with a tight urban boundary and few brownfield sites remaining within the city. The University is a major landowner, a situation which constrains ownership and development even further. Parts of the area are vulnerable to heavy flooding, which tends to push new residential development further out of the city. There is a lack of affordable housing with a dwelling stock dominated by market housing or private rented student accommodation. Coupled with a dwindling land supply and huge demand across the spectrum of the housing market, house prices are consequently very high (within the London range).

The majority of residential development within the city is brownfield, but consists largely of back-land development and infill, and as such is consequently small in scale. The largest sites to come forward in recent years have been for 200+ houses, with the Simoco site (formerly B1 – business – use) representing one of the largest of these (see p. 209). A general strategy within the local authority is to increase the housing supply (both market and affordable) within the city to reverse the trend of commuting in, whilst ensuring that whatever development takes place is appropriate in terms of quality and context.

Within the local plan the affordable housing need is set out clearly. Thus all housing sites of over 20 houses have to provide 30 per cent (by site area) of social housing in an attempt to address the waiting list of 6,000 people. An officer has also been appointed in an enabling and development role to ease the constrained land supply, in part by evaluating the land that is held by the local authority in order to rationalise and release sites suitable for development. In addition, the authority has attempted to introduce a more inclusive approach to development control through a variety of approaches. Some residents suggest that the local authority recognised that this more inclusive approach to decision-making was required because a number of major (unaccountable) planning mistakes had been made in the past. However, the need for greater community involvement and more contextually appropriate development essentially represents a response to the increasing development pressure.

Pre-application discussions

Cambridge City Council identifies an early dialogue through pre-application discussions as one of the primary methods of ensuring appropriate development as an outcome of a smooth process. Thus pre-application discussions are held in a regular slot every two weeks, using a development team approach. At each session a range of professional expertise is represented with access to senior officers as necessary.

The process is encouraged within the authority's development control literature, but is otherwise developer-led, with developers or applicants approaching the authority to request time at one of the slots. The initiative also depends upon the professionalism of all of those involved as there are no formally established procedures (something that might enhance the approach). The structure of each session depends upon the nature of the enquiry, and all applications are encouraged, regardless of scale. The authority works collectively and argues that these joint previews enable a joint awareness of the problems and opportunities associated with particular developments.

Development briefs and public meetings

Alongside early dialogue, the local authority seeks to institute development briefs, established where appropriate with input from public meetings. Development briefs, they believe, can help to establish key considerations (local or design) at a very early stage in the development process. Therefore the Cambridge City Local Plan contains a number of sites that are identified for a development brief, usually reflecting the significance of the site or development, or the level of community interest.

Usually the process is initiated when a landowner expresses interest in the site, after which the authority will undertake the brief to test out community aspirations through public meetings and workshops. The brief is subsequently refined through dialogue with the developer. The workshops or meetings are usually led by the environmental design section, with the dedicated consultation officer organising the event and taking the lead in conjunction with urban designers, a range of other officers and development control. The main resource involved in undertaking the development briefs is that inherent in organising and attending the meetings.

Development Control Forum

In contrast to the pre-application discussions and public workshops, the purpose of the Development Control Forum is to act as a safety net, ensuring that contentious proposals (perhaps a result of the applicant not engaging in a dialogue with the local authority and community) are picked up. The Development Control Forum is seen as a successful method of broadening the dialogue between the different stakeholders, and establishing direct relationships between developers and the local community. The key to its success seems to be having the forum early in the process, to get people's views before the decision-making process begins.

The purpose of the forum meeting is largely to mediate and seek compromise between the different parties on significant applications (not householder applications). Thus if there are valid planning points that arise and the committee members support them, these can be negotiated separately and agreed, or alternatively, agreement can be reached at the forum itself. During the statutory notification period, notification letters are sent to the local residents in the neighbourhood, alerting them to the fact that they can petition the Forum, in front of members of the planning sub-committee if there is enough demand. Notices are also posted at the site and on the internet. A forum is initiated through receipt of 25 or more names.

The Forum is held on a Wednesday morning, on a four-weekly cycle. The meetings are usually chaired by the director or deputy director of the planning services, and attended by the case officer, members of the planning sub-committee (usually around 8 of the 11 members attend) and is open to members of the public and press. The applicant and the petitioners are allowed three representatives each, and each is given up to 20 minutes to present their case or make comments, after which the planning sub-committee members have an opportunity to ask questions and make comments. The proceedings of the Forum are formally recorded (as minutes), ensuring that any issues arising or addressed are considered in the determination of the application.

The Simoco site, St Andrews Road, Cambridge

The process undertaken for the proposed development at the Simoco site, St Andrews Road, Cambridge, is an example of several elements of the Cambridge approach, and illustrates the way that an inclusive process can overcome tensions and begin to build productive relationships between the different stakeholders. The site on the edge of the city centre comprises several parcels of land formerly owned by Simoco, a company involved in hi-tech research occupying land situated next to the site. The existing locality is mixed, predominantly residential, and functions almost as a self-contained community. The area is an intermediate office area in the local plan, which limits redevelopment of office space to an additional 10 per cent of the original office space area on site.

The developer originally purchased the separate sites on the basis of B1 use, although preliminary investigation by local agents had indicated that residential development might be considered. The developer's agent was also aware that the authority was keen to see a reduction in office provision and an increase in residential provision on the site, although this was not identified in the local plan. A trade-off was eventually made via two planning applications. Thus the agent made an outline application for residential development on the northern site of 100–120 units (retaining some flexibility over density for subsequent purchasers), and consolidated the office space allowance in a detailed application on the southern site.

After submission of the applications a residents' association meeting was held. The high level of interest within the local community was partly a reaction to the climate of aggressive development that had been experienced previously (on other sites), and partly due to the strength of community organisation within the area. This comprised two residents' associations and an active church (which had itself been trying to get hold of part of the site). The residents felt that the publicity they generated tipped the balance and the local authority became very keen to listen and to get the developers to consider public consultation. In response – and in order to progress the application – the developers held a public meeting with an open invitation and ninety people attended, including members of the local community. At this initial meeting, the local authority planners took a back seat and the developers presented the proposals. The meeting highlighted some perceived problems, and was acknowledged to be a very difficult and hostile meeting by all of the parties involved.

A second public meeting addressed planning issues in general around the site, whilst a third public meeting (a workshop) split the residents into different small groups to consider design issues. Local traffic, density, building height and other issues were identified as key concerns.

It was felt by the residents that the meetings enabled them to educate the planners about what the local community wanted, particularly as regards the level of local traffic and the impact on the neighbourhood which previously had not been acknowledged by the local authority. Within the community it was felt that the meetings were a positive experience, and enabled the different stakeholders to find common ground and eventual compromise.

In parallel with the public meetings, an ongoing dialogue developed between the developer and a representative of each of the two residents' associations, through a series of informal meetings to test out ideas and issues that would feed back into the formal meetings. The parties involved found that this informal dialogue was a crucial platform for establishing and defining issues in a non-hostile and cooperative way. To enable this sort of dialogue, it was felt important to have someone in the liaison role (a local spokesperson), although not necessarily a councillor.

At this stage a development brief which addressed the concerns that had arisen from the public workshops and informal meetings was drawn up. The developer's consultants prepared the brief in conjunction with the authority, as time constraints meant that the authority was unable to undertake it in-house. The committee adopted the brief in January 2000, immediately prior to determination of the applications (at the same committee meeting). The authority recognises that in this example, the brief and local consultation came too late and ideally should have been undertaken at the pre-application stage, in order to address (and ameliorate) some of the issues that were eventually ironed out at the Development Control Forum.

Discussion

Since adopting a more inclusive approach, the local community has noticed a positive impact; in particular the community has been able to develop an ongoing relationship with the planners and with local government. Cambridge City Council suggests that on balance, the approach takes longer than a standard development control process, but that the outcome and quality of schemes can be greatly improved if the applicant is cooperative. They suggest that time spent in the early stages can also reduce time spent on the appeal process, as the applicant is less willing to appeal a decision that has been transparently determined with involvement of all key stakeholders.

This increase in the length of the process can be seen as a negative feature of planning in Cambridge by developers and applicants. Officers suggest, however, that initial hostility from developers usually vanishes during the course of the process, as the benefits of cooperation and collaboration become clear. The success of the approach depends upon a number of factors. The strength of the community, and their ability to engage effectively in the process is of crucial importance. For example, the strength of the two local residents associations in the St Andrew's Road area, and their collective ability to organise and articulate a response at the Development Control Forum enabled the community to negotiate effectively with the applicant. Other communities may not be so motivated or able to participate effectively at a Forum.

The residents of St Andrew's Road found that a core group of individuals is required to drive and maintain the community involvement. It was also felt that the level of community involvement and commitment to the process depended upon the extent to which the community felt threatened, and the extent to which the community felt that it could succeed by fighting. In this respect, the support that the community received from the local planning authority and the local councillors was invaluable to the residents' groups.

It was acknowledged by all of the parties within the St Andrew's Road example that the process could be improved and enhanced. With this in mind, the local planning authority are putting together a consultation strategy to make the elements of the approach explicit. This will also include the concept of the considerate applicant, which was an issue that had arisen from the recent Best Value review. Another aspect that the Best Value review identified was ensuring that all communities are aware of the approach. Currently there is a high level of awareness of the approach amongst local agents and landowners, but this is clearly lacking within many of the more marginal communities.

Greater inclusion in the planning process is a very positive way to ensure that development responds to local needs, enhances an area, reinforces existing communities and patterns of life, and utilises local knowledge (e.g. flood areas, pedestrian movement, etc.). It can also mean that communities feel involved and acknowledged in the process, consequently building community capacity and reducing the gulf between the formulation and administration of local policies.

However, if a commitment to adequately resource an inclusive process is not in place (especially from the local planning authority but also the housing provider), then moves to increase inclusion can lead to a deterioration of working relationships between the parties involved, with increased delay and mistrust of motives. Despite having senior-level support (acknowledged as a critical factor in driving the approach forward), it is recognised within Cambridge City Council that currently the process is not adequately resourced, and relies heavily on the goodwill of officers.

Recommendations

Widening the inclusion of different groups in the planning and development processes can take a significant effort, as the case studies demonstrate. But this approach pays dividends by addressing two key tensions. First, early investment and bringing a range of people on board avoids a situation where communities in general, or those with a particular issue to raise, feel disempowered by the system. This can mean – and commonly does – that development proposals face fewer objections and move more swiftly through the system. Second, the suspicion of decisions being made behind closed doors will be at least partially quashed. Therefore inclusive processes address the issues of both planning delay (see Chapter 6) and the Nolan Committee's (Committee on Standards in Public Life, 1997) suggestion that the planning system is insufficiently open and transparent.

More generally, there are three fundamental strands of an inclusive process (demonstrated in both of the case studies) which together can start to close the gulf between parties:

- Fostering a sense of ownership of the process and the outcomes to address any feelings of lack of control and to encourage a willingness to engage in the process.
- Using shared knowledge to formulate planning tools and development proposals that respond to the particular needs of a locality or community, or to the working processes of the organisations involved.
- Setting the limits, by consulting early, and with integrity, and therefore forestalling the demand for more comprehensive involvement further down the line (when it is more difficult for housing providers to respond constructively).

The principle of inclusion within the development/planning process can take different forms. It can be formal or informal, ongoing or intermittent, wide-ranging or focused, and directed towards policy formulation or feedback (but preferably both). An inclusive process should have stakeholder involvement in the realms of formulation (of policy/proposals) and feedback at both policy-based and development-specific levels. It should provide a framework for discussion, enabling relationships to develop between parties that would not normally come into contact. It should also enable wider understanding of different objectives and identification of potential cross-party aims or common ground. Finally, and ideally, it should be an iterative process, with the involvement of the stakeholders feeding back into and shaping the outcomes.

It will not always be possible to bring all partners on board with the need for more development, but at least such approaches can help move anti-development attitudes towards a more constructive acceptance of development. These processes can also be important in clarifying the role that stakeholders can play in shaping development, and indeed all stakeholders, including developers and the local community, can both initiate and run the process. The range of inclusive approaches includes the following:

Consultation exercises (housing and planning) – at the policy-based level

A wide-ranging and detailed consultation exercise undertaken whilst formulating planning tools and policy can be a means to ensure that the wider stakeholders have an opportunity to comment and make suggestions, rendering the final product more appropriate to the local and environmental context. Housing departments might also benefit from adopting similar approaches whilst formulating their housing strategies, ensuring, for example, that planning departments comment on their plans and vice versa to deliver a coordinated framework (see Chapter 13). As undertaken in Stratford-on-Avon, a consultation exercise with extended scope beyond the local context can also draw on the experience of other professionals who have experience in formulating similar tools. By such means a climate of shared experience between local authorities, academics and other organisations and individuals can be fostered. As the case study shows, if the process is established at an early stage, a more positive outcome is facilitated, and the policy or guidance is likely to be accepted as something that other stakeholders will engage with and sign-up to.

However, government guidance on the production of development plans calls for effective community involvement and participation, rather than mere consultation, arguing that 'consultation tends to mean that most of the end-product is determined by the elected members acting on officer advice, with the consultees either having only a minimal impact on all issues or a significant effect on minor issues only' (ODPM, 2002d, p. 56). The guidance argues that more fundamental forms of involvement are only likely to be successful if there is a commitment within the authority to the outcomes, a clear strategy for participation, strong and coherent project management, and the proper use of staff resources and skills. The guide advises that there are a number of aspects that must be planned and managed with great care, yet also treated flexibly as the work proceeds:

- Link into and draw benefit from any other recent or concurrent community participation, for example work of Local Strategic Partnerships (see Chapter 10).
- Be sure that any stages or participation outcomes are linked into the democratic processes.

- Start participation early and keep it going throughout with a two-way process of information exchange.
- Be as inclusive as possible, in particular amongst traditionally hard-to-reach groups.
- Use a diversity of methods and techniques, with opportunities for consultees to become involved to varying extents.
- Whatever methods are used, ensure that they are designed to build towards a consensus.

Planning for real and public workshops

A number of more fundamental approaches to participation are briefly discussed in Chapter 10. 'Planning for Real' exercises and public workshops can be undertaken at both the strategic (policy-based) and development levels. This form of focused participation requires strong management and a clearly defined set of objectives. At the strategic level, planning workshops can be used to establish local planning guidance that embraces the aspirations of the community, whilst taking advantage of local knowledge. In Stratford-on-Avon, the process is used to formulate community-led VDSs via the dedicated enabling officer. At the development level, this approach can be used to establish site-specific development briefs as illustrated in the Cambridge case study presented above, and in appropriate circumstances to develop a design in more detail.

This approach requires enabling rather than directing, and can potentially provide a framework within which detailed local issues are identified and explored. It also enables direct negotiation between the relevant stakeholders – a key part of the process in Cambridge. At the development level, Planning for Real can offer the basis for housing providers to proactively establish and maintain contact with the wider community (and councillors) at an early stage. This can identify potential sticking points and start to address any latent community opposition. The success in implementing both Planning for Real and development control fora is, however, heavily dependent upon the commitment of individuals. Within Cambridge City Council, for example, it is acknowledged that senior-level staff play a key role in driving the approach, whilst the officers are very committed and dedicated despite limited resources. The attitude of the applicant and petitioners also has a major impact on the outcome, particularly the willingness to establish a relationship as the basis for meaningful discussion and negotiation.

User fora and working groups

User fora and working groups are a good way of establishing an ongoing point of feedback or contact between the planning authority and the housing provider and other relevant parties (for example, consultants and agents) at the strategic level. In Birmingham (Chapter 11), this approach has been used to establish a dialogue between the parties as a means of monitoring the function of the planning process and potentially identifying and addressing common points of tension within a neutral (non-development) setting. The forum meets every three months (a lunchtime session, the authority providing the lunch), and is invited to discuss any relevant issues. It enables the sharing of knowledge, increases mutual understanding and can provide a ready-made context for the development and formulation of new initiatives in an inclusive manner. The continuity of the individuals involved enables a long-term working relationship to evolve. The industry representatives benefit from an opportunity to shape the process whilst establishing an ongoing relationship with the local authority.

Rydin (in Cullingworth, 1999, p. 187) usefully reminds readers that such user fora are nothing new, and in fact proved less than successful when introduced as a direct outcome of the Skeffington Committee recommendations in 1969. She notes that when originally established, Community Fora (as they were then – see p. 198) usually became a channel for one-way communication from the local authority inviting representations on its proposals. Thus fora tended not to offer up useful advice or positive proposals and were quickly passed over. The experience offers a salutary lesson that inclusion means a two-way process, and is of little value unless its outcomes are taken seriously by those with the real power to make decisions.

Consortia input

In common with user fora and working groups, a consortium approach to consultation is a proactive initiative that enables a more consolidated housing provider response, as experienced in Brent (see Chapter 13). Many smaller RSLs may have limited experience of the planning process or of dealing with developers during planning gain negotiations. The creation of consortia – and hence opportunities for sharing knowledge – may go some way towards addressing this problem.

Sharing the resource burden through a consortium (formal or informal) of housing providers can also enable an increased level of proactive input, for example commissioning or joint commissioning (with the local authority) of research and analysis, and representations on specific aspects of the process, as undertaken in Brent or Birmingham (see Chapters 13 and 11). The establishment of consortia can further provide a formal point of contact between the authority and the housing providers, enabling an ongoing relationship for feedback and participation with the potential to tie in to a system of partnering. This approach can enhance the credibility of RSLs, enabling a relationship on an equal footing with the planning officers and improving the levels of mutual understanding between the RSLs and the planning officers. It also helps to foster realistic expectations.

Development Control Forum

In Cambridge, the Development Control Forum has a different role, as a means of opening up the planning process (a form of safety valve) to enable wider community involvement in the decision-making process for significant applications. The purpose of the meeting is to mediate and seek compromise. Thus if valid planning points arise, applications can be renegotiated. Consequently all those involved in the decision-making process (including the planning committee) reap the benefit of an ongoing and detailed knowledge of the relevant issues.

Cambridge City Council suggests that the key to success is to get people's views as early as possible. The key lesson, however, is that consultation, participation or involvement of any sort takes significant resources, and although savings might be made down the line, the further the process moves along Arnstein's (1969) ladder of citizen participation (see Chapter 10) from no power, through degrees of tokenism to degrees of citizen power, the more expensive the original set-up cost is likely to be. Many commentators argue, however, that the benefits increase commensurately with the commitment to participation and the resources invested.

The route to inclusive planning

A range of other approaches to a more inclusive planning process with open decision-making are set out in Fig. 12.3. Fundamentally, inclusive planning begins with a commitment to adequately resource a more open process, through investment in skills and by assigning dedicated roles. Simultaneously, the community itself must have the capacity to participate in the process, which can be achieved by publicising the process and thereafter ensuring that people understand how they can influence decisions and the motivations of different parties, including the local authority, partner RSLs and private house builders. An early dialogue is critical, establishing the principles that will guide the process, and this may involve the formulation of consultation timetables (see Chapter 11). An inclusive process needs particular method and structured management, and some of the possible approaches have already been discussed. Management is about enabling a range of different inputs at various stages without seeking to control in a heavy-handed way. Establishing protocols is also important to lay out the game rules that establish trust and set expectations.

A number of central messages can be summarised as follows:

- Senior/director level commitment and support is crucial to drive and resource-inclusive processes.
- These processes can be resource-intensive, although potential delay in the initial stages is offset by a smoother route overall and more positive outcomes, with reduced necessity for appeal.
- Negative or defensive attitudes at the outset can be problematic, willingness to adapt and flexibility are required.

➤ **Public exhibitions, web sites and the local media** – to aid consultation and spread awareness.

➤ **End-user workshops** – formulation of design guides to include workshops with end-users as a means to identify what does (and does not) work for the residents.

➤ **Knowledge-building** – use long-term approaches to knowledge building, inclusion and involvement in built environment issues within the community. Examples include a 'suggestions box' in a public area, a formal and ongoing means of consultation and information, and enhancing local awareness of issues and impact through formal review (with objectors) of contentious schemes after completion, to address whether fears were unfounded.

➤ **Neighbourhood fora** – which enable ongoing involvement, capacity building and feedback from all parties over the long term.

➤ **Knowledge sharing and benchmarking** – to encourage consistency between authorities and identify potential for knowledge-sharing, common guidance and sharing of best practice.

➤ **Enquiry by design** – a process developed by the Prince's Foundation (2000) of involving the stakeholders in the collaborative planning and design of sustainable urban extensions. The process is similar to Urban Design Action Teams (UDATs) (see Chapter 10) with facilitators brought in to guide a collaborative and intensive process of discussion and design structured over several days. The outcome is a master plan which participants do not have to be bound by, but which they must agree to be influenced by. It provides a basis from which to negotiate in taking a development forward.

12.3 Other approaches to inclusion planning and decision-making.

- Sometimes more focused involvement is more appropriate than wider consultation or participation, avoiding issues of several tiers of public representation.
- There is a potential for 'meeting fatigue'; a core liaison group (consisting of key members of all parties) can maintain continuity, establish a strategic negotiation context and maintain the impetus of the process.
- Some established communities may be better equipped than others to engage in such processes, necessitating an element of capacity building as part of the process.
- The process should be enabled. A light-hand approach should be used within planning workshops and Planning for Real exercises to ensure that particular solutions are explored, but not imposed.
- Hostile and defensive attitudes from councillors and the wider community remain common. Capacity-building exercises within the community to explore development issues (i.e. location, design and density) can help to address this.

13

Integrated and realistic working practices

The bunker mentality

During the 1980s and 1990s 'partnership' became one of the most used and abused terms in the language of governance, just as in recent times 'corporate working' (joined-up thinking in practice) has become the leitmotif of local government. Ward (in Cullingworth, 1999, p. 232) observes, however, that partnerships have been a feature of British planning practice since the 1947 Act, initially to reconstruct the shattered commercial centres of British towns and cities following the Second World War, and from the 1960s onwards in the construction of major residential expansions. Indeed, in a broad sense, all land assembly arrangements, planning gain agreements and the very nature of planning itself can be regarded as partnership arrangements of sorts because they all involve the negotiation and agreement of outcomes that offer shared benefits for the two (or more) parties involved.

In a narrower sense, government has recently emphasised the need to establish integrated policy and working practices internally and constructive partnerships externally (see Chapter 10). Thus a string of studies, guidance notes and good practice guides (see for example, Fraser, 1991; Barlow, 1997; Housing Forum, 2000; National Housing Federation, 2000) have focused specifically on the issue of partnering as one major aspect of integrated working. In a very different sense, the Urban Task Force (1999, p. 73) also emphasised the importance and value of integration, this time in a physical sense. They argued for integrated spatial master planning as a way in which a range of skills – not available in any single organisation – could be brought together to deliver the urban renaissance. They suggested that an integrated spatial master plan requires an integrated design team, implying a broad range of cross-sectorial professional and non-professional inputs (see Fig. 13.1).

Few assessments have been undertaken, however, of the success of integrated working practices, although Littler *et al.* (1994), in work for the Welsh Office, were able to demonstrate that small local authorities in Wales were on the way to improving cooperation between planning and housing departments in general policy and the provision of affordable housing. The research identified that greater integration between departments, and hence policy, was found to rest on personal relationships between individuals, and thus where authorities were small and closely-knit there tended to be better operational integration. This is also true in authorities where the housing and

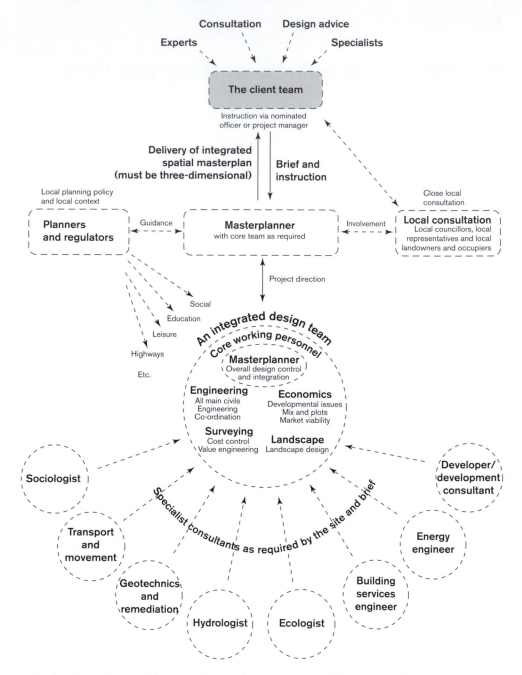

13.1 *An integrated spatial masterplan requires an integrated design team (Andrew Wright Associates in Urban Task Force, 1999, p. 76).*

planning function is shared within a single department: in such instances, knowledge of different policy areas is more likely to be shared (Gallent *et al.*, 2002). But integration does not end with local authorities, and the term, in the broadest sense, does not merely refer to local strategy and policy.

Integration – or a lack of it – occurs across a number of levels and assumes many different guises. It can refer either to policy design or product, or to the way in which organisations operate in unison. Operational links between RSLs and local authorities, for example, have been the subject of numerous studies, notably Taylor (1997a) and the National Housing Federation (2000). Within the private construction industry, partnering between contractors – and between housebuilders and other agencies – is a subject addressed by Sir John Egan (1998), as a means to innovate procurement and constructional processes, and deliver cheaper, high quality housing. In land-use planning itself, integration between different levels (local, regional and so forth) is high on the agenda both nationally (RTPI, 2001c; DTLR, 2002a) and on the European stage (Nadin *et al.*, 2002; Faludi and Waterhout, 2002).

Integration and partnership, in all its different guises, are therefore a broad objective of the range of stakeholders active in the delivery of new homes, from those concerned with their detailed construction to those concerned with control, development process, or managing the release of public finances, to those at the policy end of delivery. However, a common experience in each sector, and the main cause of concern, is the 'silo mentality' that has dogged the development process, in which individual stakeholders pursue their own goals with little regard to the objectives of others. The result is a lack of realism about how individual contributions work for or against achieving an integrated whole, or about what the conflicting objectives of other stakeholders might be and how they can be accommodated.

This chapter considers the degree of integration achieved between housing providers and local planners, examining how greater integration can and is being brought about. A second concern (although there is no artificial separation of the two in the text) is the way in which the processes and mechanisms of integration lead logically to greater realism (in policy and development aspirations) and awareness of both development constraints and socio-economic circumstances. The chapter is essentially concerned with organisational arrangements and the benefits of a variety of different partnering and collaborative approaches to the delivery of new homes.

It is the thesis of this chapter that through greater coordination and integration of working practices an enhanced understanding of (sometimes) conflicting roles and relationships can be achieved. This can lead to increased connections between activities and responsibilities, and therefore to a shared interest in, and responsibility for, outcomes. This implies interactions both within and between organisations (public and private). However, on the public side of the equation, such integrated corporate working practices should be clearly distinguished from their antithesis – corporatism – which Schmitter (quoted in Reade, 1987, p. 120) defined as

> A system of interest representation in which constituent units are organized into a limited number of singular, compulsory, non-competitive, hierarchically ordered and functionally differentiated categories, recognized or licenced (if not created) by the state and granted a deliberate representational monopoly within their respective categories.

Instead, corporate working implies joint and shared responsibility for action.

Integrated and realistic working processes

Integration and realism imply the coordination of roles, processes, mechanisms and outcomes, through integrating working practices that encourage inter-stakeholder awareness, and therefore greater realism.

Many of the tensions experienced in housing provider–planner relationships, and discussed in Part Two of the book, can be attributed to a lack of integration and realism. This can occur throughout the whole process, both at a strategic (policy) level and at the level of individual developments. Indeed, many of the problems created by the lack of integration and realism in policy have a trickle-down effect on development control and implementation processes. Moreover, inconsistencies between the different tiers of planning policy (regional, county and district) can result in uncertainty and delay (see Chapters 6 and 14) and perpetuate combative attitudes between the different parties, for example, in relation to assessments of housing need/demand or disagreements over the need for housing *per se*. A common perception is that local authority analysis and consequent policy requirements are over-simplistic, with allocations, capacity and need failing to reflect local context and market conditions. Equally, house builders' commercial assessments of housing demand may not adequately reflect issues of need and context.

The lack of coordination between different strategies on a cross-disciplinary and geographical basis can also cause problems. A lack of coordination between housing and economic development strategies, for example, can constrain land availability and viability, as housing demand (or need) does not necessarily correspond geographically with land availability. Delay, inconsistency and antagonism can be the consequence of a lack of corporate coordination between planning and housing departments (Barlow and Chambers, 1992; Tewdwr-Jones et al., 1998) or even within departments, between forward planning and development control, for example (Punter and Carmona, 1997, p. 349). This can be a major constraint when undertaking complex negotiations such as Section 106 agreements (Farthing and Ashley, 2002; DTLR, 2002a).

An inclusive planning process – illustrated in the two examples provided in Chapter 12 – potentially fosters and facilitates high levels of realism and responsiveness to local contexts, communities and commercial constraints, whilst a streamlined process (see Chapter 11) embraces issues of efficiency and integration of planning mechanisms and outcomes. The costs of pursuing these initiatives are likely to necessitate additional up-front resources (time and skills involved in establishing and maintaining systems), and increased levels of commercial openness (see Chapter 14). A willingness to participate and potentially compromise is also required. The benefits of such an approach include better outcomes and a smoother and more efficient process, both within and between organisations. The mechanisms and outcomes are also potentially more realistic and responsive, and relationships between parties are established and fostered.

The aim should be to integrate practices over time to deliver a consistent message, although this has not always proved easy. Hambleton et al. (1996b), for example, identify a range of barriers to effective collaboration (see Chapter 10) and argue that as collaborative working becomes more the norm, problems of establishing and maintaining accountability can emerge, in part because cross-cutting agendas sit uncomfortably with the more traditional sectorial responsibilities of elected members required by council structures, i.e. members responsible for housing, or planning, but rarely both. Newchurch and Co. (2000, p. 2) add four further categories of barriers:

- Financial – including the inability to fund projects, inconsistency in accounting methods and annual budgetary constraints.
- Cultural – wariness of new ways of working, resistance to change, lack of willingness or clarity on partnership working.
- Resources – limited resources to develop and implement partnerships and the inability mostly in terms of capacity, of members and of pattern organisations to support projects.
- Existing government legislation – fiscal policies that restrict authorities' funding methods and a focus on national initiatives that may divert resource from local priorities.

Nevertheless, with the strong trend towards diversity in local service provision, for example in the delivery of social housing, authorities have increasingly been keen to explore inter-agency approaches to policy delivery. A danger on the horizon, however, is the move away from internal integration within local authority departments as new council structures come on stream. Central government aspirations (see Chapter 10) support a split between the political executive (mayor and cabinet, or mayor and council manager, or council leader and cabinet) who will remain active in establishing key council policy, and the political assembly (the full council made up of councillors), who will retain regulatory responsibilities. As Hambleton and Sweeting (1999, p. 17) argue, this could set the planning profession back 20 years if policy making in planning is separated from development control.

A wide range of research has been undertaken on partnerships in their many different guises. The Housing Forum's guide evocatively entitled: *How to Survive Partnering – It Won't Bite*, describes partnering from the (Egan) perspective of delivering greater construction efficiency and quality. It defines partnering as 'an agreed method of working together as an integrated and coordinated team to achieve common objectives and shared benefits' (Housing Forum, 2000, p. 5), but adds the proviso that whatever the arrangement, success relies on individual commitment from those involved. Based on extensive survey work of public and private sector housing providers, they argue that:

- There is never just one model of partnering or a single framework that will suit all organisations.
- Partnering means radical change, not doing what is already being done slightly better.
- It does not imply a quick fix solution, but long-term commitment of the partners.
- The nature and quality of team relationships are crucial, including good communication and flexibility.
- Partnering is a means to an end, not a solution.
- It represents an ongoing learning process in which continuous evaluation should lead to concrete improvements in working practices and relationships.

Partnership approaches can be adopted for individual projects – project partnering – or as long-term ongoing arrangements – strategic partnering – and can be used between the public, private and voluntary sectors (i.e. RSLs) in any combination: public/private, public/public, public/voluntary etc. Research on the latter arrangements sponsored by the Joseph Rowntree Foundation also found considerable variation in partnership arrangements, although some agreement on principles for success (Taylor, 1997b, p. 4). These were expressed in terms of the need for:

- Clear targets – for the involvement of voluntary organisations in policy and service planning, which go beyond numbers to the depth and quality of involvement.
- Commitment – throughout authorities: front-line staff need to know they will be backed up if they are expected to adopt new ways of working.
- Clear allocation of responsibilities – within authorities, with dedicated time and resources, to develop and service partnerships.
- Monitoring, benchmarking and review mechanisms – which provide incentives for and reward partnership.
- Resources for voluntary sector partners – and time to allow them to get up to speed before all the key decisions are taken.
- Mechanisms for involvement – which recognise the many demands on organisations with limited resources and use their time effectively.
- A willingness to understand and accommodate – different cultures, values and resource capacities of voluntary organisations.

The Housing Forum (2000, p. 17) research defined its own set of success factors (see Fig. 13.2), whilst 'A Framework for Partnership' between the Local Government Association, National Housing Federation and the Housing Corporation (2001) argued that partnerships should extend across the range of housing, planning and regeneration activities that local authorities engage in, and across their respective strategies. In particular, the Community Strategy and the joint working required in its preparation was seen as an opportunity for increased communication and for establishing cross-cutting objectives.

Plan

Set clear objectives
Decide on team selection criteria
Consider whole supply chain, users and community
Involve all partners

Attitude

Embrace a new working culture
Build teams
Mix/second people between organisations

Risks and rewards

Commit resources necessary for success
Set risk/reward structure
Use open-book accountability (see Chapter 14)

Trust

Understand each partner's business
Clarify common goals
Agree the basis of an open relationship

No conflict

Clarify expectations
Use documents as tools not weapons
Agree a problem-resolution strategy

Evaluate

Set up a regular system for reviews
Agree benchmarks
Measure key performances indicators against benchmarks
Feed learning into future planning

Repeat

Build on team/experience/commitment
Work towards strategic partnering
Partner within organisations to embed a cultural change

13.2 The Housing Forum partnering code.

Although integration of work practices internally within the public sector will undoubtedly bring benefits, it should not be forgotten that partnerships between the public and private, or public and voluntary sectors effectively establish special (favoured) relationships that both exclude others, and raise issues of accountability and probity. A key test of success for the public sector, therefore, is that any losses in accountability and inclusivity must be compensated for by the overall benefits of the partnership, and this depends on the 'price' exacted for the arrangements (Ward, S. in Cullingworth, 1999, p. 248). Hambleton *et al.* (1996c) establish a number of questions to ask of inter-agency working practices that could equally apply to other partnership arrangements to help ensure their accountability:

- Does the expenditure of effort and resources represent good value for money?
- How can citizens hold those engaged in inter-agency collaboration to account?
- How do elected politicians hold those engaged in inter-agency working to account?
- Is responsibility for decision-making clear?
- How is financial accountability maintained?

The case studies

The case studies demonstrate two alternative approaches to establishing more integrated and realistic working practices. The Braintree case illustrates:

- The critical importance of effective partnership working, cross-party workshops and meetings.
- The value of ameliorating (aggressive) market forces – and removing, as far as possible, destructive competition.
- The need to share knowledge and experience, thereby developing a constructive relationship.
- The possibility of achieving gains from economies of scale and decisions in parallel (simplifying the decision-making process on multiple sites).
- The benefits that can derive from a specific forum set up with the purpose of identifying and piloting innovation.

The London Borough of Brent example demonstrates a range of collaborative approaches to project management and to understanding the complexities of local development opportunities. More specifically, it reveals:

- The value of undertaking a broad review of all aspects of operation, of thinking from first principles in order to shake off institutional separatism, and formulate an integrated strategy.
- The long-term importance of establishing and maintaining an ongoing relationship between parties.
- The benefits of and means of identifying and agreeing a consensus view between parties.
- The obvious advantages of sharing knowledge and experience between parties to improve understanding, working practices and development outcomes.
- The need for a willingness to collaborate and cooperate to achieve common housing goals.

CASE STUDY: Braintree – partnership working

Braintree in Essex is one of three market towns within Braintree District. Being located within the catchment area for Stansted Airport, the housing market in and around Braintree began to experience a boom in the 1990s with the development of the airport as a major employer and magnet for new businesses. By 2000, ongoing development within the area primarily comprised three major sites: Great Notley Garden Village (approximately 2,000 dwellings); Marks Farm (1,350 dwellings) and Maltings Lane (850 dwellings). There were also a number of smaller rural infill developments, each of around 50+ dwellings. In this respect, the supply of new private housing was buoyant, although the supply of affordable housing within Braintree was in a more precarious state.

A detailed needs survey was undertaken by the local authority housing department in 1998 which established housing need at 2,923 households, and a need to rehouse a further 1,600. The policy of the local authority was to allow for rehousing 10 per cent of this figure each year (in the region of 160 homes), although the figure was largely offset by the loss of social housing through the 'Right to Buy', which was causing the loss of approximately 100 houses annually. Consequently, despite efforts to ameliorate the deficit, the situation was getting worse.

This increasing deficit and a shift in the balance of housing stock (due to a large increase in commercial development) prompted the local authority to initiate a partnering arrangement with selected RSLs. This represented an attempt to increase the supply of affordable housing through gains made due to shared knowledge and a suspension of typical competitive market conditions. By 2000, the local authority had an objective to bring forward 100 affordable units annually; or 10 per cent of what private housebuilders would be building over the following decade.

Braintree Housing Partnership

Following the 1998 housing needs survey, the Braintree Housing Partnership (BHP) was established to streamline and improve the delivery of affordable housing within the area. The principles behind the partnership included the sharing of knowledge and experience, the establishment of a closer working relationship, and enabling commercial openness and collaboration. The aim was to allow the local authority housing department and three partner RSLs to pool their knowledge and negotiate from a stronger standpoint.

At the time, there were 25 RSLs in the area, ten of which were significant providers of housing locally. The RSLs were keen to be involved within the partnership as the mechanics of the BHP effectively guaranteed a certain workload to the partner-RSLs over the period of the partnership. The partners were selected through competitive tender, with RSLs invited to tender for two separate projects to enable cost and quality comparisons to be made.

An agreement (or charter) was established between the members of the partnership, whilst the three RSLs employed a managing agent to drive and coordinate the working process. The partnership was set up on a three-year rolling programme, with the key partner agreement renewed annually to enable close monitoring and control of the partnership, and its direction.

Great Notley Garden Village

The development at Great Notley Garden Village came on-stream at the same time as the Braintree Housing Partnership was being formed, and provided a vehicle for the principles of the partnership initiative to be tested. The development is due for completion in 2011 and will deliver market housing, 200 affordable homes and a range of other community facilities and benefits.

Initially, 8–10 sites for major residential development were identified in the Braintree District Local Plan, but following a consultation exercise Great Notley was chosen to accommodate the development. Countryside Properties Plc – a major developer based in Brentwood and operating across the country – originally had all of the options on the different parcels of land that made up the Great Notley site; therefore the site was quick to bring forward avoiding a long process of consolidation of ownership and enabling the negotiation of a comprehensive package of planning gain. Outline planning permission and the Section 106 agreement were established and agreed in 1991. Alongside the outline planning permission, the levels of affordable housing and the location of this provision were also established.

Initially the development comprised different sites with six Section 106 agreements for affordable housing, although through the auspices of BHP the affordable housing requirement was treated as one. These sites were also treated as an integrated whole in design terms to enable a coherent place-making approach to be used. Thus the development and the dwellings have a clear visual image that is easy to market, enabling the development as a whole to be branded as 'Upper Chelmsford' by the developers – Chelmsford being the desirable neighbour of Braintree.

The total site nevertheless remained divided into site parcels (with planning consents on each), and some were subsequently acquired and developed by other developers. In this respect, Countryside was operating in different roles: as landowner (selling site parcels with permissions attached); developer (on the sites that it had retained); and contractor (for example undertaking the construction of the church, village hall and dwellings for other housing providers on site).

Partnership working

Countryside Properties were not formally part of the BHP, and as such there was no partnership agreement or charter between the BHP partners and the developer, although individual contractual agreements (setting out objectives) between each of the three RSLs and Countryside Properties were established. The local authority suggests that there were benefits for the developer in involving the BHP within the development at Great Notley, not least opportunities for future development and the building of an ongoing positive relationship with the local authority.

The subsidy for the affordable housing takes the form of either free houses or free land. To deliver this, a land transfer agreement was drawn up for each site, alongside a contract between each respective RSL and Countryside Properties to establish for each site parcel the number and type of units and the design and specification. The latter amounts to a standard building contract between employer and contractor. Where the subsidy comprises free units, a nil value is attached to the building contract, whilst the transfer of the land is costed at its current market value. Where the subsidy takes the form of free land, a nil value is attached to the land transfer, whilst the building contract has the appropriate value attached to it. In essence the developer was acting as both landowner and contractor, and was therefore able to receive contractor's profit alongside developer's profit.

The RSLs collaborated to produce a standard specification for the design and construction of the affordable housing. This was a difficult process for the parties involved and required levels of compromise between the RSLs, but enabled simplification of the administration and construction process, and greater certainty in cost forecasting. The specification subsequently formed part of the 'employer's requirements' within the agreement between the RSL and the developer.

Initially each site parcel that was earmarked for affordable housing was divided equally between the three RSLs, a practice which meant that each RSL had an equal stake in the different phases of development, but had to face the increased administration (for example involvement in site meetings) that this required. As the process evolved, it was decided to divide each site between two RSLs instead, in order to minimise duplication of resources, and make the process easier and more rational to manage. Careful management of plot allocations to each RSL meant that the total numbers of units were to be equalised over the different phases of development. Rent levels were also agreed across all of the affordable housing and capped below market levels.

The working structure

The working structure included working groups and meetings to discuss strategy, attended by the partner members of the BHP and by representatives from Countryside. These took the form of cross-party partnering workshops every month, and included site meetings and strategy workshops where decisions were taken that covered general issues for all sites and further Section 106-type negotiations. Early in the process, workshops were held on issues such as partnering and innovation, as one key objective of BHP was to function as a platform to pilot innovations within the planning and development process. Key initiatives included the process of benchmarking the development and construction between the different phases in a system of constant review.

Initially the working structure led to confusion about the role of BHP and the different parties involved. There were, for example, particular difficulties with the leadership of the process, with conflicts arising regarding who should drive the process forward to ensure that necessary actions were undertaken. The developer believed that the partnership process needed to be driven by the BHP (the local authority and the RSLs) and found the lack of progress prior to each meeting frustrating. They argued that this lack of impetus in the process had much to do with absence of grant funding, the timescale for which usually enforced a discipline on RSLs.

It was concluded that the local authority had a potentially key role to play in the process, particularly in ensuring that the developer fulfils all of the necessary requirements. All of the parties subsequently acknowledged that the process had suffered from a lack of impetus and accountability, and that meetings were not efficiently managed, with heavy involvement by all parties at all meetings being unnecessary. As a result, by 2000 the programme was falling behind, and there was a general cross-party consensus that the mechanics of the process needed tightening up.

Discussion

The partnership approach reflects an attempt to address an existing (and an ongoing) imbalance in the provision of affordable housing compared to the provision of market housing. In 2000, Braintree was rarely achieving 25 per cent affordable housing in general development in the area, with the figure usually averaging around 10–15 per cent, although 25 per cent was usually the starting point for negotiation. A number of constraints were affecting delivery of affordable units, not least that the brownfield sites coming forward had additional development costs which were offset against reduced affordable housing provision. The local authority acknowledged that policies governing Section 106 social housing provision could increase the requirement to 30 per cent (to begin to address the deficit), a change that was to be considered in the forthcoming local plan review.

The function of the BHP is evolving over time and should allow the development process to improve and evolve. Of critical importance, for example, is a new streamlined and controlled system of management and commercial imperatives to drive the process. Some of the primary benefits of the approach have been the gains in scale that decisions on multiple sites made in parallel have allowed, including improved decision-making efficiency and the value of planning gain. The knowledge and experience gained in each phase of the development of Great Notley Garden Village should inform any subsequent development process, whilst the establishment of standardised specifications for the affordable housing will enable the developer to make accurate cost forecasts in future developments, and in the short term has reduced the cost of social housing provision.

However, the benefits that are gained from economies of scale and streamlining the decision-making process could potentially be offset by the dis-benefits. These could tend, for example, towards a standardised end-product, resulting in a lack of diversity and choice in housing, and in some cases to lowest common denominator design. This is a conflict that requires a careful balance, taking into account the current emphasis on delivering Best Value, both in the short term and in the long term.

The partnership process has also enabled a less combative relationship to develop between parties, enabling frank discussions and constructive negotiations, which compare well with previous difficulties in negotiation experienced by the local authority. The approach has also removed much of the competition between partner RSLs, so that all three RSLs now operate on a level playing field and cost elements are no longer inflated through competitive market forces.

As an initiative, the BHP has the ability to work with other developers, and to undertake joint commissioning. Indeed it has been suggested that the relationship which has developed between BHP and Countryside Properties might be unhealthily close, with partner developers getting an unfair competitive advantage if, for example, council-owned land is brought to the table.

Great Notley Garden Village itself has also been criticised on the grounds that it does not reach current standards on issues such as development density, or the percentage and distribution of affordable housing. In large part this is because consents were achieved in 1991, prior to the shift in national policy on such concerns. The local authority (through the BHP) has since been able to alter the distribution and segregation of the different tenures to a limited extent through negotiation, but has not been able to significantly increase the scale of provision or its location. This is perhaps an indictment of the fixed nature of consents.

The partnership can translate to other developments and contexts, which was the intention of the local authority in Braintree, which regards the renewal of a three-yearly cycle of RSL involvement as a key means to approach, encourage and implement affordable housing. Both the developer and the local authority suggest that the linking together of sites (within the context of a partnership) is beneficial, allowing optimal use of planning gain, and an enhanced ability to 'place-make'. The local authority suggests, however, that the approach would need to be adapted in areas where a large number of small sites in disparate ownerships predominate.

CASE STUDY: Brent – collaborative management and understanding

Within the London borough of Brent the issue of delivering affordable housing is a critical one; there is a very high demand for such housing coupled with a very short supply. As a consequence, in the late 1990s £6 million was spent annually on temporary accommodation for the homeless, of which the council could only claim £2 million back through grant support. In the late 1990s, with the UDP review fast approaching and the London Planning Advisory Committee (LPAC) requesting information on land and housing capacities, the local authority began to evaluate their approach to delivering affordable housing. At that time, a wider strategic objective was established within the borough to increase the total housing stock by 7,500 dwellings, at least half of which was to be affordable.

The approach taken within Brent was broad based, addressing issues about the supply of land, the housing and planning policy context, the local understanding of affordable housing issues and the efficiency of the planning process. The range of initiatives have come about largely due to the close nature of the collaboration between the planning and housing departments and the local social housing providers.

Collaborative housing capacity studies

A joint working group of planning officers and local RSLs (which meets quarterly) enables the development of a strong relationship and provides a platform to discuss issues and identify solutions. It was out of this group, for instance, that the idea to collaborate on housing land capacity studies originated. As the authority had limited funds available to undertake capacity work, a collaborative approach offered the potential to acquire the best quality of information and analysis within the given budget. Brent also wished to be more proactive in identifying the full range of opportunities for housing land within the borough and in encouraging more land to come forward.

Initially money was obtained to enable a survey of sites by planning graduates. A view of site opportunities in the short, medium and long term was required, so sites were identified that were redundant, or had current (but marginal) uses upon them. At this stage, local RSLs were asked to look at the potential sites and make an assessment in terms of desirability and developability. There were in the region of five to six key RSLs who operated frequently in the area and each of these was given a number of potential sites to evaluate. As this process was undertaken over an extended period of time, a willingness to cooperate was maintained, despite the fact that the RSLs were essentially giving free consultancy services to the local authority.

The detailed criteria for assessing the viability of each site was left to each RSL, but each assessment was design-led, and undertaken within the local planning authority's existing planning guidance. As the RSLs were very familiar with the borough they were able to draw upon considerable knowledge and experience of both the statutory requirements and the contextual factors. Issues such as contamination were only evaluated where already known or considered highly likely, whilst specific analysis (for example soil tests) was not undertaken. Outputs of the process included a classification of which sites were appropriate for immediate development, and which sites were appropriate for development if identified constraints could be overcome. This translated into priorities and a view of availability over the long term.

Officers argue that the initiative has resulted in a win-win situation, whereby the local authority gains from the knowledge and experience of the RSL, whilst the RSL gains from having a competitive edge over the land market. Thus the participating RSLs got the opportunity to move on sites first with the benefit of detailed knowledge of what the local authority required.

The process of identifying and prioritising different sites and constraints has meant that sites have been brought forward more quickly, with several sites consolidated through the use of Compulsory Purchase Orders, and others through hastening the demise of existing marginal businesses that were either failing or happy to sell up and move on. At the start of the process, the local authority estimated that if the approach had identified only an additional one or two sites, then it would have been a worthwhile undertaking in terms of housing need in the borough. By the end of 2000, planning permission had just been granted on a high-density housing scheme in Willesden (identified through the capacity study), and several more applications were in the pipeline, so the initiative has started to deliver considerable benefits in increased market and affordable housing. The local authority is also pleased that the initiative has helped to foster a more design-led approach to high-density development, as a distinct move away from the former numbers-based approach.

Cross-party lunchtime presentations

The success of the capacity initiative built upon good working relationships that had already been established between the local authority and social housing providers. This relationship has been reinforced by knowledge-sharing events attended by council members, housing and planning officers and social housing providers. As policies need to be both workable and appropriate to the parties involved, it was considered important to involve RSLs in knowledge-sharing exercises, the outcomes of which could potentially feed into the UDP review process. The local authority identified the need to investigate the issue of affordable housing in more detail, and as a result initiated a cross-party session, hosted by the Development Control Section.

The lunchtime meeting was undertaken as a type of CPD initiative to enable discussion of the wider issues surrounding planning, housing, affordable housing and homelessness. Fifty people attended, and presentations were made by the housing and planning policy sections of the authority, and from the Notting Hill Housing Trust (an RSL operating across a number of north London boroughs). Issues covered included affordable housing policies; the problems of homelessness within the borough; the difficulties with land; financing and operation of the RSLs; the problems that are experienced by RSLs trying to compete with the private sector; and why Development Control is under pressure from the RSLs. A two-way dialogue and a greater understanding of the different viewpoints resulted.

CPD presentations to local authorities were an initiative that the Notting Hill Housing Trust had already unilaterally been undertaking within different London boroughs for the preceding three years. They were therefore particularly keen to participate in the presentation at Brent as they felt that a knowledge-sharing approach could help to find solutions to some of the affordable housing constraints in the borough, and to share experience of good practice from elsewhere.

Management of planning applications

As such meetings are collaborative gatherings of the range of different parties, they provide a forum for the informal discussion of issues and an opportunity to identify and discuss potential initiatives. It was through this process, for example, that the idea of an agreement relating to the management of planning applications (similar to a service-level agreement) was identified.

The agreement that has now been adopted seeks to simplify and smooth the planning process in response to criticisms that planning delay was constricting the delivery of new housing. The agreement covers different aspects of the application process, with the local authority undertaking to do a range of things on pre-application, and to provide clear design advice at an early stage in the process. Other detailed elements of the agreement include ensuring that the Section 106 is signed off and that the broad principles are in place at specified stages, and stipulation of when decision notices are to be sent out. In return, the applicant is required to provide the correct information at key junctures, and to carry out public meetings where appropriate.

RSL consortia input for consultation on policy

A final key initiative has been the establishment of a consortium of several RSLs operating within Brent. A proposal for the consortium was made out of the regular planning/RSL meetings in order to provide early feedback on the draft housing and affordable housing policies within the emerging UDP. Acting as a consortium also enables the RSLs to engage in consultation with a stronger and more consolidated voice, and ensures they have a greater impact.

The RSL consortium commissioned the consultants Oldfield King (who had undertaken this role elsewhere on a number of other draft policies) to undertake an evaluation on their behalf. Several specific comments came out of the process (which were subsequently addressed) and the local authority felt that the amalgamated feedback was very useful, saving a lot of time during the consultation process. A further clear benefit was that the consortium were able to help Brent formulate an appropriate technical definition of affordable housing, which was also discussed at the Brent Housing and Planning subgroup. Overall, the RSLs and Oldfield King were generally very supportive of the draft policies, believing them to be both workable and achievable. This was a welcome response as the local authority were preparing to present the case through the UDP review and were therefore more confident that what was being proposed had firm stakeholder support.

Discussion

The initiatives at Brent represent a cross-party acknowledgement of serious constraints, alongside a willingness to innovate and take responsibility for addressing constraints. This process has been facilitated largely through the ongoing relationship that has been established between the planning and housing departments, and the local RSLs. This close working relationship and knowledge-sharing has meant that the supply of land for housing (both affordable and mixed tenure) has increased, and consequently the supply of affordable housing has become correspondingly greater.

Collaboration on housing land capacity studies has also enabled closer adherence to national targets, guidelines and best practice in terms of brownfield land. The RSLs in the borough (with an emphasis on family units for rent) had not previously been keen to develop sites with higher than usual densities. However, the design-led approach has delivered a greater confidence in producing higher-density housing on brownfield land, and consequently the previous heavy reliance on greenfield sites is falling off (in the 1980s the borough lost approximately 100 acres of open space).

The local authority recognises the clear benefits that have arisen from the approach, and would like to undertake more proactive initiatives. Unfortunately they also feel very constrained by demands on current staff resources. Because this type of approach is resource intensive and represents involvement that is outside the core activities of the council (and local RSLs) the time and resource issue remains decisive.

Building long-term relationships is of critical importance in improving the implementation and delivery of housing and housing land through the planning process. In this respect, the benefit of the different initiatives at Brent are perhaps less focused on the resolution of conflicts and more on developing a consensus view and on fostering levels of openness, certainty, commitment, trust and transparency.

The local authority would like to see this type of relationship extending to private housing providers. They recognise, however, that this may not be possible to the same extent, as individual private housebuilders do not operate so frequently within the same borough, and therefore their interests are more geographically dispersed. As a consequence it is more difficult to establish and maintain a relationship between the parties (although not impossible: see Chapter 11), including between developers and RSLs. The local authority suggests that private developers in Brent also tend to oppose the initiatives on affordable housing, believing that they give RSLs an unfair competitive advantage.

Finally, in its move to address the particular constraints on affordable housing in the borough, the local authority has needed to challenge and adapt some of the national guidelines currently in place. They have, for example, moved away from national targets on affordable housing in Circular 6/98 (DETR, 1998c), which sets a threshold of 25 units before afford-able provision is required – Brent now adopts a threshold of 10 units. The inflexibility within national guidance on affordable housing is regarded as particularly detrimental by officers; however, their response, along with the other initiatives, contributes to a perception that the authority and private housebuilders have very different and conflicting interests.

Recommendations

The two case study examples presented above illustrate that the key principles of integration and realism involve establishing joint working practices within and between organisations, and the formulation and implementation of policy tools and proposals that are realistic and fit within an agreed framework. Appropriate skills, shared knowledge, understanding and awareness of contexts, limitations and constraints are therefore key components in achieving and enabling realistic processes and outcomes. The way this is achieved locally will build upon:

- Integration and coordination of working practices and implementation within an organisation (both corporately and individually), between organisations (building constructive relationships), and by drawing in wider involvement.
- Integration and coordination between the different tiers of policy, the different strat-egies, policies and guidance appropriate to an area, a particular development proposal and its policy and physical context, and the different elements of a development and its totality.
- Realism through an understanding of contexts, constraints, roles and motives; through policy, process and stakeholder responsiveness; through skills availability; and finally through shared knowledge and shared undertakings.

At the strategic level, partnership – or joint – working (both formal and informal) between organisations can facilitate responsive planning tools and enable implementation processes that benefit from greater certainty and consistency. Formalising the link or working practice can enhance the relationship between different departments within the same organisations by introducing new liaison roles (see Chapter 12), interdepartmental working protocols, or through rationalising the structure of the organisation to combine or link functions where appropriate. However, the success of such corporate working initiatives is dependent upon the individuals involved and their willingness and attitudes.

The lessons are just as important for housing providers as for local authorities. For large house builders, for example, the different working practices of their various subsidiary companies/regional offices can lead to a great disparity in local practice. For local authorities, the need for coordination between planning and housing departments emerges as a key message from this chapter.

At the development level, partnership working is also a key initiative, enabling shared knowledge and integration. Formal partnerships between organisations (where appropriate) can potentially simplify the process through decision-making in parallel and coordinated project-management. Informal partnerships facilitate similar benefits within contexts where formal (or legal) agreements between the parties are not appropriate. Informal methods can also contribute to enhancing skills, knowledge and understanding within and between organisations.

Realistic policy is an end-goal reflecting the importance of establishing attainable objectives. Realism in the formulation of planning obligations is an example on which PPG1 states that obligations should be 'fairly and reasonably related in scale and kind' to the development under consideration (DoE, 1997a, para. 36). At the same time, policy realism has to be viewed as a product of both social/environmental and commercial (economic) objectives. Thus authorities need to ensure that their requirements are both appropriate to the size and scale of the project and relate to its impacts. Housing providers, on the other hand, should be prepared to ameliorate the social and environmental costs that their development generates. Policy realism is therefore a function of local understanding, and realistic planning policy can only be developed by those close to – and with an awareness of – the local context. Overall, seven key approaches to establishing integrated and realistic working practices emerged from the research.

Strategic partnerships

There are many different forms of strategic partnership. A formalised association between the local authority and selected RSLs (usually on a competitive basis) can establish certainty and continuity in the assignment of Section 106 affordable housing obligations and in joint commissioning. In the case of the Braintree Housing Partnership, the local authority or developers bring appropriate developments to the table which are shared out between the RSLs, who operate on a mutually non-aggressive basis. The partnership approach establishes a culture of shared knowledge and undertaking between partners, enabling innovative approaches to the sharing and management of information. As well as benefits at the development level, partnerships can also function as ongoing fora or panels for review, feedback and proactive involvement. Authorities need to be careful, however, that partnerships include a range of partners (which are regularly reviewed) in order to avoid conflicts of interest or the stifling of local competition.

Research on the delivery of affordable housing from the RICS Policy Unit (2001, p. 25) revealed that considerable confusion exists in local authorities about the relative merits of open competition versus partnering, and about how these two processes are best welded together. The research reported in this chapter revealed that partnerships offered a valuable means to focus resources and energies, but represented a supplement to, rather than a replacement of, healthy competition. Important features therefore included:

- An open and accountable selection process, with clearly established criteria for selection.
- Means to measure and track the added value delivered by the partnership arrangement.
- An ongoing process of monitoring membership and if necessary a rotation of members in order to maintain fresh thinking and innovation.
- The need for a win-win scenario that offers clear benefits to the authority, to partner RSLs and if involved to private housebuilders as well.

Liaison or enabling officers

Formalising links or working practices between local authority departments (particularly housing and planning departments) can contribute to smooth internal and external processes, whilst ensuring that the remit of one department is thoroughly acknowledged within another. Key benefits accrue through establishing a liaison (or enabling) role between the planning and housing departments, as in Stratford-on-Avon (see Chapter 12), whilst the interface with housing providers is enhanced and the interests of RSLs are prioritised.

Corporate working – integrated and joint strategies, policies and guidance

This initiative operates at different levels. It can overlap with the concept of strategic partnerships where an area-based approach is undertaken with combined housing and development strategies, common objectives and partners (from both private and public sectors), as in Birmingham (see Chapter 11). It can be expressed through a more thorough integration of planning policy and housing strategies, for example in Cambridge (see Chapter 12). It can also include methods of corporate and inclusive working within and beyond the local authority to produce policy tools that reflect common interests and acknowledge requirements specific to the local context, for example the formulation of SPG on affordable housing in South Lakeland (see Chapter 14).

There can nevertheless be potential constraints to close working between housing and planning departments, reflecting the different frameworks, targets, budgets and legislation. This can be alleviated to an extent by enhancing shared and dual skills, through establishing an ongoing working relationship or protocol, or alternatively by undertaking a major joint-working exercise (see Birmingham or South Lakeland). Corporate working requires authorities to move beyond closely defined roles and responsibilities to consider how by working jointly and collaboratively between departments shared objectives can be identified, resources can be pooled and more efficient and effective processes can be put in place. Effective corporate working requires:

- agreed authority-wide corporate objectives based on a strategic vision;
- a willingness to share information and resources;
- commitment to joint working at the highest level;
- a desire to seek collaborative shared solutions to problems.

In the specific context of planning and housing it might imply:

*   coordinated policy frameworks (development plan/LDF policy and housing strategies);
*   keeping in touch – meeting to discuss joint interests and initiatives and projects in the pipeline;
*   preparing joint guidance or protocols;
*   pooling resources on, for example, consultation exercises;
*   interdepartmental meetings early in any project's lifespan;
*   funding joint liaison positions;
*   including housing departments on the statutory consultee list;
*   moving in time beyond bilateral to multilateral modes of working – interdepartmental, inter-agency and inter-authority;
*   investing time and effort up front to reap the rewards further down the line.

Sharing knowledge and information

Actively building relationships is an essential means of gaining greater knowledge and awareness. This can involve gathering local intelligence and sharing this information between partners. It can also involve raising awareness of the different constraints faced by partners. The initiatives in Brent involving lunchtime presentations and seminars undertaken in conjunction with a leading local RSL, or the RSL partnership in Braintree, directly or indirectly aim to build relationships whilst recognising the limitations of going it alone. The initiatives illustrate the complementary nature of partners' skills bases (and some of the gaps) and the importance of investing time in shared learning. These relationships represent an acknowledgement that no one stakeholder has a monopoly over skills or knowledge. They also represent a recognition that by bringing skills together, better outcomes can be achieved.

Guidance produced jointly by the Local Government Association, National Housing Federation and the Housing Corporation (2001) argues that local authorities have detailed local knowledge and the networks to gauge community aspirations, whilst housing providers often bring a wider pan-regional knowledge about housing trends. Together these complementary sets of knowledge and data on housing markets, community needs, innovative practice and community consultation offer the basis for more effective action on housing – both market and affordable – and for establishing single unified research programmes to further inform decision-making.

Development partnerships

Development-based partnerships can provide a means of achieving development more smoothly. They also offer a means of establishing a formal or informal dialogue between the different parties at an early stage in the process, thus helping to ensure developments are achieved in an integrated and holistic manner. Different types of partnership may be appropriate in different contexts, for example reflecting the different scales and nature of development. Levels of commercial openness and trust are required, as is strong management (establishing who will drive the process) and efficient administration to avoid unnecessary duplication of tasks.

Key elements of the approach can include regular cross-party meetings, partnering workshops, joint decision-making and accountability, and sharing the burden of technical and management resources. The development at Great Notley Garden Village, for example, is essentially an extension of the activities of the Braintree Housing Partnership (a formal association) and its (largely informal) interface with a developer (Countryside Properties). Other formal partnerships or associations between local authorities, the private sector and RSLs (for example the Estate Renewal initiatives in Birmingham – Chapter 11) can offer an inclusive, responsive and strategic way of delivering housing in a joined-up manner.

Integrated project management and negotiation

Coordinating project management and negotiation between parties without a formal mode of association can become critical at larger scales of development. This approach represents a multilateral commitment to achieving agreed outcomes. As mutually agreed objectives often have no formal basis, as in Newcastle (see Chapter 15), they depend heavily on the attitudes of the organisations and individuals involved. Integrating the management of the process requires an early establishment of (and commitment to) mutual objectives alongside the coordinating of outputs and timetables (both planning and commercial). Establishing a hierarchy of negotiation and decision-making (with preparatory interdepartmental negotiation leading to 'one-stop-shop' senior-level decision-making) can also be crucial. Unfortunately coordinated project management can become very unwieldy in terms of administration and communication due to the large numbers (and hierarchies) of people involved. Tight control and strong management is therefore important.

Integrated development proposals

The outputs of the process also need coordinating and integrating. In large part this is the role of better urban design, ensuring that large projects are coordinated between phases and that small projects positively reinforce and add to their context to create a coherent whole. Design principles for housing development have been discussed in Chapter 8. Better integration involves understanding and responding to the existing context and relationships, coordinating services, amenities and infrastructure as well as addressing issues of character and place, and the wider impact of the development in social and economic terms, e.g. the master plan at Sedgemoor (Chapter 14).

Phasing of a development can be an important tool with which to tie a development to its context and ameliorate the impact of construction and development. Unfortunately existing residents may wish to throw up barriers around their established communities, leading to disconnected and inherently unsustainable developments. This should be resisted, not least by seeking to explain the benefits of more integrated solutions. Fundamentally the domination of the limited and sometimes oversimplistic design objectives of single stakeholders, e.g. highways authorities or planning amenity standards, can undermine the delivery of good design. The objective should be an integrated design product, delivered through an integrated development process. That, however, is easier said than done (see Fig. 13.3).

The route to integrated and realistic working practices

Additional approaches and strategies for establishing more integrated and realistic working practices are listed in Fig. 13.4. It is clear that, as with the other strategies outlined in the Part Three chapters, the path to greater integration and realism starts with

13.3 From theory to practice (Louis Hellman, 1996).

early dialogue. This dialogue should establish the rules of engagement (for want of a less confrontational phrase) and protocols, and it should also look at how and why past practices have failed and have not resulted in constructive partnerships. From this point, there is a need to review existing planning tools, the relationship between tools and how far they are tailored to the peculiarities of the local socio-economic context. The task

➤ **Acceptance of national targets and policy** – authorities should avoid 'undershooting' and embrace the role of 'enabler'; housing providers should adapt to emerging policy requirements, including the need for wider community involvement and better design.

➤ **Locally set performance indicators** – adopt and adapt local Best Value indicators to identify and monitor key problem areas. To cut across key policy areas and to measure and encourage holistic working practices, cross-disciplinary local indicators might be adopted.

➤ **Address cross-disciplinary skills and expertise shortage** – design, planning, housing management and development economics skills need to be addressed through continuing professional development and further training.

➤ **Corporate strategies** – which under the Best Value regime provide the opportunity to coordinate local authority activities and place the planning vision firmly into the broader holistic and cross-departmental/disciplinary vision for the local authority area.

➤ **Matrix management structures** – including cross-departmental committee structures and cross-disciplinary management arrangements and objectives. At Wycombe District Council, matrix management is used across the authority, with cross-departmental committees and corporate priorities based on MORI surveys every two years (see Chapter 10).

13.4 Other approaches to integrated and realistic working practices.

then is to assess the relationship between organisations, the delimitation of roles and the assigning of tasks. These are the broader ground rules that feed into a project management structure that is adequately resourced, is clear on the issue of partner responsibility, has agreed outputs and integrated decision-making, results in the sharing of knowledge, and is subject to ongoing review.

This is an ideal framework; in the real world the achievement of integrated and realistic working practices may be constrained by a number of factors. The following points should be borne in mind:

• Conflicts of interest that can potentially occur in partnership arrangements where the local authority is involved as a partner. Such arrangements can render potential commercial advantage to existing partners, prejudicing future competition. The motives of local authorities can therefore be an issue (whether controlling or promoting development?).

• Due to the large number of people involved in project management, the process can become unwieldy and a drain on resources. Streamlined means of involvement, administration and communication can help (see Chapter 11).

• A commercial motive driving the process can potentially ensure levels of accountability, and can also ensure that targets and timescales are met and undertakings are sanctioned.

• Local authority implementation processes may not be as geared up as commercial project management skills and programming; benefits can therefore be found through enhancing these skills and systems.

• Without formal agreement between organisations, it can be difficult to maintain impetus and participation internally. High levels of trust are required, enabled by an overarching commitment to the desired outcome. There is also potentially a lack of leverage without a formal agreement.

- Institutional and corporate unwillingness to change remains a key constraint.
- There is a need to spread responsibilities according to recognised skills. Leadership is important but projects should not rely excessively on the input of particular individuals or parties.
- Ongoing investment in the development of human resources and skills is essential.

14

Certainty and transparency

Starting from the top

The benefits and drawbacks of a discretionary planning system which seeks to balance broad strategic certainty and local flexibility in decision-making were discussed in Chapter 7. Recent research into the delivery of affordable housing through planning has revealed a view, often held locally, that national policy is 'deliberately ambiguous', accentuating uncertainty for developers (Smith, 2002, p. 108). The concern of private housebuilders over the lack of predictability in the system is long established, and represents a particular source of frustration when commercial judgements need to be made. The desire to offer guidance rather than prescription, and hence leave the detail of decision-making or negotiation (in the case of planning obligations) with local government partially explains this apparent ambiguity. But there are also more fundamental factors at work.

For example, there is a blurred division in the British planning system between law and policy. Law, as set out in primary legislation, appears fixed, but may be difficult to apply in different local situations. It also needs interpreting in the courts, and often the exact meaning of legislation takes several years to be fully established following the passing of an Act of Parliament. In the intervening period, progress on many fronts is curtailed. The fact that establishing a working meaning of legislation is inherently an uncertain process, explained some of the reluctance of the House Builders Federation (HBF 2002b) to support radical change to the planning system in the run-up to the 2001 Planning Green Paper (see Chapter 2); this despite their constant complaints that the old system was failing – a case of better the devil you know.

To clarify the purpose and meaning of national planning policy, the system of planning policy guidance notes (PPGs) was introduced in 1988. However, it has been suggested that national 'planning law is not neatly codified' (Cullingworth and Nadin, 2002, p. 131), and instead the direction of policy is determined by the whims of successive planning ministers who in the most extreme cases announce new policy, thereby establishing material considerations, during after-dinner speeches (Read and Wood, 1994, p. 13). The most recent example of this was Lord Falconer's suggestion soon after the publication of the Planning Green Paper that local planning authorities should take for granted that its content would become policy and should apply its key principles to local practice. Given that the paper had at that point not been subject to consultation (the purpose of a green paper), the Planning Minister's remarks might at the very least have been viewed as jumping the gun.

Clarity of national policy, and what influences that direction, are significant concerns in a political regime that hands wide-ranging policy portfolios to individual ministers. This approach to government has inevitable strengths and weaknesses, but at its worst can lead to wild ideological swings in policy, for example, between the anti-planning views of Nicholas Ridley in the mid-1980s, and the pro-planning views of Chris Patten in the early 1990s (see p. 109). Since the mid-1990s, however, and despite frequent ministerial changes, a more settled system has gradually emerged. Nevertheless, the equally frequent changes in policy through the continual rewriting of the PPGs can and do cause frustration as policy at the local level is delayed or usurped, and as the implications of new policy are worked through and often found wanting. Since 1988, for example, new versions of the guidance in PPG1 have been issued on three separate occasions and the guidance is being rewritten in 2003. A life span of 5 years for the PPG that lays down the basic policy and principles for planning in England is not very long.

With such a fast-moving national policy framework, inconsistencies between different pieces of policy guidance are inevitable, and reinforce the discretionary nature of decision-making in which different national policy objectives (let alone local objectives) may be in conflict and need to be balanced. Furthermore, it is usually unclear in most national policy statements which elements are policy, and must be taken on board by local planning authorities, and which elements are guidance, about which discretion exists at the local level (Morrison and Pearce, 2000). Equally, local policy can be inconsistent with regional or strategic policy (i.e. policies in structure plans or in the future in subregional strategies), and although government advice suggests that the most up-to-date adopted guidance will in the future take precedence (ODPM, 2002c, para. 8), such inconsistencies can be a source of further confusion and uncertainty.

The major concern in this chapter, however, is with transparency in local policy-making and in the dealings between the public and private sectors. Therefore, although there are inherent uncertainties in the wider policy framework, the discussion focuses on the way in which greater certainty will emerge from more certain processes at the local level. In development control, for example, inconsistency occurs when different officers interpret planning policy and planning problems in different ways. To some extent that is inevitable when individuals are asked to weigh up evidence and make informed value judgements. Nevertheless ensuring that such judgements are made in an objective, open and fair manner is the job of the professional planner, although private housebuilders have long bemoaned the inconsistencies and indecisiveness of the local planning process (DoE and HRF, 1976, pp. 49–53), complaining about:

- a perceived tendency for councillors to ignore the advice of officers (thus rendering pre-application discussions useless);
- local authority bureaucracy and indecision;
- the disregard displayed by authorities to the financial implications of planning requirements or to the saleability of developments and preferences of potential purchasers;
- the lack of clear policies and guidance for particular sites;
- the tendency to stray from legitimate planning grounds established in government guidance.

A clear and consistent framework of policy and guidance as demanded by the plan-led system should help to overcome problems of inconsistent interpretation. Nevertheless inconsistencies also exist within most development plans as a result of: different chapters being formulated by different authors with insufficient attention being paid to harmonisation and integration; and the fact that although plans are required to be in general conformity, this inevitably means that – as with national guidance – different policies will be pulling in different directions. In considering this state of affairs, Tewdwr-Jones (2002, p. 172) has argued that the planning system has an in-built and deliberate recognition of

> The importance of retaining policies that pull in opposite directions in order to provide certainty with flexibility, and for local authorities to determine each case on the merits of all relevant policies of the local plan and other material considerations.

Thus certainty in the British planning system can only be delivered up to a point.

The lack of transparency that flows from such a system was recognised by the Nolan Committee on Standards in Public Life (1997 – see Chapter 12) in the context of planning gain. Nolan argued that in the case of planning obligations there has been insufficient transparency and consequent uncertainty in their use, such that they convey an 'impression to the public of planning permissions being bought and sold' (Campbell *et al.*, 2001, p. 2). Research funded by the Joseph Rowntree Foundation (2001), for example, indicated considerable variation in the interpretation of affordable housing policies across England, resulting in wildly different levels of affordable housing being obtained (where it is obtained at all) from typically 11 per cent in the north east, to 27 per cent in the south east. Authorities pointed to the lack of clarity in the policy framework set up by central government as the main problem in achieving affordable housing through Section 106 agreements. Recognition of this problem of inconsistency and perceived impropriety was behind the proposals to move towards a published system of tariffs as the basis for negotiating planning gain (see Chapter 9), a system, following consultation, rejected by government in the 2002 'Sustainable Communities' Planning Policy Statement (ODPM, 2002a, para. 53).

The role of authorities in driving forward a process that is inherently more transparent and therefore generates increased certainty is fundamental to addressing the key tensions inherent in the discretionary nature of British planning (see Chapter 7). The research indicated that:

- Local authorities have a pivotal role to play in generating greater certainty, which is essential if high-quality housing developments are to be brought forward.
- Authorities can achieve this by ensuring that they establish a robust local planning framework that is complemented (and not supplanted or confused) by additional supplementary guidance.
- With discretionary power comes the responsibility to ensure that decision-making is also transparent. If this is the case, then there is a greater likelihood that other stakeholders will understand how decisions were arrived at, which will achieve greater acceptability and reduce the friction that frequently results in appeals and delays.

Certainty and transparency

A certain and transparent planning process implies the promotion of more certain and transparent policies and development processes, through sharing information and objectives.

At its best, a plan-led yet discretionary planning system can offer housing providers the certainty they require to make informed and dependable financial and development decisions. It also offers other stakeholders – including the community – the certainty of a reasonably stable planning framework. At its worst it can degenerate into an *ad hoc* and unpredictable system in which decisions are based on who shouts the loudest, on political dogma or on deals done behind closed doors. The objective of a certain and transparent decision-making process is to overcome such problems and by sharing knowledge develop clear and inclusive policy frameworks. In this regard there is some overlap between the topics addressed here and the two preceding chapters: transparency has much to do with the inclusion of different groups in decision-making (Chapter 12), and also with the degree of integration across an authority and between organisations (Chapter 13).

Unfortunately, public–private sector frictions are commonplace, as are clashes of personality which all too frequently act to evaporate trust, heighten suspicion and undermine transparency. In particular, some housing providers (interviewed during the course of the research) pointed to the idiosyncrasies of individual local authority officers as a cause of inconsistency and subsequent lack of certainty in the planning process. Of course personal communication is always going to be the unknown factor in any form of democratic system and it can only be hoped that in the majority of cases it contributes to a positive outcome. In other cases, shared leadership, consistent policy, and strategies for building better relationships can act to ameliorate negative impacts and help build trust.

These are management problems. Research commissioned by the RTPI to examine the key aptitudes required by planners as managers revealed a broad range of competences that planners require, including intellect, personal integrity and flexibility, a drive to achieve, and skills in strategic management, political awareness, decision-making, communication, negotiation, self- and stress management, people management and relationships, analysis and problem solving, change management, business and commerce, influencing people and the ability to deliver results. Many of these generic skills are required by all professionals, including housing providers, but the complex nature of many planning problems means that team-working is particularly important to overcome individual inadequacies and ensure a consistent line is taken on key policy issues. The RTPI (1995b, p. 77) research revealed that five significant management gaps need to be bridged:

- The need for better developed people management skills.
- The need to better cope with the constantly changing professional context faced by planners.
- The need for better self- and stress management skills in the light of increasing workloads.
- The need for enhanced business and commercial skills in view of the interface between planning and development activity.
- The need for better management of information in the era of IT and the information society.

➤ Accessible to all stakeholders, including groups that traditionally are hard to reach
➤ User-focused and responsive to the needs of stakeholders
➤ Ensures stakeholders are kept informed
➤ Demonstrates transparency, probity, fairness and consistency in decision-making
➤ Operates within a development framework, which is rooted in an up-to-date development plan
➤ Proactive in securing a high quality outcome
➤ Responsive to government and national initiatives and policy
➤ Takes a corporate approach to the development process
➤ Establishes strong and effective relationships and partnerships with other authorities and external bodies
➤ Ensures provision of appropriately skilled and competent staff
➤ Provides an effective, well-managed service

14.1 Towards an excellent service: critical factors (POS, 2001, pp. 3–4).

The work also argued that to be competent in their jobs and focused on delivery, planners need to have the capacity to reflect and think, the confidence to take risks when required, and the sensitivity to develop good working relationships. Responding to the management challenges facing planners, the Planning Officers Society produced a series of 'Excellence Matrices' to establish the critical factors that shape an excellent planning service, including matrices for development control, planning policy and design and conservation. The eleven critical factors for development control encapsulate the key arguments (see Fig. 14.1) that, in order to be transparent in decision-making and to offer certainty, development control (like policy making) needs to be user-focused, driven by a clear vision of what it is trying to achieve, and resourced to deliver on policy aspirations. Authorities therefore need to show a clear commitment to the policies they adopt and the decisions they make. This should relate in turn to a clear strategy about what kind of place they wish their plan area to be.

Advice in *Making Plans* from the ODPM (2002d, p. 8) argues that 'the strongest and most immediate commitment comes from realising the value of the plan for the local authority with a vision and a strategy firmly grounded in the community'. The guidance identifies a number of benefits that having an up-to-date and effective policy framework can bring:

• Community commitment to the future of the area.
• The influence that making the plan provides on the determination of the scale and location of development at the strategic level.
• The role of plans in promoting regeneration and investment, by creating confidence in commitment to change and improvement.
• The success that being able to link bids for funds to a strategy for an area has brought.
• Providing a strong basis for successful negotiation on development proposals, and on developer contributions.
• The contribution that the plan has enabled the authority to make to the provision of affordable housing.
• Providing a means of coordinating the activities of different departments, and different authorities and organisations.

To these can be added the certainty that comes with confidence about the future of an area, which only the public sector can deliver. Transparency and equity in decision-making are therefore clearly issues for the public sector. But the openness and integrity of developers are also important; for example, their willingness to make clear the overall costs of development schemes or to negotiate openly with local authorities. Local authorities are required to be transparent in the preparation of development plans and in making decisions, but political and commercial openness and integrity by all parties can lead to a more efficient and effective system with better outcomes for all concerned.

The case studies

As in the previous chapters, the case studies set out below demonstrate two broad approaches adopted within different local authority areas to achieve greater certainty and transparency. The case of South Lakeland shows:

- How it is possible to implement cross-departmental corporate working in order to achieve balanced and workable policies and guidance.
- How cross-party support (local authority departments, housing providers, council members, and other agencies) can be achieved through meaningful consultation and open debate.
- The importance of policies and guidance being transparently based upon good quality housing needs assessment (HSAs).
- The means of reducing uncertainty within the process through clarity of policies and transparency in requirements and determination.
- The potential for reducing delays through clarity and transparency of Section 106 agreements and related guidance.

The Sedgemoor case looks more specifically at the nature of the public–private relationship in housebuilding, and at how particular trust issues might be resolved. It also demonstrates:

- How all parties collaborating as a team from pre-application stage can deliver more creative problem solving.
- The importance of breaking down the public/private taboos regarding the sharing of knowledge and information, particularly financial information.
- The benefits of developing a shared understanding of the aims and objectives of the process, including the definition of quality in outcomes.
- The value of testing alternatives through the design process.
- The benefits accruing from the preparation of detailed development briefs to provide a framework for future planning applications.

CASE STUDY: South Lakeland – clarity through a corporate approach

South Lakeland District Council is responsible for an area of Cumbria that contains the Yorkshire Dales National Park and the Lake District National Park. Administrative control is split between South Lakeland District Council and each National Park Authority. The Park Authorities have responsibility for planning (including preparation of Local Plans) within the parks, whilst South Lakeland District Council has responsibility for housing within the whole area, alongside a responsibility for planning within the remainder of the district. South Lakeland is a rural district, and as a result there are few brownfield sites (less than 20 per cent of development). Unemployment within the district is reasonably low, although a large proportion of employment is seasonal and consequently incomes are low. Nevertheless, as a consequence of the environmental qualities and the market in second homes and retirement homes, land and property values within and around the Parks are very high.

These high land and property values, coupled with the fact that there is no allocation for affordable housing within the National Parks, mean that there is significant pressure for the provision of affordable housing in the remaining areas within South Lakeland. A housing needs survey of the district is undertaken every five years by consultants based upon a questionnaire examining future need for housing both within and outside the National Parks. Most existing residents are satisfied with their accommodation, although the latest survey (undertaken in 1997) identified a potentially large group of people who could not afford the available housing. The survey also found that an income of £17,500 or more was needed to access the housing market in the majority of the district, but that 75 per cent of the newly forming households within the area had a lower income than this.

SPG on affordable housing

The local authority acknowledged that the shortage of affordable housing within the district was exacerbated by constraints on the supply of such housing. In particular the local authority highlighted planning delay and delays in negotiating Section 106 agreements as a primary obstacle, as delays frequently meant that RSLs missed out on funding because of the tight time scales involved in the grant-funding process. Following the detailed housing needs survey of 1997 it was decided to produce Supplementary Planning Guidance (SPG), dealing with the requirements for, and provision of, affordable housing in the district. The SPG aimed to clarify the position of the local authority up front in the process by establishing quite detailed and prescriptive requirements, and in so doing reduce the propensity for delay through protracted negotiation.

The SPG (completed in March 2000) is only applicable to the areas of South Lakeland outside of the National Parks and is intended to provide a background to the issues as well as practical guidance to the parties involved, in particular to developers. The local authority felt that a key part of the SPG was a justification of their requirements in order to make the principle behind the approach transparent, and in this way get the developers (as far as possible) on board. To achieve this, a summary of the findings of the housing needs survey of 1997 was included within the guidance, identifying the key issues and problem areas.

The SPG gives a comprehensive definition of what is meant by 'affordable housing' within the context of South Lakeland and states that there will be a requirement (within any Section 106 agreements) that the housing remains affordable in perpetuity. It also identifies specific housing sites allocated within the local plan which do not already have planning permission, and upon which affordable housing will be required. Where the provision of affordable housing is to be market housing at a discount, the SPG specifies that a general discount of 20 per cent on the market value will be required, with some flexibility depending upon property type, location and the market price of housing in that area. The discount can also be averaged over the total number of affordable units on site, enabling a mix of income levels to be accommodated. However, the discount is only to be applied to housing within the range of the average house price for the area, effectively stopping 20 per cent discounts being offered on higher-value housing, which would be of little benefit to those on low incomes.

The guidance also covers the standards that would be required, addressing issues of the mix, balance and integration of housing types and tenure types, alongside the quality of design, materials and construction. Detailed issues of design are not covered within the guide as this aspect of affordable housing is dealt with in policy and guidance elsewhere. Nevertheless, the local authority recognises that the standards of design of affordable housing are sometimes poor, and that there is the potential to improve guidance in this respect.

Consultation process

It was recognised by the local authority that if the guidance was to be effective, then it was of prime importance that the requirements within the document should relate to the findings of a thorough housing needs survey (as was the case in South Lakeland). The developers within South Lakeland concurred with this view as they did not wish to be 'conned' (in one housebuilder's words) into providing something for which there was no need. Alongside the identified need for robustness and transparency in the principles contained within the guidance, it was believed to be important to ensure that all of the relevant parties were consulted and involved, so that the guidance would be accepted by the different stakeholders in the process.

A corporate approach was taken to the development of the guidance. An umbrella group consisting of representatives of the planning and housing departments was established; they drove the process forward and initiated regular meetings that were usually informal in nature. Representatives from other departments and organisations supplemented this core group as required, whilst council members were involved in commenting upon and shaping the evolving document. Once the draft SPG was complete, it was sent out to a wider range of organisations for feedback (e.g. the HBF, Environmental Health etc.), and further meetings were held as a result of the feedback received.

The meetings increased in size as more people became interested and involved. At the second consultation stage it was decided that as the SPG was seeking to go beyond the usual remit of guidance (its prescriptive nature tends towards policy rather than guidance), it should subsequently be adopted as part of the local plan.

The guidance was formulated, consulted upon and refined within the space of a year. Those involved in the process suggest that this speed reflected the level of support and commitment that the process received from all of those involved. In particular, it owed much to the already good working relationships between the planning and housing departments of the local authority, which also helped to ensure that the guidance was well balanced and coordinated. The good working relationship was enabled in part by the fact that the local authority departments were all located within one building, on one site. Consequently officers within the different departments are more aware of each other, and able to forge and reinforce informal working relationships.

Discussion

The development of this SPG for affordable housing has subsequently been regarded as good practice in Cumbria, where South Lakeland is now considered a model authority with regard to affordable housing. Within the county there has been a ripple effect, where this instance of good practice has influenced the practices and approach to development within other authorities. The SPG on affordable housing has most crucially helped to bring forward an increased quantity of affordable housing more efficiently, which to some degree has begun to address the desperate shortage.

Local developers welcomed the opportunity to become involved in the process and express their opinions, and consequently are broadly happy with the content of the guidance. They argue that the SPG increased certainty as all applicants are now treated fairly, in contrast to their previous experience when they believed that developers from outside the district were getting preferential treatment. In particular, there was a view that local developers were required to fulfil more onerous Section 106 obligations, increasing their costs and enabling developers from outside to undercut them. Conversely, the local authority asserted that local housing providers (both private developers and RSLs) were easier to work with, in contrast with housing providers from outside the district. This highlights a difference in perception about the different working relationships involved, and also illustrates the level of tensions that can arise during negotiations.

The actual process of developing the guidance has also had long-term benefits. In particular, local developers have identified that since the process of formulating the SPG began, the local authority has started to function as one organisation instead of three separate organisations – their view previously. Although some vestiges of tension remain following the introduction of the approach, the process has clearly improved the nature of corporate working within the local authority.

A potential constraint to this type of approach being adopted elsewhere is the general resistance to change within most local authorities. This is a critical issue identified by both parties (housing providers and the local authority) especially when coupled with a lack of resources. The process of identifying needs, recognising where change within current practice is required, and subsequently implementing a collaborative process to establish detailed and contextual guidance has been extremely resource-intensive. The local authority in South Lakeland admits that had the affordable housing situation not been so critical, then the process would never have been undertaken. This type of detailed and contextual guidance also represents an ongoing resource commitment, as the prescriptive elements of the guide are based on local data, which will continually change over time requiring frequent review and updating.

Despite the obvious gains, some problems have been experienced. These reflect a frequent mismatch between the locations where housing is needed compared to where it is provided. This is a particular problem within South Lakeland due to the pressure exerted by the National Parks which have no land allocations for new housing, yet still have a large population of existing and newly forming households that require affordable housing. Another constraint identified was the NIMBY attitude towards affordable housing, both in the local community and in the local political sphere. In 2000, local developers suggested that it was this issue (alongside the council members who exhibit and support NIMBYism) that was the weakest link in the process, not planning guidance or planning officers.

Furthermore, the local authority suggested that even when all of these different constraints have been overcome and affordable housing provision for a site has been agreed (the Section 106 agreement signed off), it remains very difficult to monitor the provision of affordable housing and ensure that all of the agreed requirements are being fulfilled. As the success of this approach relies on the clarity of guidance and the strength of the Section 106 agreement, this weakness is of critical importance. The local authority in South Lakeland felt that this issue was the next big challenge; updating their development control processes to enable effective monitoring to take place, both within the context of affordable housing provision and within a wider planning context.

CASE STUDY: Sedgemoor – certainty, transparency and trust

As one of only three larger urban centres in Somerset, Bridgwater had been the recipient of a large proportion of the county's housing allocations in the 1980s, most of which developed in a fragmented manner resulting in poor-quality urban sprawl with little sense of place, community, or inherent quality. In the 1990s the expansion of the town had become physically constrained, although parts of the periphery continued to expand further into the surrounding countryside. Nevertheless, in the face of mounting pressure for new residential development, Sedgemoor District Council allocated two significant parcels of greenfield land for 1,400 new homes in the 1991 local plan.

The scenario faced by the local authority (because of the fragmented ownership and heavy infrastructure costs) promised to deliver yet more suburban sprawl, with little chance of delivering the required infrastructure improvements or the sustainable environment the authority wished to see. Fortunately, a successful bid to the 'Quality in Town and Country, Urban Design Campaign' fund of 1994–5, organised by the Department of the Environment, gave the council the spur it needed to rethink their approach to residential design.

Avoiding confrontation

The local authority argued that a positive approach to residential development was required, an approach which would avoid the confrontational and reactive review of residential design. They were concerned that the sequential process of private developer proposal, followed by local authority intervention based on little preconceived design policy or guidance (as was previously the case in Sedgemoor), would inevitably end in an appeals lottery in which the authority would take its chances alongside the developer.

The identified solution was to involve the housebuilders at the start of the process (pre-application) in a collaboration with the council in order to build a culture of cooperation in which all parties could achieve shared objectives: high-quality, contextually appropriate, profitable residential development. To pursue the aim, a steering group was established which represented the broad range of stakeholders in the area: the county, district and town councils; representatives of the landowners and developers; together with an academic input to act as an independent arbitrator when required. A project specification was drawn up to identify the roles, interests and needs of the different stakeholders, together with the benefits each expected from the process (see Table 14.1). This key innovation (to which all parties signed up) clarified issues, ways of working and decision-making as well as common aims, objectives and outputs. An appendix to the specification laid out these concerns and meant that there was less room for disagreement during the later stages.

The aim of the initiative was to create a team capable of solving problems in a collaborative way, to avoid defensive posturing and to utilise the resources and skills of both public and private sectors effectively. Consequently the primary public/private taboo was broken, with members of the team sharing knowledge and information (including operational costs) from the outset.

Defining quality

As there were many different parties involved in the approach, a key task was to establish the criteria within which the proposals would be evaluated. Central to this discussion was the identification of the common definition of what was meant by 'quality'. To reach an

Table 14.1 South Bridgwater stakeholders, interests, needs and benefits

Stakeholders (People and groups with an interest)	Role/interest (The role of the person or group and the interests they have)	Needs (The needs the person or group may have)	Benefits (added value) (The benefits that the person or group hope to gain)
Consumers/users Future residents The local community	Participation in process. Influence process and outcomes. Quality environment which meets a variety of needs including private economic investment.	A development which caters for basic local needs, built to contemporary acceptable standards and which minimises the need for public financial investment.	A product which exceeds expectations and improves upon contemporary residential standards, delivers wider/ enhanced public benefits and creates new choices and opportunities. Provides improved comparative financial return on investment.
Providers Landowners Developers Financiers/ investors Agents/consultants	Participation in process. Influence process and final outcomes. Responsible for resource inputs of land, finance and expertise. A marketable product which will attract consumers/users.	Effective use of resources (control of costs). Acceptable return on money spent. Minimum delay in processing. Implementation which fits with corporate business plans. A competitive product. Maintenance/ enhancement of corporate image.	Reduced costs. Improved return on money spent. An expedient process. A competitive product which generates high sales values/sales volume in a year. Market-leader image.
Those who make the decisions Local Planning Authority Local Highway and Education Authorities	Management of process. Coordination of public participation. Identification of needs and requirements. Supervising role over outcomes. A quality environment which meets local needs and which delivers wider public benefits.	An open participatory approach which involves local interests. Delivery of identified infrastructure requirements. The maintenance of environmental assets. A development which does not cause material harm.	Public approval. Reduced processing and other public costs. A distinctive 'quality' environment. A range of benefits targeted at both direct consumers and indirect users.

Table 14.1 continued

Those who have an influence over the outcome Town Council Civic Society Environment Agency Wessex Water Ministry of Agriculture Fisheries and Foods Wildlife Trust Countryside Commission	Participation in process. Influence process and outcomes. A means of enhancing existing environmental assets and creating new ones. A development which adds value.	A development which does not cause material harm, and which safeguards particular environmental assets. Delivery of identified infrastructure requirements.	The enhancement and creation of particular environmental assets.

understanding, the team went back to first principles and identified the concept of 'quality thresholds' as a means to measure the satisfaction of differing aspirations by alternative courses of action. It was recognised that quality would be achieved when the development proposal exceeded the expectations of the greatest number of stakeholders.

- Basic threshold: a development which conforms to the specification of planning policy and guidance, is fit for its purpose of providing a basic range and level of needs and expectations, and provides some value for money to some stakeholders.
- Intermediate threshold: a development which exhibits superior attributes and provides added value because it is unique (product differentiated) and delivers a range of benefits which exceeds basic needs and expectations, i.e. it has competitive advantage.
- Optimum threshold: a development that is sustainable and responsive across the broadest range of environmental and needs-based criteria within the structural constraints of any given context.

The assumption was made that a development which met the basic and intermediate thresholds, but which was not sustainable or people-centred, would ultimately produce a significant environmental and social cost, and that this public cost would be greater than the private costs associated with higher quality.

Development of a masterplan

To pursue the theory it was decided to prepare development options for the allocated land corresponding to each identified threshold. Of these, the optimum quality masterplan was finally chosen (see Fig. 14.2). It aimed to create a unique sense of place by drawing on local contextual themes identified through rigorous analysis. The concept involved the creation of two different neighbourhoods reflecting a village theme. One of the neighbourhoods was internally structured with clearly defined, traffic-calmed streets and a legible street pattern accessible to public transport, whilst the other was more externally structured with soft edges. A country park was situated between the two development sites as a strong and integrating link. Within the developments themselves, issues such as housing density and building type,

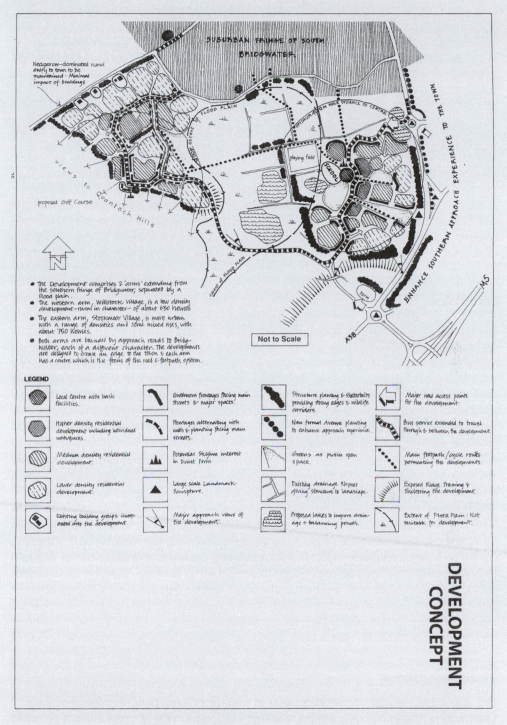

The content within the figure includes:

SUBURBAN FRINGE OF SOUTH BRIDGWATER

Hedgerow–dominated rural entry to town to be maintained · Minimum impact of buildings

Views to Quantock Hills

proposed Golf Course

OPTIMUM 400M WALK DISTANCE TO CENTRE

ENHANCE SOUTHERN APPROACH EXPERIENCE TO THE TOWN

playing field

School

Extent of flood plain

Extent of flood plain

Farm

N

M5

A38

Not to Scale

- The Development comprises 2 'arms' extending from the southern fringe of Bridgwater; separated by a flood plain.
- The western arm, Willstock Village, is a low density development – rural in character – of about 630 houses.
- The eastern arm, Stockmoor Village, is more urban with a range of densities and some mixed uses, with about 750 houses.
- Both arms are bounded by approach roads to Bridgwater, each of a different character. The developments are designed to create an edge to the town & each arm has a centre which is the focus of the road & footpath system.

LEGEND

- Local Centre with basic facilities.
- Higher density residential development including individual workspaces.
- Medium density residential development.
- Lower density residential development.
- Existing building groups incorporated into the development.
- Continuous frontages facing main streets & major spaces.
- Frontages alternating with walls & planting facing main streets.
- Potential Skyline interest in built form
- Large scale Landmark Sculpture.
- Major approach views of the development.
- Structure planting & shelterbelts providing strong edges & wildlife corridors.
- New formal Avenue planting to enhance approach experience.
- Greens as public open space.
- Existing drainage Rhynes giving structure to landscape.
- Proposed lakes to improve drainage + balancing ponds.
- Major new access points for the development.
- Bus service extended to travel through & between the development.
- Main footpath/cycle routes permeating the developments.
- Exposed Ridge. Framing & Sheltering the development.
- Extent of Flood Plain · Not suitable for development.

DEVELOPMENT CONCEPT

14.2 *South Bridgwater development concept.*

form and height were clustered to create areas of character and to provide focal points for the development.

In 1998, following the initiative, Sedgemoor prepared a detailed development brief for South Bridgwater, setting out the parameters by which subsequent planning applications would be made and evaluated. Furthermore, in contrast to previous practice, the emerging local plan was intended to contain policies aimed at enhancing the quality of the new development within Sedgemoor.

By 2000 the brief had still not resulted in a planning application and some of the early collaborative thinking was beginning to break down as Charles Church (one of the two initial housebuilders together with Bloor Homes) sold their interest to Beazer Homes, who were more determined to impose their standard products on the site. The authority was also experiencing problems encouraging the two housebuilders to collaborate in submitting one coordinated application, as well as a coordinated package of infrastructure improvements (an overall contribution of £5 million was required). Nevertheless, the brief has already brought benefits in effectively forcing the appointment of urban designers by both housebuilders and their engagement with the authority in taking forward the urban design framework.

Discussion

Despite lingering doubts over whether it is possible to deliver the quality sought in the brief, the experiment has been viewed as a success because of the new collaborative working relationships that have been engendered in the district. The success of these relationships has been largely dependent upon participants being willing to move beyond professional and institutional barriers, and approach the initiative with commitment and enthusiasm. Consequently, the planners have had to question the existing rigid standards and practices in the authority, whilst the housebuilders have had to question the philosophy that 'quality does not pay'. Overall, both parties suggest that the initiative has required a higher resource cost than the traditional sectoral approach, but has the potential to achieve better quality outcomes alongside time savings further down the line, better returns on investment for the house-builders, and the avoidance of negative environmental and social costs.

Peripheral town expansions of the nature proposed in Bridgwater remain important contributors to housing requirements and need. However, many authorities have little more by way of policy or guidance for guiding residential design than Sedgemoor had in the early 1990s. Nevertheless, by adopting an approach that harnesses collaboration as a means to deliver quality, and by pre-empting the development process (by getting in first before positions harden on design), the local authority should be able to favourably influence the process of delivering residential development. Furthermore, it is to be hoped that with the right process in place, the right product will follow.

Recommendations

The above case studies demonstrate that at a strategic level, the policy frameworks and approaches that an authority wishes to adopt need to be in place at the earliest possible opportunity. This, of course, is a common theme across all the Part Three chapters, and is in line with government guidance (DoE, 1997b). These frameworks must be clear and legible, whilst standard documentation – such as Section 106 agreements – should be accepted amongst the different users. Where supplementary planning guidance is produced, this needs to be well thought out and should be taken into account consistently during the life of the local plan (although the plan retains primacy).

The clarity of policy is an issue at the heart of coherent decision-making and at a strategic level, achieving greater certainty and transparency has much to do with clear leadership. Thus the planning authority has an obvious role to play in ensuring that what happens on the ground bears a close resemblance to the vision established on paper. But this vision itself must be acceptable to all the key stakeholders. The acceptability and joint ownership of the policy framework are central to the way in which the stakeholders build trust. Furthermore, private developers may be less inclined to be completely open about the costs of particular housing schemes if they do not believe that the frameworks within which they are operating are right, or at least democratically derived. As one RSL commented:

> Clarity is what everyone strives for. Whether it's building cost, land value or planning consent. If they know what they're buying into, then they're much more willing to do it quickly and efficiently.

At the development level, if consistent, clear and transparent policy has already created the conditions within which trust and positive planning can thrive, the need then is to ensure that better relationships result in better housing products. For the key stake-holders, this will mean open negotiations where all concerned have a clear grasp of the costs of a particular scheme and the planning gain requirements. For housing providers, the willingness to engage in more open processes of negotiation seems fundamental if confrontation is to be avoided.

Council members (for their part) can sometimes be thought of (perhaps unfairly) as the weak link in the housing development process. They are accused of making decisions behind closed doors, but being unwilling to take responsibility for particular developments, defend the decisions of the council, or work with local people to ensure greater political transparency and acceptability. In some instances, it is argued that members have a poor understanding of development economics, leading them to request ever greater gains from planning without due regard to the impact this will have on the viability of a scheme. Of course members have a critical role to play in making sure that the public comes to trust the actions of the local authority. Nevertheless, they may be better placed to fulfil this role given additional training.

Once the policy and decision-making process extends beyond the local authority, its transparency (and hence acceptability) increases. So whilst members have a role in articulating and justifying policy to the public, officers should be proactive in drawing the widest possible range of groups into the area of policy design. Housing providers need to be willing to engage positively in this process. The case studies set out in this chapter reveal how stakeholders might work together more effectively at both the strategic and development level. The examples point toward a more transparent way of working, resulting in less conflict, fewer delays and therefore greater certainty. In all, they help to illustrate five key approaches:

Establishing a policy framework

The first requirement of certainty is the establishment of a clear, stable and broadly accepted policy framework as the basis on which negotiation will commence and decisions will be made. First and foremost will be the development plan (the LDF), that should be up to date, adopted and under constant review. Guidance produced for the RTPI on the writing of development plans argues that in the days of Best Value (see Chapter 10) 'it is self-evident that a good development plan is one which is well related to other plans' (Crow *et al.*, 2000, p. 13), and that consistency within and between plans is vital, although one of the most difficult elements to achieve in practice. A good development plan is identified as one that:

- is well related to other plans, both hierarchically and horizontally;
- expresses a spatial interpretation of a commonly held vision;
- adequately guides (but does not attempt to anticipate) development control decision-making;
- gives long-term guidance to the plan-making and investment of other public sector organisations;
- acts as a source of information about development intentions, guiding investment decisions by the private and the voluntary sectors;
- may (if required as such) act as a marketing or boosting tool, attracting investment, visitors or general interest in an area;
- by setting out the locations in which community and other action may take place and the essential parameters of policy which relate to that action, both legitimates and guides that action.

Beyond the plan non-statutory supplementary planning guidance also has an important role to play (see Chapter 15). South Lakeland's SPG on affordable housing, for example, has been greatly welcomed by developers and RSLs alike, and the exercise has brought both strategic and development level benefits. At the strategic level has come the realisation that different stakeholders can work together effectively and there is now a greater commitment to use this realisation in other policy areas. At the development level, the entire process for delivering affordable homes is now smoother, more transparent and defined by frankness and trust rather than misunderstanding. Planning is in large part about reconciling interests, and establishing a clear policy framework is the first and most crucial part of this endeavour. Positively engaging in this process beyond partisan site-specific representations can be an important role for housing providers.

Consistent implementation and interpretation

The second part is the consistent interpretation and implementation of that framework. Ensuring that an organisation (especially a local authority) is operating in a consistent and coordinated manner in the implementation and interpretation of policy tools enhances the levels of certainty and consistency within the process. This represents a key issue for housing providers and their ability to project-plan and undertake commercial operations.

Consistency can be achieved through a system of comprehensive knowledge acquisition and sharing such as the lunchtime CPD sessions on their design guidance and its interpretation undertaken in Stratford-on-Avon (see Chapter 12), or it might involve the adoption of formal working practices and protocols to enhance consistency. It requires authorities to move beyond the 'learning on the job' approaches to staff development that still characterise many areas of local planning practice (Arup Economics and Planning, 2000, p. 11). It can also include the employment of dedicated (and appropriately skilled) local authority officers who comment and report on specific issues (for example, on social housing or design) for each application, therefore ensuring continuity. Fundamentally, it requires having a robust policy and guidance framework in place in order to inform decision-making.

Open-book accounting

The financing of schemes, and the extent to which the development economics of each allows – or not – the funding of public sector aspirations (infrastructure, social gain, better design, and so forth) represent the root cause of much provider/planner tension. An open-book process provides a possible way forward. Whilst some partners seem to be embracing the need for greater openness (see, for example, the RSLs at Braintree – Chapter 13), developers remain unhappy with the extent of some gain requirements and the consequent prolonging of Section 106 negotiations. Many believe that full cost disclosure could leave the private sector vulnerable to further gain demands and may compromise commercial confidentiality in a sometimes cut-throat industry. For these reasons open-book examples are rare, although the experience at Sedgemoor of an open and shared process quickly allowed the parties to bypass defensive posturing to clarify shared objectives and, because the explicit aim was to optimise outcomes for all those involved, deliver win:win scenarios for all parties.

Guidance on the benefits of partnering by the Housing Forum (2000, p. 6) argues in favour of open-book approaches across the industry. They suggest that:

> An open book approach to partnering (where each member of the team lays open their part in the contract, estimated profits, overheads and costs) means that an understanding of the component costs is required by different members of the team. This will lead to improvement in the processes of value management and risk analysis. The trust on which such an approach is based will also result in a greater sharing of skills and expertise.

A shared appreciation of development economics and social costs

Open-book approaches on the part of developers and RSLs can be matched on the part of planning authorities by a commitment to a comparable level of clarity and openness. This might, for example, involve significant improvements to the way Section 106 agreements are laid out and issued, for example, in specimen form (as has been the case recently in Stratford-on-Avon – Chapter 12) to build on increased certainty and transparency in the policy process. Unfortunately, where planning gain is concerned, planners can ask for gain requirements that are impossible to deliver on a particular site. Through training, and therefore a greater appreciation of development economics, officers and members can develop more informed ideas about what is, and is not, feasible. The early involvement of local authority estates departments will also help overcome the lack of understanding that permeates many Section 106 negotiations.

Knowing what is economically possible should pave the way for greater certainty. In particular, the need for greater certainty about the costs of planning permission (including any planning gain requirements) remains crucial for the developer when deciding how much to pay for land. The more these costs are known in advance of purchasing land or taking out an option, the less confrontational the planning process is likely to be. Equally, if developers have an awareness of the social costs of their developments, then they are likely to be more willing to factor these costs into their calculations. Education in this sense is a two-way process.

Negotiation based on trust

Whilst the clarity of policy statements and guidance is a key element of bringing about greater certainty, there is also a need to balance consistency with flexibility. By these means it is possible to ensure that developments are appropriate to context and that partners can tailor schemes and requirements to changing physical and economic settings. This is likely to mean, for example, being prepared to amend briefs following pre-application discussions with developers. However, flexibility within an agreed framework should not be mistaken for, or substituted with, inconsistency. The operation of Midas Homes in Torbay illustrates the importance of pre-application discussions, and negotiation on the basis of frankness and equity (see Chapter 15). Without flexibility (a willingness to compromise or accept modification) on both sides, such discussions become meaningless. The negotiation of affordable housing targets, phasing and location between RSLs, housebuilders and local authorities offers a case in point where open negotiation based on trust can help to resolve tensions. Key prerequisites for successful affordable housing (or Section 106) negotiations include:

- up-to-date, rigorous and publicly available baseline data on local housing needs;
- realistic aspirations based on commercial realities about what a site can sustain;
- a willingness to balance affordable housing requirements with other planning gain objectives of the planning authority;
- realistic phasing requirements, matching agreed market provision with the staged delivery of affordable housing requirements;
- a willingness from all stakeholders to build integrated and mixed communities, rather than separated and segregated estates;
- an agreed timetable covering pre-construction, construction and post-construction stages.

To aid this process it may be worthwhile considering employing an impartial facilitator to work with all parties in the role of honest broker. To avoid conflicts of interest, all negotiating stakeholders should share in the financing of such a position. In the long term the investment may actually save resources because of a reduced need to fight acrimonious and expensive appeals. Partnering approaches, as dealt with in Chapter 13, offer similar benefits.

The route to certainty and transparency

Additional approaches and strategies for establishing greater certainty and transparency are highlighted in Fig. 14.3. The case studies suggested that greater certainty and transparency at both a corporate and an individual level rely heavily on:

- The formulation and content of planning tools especially the adopted policy, which needs to be a product of careful and sensitive appraisal of local circumstances, be inclusive, have clarity of content, establish a clear framework for the development process, and provide a basis for negotiation (see also Healey *et al.*, 1993). Such a framework should also be consistent (with other policy frameworks at other tiers and

➤ **Planning committee knowledge building** – to reduce the instances of planning committees interpreting national advice incorrectly or over-ruling officer advice (despite often extensive prior negotiations between officers and housing providers to ensure an acceptable scheme). Planning committee knowledge-building exercises can be valuable on key areas of ambiguity and interest – legal responsibilities, design objectives, regional and national responsibilities, etc.

➤ **Planning committee representations** – making time for applicants, agents and community representatives to address the planning committee directly to present their proposals and field questions.

➤ **Evaluating outline permissions** – the use of outline permissions can both increase certainty by establishing the principle of development early on, but can also create uncertainty about the eventual form a development is likely to take. Carefully considering where outline permissions are and are not acceptable (perhaps in published guidance) can help to strike the right balance. The provision made in the 2003 Planning and Compulsory Purchase Act to offer an alternative to outline permissions, and in time perhaps to replace them with 'Statements of Development Principles' (ODPM, 2002a, para. 49), does not alter this advice.

➤ **Investing in rigorous enforcement** – despite the intentions of this guide and the good intentions of most housing providers, sometimes developments are not implemented in the way envisaged in the planning application. Enforcement is too often the neglected sector of the planning process, but is fundamental if the certainty enshrined by a credible planning system is to be realised.

➤ **Mediation** – which aims to resolve objections to development plan policy is being piloted by the London Borough of Barnet. Barnet is seeking to deal with specific objections to proposals in the emerging UDP. The aim is to resolve disputes quickly and amicably in advance of the public inquiry. This strategy is being promoted by the Planning Inspectorate who have also recommended mediation – and therefore more constructive appeals – as a means of resolving disputes at the other end of the planning process. Research undertaken for the DETR (2000i) found that mediation was particularly valuable as a non-confrontational means to resolve disputes in smaller applications, but was only effective where there was a willingness on all sides to enter into negotiations. It was most effective in resolving disputes surrounding design and layout considerations, and least effective at resolving fundamental policy disputes.

14.3   Other approaches to certainty and transparency.

national guidance) and be comprehensive, aiming to anticipate different contexts (locally), events and circumstances.

• Establishing mutual trust between different stakeholders and between stakeholders and the community. This could mean building ongoing relationships between different groups and establishing formal working structures. It will certainly depend on a willingness to act in good faith, to negotiate openly, and, where possible, to make clear commercial, political and planning agendas.

Clarity in the framework, and trust between partners, are central to establishing the certainty and transparency that providers, planners and the general public require from the system. But recent national proposals, such as the increased use of criteria-based policies, or to move away from negotiated obligations to predetermined development tariffs (DTLR, 2001a) represent evidence of a failure to establish clarity and trust in a discretionary process. Drawing on the case studies, a few final points are worth emphasising:

- An adopted plan is essential to the working of the whole planning process, but plans will never be completely up to date or represent end-states in themselves. It is better to have a plan adopted (even if partly out of date) and be working on its revision rather than never having an adopted plan in the first place.
- Transparent strategies need also to be inclusive – RSLs, developers and other interested parties should have early involvement in their preparation.
- There is no point in continually reinventing the wheel. Sample agreements or standard drafted policies should be shared between local authorities, although they will always need to be adapted to fit the context. Web sites might be useful for this purpose.
- Flexibility is often viewed as particularly important in relation to issues of design and development density, but that should not discount the need for comprehensive policy in these areas.
- Consistent interpretation of national frameworks (for example, PPG3) is required in order to avoid general and cross-party confusion. This might involve consultation between authorities and their partners (including the Government Regional Offices) over the implications of government policy.
- Transparency and inclusivity in the policy-making process are increased when the different interest groups have easier access to the decision-makers (the chief officers and members). This cannot happen all the time, but should occur at various key stages in the process.
- The active involvement of communities (and public consultation) should be viewed as an integral part of the development process rather than as an afterthought.

15

Positive and proactive planning

Negative and reactive planning

A range of fundamental criticisms of the planning system have revolved around the tendency of many local planning authorities to resort to reactive and largely negative approaches to planning, in so doing, losing sight of the proactive and positive role envisaged for planning when the comprehensive system was introduced as part of the attempt to build a new and fairer society following the Second World War. Reflecting on the fiftieth anniversary of the 1947 Town and Country Planning Act, for example, Cullingworth (1997b) argued that planning in the UK has lost its vision. Thus although restrictive controls were (and remain) a necessary part of the machinery of the planning system as envisaged in 1947, these were originally merely intended to be the under-pinning for the positive purposes of planning – to rebuild the cities, build the new towns, locate development in the public interest in accordance with plans, and protect buildings and landscapes of community value. In that sense, he argued, planning was central to the reconstruction programme that also included plans for education, economic development, health and agriculture. Today, however, although plans continue to exist, these have been restricted in scope and are restrictive in character, containing little of a positive or coordinating nature. Thus, he suggests, positive planning has been jetti-soned in favour of negative planning (Cullingworth, 1997b, pp. 949, 956).

The issue of resources, or more particularly the lack of them, might explain some of the criticisms as regards the widely perceived underperformance of the planning system, and the difficulties planners face in setting the planning agenda as opposed to reacting to events. The *Resourcing of Local Planning Authorities* report has already been discussed in Chapter 11, and revealed a siphoning of resources away from policy-making processes to development control. An earlier and complementary report from English Heritage (2001) revealed much the same story for conservation; that the highest priority for resources are the reactive and demand-led services such as development control and grant-aid schemes, rather than longer-term proactive tasks such as appraisals, enhancement or even enforcement. The study revealed that expenditure by local planning authorities on the historic environment had declined in real terms between 1996/97 and 2000/01 by £3.5 million net or 8 per cent, and on staff by £3.1 million or 10 per cent.

But the recent under-resourcing of planning represents just part of the problem. Fundamentally, as the proportion of private sector development (both large and small scale) has dramatically increased as a proportion of total development activity in the UK, a system designed to cope with what was believed would be the relatively small rump of private development (see Chapter 2) has increasingly found it difficult to deliver. Nowhere is this more obvious than in the seeming inability of the system to plan positively for housing. Thus, for example, in the post-war period most housing development was delivered by the public sector – much in the visionary New Town programme – but as the public sector has increasingly withdrawn from direct supply of housing, the planning system has become the major mechanism to plan for, manage and control the delivery of new homes. The poor quality of much new housing (see Chapter 8), the obvious resistance within many established communities to most new allocations (see Chapter 11), and the increasing concern amongst providers that a housing crisis is looming of equivalent magnitude to the rail crisis of 2001 (Stewart, 2002, p. 6) confirm the inability of the planning system to rise to the challenge.

Cullingworth (1996, pp. 172–3) has argued that the increasing failure of the British planning system to plan positively for the challenges of the late twentieth and early twenty-first centuries relates to its in-built inability to cope with change. Thus as the assumptions on which the post-war planning system was founded – modest economic growth balanced between the regions, low population growth, little migration (either internally or from abroad), stable patterns of household formulation, stable (low) patterns of home ownership, and slow technological advance – have proved incorrect, debate has increasingly focused on improving the efficiency of the planning system, rather than on questioning its underlying assumptions and processes.

> There has . . . been little attempt to deal with the problems which stem from the growth of population, of activities, of wealth, of new lifestyles and increasingly – of uneven opportunities. Planning policy is still largely geared to dealing with 1947-style problems of physical redistribution of a fixed amount of activities. An unprecedented range of land-using activities have grown, and will continue to grow, over the country as a whole. The objective should be to decide how these are to be dealt with, and to plan for the land use implications. This involves far more positive and interventionalist planning than is currently popular. Some vision such as that of the early post-war years is needed, but adapted to the very different conditions of a dynamic society.
>
> (Cullingworth, 1996, p. 174)

The Urban Task Force came to much the same conclusion, calling for a more creative planning system which is more committed to making things happen and an overall emphasis on achieving positive change. This, they argued, 'must be based on partnership between the local authority and the project stakeholders, with the full involvement of the local community wherever possible' (Urban Task Force, 1999, p. 191). Based on their analysis of northern European approaches to planning (particularly those in the Netherlands and Scandinavia) which demonstrated the strength of strategic planning at the heart of the development process, the Urban Task Force recommended:

- That development plans should become simpler, more flexible and strategic documents, closely integrated with other local strategies, and avoiding the inclusion of detailed site-level policies.
- The formulation of detailed planning policies as part of the area planning process, including the preparation of integrated spatial masterplans that provide more meaningful opportunities for local communities to participate in decision-making.

Their proposals reflect those in the later Planning Green Paper (see Chapter 2), and were based on the observation that an early investment in spatial masterplanning combined with genuine public participation leads to a quicker and more straightforward system of development control. A key contribution from the RTPI Think Tank on Modernising Local Government (2001, pp. 46–8) to the debate concluded that planners would be judged in the future much more on their ability to deliver policy objectives, than on their ability to police the environment. They identified three complementary sets of writing on the future of planning:

- The first recognises the increasing malaise in the profession, but also the value of traditional planning and its achievements. Writers within this vein criticise the over-bureaucratic and managed nature of planning which is stifling its potential, and argue in favour of freeing planners from this burden, leading to a greater application of core skills, and renewed vision and sense of purpose.
- The second set believes that planners need to respond more directly to the wider realities of the economy and government, by recognising the complexity of modern society and the limitations of planned intervention. This, more incremental, school of thought believes that working more closely with the market and political processes in a partnership for public good will deliver better results by harnessing these powerful forces.
- The final set envisages the need for a far more radical set of policy approaches and political actions informed by the increasingly urgent environmental imperative facing society. For them, planners will have less autonomy to set the land-use policy agenda, and instead a coalition of allied professions, scientists, politicians and the public will set the policy agenda.

The Think Tank concluded that all three approaches have their merits, and what is clear is that planning cannot stand still. Echoing a call of the Town and Country Planning Association Inquiry into the Future of Planning (1999), they argue that this might in time mean fundamentally 'reinventing planning' as a more radical and interventionist (or at least prescriptive) force for change.

Being positive and proactive

Positive and proactive planning implies a planning process that drives change rather than follows it, through vision, proactive interventions when required and through establishing a positive policy framework well in advance of development.

To some extent this last route to better working practice is an overarching one that encompasses and brings together the others discussed in the four preceding chapters. Thus moves to create more streamlined, inclusive, coordinated and realistic, certain and transparent processes will all be positive moves aimed at addressing frequent and recurrent shortcomings in the relationships between planners and housing providers. Nevertheless, a recurrent comment in the survey of practitioners (including planners) was the need for a more positive (less negative) and more proactive (less reactive) planning process.

A concern for positive and proactive planning is not new. In calling for a more positive planning process, past-RTPI president Brian Raggett (1999) observed that more than 60 years ago Thomas Sharp wrote, 'Any future planning must be positive planning: not merely planning that restricts and controls, but planning that performs.' Sharp's comments in turn echoed sentiments inherent in the evolution of the planning system in the UK as a forward-looking visionary process. Raggett himself called for a new invest-ment in planning that recognises the need to:

- put high-quality joined-up plans in place on time;
- emphasise quality not speed of decision-making;
- deliver flexibility in plan making by treating plans as living documents subject to annual reviews of progress and adopting supplementary planning guidance for more detailed concerns;
- modernise planning services through better use of IT;
- be user-friendly by engaging with the public, for example through 'planning for real' exercises;
- be forward-thinking and creative, by anticipating trends and change;
- be tough through more rigorous, better-resourced enforcement;
- be clear and consistent in all negotiations, particularly planning gain.

The danger remains that the squeeze on resources in recent years has left much plan-ning practice retrenching to its core and structurally flawed statutory responsibilities. The resulting marginalisation of planning within local authorities (and nationally) has as a result often left local planning services unable to exert an influence on the environment and populations that they seek to serve beyond their narrowly defined control function. In this regard, Raggett (1999) has also criticised the tendency to separate development plans and implementation work (urban design, conservation, regeneration) from develop-ment control, on the grounds that development control can be treated as a lesser regulatory function. Such practices are likely to reinforce the perception – not least amongst housing providers – that planners simply say 'no' or remain uncommitted, without positively setting the agenda or thinking creatively about development solutions.

The criticisms drove the housing and planning group Room (2000) to try and define a new (positive) planning agenda, explicitly linking the role to the successful promotion of urban renewal and regeneration. In setting the agenda for positive planning, Room suggests that principles should include: clear objectives from the outset; a land use dimension that contributes to wider social progress; a reasonable measure of consensus that the intended outcome should represent an improvement on what existed before; that the planning process should drive or significantly influence outcomes; and that the skills used should be those for which trained planners are particularly suited. A subsequent checklist for action by local authorities (Room, 2002) suggested that authorities should:

1. Be alert to the changing national planning policy context, including both new formal requirements of planning policy and opportunities to use planning to deliver land use aspects of other policy initiatives.
2. Decide on the fastest and most efficient means to implement new government policy locally, for example, by incorporating it into a development plan review which is already under way, or adopting supplementary planning guidance.
3. Consider how best local communities can present their views to shape rather than just respond to emerging planning policy, with staff acting as facilitators and advisers more than instructors.
4. Review the role which the planning department might take in coordinating the corpo-rate activities of the authority, particularly where planning staff have relevant skills, for

example in public involvement, mediating between different interests and evaluating policy options.

5. Promote and explain the role of planning in local communities, both as the means of achieving community-inspired objectives, for example, as defined through local strategic partnerships and community strategies, and as a process of reconciling conflicting views.

6. Pursue high standards: quality in planning practice brings out the best of local contributors and generates support for further achievements.

7. Be clear about objectives without being too prescriptive about how they will be achieved.

8. Not try to force the pace of public involvement in planning processes that depend on partnership or consensus among local people, but keep inspiring contributors.

The Royal Society for the Protection of Birds (RSPB) have also called for a more positive approach to planning, criticising the 'deadening places' we get without it – bleak suburban housing estates that are cut off from the services and life of the community, decaying high streets, and neglected and car-dominated streets and public spaces. For the RSPB, positive planning is not just about protecting the country's valuable built and natural heritage (important though they recognise this is), it is about 'encouraging development – securing the right development, in the right location, at the right time – so that places evolve in a sustainable way, serving new needs and enhancing quality of life' (RSPB, 2002, p. 16). In short, they contend, positive planning requires:

- visionary planning aimed at achieving high quality development
- policy that promotes sustainable developments and patterns of land use
- systematic assessments of benefits, needs and environmental impact, using sustainability appraisal techniques
- a focus on environmental resource efficiency
- environmental enhancement as part of all developments.

Research on the role of planning in local government also came out firmly on the side of a positive and proactive agenda. Cowan (1999) argued:

> There's a paradox. Rarely has planning been so high on political agendas as it is today. Hardly anyone believes that central and local government's objectives on economic development, regeneration, environmental quality, social equity, transport and urban management can be achieved without planning. Yet the planning system – through which the use and physical form of development are guided and controlled in the public interest – is widely regarded as little better than a bureaucratic obstacle to action.

The report outlines a wide-ranging agenda for action (summarised in Fig. 15.1), based on the notion that planning is a powerful tool for harnessing public and private development activity to deliver action within a dedicated legal structure. At the heart of good planning, it is suggested, is therefore a direct engagement with the processes of development, but this requires a proactive recognition of commercial opportunities and realities, alongside the active promotion of local community aspirations and articulation of public objectives. Thus proactive planning not only has vision, but is dynamic, enabling, supportive, and accessible. However, in an echo of Ragget's position (see p. 262)

➤ The planning system is the most powerful tool a local authority can use to achieve its objectives

➤ Planning has the capacity for agreeing visions, analysing problems and opportunities, organising consultation and collaboration, setting policy, guiding design and implementing action, all within a dedicated legal structure. It is a flexible mechanism that can work within the timescales of 10 to 25 years that the processes of development and urban change often take, reconciling the need to think long term with the more immediate requirements of grant regimes and politics

➤ Planning is a process through which difficult decisions involving major conflicts of interest can be taken openly, fairly and accountably

➤ Development is the key to making things happen. The planning system's enormous potential lies in its statutory power to guide and control development

➤ None of the various plans produced by local authorities are based on such wide economic, social and geographical analysis as a development plan. No other plan has such a direct impact on what happens on the ground

➤ At the heart of the best planning practice is a real engagement with the process of development. The planning service should take a proactive approach, rather than merely fulfilling the statutory planning function

➤ Proactive planning has vision, its approach is positive and enabling, rather than reactive and bureaucratic

➤ Proactive planning is dynamic. It sees commercial feasibility as a key to harnessing the development process to achieve goals of public policy, rather than an extraneous factor planning can ignore

➤ Proactive planning is supportive. Development control must be seen as a positive means of guiding planning towards fulfilling both their own objectives and the objectives of public policy

➤ Proactive planning is accessible. It helps local communities express their views and become constructively involved in bringing about the development their area needs

➤ All local authority planning functions – including strategic and transport planning, development control, enforcement, implementation, urban design, conservation, and monitoring outcomes – should be integrated within a single directorate, not split between different management structures. The scope for creative, proactive planning lies in the connections

➤ Development planners and development controllers should work closely together in pursuing common objectives

➤ In each planning authority one council officer (a qualified planner) should be clearly identified as the head of the planning service. This is necessary to provide a credible focus for the professional planning advice on which the council relies. The importance Of this advice reflects the quasi-judicial nature of the statutory planning function

➤ The head of the planning service should be responsible for advising the authority, with direct access to councillors as their professional advisor on planning matters. The head of the service may be responsible to the director of a multidisciplinary department or directorate who is not a professional town planner. But that senior officer should not have the power to keep elected members of the council in ignorance of the professional advice of the head of the planning service

➤ A council which does no more than go through the motions of statutory planning procedure will find its low expectations of planning justified. The local authorities for which the planning system really works are those which appreciate the potential of their most powerful weapon

15.1 A manifesto for getting the best out of planning (Cowan, 1999, summary of RTPI, 1999).

and against the increasingly common practice in local authorities, it is argued that such characteristics are dependent on joining-up the planning function, and avoiding the marginalisation of the service through splitting policy-making and development control activities, where the latter is treated as just another regulatory function (RTPI, 1999).

Of course, being positive is not just important amongst planners, it also relies on providers being positive in turn in their reactions to any proactive frameworks advanced through the planning process. Providers can themselves be accused of being negative and reactionary if they are not able to adapt their own approaches to particular contexts. Furthermore, Room (2000, pp. 14–15) argue that the changes in power relationships between providers of development and local authorities make such approaches the norm rather than the exception, particularly in parts of the country where competition to attract valuable footloose employment is a priority. In such places it is even more important for authorities to demonstrate the added value that planning brings, by identifying opportunities and showing how to overcome constraints.

The case studies

The case studies demonstrate two alternative approaches to positively addressing the local agenda. The Newcastle case illustrates an approach to a particular major development that:

- innovatively responds to local need whilst balancing conflicting policy objectives;
- responds to an externally imposed commercial imperative by internally reorganising resources, and in doing so reduces the commercial risk and raised confidence;
- participates in an effective public/private collaboration to deliver the new development without undermining the need for thorough local public consultation;
- ensures local political support and senior officer backing throughout;
- delivers significant planning gain for the city, and a major long-term development opportunity for the developers.

In response to a particular local problem and housing pressures, Hammersmith and Fulham have instituted a process that:

- evaluates the local context (physical, social, economic and policy) to fully understand what the local issues are;
- innovatively formulates and administers policies that respond to the specific needs of the locality;
- utilises clear and well-justified policies to enable consistent and careful determination of applications;
- delivers consistency across the different tiers of policy as a corporate objective;
- ensures careful management of planning applications for affordable housing to achieve the best outcomes.

CASE STUDY: Newcastle – an approach to fast-tracking

The development at Newcastle Great Park is an example of how the different parties can engage proactively in the process, effectively managing different elements and outcomes. Both the local planning authority (Newcastle City Council) and the developer consortium (Beazer, Leech and Bryant) acknowledged the development as being of strategic importance to the social and economic growth of the city, which helped to ensure that the impetus of the process was maintained.

Situated four miles to the north of Newcastle City centre, the development will comprise 2,500 homes, 80 hectares of land for employment uses and a country park, all to be completed over a period of ten years. By 2000, outline planning permission was in place and the developer consortium were in the process of achieving the individual detailed planning applications (reserved matters) for the different packages of land within the overall site. The greenfield site at Newcastle Great Park was not typical of the majority of development occurring within the city; the larger sites are usually in the magnitude of 200–400 dwellings, whilst over the preceding 10 years more than 88 per cent of development in the city has been on brownfield land.

A driving force behind the development was the recognition that new development would serve to reinforce the emerging knowledge industries in the area and reduce the decline in resident population. As such, it was viewed as a key element in the city-wide regeneration strategy. The local authority identified that within Newcastle, the percentage of detached housing stock is 5 per cent, which is much lower than the national average of 26 per cent. This disparity has arisen because of the historical prevalence of heavy industry in the area, with its corresponding high demand for smaller, cheaper housing. By the late 1990s, the growth in new businesses had introduced higher-income populations, and housing demand changed accordingly. The limited supply of detached housing contributed to the mobile 25–45 age-group population moving out of the city to outlying areas, with estimates suggesting that four families per week have been moving out of the area.

Project management and negotiation

The site was allocated in the draft UDP as a significant allocation that had been identified independently (prior to the UDP public inquiry in 1995) as appropriate for development by both the local planning authority and interested developers. The UDP was adopted in early 1998 (allocating the Newcastle Great Park site for development), and a consortium of developers embarked upon the process of converting the allocation into a planning consent. A constraining issue at the outset was timescale: the land options were shortly to expire (having been negotiated by the developers ten years previously) and the developers required a level of certainty in the process before they were willing to invest further. The local authority acknowledged the strategic importance of the site, and responded with a commitment to resource and facilitate the process accordingly.

In order to achieve the timescale imposed by the developers, a detailed programme for the application period was agreed between the parties at the outset. Within the authority a full-time project officer was appointed to the project whilst the developer consortium employed a project management team to maintain a level of control on the complexity of the project and the people involved. The developers, for example, found that due to the scale of the project, strict control was required over the numbers of consultants utilised and the amount of paperwork generated. A formal working group was set up (to include members of the planning committee) and informal networks were established. A special planning subcommittee was also constituted and given powers to deal with all matters except development control (i.e. to approve the development brief and masterplan but not the planning applications).

The mechanics of the approach

In order to fast-track the application within the local planning authority it was decided to maintain the existing management structures, but to reorganise resources and reprioritise workloads to meet the imposed deadlines. Meetings were held weekly or fortnightly between the three parties and the consultants, although initially the process did not gel. In hindsight both the developer and planning officers acknowledge that the authority lacked motivation because of their uncertainty that the proposal would proceed to application stage, in large part because of the likelihood of an Article 14 Direction calling in the application to be determined by the Secretary of State. The resource-intensive process was nevertheless established at the pre-application stage, and represented a significant investment (with no guaranteed outcome) on the part of the local authority.

By 2000, the different parties and individuals had become more committed and enthusiastic as the threat of an Article 14 Direction receded, and consequently the project management structure between the parties evolved. Within the developer consortium there were a number of teams:

- Consortium principals, meeting once a fortnight with an overarching remit to review progress and make decisions.
- Commercial area team, meeting once a fortnight to drive the commercial element of the mixed-use scheme forward.
- Residential technical working group (led by a consortium principal) driving forward the detailed design of the different residential land parcels and ensuring compliance with the overarching masterplan principles through production of DSSSs (development site strategy statements).
- Commercial technical working group (led by a consortium principal) driving forward the detailed design of the commercial development.

Streamlining negotiation

A Core Implementation team was also established comprising senior representatives from both developers within the consortium, the lead project manager and a cross-section of officers from the local planning authority (development control, policy, traffic and other relevant parties). This regular forum enabled negotiation and decision-making on the spot, whilst any issues that could not be resolved through the Core Implementation team were referred to a higher level (Chief Executive level) when required.

During the Section 106 negotiations in 1998, similar principles were adopted to avoid a lengthy and protracted process. The basis for the S106 negotiations were established transparently with the local authority undertaking a scoping study and the developers a series of impact studies (e.g. Travel Impact Assessment and Environmental Impact Assessment). Initial negotiations took place at a technical level between all of the interested parties (developers and local authority), and final negotiations and decision-making were undertaken at a senior level within the local authority by a senior level officer with across-the-board knowledge and

experience. This single point of contact for decision-making within the local authority significantly contributed to reducing the length of the process. Thus the bones of the Section 106
agreement (a package comprising £23.5 million, including infrastructure, landscaping, the
country park, public transport contribution, contribution to non-car initiatives, and affordable
housing) was established in six weeks.

Despite these measures to simplify and streamline the process, the complexity of the project
increased as the emerging raft of new government planning policy began to impact. The
publication of draft PPG3 and the Urban Task Force Report in 1999, with the increasing
emphasis on high-density, brownfield development, combined with the high profile and
politically sensitive nature of the proposal (a greenfield site and former green belt deletion)
conspired to create conflict and increase the complexity of the process. Consequently the
resolution (planning consent) required by the developer was not achieved prior to the land
option renewal, although the local authority gave a formal indication that they were 'minded to
approve', which acted as sufficient reassurance to enable the developers to purchase the land.

The nature of the development

This conflict between the emphasis in national policy and acknowledged regional needs
highlights the difficulty of administering broad-brush national policy within different regional
socio-economic contexts. Within Newcastle, a Joint Venture Agreement was established to
address the balance between local needs and national policy. The Joint Venture Agreement
stipulated that development of Newcastle Great Park was limited to 250 new houses per year
(to avoid stifling the development of brownfield residential development in the city). Another
important aspect of the agreement was that if the brownfield targets fell below 60 per cent
(of total development within Newcastle, averaged over a three-year period), then the developers would have to undertake financial viability appraisals on selected sites, and (depending
upon their viability) undertake the development. In effect, this type of mechanism represented
the developer underwriting additional brownfield development in the city for a specified period.

In addition to addressing the mechanics of the process, the approach taken at Newcastle
Great Park also sought to influence the nature of the outcome. The site has been planned
strategically with regard to the rest of the city, and as a key part of the city-wide strategy the
elements of gain will be strategic in their impact. Furthermore, a system was developed to
ensure that the development of each cell of land sat within a design framework for the whole
scheme (a DSSS was produced at the detailed planning stage for each cell to illustrate this).

The mixing of uses across the site is potentially less successful, however, reflecting to some
degree the zoning of the site into residential, commercial and amenity areas. The affordable
housing provision on the site is also clustered around the amenities and public transport, which
as a consequence leads to pockets of affordable housing. In some respects, this configuration
responds well to the needs of the residents of affordable housing, however, it has resulted in
a layout lacking a fine-grained mix of use and tenures. This reflects the conflicts and constraints
that arise when combining commercial development with low-rise, low-density residential
development in a peripheral location.

Discussion

The process that was established at Newcastle evolved over time and both the developers
and the local planning authority felt that commitment and skills had increased over the course

Table 15.1 Key stages in the process

Dates	Key Stages
1988–1989	Land options signed up
1995	UDP public inquiry
1997	UDP PI/Inspectors report
January 1998	UDP adopted
Spring 1998	Teams emerged; developers set up the system of weekly/fortnightly meetings with three main parties and consultants
Summer 1998	Consultation on masterplan
August 1998	Planning application submitted with Traffic Impact Assessment and Environmental Impact Assessment; decision wanted by end of 1998
Autumn 1998	'Bones' of Section 106 (planning gain) agreed in 6 weeks
October 1998	Total sum of Section 106 money agreed
End of 1998	LPA 'minded to approve'; developers renewed the land options
14 February 1999	Scheme called in by Secretary of State
25 August 1999	Developers took legal decision to withdraw from the inquiry
1 September 1999	Outline planning application resubmitted
14 July 2000	Cross-party 'working day' (led by developers) to finally clear up all outstanding matters
6 October 2000	Outline planning permission granted
2001–2002	Development Site Strategy Statements preparation and reserved matters applications

of the project (see Table 15.1). A key element contributing to the successful partnership between the developers and the local authority was the proactive approach taken when dealing with some of the unforeseen complexities and constraints that emerged throughout the process. The adaptation of the scheme (in line with emerging policy) and the establishment of links between the development at Newcastle Great Park and brownfield development in the city centre through the brownfield/greenfield agreement (2 to 1; in line with national policy) reflected this inherent flexibility in the process. The approach and attitude of senior local authority officers were also crucial, enabling a proactive (rather than reactive) approach, alongside the collaborative attitude of the developers.

Another important part of the process at Newcastle was the high level of mutual trust. In this case, both parties acknowledged that the stakes had been high enough for them to countenance the risks and engage with the process, even through no formal agreement was ever signed between the local authority and the developers. From the developers' perspective, the risks of engaging in the process were reduced as two different development companies were involved which helped to spread the risks. This involved a level of commitment and trust between the developers, although elements of commercial coyness remained.

The informal nature of this working process (up to the signing of the Section 106 agreement) meant that the local authority had limited power over the process, which was largely driven by the developer. If there had been a formal relationship, outcomes might have been further streamlined, as attitudes may have been more positive and collaborative from the start. Alternatively, it has been argued that a more formalised relationship could have been problematic, particularly during the public consultation exercises, with the local authority being seen to promote the development, yet control it at the same time.

Some of the initiatives and approaches that have been developed within Newcastle can clearly translate to other contexts. These include the mechanisms of the working process and the resourcing of the project. Other aspects are specific to a very large and complex site, including the brownfield/greenfield (joint venture) agreement, which the authority admit they are unlikely to use again following the clear national guidance in PPG3 delivering a sequential test for housing development (see Chapter 5). The innovative nature of the agreement nevertheless demonstrates a positive approach to planning that ensured that both the developer and authority met their agreed objectives.

CASE STUDY: Hammersmith and Fulham – meeting local need

Hammersmith and Fulham is a very urban London borough; there are few sites for development and on average there is only between 100 and 300 new houses completed within the borough each year. Within Hammersmith and Fulham (as in much of the south east) there is a crisis in the affordable housing sector, with a geographical haemorrhaging of key workers out of the area due to a lack of affordable housing for people on modest incomes (between £15,000 and £25,000 per annum). At present there is provision for the very rich or the very poor, and a big gap in the intermediate (key worker) sector. There is also a lack of availability of land for employment uses in the borough; potentially another constraint to the creation of a balanced, vibrant and sustainable district. Within the local authority, the issue of affordable housing has a high priority, with much attention being focused on the objective of delivering adequate numbers of high-quality affordable homes.

Within Hammersmith and Fulham it was decided to tackle the affordable housing crisis in a proactive manner, by introducing a planning policy which would seek to reduce the opportunities for developing market housing in particular circumstances, whilst encouraging the development of affordable housing, and the development of land for employment uses. The new policy (based loosely upon a rural exceptions policy) resists change of use (on certain sites) from employment to residential, unless the residential development is 100 per cent affordable housing provision. This safeguards existing vacant employment land for future employment uses or for affordable housing. A similar policy applies to land in former community uses, where change of use is refused unless it is for affordable housing. The local authority believes that both policies are unique to the borough, and have been very successful in achieving a high proportion of affordable housing. In addition, the local authority has policies in place that seek to secure the maximum proportion of affordable housing provision within residential developments brought forward in the normal way.

The development of the new policy

The change of use exceptions policy was adopted as part of the UDP in 1994, but had been in operation for a number of years previously. Prior to that, the approach to affordable housing within the borough was based upon the simple principle that a percentage of the total housing on each site was to be affordable. The change in approach was justified and underpinned by thorough housing needs research.

In the early stages of developing the policy, a loophole was discovered by an RSL who sold land bought in this way for commercial redevelopment at a significant windfall profit. Although in that case the windfall was subsequently reinvested in affordable housing, the issue of affordability in perpetuity is now tightly controlled, with a standard Section 106 planning obligation used to ensure that the housing remains affordable and that the land will not be disposed of other than for certain prescribed purposes.

The policy mechanism

The policy works by allowing a change of use to affordable residential uses only, and only outside of designated employment zones and if an employment site has not been in use for a number of years, or is unlikely to be used for employment in the future. The site is also identified and assessed against criteria (established by the policy) to see if it is appropriate for affordable housing. Delivery occurs via a network of officers within the planning and housing departments alongside local RSL partners who are constantly in the process of identifying suitable available sites. The relationship between the authority and its partner RSLs has also evolved over time. Initially the authority had two RSL partners, but has since opened up the market to increase competition. Hammersmith and Fulham now has six RSL partners, including the original two.

The process can be initiated in a number of ways; the vendor may discuss the site initially with the housing department, or an RSL may identify the site and work in partnership with the borough to develop it. A system of joint commissioning is used if the borough (or the vendor) identifies the site, in which case a competition between three or four RSLs is undertaken. Subsequent planning applications follow the traditional route; the applicant applies for the appropriate change of use, with the policy treated as a material consideration in determining the application.

The planning histories (and consequently land use status) of different sites are often mixed, which can make the process more complex, enabling a proportion of market housing to be included in the proposal alongside the affordable housing. This contrasts with the typical housing negotiation process elsewhere, where instead of negotiating about affordable units, the negotiation is based upon how many market units should be conceded.

Responding to local need

Being constrained by Housing Corporation funding limits, before the change of use policy was introduced, RSLs operating in Hammersmith and Fulham found it difficult to compete for land in the open market. This impacted seriously upon the scale of operation of the RSLs and on the numbers of properties that could be delivered on an annual basis. Delivery of new affordable units was therefore almost exclusively reliant on the vagaries of Section 106 negotiations.

As the policy affects the price of the land (in essence it sets a cap on the land value to the price that the RSL can afford to pay), RSLs can now acquire greater land holdings and undertake greater levels of development. Consequently, the landowner, rather than the developer (where one is involved) loses out, as developers are still able to make profits based on lower land values which are simply passed on to landowners. In response, some landowners have tried to hold back their land from the housing market, hoping that over time the policies will change again and they will be able to capitalise on developing market-sector housing for a higher profit in the future. This type of action has had a minor negative impact on the overall supply of land for housing in the borough.

Lime Grove Studios: Notting Hill Housing Trust

The development at the Lime Grove Studios (a site formerly owned by the BBC) is an example of the policy in action. The completed and occupied development comprises 50 homes shared and rented at a discount to the open market (in perpetuity). The Notting Hill Housing Trust (an RSL that operates primarily within north, west, and central London) manages the development. Notting Hill Housing Trust is quite active, managing between 10,000 and 15,000 properties and with an annual development programme that typically comprises 250 properties for rent and 250 properties for shared ownership.

The studios had been vacant for some time, and the site was not considered appropriate for other employment uses. A developer got involved with the site, and entered into a back-to-back deal with Notting Hill Housing Trust on the day that the developer bought the site (i.e. the site was bought and sold twice on one day), hence the developer got a mark-up. The developer and land vendor accepted the policy, because it was a well-established policy in the area. Conflicts subsequently occurred with adjacent residents on Lime Grove who were not keen on affordable housing in the locality. However, as the policy principles had been clearly set out in the UDP the objections were not upheld.

Management of planning applications for affordable housing

To complement the initiative, and in order to streamline the affordable housing process the authority also attempts to carefully manage and resource the application determination phase. When a developer comes forward with a site, pre-application discussions are encouraged to examine the proposals and ensure that they will comply with all relevant criteria established in the UDP.

The local authority is primarily concerned with the nature and quality of the outcome rather than with the speed of determination of planning applications. They feel that the issue of fast-tracking certain applications is not appropriate and are quick to refute the suggestion that their approach embraces the concept of fast-tracking, whilst identifying the tensions that could arise between the different stakeholders if preferential treatment was awarded to certain types of application. Nonetheless, careful management of affordable housing applications, and ensuring that applications are not delayed due to lack of resources, effectively delivers a streamlined system for this type of development.

The authority feels that communication, cooperation and the sharing of common objectives are the cornerstones of the approach. Therefore, within the borough there is an Officers' Steering Group every six weeks that is attended by all key departments with land interests. This group provides an important link between the housing and planning functions of the local authority, and is the principal interface between different departments, enabling ongoing informal communication.

As the local authority has achieved success in delivering a high proportion of affordable houses, this is reflected in the level of Social Housing Grant secured within the local authority area. The issue of affordable housing is such a corporate objective that the whole process of funding, implementing and delivering is under continual scrutiny to minimise inefficiency. So, for example, whenever there are changes in the make-up or administration of the social housing funding process, the local authority responds to maximise the scope of each potential grant.

Discussion

The experience at Hammersmith and Fulham highlights that national broad-brush policy is often unresponsive to local circumstances. For example, the borough feels that the guidance given in Circular 6/98 on affordable housing is not fine-tuned sufficiently for their context. The largest impediment to achieving affordable housing is the threshold of 15 residential units (or 0.5 hectares of land), below which Section 106 negotiations are not triggered in central London. This criterion in effect rules out a third of the possible Section 106 affordable housing programme due to the small size of many of the urban sites in the borough.

To overcome the problem, approaches such as Hammersmith and Fulham's require resources. Typically, the local authority spends more time on developing appropriate policies and administering and determining applications to ensure that they get the best outcomes, so consequently the cost of planning in the borough is high. This also means that more time spent on certain (priority) applications means less time for others. However, the local planning authority has strong support from the members of the council, who see this investment as good value, and as such have supported the appointment of additional staff (despite budget restrictions elsewhere).

The local authority feels that this innovative and positive adaptation of policy has been very successful, enabling them to achieve an annual affordable housing percentage of 65 per cent (of the total housing constructed) over the past ten years, despite the periods of growth and recession which the development industry (and the economy as a whole) have weathered. They assert that by 2000, they were achieving the highest percentage of affordable housing of any London borough, and were the only authority to achieve over 50 per cent.

The approach pursued at Hammersmith and Fulham would clearly not be appropriate everywhere, for example, where land values are low, or sites are poorly serviced by facilities, amenities or public transport. Nevertheless, as Hammersmith and Fulham is such a dense urban borough, with generally good public transport and provision of facilities, coupled with a high need for affordable housing, the approach usually works well. Officers nevertheless point out that the approach will only be effective as long as it is backed up by national government policy (through policy and guidance), as they need to operate within the limits of what will stand up to scrutiny at appeal.

Despite the fact that it has succeeded in reversing the decline in affordable housing, and enabled the local RSLs to operate outside of the usual funding constraints, there are divided opinions on the policy. For example, the policy continues to create tension with developers who feel it is unduly restrictive and unrealistic within the market context, consequently depressing the price of land. Despite this, the principles of the policy are now widely known and accepted by developers operating in the area, and it remains an integral part of the UDP. To avoid criticism, the local authority ensures that it is even-handed and that the policy is applied to land held by the borough alongside privately owned land.

Negative perceptions also continue to abound within the community, despite the emphasis being placed firmly on bridging the housing gap for key workers. For example, the local authority still encounters a backlash whenever there is a proposal for affordable housing, although they suggest that it is perhaps a more sophisticated backlash than in recent times. Thus today, residents will no longer directly object to social housing, but will find other means of raising objections, suggestive of a hidden NIMBY agenda. The authority finds that it is difficult to reduce objections even in the poorer areas, where there are concentrations of affordable or social housing with desperate need for more. Successful capacity building to counteract this can be undertaken effectively at the local level, but it is very difficult to undertake a similar process at a more strategic, district-wide level.

Recommendations

Fundamentally a number of key qualities seem to characterise a positive and proactive planning (and development) process:

- Thinking ahead – the need to think ahead and pre-empt development by putting in place a coherent policy framework. The very act of plan-making is by its nature a positive activity, although the tendency for plans to be out of date before they are adopted and to focus on a protective rather than future-oriented view of plan areas has tended to give even this process a negative image. The updating of policy frameworks is critical, whilst still offering certainty over the long term – a fundamental goal of the planning system.
- Doing the groundwork up front – this might encompass the need to adequately prepare the ground for future development activity. For example, with policy frameworks based on thorough analysis of the existing situation (local and strategic) available for house providers to use, backed up by supplementary guidance, development briefs, design frameworks or masterplans building on policy already articulated in the policy.
- Being creative – by thinking around problems and advancing new policy solutions. Both the Newcastle and Hammersmith and Fulham examples above illustrate such approaches, through respectively innovative use of negotiated and policy solutions that directly address local problems. The examples illustrate the need for creative thinking in both development control and policy writing.
- Being visionary – much of the discussion in Chapters 11 to 14 has focused on the processes inherent in building better relationships, but positive and proactive planning is also about defining a future vision for a sustainable environment. This should inevitably encompass a physical vision for environments from strategic (two-dimensional) to site-specific (three-dimensional) scales, and should also encompass a social and economic vision, not least as regards how new housing (private and social) fits into future plans. Planning is, in significant part, a design discipline and this part of its remit needs to be rediscovered.
- Selling the vision – because once devised, any vision will need to be sold both to those who have to operationalise it internally and to those on whom it will most directly impact – the community and development interests. Without these constituents signing-up to the vision, its implementation is never likely to move beyond a paper dream.
- Balancing certainty with flexibility – by all these means offering greater certainty by clearly setting the agenda preferably well in advance of development interest, although avoiding the over-rigid implementation characteristic of some planning schemes in the past. So, as with all the routes to better practice, regularly monitoring implementation processes – including any physical vision – is fundamental, to ensure they are still relevant and valued.

Although much of the responsibility for creating and managing a positive and proactive planning process falls on planning authorities, housing providers also have an important role to play and the key qualities above can apply equally to the development process. The role requires engaging in the process of policy generation and review, and being prepared to respect local priorities and aspirations once agreed. Five key approaches emerged during the research.

Appraisal

The need to adequately prepare the ground for the development of policy and for making decisions on various development options as they arise has always been a fundamental part of the planning and development process. Indeed appraisal represents both the start and the end of the planning process – analysis of the existing situation as a basis for making decisions, and evaluating the impact of decisions once implemented in order to monitor the broader impact of policies. Ensuring that authorities are fully cognisant of the various development scenarios and the strengths and weaknesses of each is therefore an important part of a positive approach to planning. However, this process needs to be thorough, up to date, and publicly available if it is to make a positive and timely impact on the decision-making of both authority and development interests. The proactive gathering of contextual data is therefore an ongoing – if unfortunately resource-intensive – process, which, if properly undertaken, can help to identify development

Table 15.2 Assessing urban housing capacity (DETR, 2000j)

Key stages	Housing capacity approaches
Identifying capacity sources	➤ Identify urban areas to be assessed ➤ Consider all sources of capacity (subdivision of existing housing, flats over shops, empty homes, previously developed vacant land and buildings, intensification of existing area, redevelopment of existing housing, redevelopment of car parks, conversion of commercial buildings, review of existing housing allocations in plans, review of other existing allocations, vacant land not previously developed)
Surveying the capacity	➤ Start with what you know (from existing studies) ➤ Use existing data (before commissioning new data, but be wary of assuming past trends will reflect future activity) ➤ Do new survey work 1. comprehensive surveys – of the whole plan area (the most robust approach) 2. priority area studies – of areas likely to deliver greatest yield, or most suited to meet key policy objectives 3. typical urban area studies – of a range of 'homogenous character' areas from which trends can be extrapolated to the whole plan area
Assessing yield	➤ Use density multipliers to calculate total housing numbers from the site areas identified (taking care to vary multipliers to reflect context types and size of site) ➤ Alternatively, use design-led approaches, by developing design solutions for a range of typical sites, and using any resulting toolkit of approaches across the plan area ➤ Use yardsticks to assess yield from 'windfall' (sites not specifically identified as available for development, but which subsequently come forward) and other hard to measure sites, based on past trends or studies of potential
Discounting potential	➤ Discount capacity, to convert the 'unconstrained capacity' so far calculated to a likely capacity, by discounting against agreed norms. Discounting should reflect developability, market viability, local character and planning standards ➤ Test the results against recent housing activity

options that might otherwise have been overlooked. In both Brent and Cambridge (see Chapters 12 and 13) this was the case, whilst in the former example ways were found to help spread the cost between authority and producers, offering in the process distinct benefits for each.

Appraisal and survey work take many forms – housing need assessments, development feasibility studies, market testing, area appraisal, urban design and site analysis, public opinion surveys, environmental impact assessment. All need reliable methodologies that enable them to be used as appropriately robust bases for policy or development planning. As regards the delivery of new housing on brownfield land, the undertaking of rigorous capacity studies is a particularly important form of appraisal (see Chapter 5), and a developing science integral to the 'plan, monitor and manage' approach to housing provision supported in PPG3. Government guidance on the preparation of capacity studies – *Tapping the Potential* – advises that many different parties will draw on the information in capacity studies, so it is crucial that all aspects of the process of assessment are readily understandable, transparent, and rigorous; key principles for all forms of planning analysis which, wherever possible, should also be readily available to users outside the local authority. Furthermore, reflecting the experience at Brent, the guidance advises that authorities should seek to develop a partnership with other participants in the development process in order to pool knowledge skills and experience. Working in partnership with landowners and housing providers can also help to reduce disputes about the capacity process and the assumptions on which it is based (DETR, 2000j, pp. 6–7). The key stages in assessing housing capacity are summarised in Table 15.2.

Creative policy-making approaches

The adopted plan carries the greatest statutory weight and therefore potentially offers the greatest certainty to housing providers and communities. It is important, however, that the policy offers more than bland generalities and presents instead a broad vision of the future development directions in local authority areas. This can be done through the design of plan areas at a strategic scale, as well as by thinking creatively about policy objectives and the opportunities and constraints impacting on particular areas. The case studies provided a number of examples of authorities thinking creatively about how to solve particular policy problems. Although not necessarily transferable, Hammersmith and Fulham's change of use policy has enabled the authority to address the acute shortage of affordable housing in the borough. Alternatively, Newcastle's equally unique joint venture agreement has allowed the authority to address the perceived need for a particular form of market housing in the city whilst still maintaining the successful regeneration of brownfield sites. The examples illustrate that planning should not be seen as a rigid activity imposing unbending standards on places, but instead as a creative and flexible problem-solving process in which housing providers are partners.

The most recent guidance on the nature and quality of development plans from the RTPI argued that a good plan is more than a compendium of policies, indexed on a proposals map. Instead they should offer a clear spatial strategy of future development, conservation and regeneration objectives, including adequate allocations of sites for the proposed growth. Plans should also set out priorities as a means to make clear the authority's approach to the resolution of conflicts (RTPI, 2000, pp. 13–14). The advice (discussed further in Chapter 14) relates equally well to the new forms of planning guidance emanating from the 2000 Local Government Act and 2003 Planning and Compulsory Purchase Act – Community Strategies and LDFs.

Supplementary planning guidance (SPG)

Birmingham's design-led approach to planning and regeneration has been recently and explicitly extended to residential development through the preparation of a new residential design guide, an approach that Stratford-on-Avon is now also pursuing (see Chapter 12). Both authorities see their design guides as means to move away from the standards-based approaches to housing pursued in the past towards more creative higher-quality development solutions. Such approaches also reflect the higher quality, higher density, approaches to development being sought by government through PPG1 and PPG3, and provide a ready means to clarify more comprehensive design agendas than has been the case in the past. Like development briefs (see below), they ensure the design requirements of authorities can be fully factored into the projected development costs of projects before housing providers purchase sites. Research

➤ **Community Strategy** – Because the community strategy establishes the corporate vision for the authority, it is important to establish within it a broad environmental and design quality agenda, as well key objectives and targets for its delivery. This will subsequently apply across local authority services, including planning, highways, housing, economic development and urban and environmental management departments, and will help emphasise design and environmental quality as core themes.

➤ **LDF Core Strategy and Proposals Section** – The local development framework incorporates the next three layers in the hierarchy. It should be viewed as a delivery tool, rather than as a regulatory device, to establish, spatially articulate, and prioritise the social, economic and environmental future of the authority, its sub-areas and key sites, and to establish the quality thresholds expected by the council and the criteria by which the grant of planning permission will be decided. The broad vision set out in the community strategy is initially interpreted in the particular context of planning in the core strategy of the local development framework. This should cover the fundamentals of design policy, including the conceptualisation of design adopted, the need to base design proposals on a clear understanding of context, and the contribution of better design to achieving sustainable development objectives. A broad authority-wide, map-based spatial strategy with detailed proposals should also be prepared and adopted at this level.

➤ **LDF Authority-wide Design Statement** – The fundamentals of design policy can be expanded upon in the authority-wide design statement that should take the form of a comprehensive yet concise statement of design objectives with associated policy to deliver them. The aim should be to articulate the generic principles and policy (rather than area-wide or site-specific policy) that will apply across the authority's area, and to indicate how the vision and fundamentals outlined in the Community Strategy and Core Strategy will be delivered. These types of policies will relate most closely to the 'general design policies' described in 'By Design' (DETR and CABE, 2000, p. 45).

➤ **LDF Area Action Plans** – Finally, the authority-wide policy should be elaborated as regards design in the range of more detailed area action plans (area masterplans, neighbourhood and village plans and area design statements, for example). The aim here should not be to repeat wholesale policy at the authority-wide scale, but to interpret it to the range of different contexts found in the locality, including areas for regeneration, major development, or conservation, and important opportunity sites. The policies found in these plans will relate most closely to the 'area, site and topic' related policies described in 'By Design' (DETR and CABE, 2000, p. 46).

15.2 The future design policy hierarchy (Carmona et al., 2002).

discussed in Chapter 8 has indicated that design guides work most effectively as part of a hierarchy of design guidance elucidating generic policy in the development plan above and outlining the key principles to be reflected in development briefs, design frameworks and codes below.

The value of supplementary guidance extends beyond design guidance as South Lakeland's SPG on affordable housing illustrates (see Chapter 14). Whatever its focus, clear supplementary guidance which is applied consistently, and that sits comfortably within the primary framework provided by the development plan (LDF), can help ensure that the vision set out in that plan remains flexible and therefore relevant. It should never, however, be viewed as a means to bypass the development plan.

In the longer term the relationship between SPG and adopted policy will change as supplementary guidance of all types – district-wide, area-wide or site-specific – becomes incorporated into emerging LDFs, many as action plans and Development Plan Documents (see Fig. 2.3). Anticipating this change research by Carmona *et al.* (2002) has suggested how design policies might be articulated in the new policy hierarchy (see Fig. 15.2). Relating the findings to housing, key principles include:

- Rooting the housing policy hierarchy in the community strategy, for elaboration within the 'Statement of Core Policies' of the LDF, which in turn will inform policy in any action plans.
- With the slimmer and swifter agenda now informing the production of policy frameworks, opportunities for authorities to define a set of authority-wide housing policies should not be lost. In recent years, those authorities that have been most successful in proactively delivering high quality new development have defined a robust policy agenda in their development plan, which is then detailed through development frameworks and briefs at sub-area and site-specific scales.
- In developing this new policy hierarchy, policies will become progressively more detailed and specific as they move towards the action plan level. It is important, however, that the policy hierarchy maintains a consistent policy agenda that aims to join up key contributions to delivery both from within and outside of planning practice.
- This does not imply repetition of policy, but instead a development and application of the key principles to the different objectives of each policy document: to meeting broad community objectives and the achievement of sustainable development in the case of community strategies; to articulating a vision for promoting and controlling development in the case of the statement of core policies; to the specifics of design or other areas of housing policy in the authority-wide design or housing statement; and to the planning needs of local areas and specific development opportunities in local action plans.

Development frameworks/briefs/masterplans

Of greatest importance to the successful implementation of proactive planning approaches is the need to clearly articulate policy and development aspirations at the earliest possible opportunity, therefore avoiding – as far as possible – being reactive, and instead increasing the level of certainty within which housing providers operate. Development frameworks and briefs provide an important means to lay out development-specific requirements and to clarify how more generic policy approaches outlined in the plan/LDF and other district-wide SPG/action plans relate to particular sites. They also provide a means for authorities to outline more visionary approaches through presenting

Urban form and public space

➤ relationship between development and wider metropolitan or regional context
➤ urban structure and grain of streets and public routes
➤ identity and sense of place
➤ design, shape and scale of major public spaces
➤ variety of built form and urban block structure
➤ location of building entrances along streets and public spaces
➤ distribution of residential, commercial and community facilities
➤ development densities, plot sizes and ratios
➤ intensification of public realm
➤ landmarks and public buildings
➤ public art
➤ use of natural features including trees, planting and water
➤ design and materials of hard and soft landscaped areas
➤ pavement widths and street furniture
➤ lighting and safety
➤ 24-hour use

Movement

➤ integration with existing pedestrian, vehicular and public transport routes
➤ location of public transport facilities
➤ integration between different movement modes (foot, cycle, car, public transport)
➤ accessibility of facilities within five- and ten-minute walking and cycling distances
➤ car parking standards and location of car parking spaces
➤ traffic calming measures
➤ disabled access

Building design

➤ building layout and orientation
➤ variety of massing, materials and architectural expression
➤ flexibility of internal layout
➤ work/live and lifetime homes
➤ disabled access
➤ materials maintenance
➤ visual link between buildings and streets – openings and entrances
➤ use of external spaces – balconies, roof terraces, porches
➤ overlooking distances

Environmental design

➤ massing and thermal performance
➤ passive environmental design
➤ exposure to sunlight and natural daylight penetration
➤ energy efficiency
➤ renewable energy sources
➤ Combined Heat and Power (CHP) provision
➤ grey water recycling
➤ reedbed filtration
➤ thermal and acoustic insulation
➤ household waste management
➤ landscape, biodiversity and ecology

Community issues

➤ play areas and community facilities
➤ proximity to existing or proposed school facilities
➤ adult education and family learning opportunities
➤ sports and childcare facilities
➤ training opportunities and job creation
➤ management and stewardship
➤ the wired community
➤ complementary community initiatives

15.3 Spatial masterplanning – checklist of design issues (Urban Task Force, 1999, p. 74).

two and three-dimensional indicative design solutions. The latter, in the form of three-dimensional masterplans (see Fig. 15.3), was heavily endorsed by the Urban Task Force (1999, p. 73) because they:

• are visionary and aid the deliverability of development, thus raising aspirations and providing a vehicle for consensus;

- provide the means for a more participative process, by allowing all stakeholders to understand proposals and therefore articulate their needs and priorities;
- allow a greater understanding of what the public spaces between buildings will be like before they are built;
- show how the streets, squares and open space of a neighbourhood are to be connected;
- determine the distribution of uses (and potentially tenures), and whether these uses should be accessible at street level;
- control the network of movement patterns for people moving on foot, cycle or public transport;
- allow an understanding of how well a neighbourhood is integrated with the surrounding urban context;
- provide a basis for negotiation and dispute resolution, if seen as part of a flexible land-use planning process;
- are equally suited to rethinking the roles, functions and forms of existing neighbourhoods;
- allow the full development potential of the site to be exploited.

In this latter role, research has consistently indicated how effective development briefs are as a means of presenting design aspirations (Carmona, 2001b, pp. 287–8). However, guidance on such matters should be realistic and flexible if it is not to create more tensions than it solves. Briefs can be prepared whether interest has been expressed or not in a site (they are useful promotional tools) and can be prepared by housing providers and authorities alike. However prepared, they form a valuable basis from which to negotiate, particularly if made the subject of public consultation and formally adopted as supplementary guidance, preferably, as action plans of the LDF. Both Cambridge and Birmingham valued the role of design briefs (see Chapters 11 and 12), the latter as part of a sophisticated design-led approach to planning and regeneration, while a major output from the process at Sedgemoor (see Chapter 14) was the detailed development brief as a means to articulate mutually agreed development objectives between housebuilders and the authority.

Urban design skills

Unfortunately, government guidance on the preparation of development briefs cautions that the preparation of design briefs (and by implication other forms of proactive guidance) commands significant resources, not least in skilled manpower, and where this does not exist, briefing can have an unintended negative impact on development quality; either by asking for too little, or by promoting unrealistic objectives. The guide concludes that 'if a planning brief is to be worth preparing, it should aim to secure a higher standard of development than would have been achieved without it' (DETR, 1998i, paras. 2.2 and 2.5). The question of design skills, or the lack of them, pervades debates on delivering both more proactive planning and better quality housing development.

The equal failure of both planning and housing providers, for example, to adequately value the importance of place-making in their activities has undermined the image of both in the public's eyes. The realisation of the importance of urban design is now fully reflected in a range of government guidance, much of which makes the case that standards of design are unlikely to improve without an increased awareness of design by non-designers engaged in the production of new housing environments and in the form of staff with dedicated urban design skills. Of the housing providers interviewed, Countryside Properties showed the greatest commitment to urban design, with expertise in-house to call on and an ability and willingness to depart from more run-of-the-mill development solutions (see Chapter 13). Of the planning authorities, both Birmingham and Stratford-on-Avon have dedicated urban design officers within their planning departments (Chapters 11 and 12). These officers have been able to bring forward design guidance, run knowledge-building CPD exercises for other staff, provide design advice on specific applications, help to bridge the gap between development interests and planners and councillors, and generally act as development enablers. Both Birmingham and Countryside Properties have also brought in outside expertise as and when required.

The route to positive and proactive planning

Other approaches to positive and proactive planning are listed in Fig. 15.4. Fundamental to all the approaches discussed above is the need to question the status quo and consider creatively how local problems can be overcome, perhaps by developing a new way of working, a new policy response, or by considering new development opportunities. Whatever solution is advanced, there is need to build a consensus around a clear vision, consider implementation and develop the necessary tools and resources (including the right skills). Positive and proactive planning can mean many different things in different places, and will result in very different solutions to a wide range of problems. It does, however, imply planners and housing providers working in a problem-solving mode and directing their efforts to clearly defined goals.

Finally, based on the case study experiences five further observations are offered:

- The pursuit of more positive and proactive planning approaches should not suggest that the very necessary reactive development control activities of authorities are not valuable, or that authorities should not say 'no' when proposed housing does not meet their policy objectives. Planners are often to be congratulated as much on what is not seen on the ground as on what is.
- Design guidance needs to be the subject of the broadest possible consultation to ensure it has political, community and housing provider support. For example, that it is recommending design solutions that are likely to have a market, that it is sensitive to context (including cultural differences in areas with significant minority populations), that in the case of social housing it complies with RSL funding guidelines, and that it is realistic and viable in all other respects.
- Once prepared, authorities have a responsibility to ensure that all policy and guidance is signed up to and interpreted consistently by officers and councillors, but that adequate flexibility is built into the guidance to allow interpretation in the light of local circumstances.
- Authorities – like housing providers – also need to be prepared to take on their responsibility for achieving higher quality, for example, by being prepared to adopt and manage new public spaces, and demand high design quality when selling land for development.
- If the cost of in-house urban design expertise is prohibitive in the short term, it may be worth considering shared posts between authorities or joint funding an urban design service with other agencies, such as highways or housing departments.

➤ **Design codes** – which are used by some proactive developers and local authorities (particularly by New Urbanists) to establish a loose set of design and development principles for large housing developments against which individual proposals can be measured as and when they come forward. Often design codes go hand in hand with a two-dimensional masterplan.

➤ **Housebuilder design guidance** – which has been prepared by a small number of private housebuilders such as Barratt and large RSLs such as The Guinness Trust to try and ensure greater consistency between their constituent companies/regional sections. The aim is to increase quality overall by defining generic characteristics of good design, and in so doing to encourage the smoother passage of their schemes through the planning process.

➤ **Urban regeneration** – which to a greater or lesser extent all the case study authorities and many housing providers were engaged in, and which the planning process should be leading as the ideal vehicle to coordinate regeneration with other development activity.

➤ **Land assembly** – which is a constituent part of urban regeneration activity, and a proactive means for planners to deliver their plans. Primarily operated through the mechanism of compulsory purchase, land assembly has not been operated effectively by planning authorities largely because of the time and expense involved. New arrangements introduced by the Office of the Deputy Prime Minister (2002e, para. 43) aim to strengthen planning authority powers to purchase land, improve the compensation arrangements and speed up the whole process. Compulsory purchase remains a powerful tool at the disposal of local authorities, and one which should be used more often and more effectively to deliver land (particularly brownfield land) for housing. The new arrangements enacted through the 2003 Planning and Compulsory Purchase Act enable authorities to acquire land if they believe its development will be of economic, social or environmental benefit to their area (Section 73).

➤ **Exemplar projects** – which authorities can help to promote on small and larger scales, by adequately publicising the development successes in their area (for example, through award schemes) and by encouraging innovative new developments in the first place, including by competition.

➤ **Integrated plan-making** – the writing of development plans provides an important opportunity to coordinate new infrastructure projects with development opportunities. In the pursuit of sustainable development objectives, the coordination of local transport plans and economic development strategies with development plans (LDFs) seems an ideal place to start (see Chapter 16). The integration of development plans with housing strategies is also critical (see Chapter 12).

➤ **Urban Design Action Teams (UDATs) or Action planning** – which are usually initiated by a community, and involve design professionals working with the community over a weekend or short period of time to brainstorm a set of solutions to particular design or planning problems.

➤ **Design competitions** – which can be used to raise and set the standards of development for particular prominent architectural, urban design or planning projects, and/or to promote particular development opportunities.

15.4 Other approaches to positive and proactive planning.

16

Moving on

Processes, planners and providers

This book has been structured to take readers on a journey. It started with the three overarching processes governing the delivery of new homes, then moved on to discuss the six key areas of concern and consequent sources of tension facing planners and providers in navigating these processes. It ended with five fundamental routes to better practice (illustrated by numerous proposals) that – within the confines of prevailing practice – should act to clear the way to better meet housing need.

As the previous five chapters have already offered recommendations on what the ingredients of a more effective process of planning for housing might be, this final chapter aims to think outside of the box of prevailing policy and practice, to reflect on what the key features of a more responsive planning process might be in the future (responsive to stakeholder needs; including the overarching need for more sustainable housing development – more housing, of the right quality in the right place). This discussion cuts across the six key areas of concern outlined in Part Two of the book. The chapter concludes by examining how the key stakeholders have viewed the first major overhaul of the planning system in over 50 years in the guise of the 2001 Planning Green Paper and 2003 Act, and whether the changes meet the aspirations established in this book.

As the research on which this book is based began, it quickly became apparent that the interface between planning and housing and the relative success or failure (depending on your viewpoint) of that relationship are largely determined by the interaction between three very different and often conflicting processes: the planning, development and social housing processes. What becomes clear on even the most rudimentary examination of these processes is that their flawed nature too often leads to suboptimal outcomes for all parties – private housebuilders, RSLs, planners, and their respective customers:

- Far from increasing certainty and proactively bringing forward development options for public debate, the planning system is slow, stultified by lack of resources and political vision, and largely unable to meet the increasingly complex environmental and social challenges it faces – this despite grand theoretical visions of the potential of planning, and a widespread acceptance of its importance by public and private interests alike.

- The private housebuilding process, by comparison, has for so long relentlessly pursued its single-minded market-led approach to housing provision that almost any proposals for new housing development are met by concerted public opposition, whilst an inability to innovate results in the same poor quality housing environments being repeated *ad infinitum* across the country – this despite a largely captive market for their products.
- For social housing, the move from mass (if often less than successful) provision by the state, to the state acting as enabler has left the planning system, through the mechanism of planning gain, in a position it was never intended or equipped to fulfil, as one of the main providers of new social housing – this despite demand increasing and stock dramatically reducing in recent years as a consequence of the 'right to buy'.

The result of imperfect markets and imperfect government in this case has been a reduced supply of (too often) imperfect new homes – both private and social; and a range of seemingly intractable tensions that have dogged the central relationships in the process of delivering new homes – between planners and providers. Examination of these tensions provided the substance of Part Two of the book, and revealed that more effective delivery of new homes must be grounded in:

- a consensus about the need for more housing in the first place – an inquiry for the Joseph Rowntree Foundation predicts a housing crisis with a shortfall of 1.1 million homes by 2022 in England (two-thirds in the South East – Barlow *et al.*, 2002);
- a recognition that conflict between the key stakeholders is wholly destructive and serves no one;
- an understanding of the pressures on key players, which more often than not are both intense and all-pervasive.

Bar charts at the end of Chapters 5 to 10 revealed the comparative views of the three stakeholders. In some instances, RSLs rated a tension as more important, whilst private housebuilders or planning authorities felt it to be of lesser significance. The patterns of ratings are different for each of the tensions; information brought together in Fig. 16.1. Significantly, however, Fig. 16.1 reveals that generally housebuilders considered almost all points of concern to be of greater significance than planners, with RSLs somewhere in between. Perhaps this is inevitable – users of a service are always more likely to find fault with it than its providers – but it might also suggest a degree of complacency amongst planners about the value added by the planning system.

Unsurprisingly, RSLs rated the delivery of affordable housing as the source of greatest tension but were also concerned about internal working arrangements within local authorities, particularly the relationships between planning and housing departments. The issue of land allocation for affordable housing (or the lack of it) was also a significant worry. For private housebuilders, delay was by far their greatest concern although again issues of land allocation and the new requirement to build at higher densities were high on their agenda. The perceived uncertainty derived from the discretionary nature of the planning system also gave cause for concern. For planners the main worries focused on the issue of land identification and allocation, but significant unease was noted over the new emphasis in central government on higher density and better designed housing and how planning authorities would deal with such concerns. For planners, issues of the discretionary nature of planning and of planning delay were not regarded as major concerns.

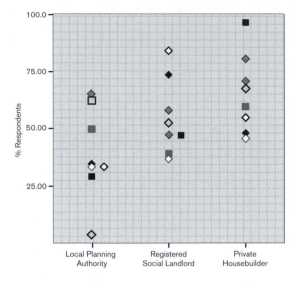

16.1 Stakeholder weighting of key tensions (% rating as significant).

The different emphases placed by stakeholders on the tensions helps to illustrate their divergent interests, and the need for cross-cutting solutions that address both public and private objectives. The solutions advanced in Part Three of the book in the form of five fundamental routes to better practice each address several of the tensions (see Table 16.1). Although the routes are on the face of it simple and perhaps even commonsensical as headline messages, the discussion in Chapters 11 to 15 indicates the complexities involved in adequately addressing any one, let alone all five at the same time. The result of not addressing them, however, will be the continuation of combative rather than constructive relationships between the parties. The mistrust and dogmatism that results lead the whole process into a downward spiral from which it is difficult to recover. Much of the case study work and the resulting recommendations consequently focused on identifying practical means to pursue the five routes. Unfortunately, because the routes are not mutually exclusive, but instead interrelated in a whole series of ways, a sea-change in practice is only likely to occur if all five are addressed concurrently.

Research of the nature reported in this book can never provide perfect answers for dealing with the nuances of every different situation. Market contexts, for example, vary significantly, and local practice inevitably centres on local conditions and circumstances. For that reason, the recommendations in previous chapters have tended to focus on broad principles rather than local detail. Whether the principles are followed or not will depend on local attitudes and the willingness amongst local stakeholders to think and act positively. Attitudes are therefore critical. An unwillingness to embrace change or an inability to see and understand other perspectives will place enormous constraints on any process. Senior professionals, in particular, will need to take a lead in encouraging their colleagues to think more laterally about the development process, including how to actively forge better working relationships with other stakeholders based on trust and transparency rather than on suspicion and misunderstanding.

Planners have a pivotal role to play if real advances in the way houses are built are to be achieved, but the other stakeholders – particularly RSLs and developers – need

Table 16.1 Routes and tensions compared

Routes to better practice	Tensions addressed
Strive to streamline implementation processes	➤ planning delay ➤ corporate working ➤ land identification and allocation
Adopt inclusive planning and decision-making processes	➤ planning delay ➤ discretionary planning ➤ design guidance ➤ development density
Adopt integrated and realistic working practices	➤ discretionary planning ➤ planning agreements ➤ corporate working
Strive for certainty and transparency	➤ planning delay ➤ discretionary planning ➤ design guidance ➤ planning agreements ➤ affordable housing
Adopt a positive and proactive approach to planning and development	➤ discretionary planning ➤ design guidance ➤ affordable housing ➤ development density ➤ land identification and allocation

to subscribe to the same principles, encouraged by a planning process that also takes their concerns and aspirations to heart. The case studies revealed that working successfully together is, to a large extent, about understanding, but also, sometimes, about compromise. They also revealed that this is possible.

An optimum process (takes time)

Some of the key overarching themes emerging from the case studies and the discussion of the five routes in Chapters 11 to 15 are outlined in Fig. 16.2. Drawing on the discussion of development process models in Chapter 3, Fig. 16.3 summarises an optimum housing delivery process, by indicating the series of interlinked and interacting processes over time, the key stakeholder roles and relationships within those processes, and how the different public/private objectives play themselves out in terms of the powers to control, influence, invest, negotiate and coordinate the actions of others.

Fig. 16.3 demonstrates the importance of building relationships from the ground level and getting the stakeholders together at the earliest opportunity. Practically, this means a closer working relationship at the pre-development and pre-application phases, which helps to smooth the path of the development process once a planning application is received. The figure graphically illustrates that to get it right at the post-application stage requires a huge and continual investment before an application is received, even before

➤ **A commitment to change** – is required. Stakeholders need to question and carry on questioning established practice – are they doing everything possible to build better, more constructive relationships – and address the needs of the other stakeholders on which they rely.

➤ **Understand the pressures** – all stakeholders are under immense pressure to deliver simultaneously on many fronts, but by understanding some of those pressures it may be possible to begin to understand differing aspirations and also to find common ground.

➤ **Invest up front** – which is perhaps the most fundamental of messages, inherent in achieving greater certainty by building relationships, coordinating efforts within and between organisations, doing the ground-work and in establishing clear frameworks of policy and guidance.

➤ **Agree and write it down** – to establish certainty by clarifying roles and responsibilities, what has been agreed and what remains to be decided, and what the roles and responsibilities of the different parties will be.

➤ **Meet early and often** – to establish dialogue and share aspirations as early as possible and to avoid, as far as possible, abortive work and divergent objectives.

➤ **Be proactive (both sides)** – to, as far as possible, avoid reactive and negative relationships and to move beyond formulaic solutions. This requires the positive engagement of all parties in suggesting and finding solutions to problems.

➤ **Be constructive** – by working to build trust through adopting honest, inclusive and transparent approaches to negotiation, and accepting that sometimes this may take a little longer in the short term, but save time over the long term.

➤ **Continual review** – by asking again and again how can this be done more effectively and more efficiently and how can others help in that process?

➤ **There is no single route to best practice** – everywhere is different and must find its own route to best practice, nevertheless, sharing knowledge and experience will always pay dividends.

➤ **The shared objective** – that all sides should be striving for more, better quality housing, for which there is a clear national need.

16.2 Overarching themes.

any development is mooted at all. This investment can and should significantly exceed that made at the post-application stage, and if it is not made, the post-application process is unlikely to be smooth.

By investing up front, an optimum process is also likely to be a faster process in the long run. This is because stakeholders will be well aware of their responsibilities and of the aspirations of the different stakeholders at an early stage in the overall process before key decisions (such as the price to be paid for the land) have been made. A key issue arising from the research is that by taking other stakeholder aspirations on board early, tensions and delays can be avoided further down the line.

In this regard, although it has been argued in Chapter 11 that authorities should make every effort to streamline their decisions by being as administratively efficient as possible, what is also clear is that good planning takes time; that this time increases with the complexity of the application; and that few applications are more important to get right (or are more complex) than those for new housing development. Thus planning should always take the long-term view that quality of decision-making is more important than speed, and central government should recognise this and reverse the undue emphasis placed on the speed of decision-making in the national monitoring of planning system effectiveness through Best Value processes.

OPTIMUM HOUSING DELIVERY PROCESS (STAGE 1: PRE-DEVELOPMENT)

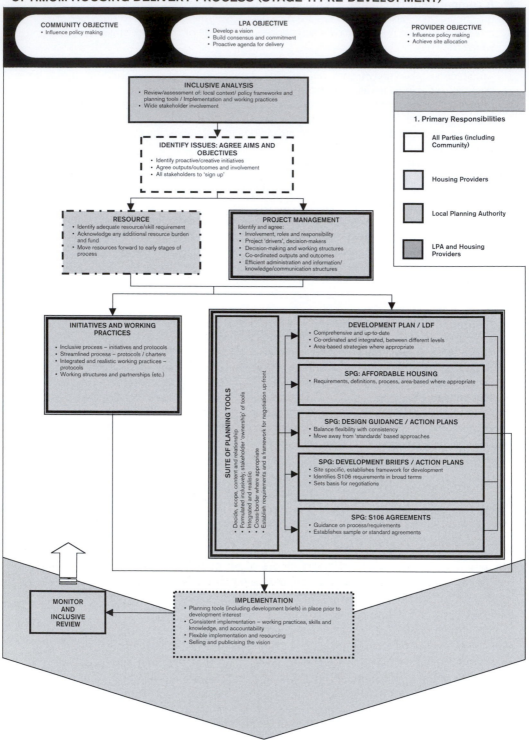

COMMUNITY OBJECTIVE
• Influence policy making

LPA OBJECTIVE
• Develop a vision
• Build consensus and commitment
• Proactive agenda for delivery

PROVIDER OBJECTIVE
• Influence policy making
• Achieve site allocation

INCLUSIVE ANALYSIS
• Review/assessment of: local context/ policy frameworks and planning tools / Implementation and working practices
• Wide stakeholder involvement

IDENTIFY ISSUES: AGREE AIMS AND OBJECTIVES
• Identify proactive/creative initiatives
• Agree outputs/outcomes and involvement
• All stakeholders to 'sign up'

RESOURCE
• Identify adequate resource/skill requirement
• Acknowledge any additional resource burden and fund
• Move resources forward to early stages of process

PROJECT MANAGEMENT
Identify and agree:
• Involvement, roles and responsibility
• Project 'drivers', decision-makers
• Decision-making and working structures
• Co-ordinated outputs and outcomes
• Efficient administration and information/ knowledge/communication structures

1. Primary Responsibilities

All Parties (including Community)

Housing Providers

Local Planning Authority

LPA and Housing Providers

INITIATIVES AND WORKING PRACTICES
• Inclusive process – initiatives and protocols
• Streamlined process – protocols / charters
• Integrated and realistic working practices – protocols
• Working structures and partnerships (etc.)

SUITE OF PLANNING TOOLS
• Decide, scope, content and relationship
• Formulated inclusively; stakeholder 'ownership' of tools
• Integrated and realistic
• Cross-border where appropriate
• Establish requirements and a framework for negotiation up-front

DEVELOPMENT PLAN / LDF
• Comprehensive and up-to-date
• Co-ordinated and integrated, between different levels
• Area-based strategies where appropriate

SPG: AFFORDABLE HOUSING
• Requirements, definitions, process, area-based where appropriate

SPG: DESIGN GUIDANCE / ACTION PLANS
• Balance flexibility with consistency
• Move away from 'standards' based approaches

SPG: DEVELOPMENT BRIEFS / ACTION PLANS
• Site specific, establishes framework for development
• Identifies S106 requirements in broad terms
• Sets basis for negotiations

SPG: S106 AGREEMENTS
• Guidance on process/requirements
• Establishes sample or standard agreements

MONITOR AND INCLUSIVE REVIEW

IMPLEMENTATION
• Planning tools (including development briefs) in place prior to development interest
• Consistent implementation – working practices, skills and knowledge, and accountability
• Flexible implementation and resourcing
• Selling and publicising the vision

OPTIMUM HOUSING DELIVERY PROCESS (STAGE 2: PRE-APPLICATION)

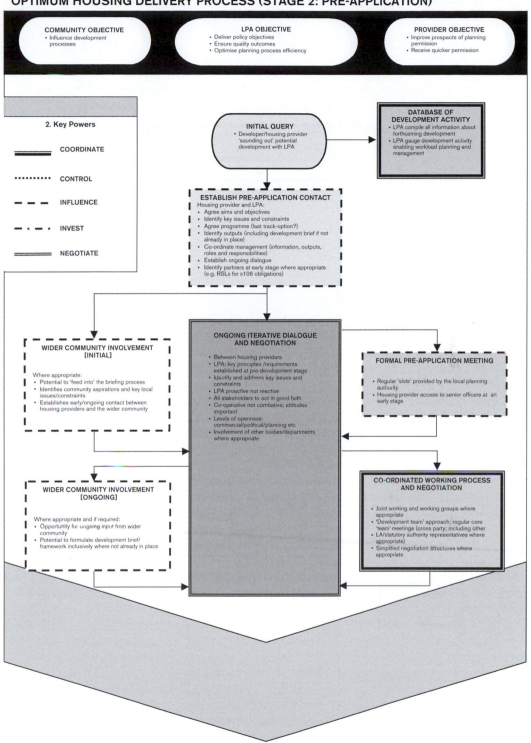

COMMUNITY OBJECTIVE
- Influence development processes

LPA OBJECTIVE
- Deliver policy objectives
- Ensure quality outcomes
- Optimise planning process efficiency

PROVIDER OBJECTIVE
- Improve prospects of planning permission
- Receive quicker permission

2. Key Powers

—————— COORDINATE

·········· CONTROL

— — — INFLUENCE

— · — · INVEST

══════ NEGOTIATE

INITIAL QUERY
- Developer/housing provider 'sounding out' potential development with LPA

DATABASE OF DEVELOPMENT ACTIVITY
- LPA compile all information about forthcoming development
- LPA gauge development activity enabling workload planning and management

ESTABLISH PRE-APPLICATION CONTACT
Housing provider and LPA:
- Agree aims and objectives
- Identify key issues and constraints
- Agree programme (fast track-option?)
- Identify outputs (including development brief if not already in place)
- Co-ordinate management (information, outputs, roles and responsibilities)
- Establish ongoing dialogue
- Identify partners at early stage where appropriate (e.g. RSLs for s106 obligations)

WIDER COMMUNITY INVOLVEMENT [INITIAL]

Where appropriate:
- Potential to 'feed into' the briefing process
- Identifies community aspirations and key local issues/constraints
- Establishes early/ongoing contact between housing providers and the wider community

ONGOING ITERATIVE DIALOGUE AND NEGOTIATION

- Between housing providers
- LPA: key principles /requirements established at pre-development stage
- Identify and address key issues and constraints
- LPA proactive not reactive
- All stakeholders to act in good faith
- Co-operative not combative; attitudes important
- Levels of openness: commercial/political/planning etc
- Involvement of other bodies/departments where appropriate

FORMAL PRE-APPLICATION MEETING

- Regular 'slots' provided by the local planning authority
- Housing provider access to senior officers at an early stage

WIDER COMMUNITY INVOLVEMENT [ONGOING]

Where appropriate and if required:
- Opportunity for ongoing input from wider community
- Potential to formulate development brief/ framework inclusively where not already in place

CO-ORDINATED WORKING PROCESS AND NEGOTIATION

- Joint working and working groups where appropriate
- 'Development team' approach; regular core 'team' meetings (cross party; including other LA/statutory authority representatives where appropriate)
- Simplified negotiation structures where appropriate

OPTIMUM HOUSING DELIVERY PROCESS (STAGE 3: POST-APPLICATION)

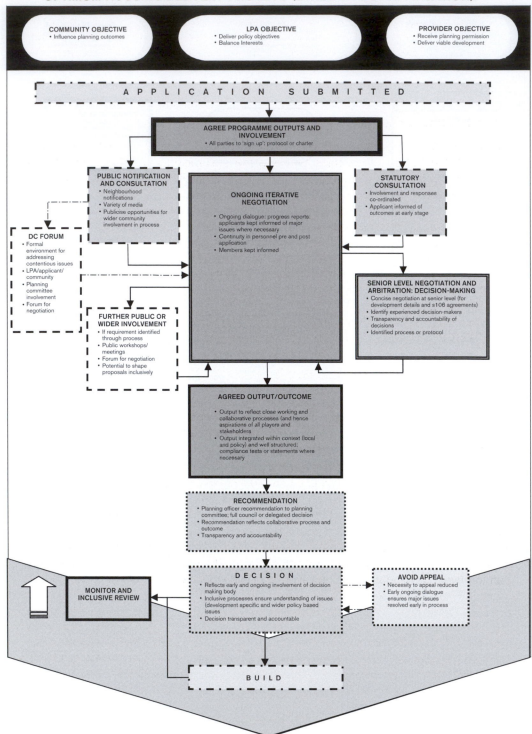

16.3 An optimum housing delivery process.

The recognition in the 2002/2003 national indicators that major developments take longer to determine than smaller developments (see Chapter 6) represents a step in the right direction. Nevertheless, to balance the concern with speed for a concern for the quality of outcomes, qualitative concerns should be reflected in the choice of national indicators and in Best Value service reviews. The various 'Excellence Matrices' from the Planning Officers' Society (2001; 2002a; 2002b) illustrate this broader quality-based agenda (see, for example, Table 16.2).

Building relationships (and new tensions)

The research confirmed that key stakeholders rely on each other to meet their objectives, and that better relationships between the stakeholders generally allow these objectives to be met more smoothly. In a biological sense, relationships should be symbiotic, rather than parasitic:

- Planners rely on housebuilders to deliver their housing allocations and on RSLs to meet their social objectives – a decent home for everyone.
- Private housebuilders rely on planners to deliver planning permission (including overcoming any local opposition), and on RSLs to manage (and sometimes also deliver) the increasingly frequent demand for affordable housing as an obligation alongside the right to develop housing for sale.
- RSLs for their part rely on planners to negotiate social housing and to deliver planning permission, and on housebuilders to effectively subsidise the delivery of new affordable homes.

Yet despite the best intentions, relationships are sometimes difficult to establish. Brent, for example (see Chapter 13), has achieved a close working relationship between the authority and local RSLs, but suggests that relationships with developers are hard to establish because developers frequently operate throughout a region or even nationally and so deal less often with individual authorities. In Torbay where a closer working relationship has been established, it is noticeable that the developer in question has up to now remained largely local in its interests (see Chapter 11).

Relationships can also be ambiguous. Private developers interviewed during the research, for example, argued that the close working relationship between some authorities and local RSLs gives unfair advantages to RSLs, whom they often regard as local authority offshoots. This identifies a potential conflict of interest, as in some respects the objectives of many RSLs are closer to those of local authorities (i.e. a public interest) than to private developers. This, however, is to misunderstand the role of private developers, who although operating in their own private interest, and primarily in the housing for sale market, also contribute towards the public interest by helping to meet national and local housing need. In this regard developers and RSLs are competing within different parts of the same market, i.e. they both compete for land, and RSLs can equally be regarded as quasi-developers. RSLs, for their part, observe that developers usually have the upper hand in commercial markets and that some rebalancing of the relationship is necessary to allow them to compete.

Table 16.2 Critical factors and their performance measurement (POS, 2000a)

Critical factors	Performance measurement process-based	Performance measurement outcome-based
Focus on quality outcomes – stewardship	▲ Characterisation of whole of local planning area is either planned, underway or complete. ▲ Monitors at least 20 per cent of all historic assets annually. ▲ Sites and Monuments Record meets national standards, and is expanded to include historic building other records. ▲ All conservation areas are covered by Section 71 studies. ▲ Implementation of joint working arrangements, within set timescales. ▲ Number of owners and developers seeking advice from council. ▲ Number of agreed protocols. ▲ Level of compliance with protocols and plans. ▲ Percentage of enquiries answered within 14 days. ▲ Local awards scheme in place. ▲ Number of refusals on urban design grounds (and number of appeals dismissed). ▲ Compliance with protocols. ▲ Number of staff/members who have undertaken urban design and conservation awareness training. ▲ Reviews quality of planning applications, and assesses them against the guidance that has been issued. ▲ Adopts SPG to best practice standards set out in national guidance. ▲ Success rate at appeal. ▲ Production of guidance for significant sites. ▲ Ensures that stakeholders' comments on draft development briefs are assessed and responded to. ▲ Number of briefs prepared. ▲ Number of developments following agreed briefs. ▲ No undue delay in processing applications. ▲ Fall in number of applications returned for further information. ▲ Number of applications valid at first attempt. ▲ Number of applications providing correct information and not amendment. ▲ A fall in the rates of appeals submitted.	▲ Reviews and assesses the influences and effect of policies and proposals on promoting, facilitating and achieving high quality development, refurbishment and public realm. ▲ Number of national awards. ▲ Includes awareness of urban design and historic environment in users satisfaction surveys. ▲ Quality of outcomes. ▲ Increase in quality of proposals.
Focus on quality outcomes – consistency of decisions	▲ Decisions are peer reviewed. ▲ Compares advice on application with final decision. ▲ Success rate of appeals. ▲ User or surveys regularly undertaken to test perceptions of fairness and transparency in decision-making. ▲ Tests recommendations against national planning guidance, BS7913:1998 (The principles of the Conservation of Historic buildings) and other national and/or international best practice criteria as appropriate to the specific case. ▲ Reduction in the number of complaints over time. ▲ Reduction in the number of cases referred to and upheld by Ombudsman.	▲ Undertakes post-completion evaluations of applications. ▲ Review systems in place to evaluate the outcome of decisions made by officers and Committee, including those not according with recommendation.

Table 16.2 continued

Focus on quality – ensuring compliance	▶ Uses an accredited process, especially in respect of site monitoring and discharge of condition. ▶ Achieves target response rate to requests for on-site advice. ▶ Achieves target response rate to complaint.	▶ High levels of maintenance.
Integrated service provision	▶ Extent to which management processes and performance management within all relevant departments work together to provide integrated service delivery (e.g. for Part L of Building Regulations). ▶ Quality/clarity of advice provided. ▶ Successful implementation of 'joined up' approach. ▶ Successful development of key partnerships within and outside the local authority. ▶ All relevant information available to prospective purchasers prior to exchange of contract. ▶ All relevant information available to prospective purchasers prior to exchange of contracts. ▶ Whether different parts of the council provide contradictory advice. ▶ Implementation of arrangements/protocols, within set timescales. ▶ Number of owners and developers seeking advice from council expertise. ▶ Level of integration of service delivery.	
Resourced service provision	▶ Monitors compliance with staff CPD requirements. ▶ Systems in place to evaluate the effectiveness of recruitment and training. ▶ Measures performance against the pace of the development process, rather than independently of it. ▶ Measure performance of conservation and urban design through user and other stakeholder satisfaction surveys. ▶ Objectives and priorities have clear targets/milestones, which reflect the policy on speed versus quality, and are monitored. ▶ A safety conscious workforce. ▶ Number of risks minimised.	▶ A process is in place for regular assessment of additional value and the quality of outcome achieved, using a range of measures e.g. internal quality audits, peer group reviews, end-user surveys and design award schemes. ▶ Measures performance against annual 'state of the environment' report.
Influential service	▶ Extent to which urban design and conservation are included in goals and objectives of strategic and corporate plans. ▶ Implementation of joint working arrangements within set timescales. ▶ Number of developers seeking advice from council expertise. ▶ Demonstrable inputs to evolving national and local policy and strategy, etc. ▶ Regularly reviews performance in user satisfaction surveys.	▶ Satisfaction surveys of customers and stakeholders.

Table 16.2 continued

Accessible service

➤ Regularly reviews policies, practices and procedures in consultation with users and revises them to increase access to services and information.

➤ Regularly reviews facilities, office opening times and availability of professional advice to meet customer expectations.

➤ Collects evidence to confirm that policies are being applied consistently.

➤ Regularly monitors staff awareness of policies and processes and identifies appropriate levels of training.

➤ Monitors participation levels (e.g. attendance at meetings) by hard-to-reach groups (in relation to proportion in population and needs indices).

➤ Regularly monitors customer satisfaction levels of any target or hard-to-reach groups.

User-focused service

➤ Regularly monitors involvement and participation of all sectors of the community in issues affecting local urban design and the historic environment.

➤ Regularly monitors progress against locally agreed targets based on user experience of the service.

➤ Maintain audit trails from initial advice through decision and outcome.

➤ Post-completion reviews of new development by members, peers/outside experts, amenity/resident groups and users.

The need for leadership

Even where the objectives of developers and local authorities coincide, developers are usually perceived by the public to be pursuing their own 'selfish' agendas. In Newcastle, for example (see Chapter 15), the authority wished to promote the Great Park development because they felt that it was a necessity for the economic development of the region. They nevertheless found themselves in an awkward position, not wishing to be seen to actively support the development during the public consultation, but also not wishing to encourage public reservations either. Planning authorities (comprising politicians and officers), it seems, often sit in the middle of such polarised arguments. On the one side the developers are trying to build houses, whilst on the other the public and pressure groups will seek to inhibit developers, and will expect the authority to act in their narrowly defined interests. Planners are therefore too often in the awkward position of trying to fulfil both sets of expectations; effectively sitting on the fence.

The Audit Commission (1999) advises that this potential conflict between the dual roles of authorities as promoters of development and as regulators can lead to inconsistencies in advice (with one part of the authority encouraging a development, and another part unable to commit). The solution, they argue, is clearer consultation and communication within local authorities to ensure that developers feel they are speaking with a single coordinated voice. In such situations, authorities also need to show leadership – having the courage of their convictions, and based on a clearly defined vision, being willing and able to promote development where that is required, or resist it if necessary. In other words, clarity of decision-making is required based on reasoned arguments.

What is clear is that, despite severe housing need, the questions of where new homes are to go, who are they for, how they should be delivered, and what form they should take are not being addressed in the local public arena, beyond knee-jerk reactions to particular developments. The result is that the public has not secured ownership of the concepts, and consequently NIMBYism and distrust of developers are rife. As the issues are not being addressed in the public (political) arena, inevitably they have to be addressed at the coal face (at the time of the application) by planning authorities, leading to further tension and distrust of local planning authorities. The move from a 'predict and provide' to a 'plan, monitor and manage' system is likely to further exacerbate these trends as national debate is suppressed, and the buck is effectively passed downwards. To operate successfully, the system requires a strong strategic planning framework to allocate non-negotiable housing requirements for local planning authorities to implement. This calls into question the move in the 2003 Planning and Compulsory Purchase Act to abandon structure planning at the county level (see Chapter 2), unless robust arrangements for subregional planning can be made to fill the gap – still an open question.

Public perceptions of RSLs are different again. In some cases there are very strong NIMBYish reactions to affordable housing (Gallent, 2002), and again many authorities seem nervous of offering decisive leadership on the issue. Other authorities, such as Hammersmith and Fulham (see Chapter 15) recognise a strong obligation to satisfy local housing needs, and so feel confident in standing up to local resistance. Again, the decisive factor is leadership, which, as national resources for social housing have declined, is having to come from the local level, and increasingly from planning authorities.

Leadership, however, sometimes involves making unpopular decisions, which local councillors can understandably be unwilling to take. The structure of local government was briefly discussed in Chapter 10, from which it was clear that new models are being experimented with, in part to reinvigorate local politics, but also to deliver stronger leadership and vision from local authorities. In London, the election of the London Mayor and preparation of the London Plan have demonstrated how planning can become a more significant local issue if taken to heart by a charismatic leader with a clear vision for the future of their area, and a strong electoral mandate. The experience has been repeated elsewhere in much smaller authorities – in largely rural and suburban Horsham District Council, for example (Cadell *et al.*, 2000), where a strong leader with a clear vision has been determined to deliver change. The election of local mayors in other parts of the country (perhaps with longer terms than the current five-year electoral cycle) may provide a means to reinvigorate local politics and local planning as well.

Sweetening the pill – by design

Leadership involves more than establishing appropriate policies and driving them through. It also – where necessary – necessitates a long-term process of winning over hearts and minds by explaining the case for a certain form of development. Savage's (2001, pp. 159–63) analysis of established resident objections to new development in Basildon, Essex (see Chapter 11) identified three key approaches to reducing local opposition to new development.

First, improved participation, to break the predominant 'decide, announce and defend' stance to decision-making taken by many authorities, and to understand the conflicting rationalities between residents, planners and providers. If nothing else, improved communication will help to make the case for new housing in a more open and transparent manner, although there will be a cost – time (CEBR, 2002). In this regard a tension at the heart of the moves to reform of the English planning system (DTLR, 2001a) is the assumption that plans and policies can be adopted more quickly and planning decisions made with greater haste, whilst also allowing increased opportunities for community participation in planning decision-making. It may be that it proves impossible to square this circle, although the research indicated that, within reason, the time it takes to get greater understanding (and ideally acceptance) of proposals is a price worth paying for housing providers.

Second, offer compensation to those most directly affected by new development, those living adjacent to proposals. Although the principle of offering direct financial compensation has never been taken up in British planning (with the possible exception of compulsory purchase orders), compensation through the operation of planning gain in the form of enhanced local facilities and amenities for an area affected by a development can be an effective method of sweetening the pill. Nevertheless, recent work undertaken for the right-wing think tank, the Institute of Economic Affairs, has argued that the conflict between local interests and development interests is so intense that it can only be resolved by effectively rebalancing individual incentives, first, by awarding development rights to local communities rather than to the state (effectively putting local communities in control and de-nationalising the right to develop land), and, second, subsequently allowing communities to sell those rights, in so doing providing a financial incentive to allow development (Pennington, 2002). This argument that communities will always act rationally and hence deliver a perfect market for development thus 'liberating the land' is clearly optimistic, it would also effectively bring to an end the system of development funding wider public benefits such as social housing, as financial gain rather than the delivery of public goods becomes the motive for granting development rights.

Third, improve the quality of new residential development, which has long been seen by central government as a way of reducing local opposition. For example, the

1992 version of PPG3 argued 'A well-designed scheme that respects the local environment can do much to make new housing more acceptable to the local community' (DoE, 1992a, para. 4). Clearly, the poor public perception of, and widespread disdain for, the quality of new housing remain key factors driving opposition to new housing as research of potential customer and non-customer attitudes to new-build residential design has revealed (Popular Housing Forum, 1998). Nevertheless, the findings from Savage's (2001, p. 163) work suggest that improved design (including safeguarding local ecological assets) can make new residential development more acceptable to local communities, although as with public compensation and involvement in decision-making, only after the need for any development at all has been conceded.

To some degree the third approach can also offer the means to deliver the other two, through encouraging direct local involvement in the design of future developments, including discussion of the planning gain that local residents would wish to see. The example of Caterham Barracks (see Chapter 10) provides a case in point, where local opposition was quickly turned into local support, and a higher density development than originally anticipated was delivered. The example also demonstrates a housebuilder willing to think outside of their own immediate objectives and to respond to the character and quality of the locality, so helping to win support for their proposals.

Proposed changes to the English planning process discussed in Chapter 2 indicate a much greater emphasis in the future on delivering stronger physical visions for local areas and sites in the form of action plans. The problem has been that although design has since 1992 been identified as a material consideration in the planning system, and since 1997 explicitly promoted as an underpinning theme of the planning process (see Chapter 8), it remains just one of the range of material considerations that authorities have to balance. Furthermore, in much of the country, planning authorities are ill-equipped (lack the design skills base) to deliver better design. The result is that good housing design remains all too rare.

An alternative might be the explicit separation of design from planning, with specific and separate urban design legislation to sit alongside planning legislation. Key powers might include: a statutory responsibility on authorities for both the design and management of all public space aimed at joining up current disparate powers in planning, highways, urban regeneration, urban management and so forth; a statutory duty on both local authorities and developers to enhance the public realm through their development activities and regulative powers; and the establishment of design review panels with their own decision-making powers as is common in the USA.

In such circumstances development proposals would need to receive planning permission as well as permission from the design review board. Such a system gives design a higher status, with its own administrative apparatus, but also runs the risk of artificially separating key planning decisions – the mix of uses, density, provision of infrastructure, etc. – from their design implications, potentially also circumscribing the remit of design. Such a system might also run the risk of increasing bureaucratic complexity, although it could reduce the overall time taken to receive consents by considering design and planning issues concurrently, rather than in sequence as is sometimes currently the case. It would also deliver more transparent and considered decisions on design and necessitate the re-skilling of local authorities to deliver the process. Figure 16.4 illustrates integral and separated models of design review/control.

Model 1: Integral design control/review process

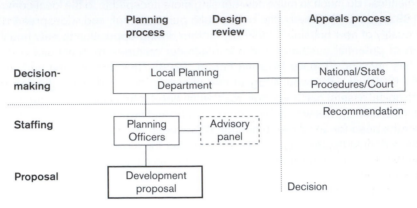

Model 2: Separated design control/review process

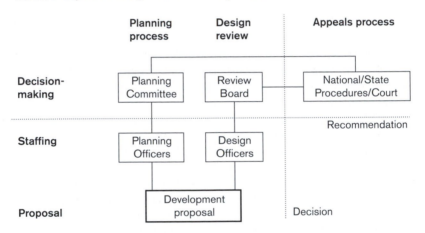

16.4 Integrated and separated models of design review/control (after Blaesser in Case Scheer and Preiser, 1994).

Sustainability – beyond land use planning

The brief discussion of public attitudes indicates the wider set of challenges and debates into which this research fits. In focusing on perhaps the core relationship at the heart of delivering new homes – between planning authorities and the providers of new housing – the work has indirectly dealt with a wide range of other relationships, through the various constituents the core parties can be said to represent, particularly local communities, house buyers, and tenants.

There is, however, a further dimension of house building relationships that should be discussed, inherent in the position of planning within the wider local (and national) government agenda. The marginalisation of planning has already been discussed, not helped by the tendency for planning to be split in recent local government reorganisations between its forward planning and regulatory function, thus undermining the essential synergy required for good planning (Cowan, 1999). Thus, advice from the RTPI (1999) on the position of planning within local government has argued that all local authority planning functions should be integrated within a single directorate, as the scope for creative, proactive planning lies in the connections, and that development planners and development controllers should seek to work more closely together in pursuance of common objectives than has often been the case in the past.

But land use planning is just the start of the public sector planning processes required to deliver new homes. Thus, as authorities and related agencies are required to prepare more plans than ever before, the demand for planning (broadly defined) is exponentially increasing. Of direct relevance to the delivery of new homes are:

- development plans (local development frameworks)
- housing strategies
- neighbourhood renewal strategies
- local transport plans
- corporate strategies
- community plans
- Best Value performance plans
- Local Agenda 21 strategies
- economic development strategies (produced by Regional Development Agencies).

The significance of integrated thinking has already been discussed as regards individual development in Chapter 13, but in view of the increasingly complex policy context, and acceptance that narrowly defined sectorial thinking has not delivered in the past, increasingly prescriptions for planning thinking beyond the 2001 Green Paper are emphasising the importance of a more integrated approach to the broader planning agenda. The Twenty-third Report of the Royal Commission on Environmental Pollution (RCEP, 2002) on Environmental Planning, for example, came out at the same time as the Planning Green Paper and offered a more radical set of recommendations, including the preparation of integrated spatial strategies, covering all uses of land and spatially related aspects of the environment. It argued that the proposed changes to the statutory planning system have ignored the real purpose of planning – to plan for the future – in favour of tinkering with its ability to more efficiently control development.

In their agenda for the future of planning, the RSPB (2002, p. 29) also call for more integrated planning, with sustainability at its heart. In meeting this objective they recognise the role of community strategies as potential tools for joining up other policy instruments (see Chapter 10), but also that – so far – it is unclear how effective they will be. For the Royal Commission on Environmental Pollution, equally important to the processes of integrating policy is the need to establish a new integrative purpose for planning that strives for more sustainable patterns of development by connecting social and economic objectives with environmental ones. Thus, they argued, a new statutory purpose for the system should be defined 'To facilitate the achievement of legitimate economic and social goals, whist ensuring that the quality of the environment is safeguarded and, wherever appropriate, enhanced' (RCEP, 2002, p. 9). For the Royal Commission, the Green Paper offered simple solutions to complex problems, whereas integrated decisions on development should be made in the light of plans that cover all forms of land use. The subsequent Planning Act in fact required planning authorities to exercise the planning function 'with a view to contributing to the achievement of sustainable development' (Section 38). Building on this very broad statutory purpose, government now has the opportunity to begin to remove the shackles from the statutory process – only time will tell.

For housing these debates are important because planning for housing aims towards a range of social, economic, and environmental objectives, and very crudely it might be argued that in recent years the main protagonists (RSLs, developers and planners) have respectively tended to concentrate on their individual objectives to the exclusion of the greater sustainable whole. Good local planning is needed to make the connections, and should be the means through which the full range of key public and private investment decisions are debated and made, across the different areas of professional responsibility – land use planning, housing, transportation, recreation, health, etc. Community strategies are a start, but, as presently constituted, lack teeth in terms of a proper statutory mechanism for delivery. Planning could be that key mechanism, but would need to move beyond its existing narrowly defined land use responsibility.

Setting local planning (and planners) free

The research revealed a widespread perception that good local planning has in recent years been stifled by the weight of increasingly robust national policy, and control at every level by national government of the planning process, of local planning policy, land use allocations, planning decisions, and planning processes (see Chapter 2). This national policy framework is increasingly sophisticated and, it can be argued, helps to guarantee a minimum provision and set of broad policy objectives (Hall, 1995, pp. 18–19). Nevertheless, as the case studies indicated, it also contributes to delivering a system that is potentially less responsive to local needs, objectives and idiosyncrasies.

In Stratford-on-Avon (see Chapter 12), for example, the vast majority of sites have been urban windfall sites in recent years, usually delivering less than ten units. The result is that most housing development falls below the 25 unit (or one hectare) threshold prescribed in Circular 6/98 for sites outside of London, above which developers can be required to provide social/affordable housing. As a consequence, despite local need, the authority finds it very difficult to negotiate affordable housing via Section 106 obligations.

In Newcastle, by way of comparison, the city has been more successful at overcoming national advice, but only after considerable time and effort and a battle with the Government Regional Office over an apparent contradiction of the requirement in PPG3 for sequential testing of all new housing development. In that case (see Chapter 15), Newcastle had long had an oversupply of both inner city redundant brownfield land and high-density urban housing, and at the same time a perceived undersupply of detached, lower density housing that typically attracts mobile, middle-class families. As a consequence, mobile middle-class families have been moving out of the city. Newcastle therefore identified the need for middle-class suburban development at lower densities as a key part of its economic development strategy, and in order to complement the existing urban provision.

In such cases there is need for a more intelligent approach to planning, with greater freedom granted to local authorities to override national and regional guidance when local circumstances require. A key justification for planning is its democratic legitimacy, which is much more direct and apparent at the local level if operated through local government, rather than through the Secretary of State at the national level. It can be argued therefore that local authorities should be set free to define their own democratically derived planning agendas, which should be capable of extending beyond strict land use planning concerns to the broader integrated agenda discussed above – including local housing policy.

With greater freedom to act locally and to innovate local solutions to local, regional and national objectives, planning might once again become a significant local political issue (beyond NIMBY objections), with communities (through their political representatives) deciding what sort of place they want their locality to be, and planning accordingly. The misconceived actions of the occasional wayward authority would seem a small price to pay to reinvigorate local planning, whilst national government could concentrate on promoting good practice, and on establishing broad policy objectives to be interpreted in the light of local circumstances.

The 2003 Local Government Act, following on the heels of the Local Government White Paper – *Strong Local Leadership, Quality Public Services* (see Chapter 10), offers a potential – if so far tentative – way forward. The Act aims to return greater independence to local government, such as the freedom to borrow to pay for major projects – including buildings, infrastructure and environmental improvements – or to charge for discretionary services such as pre-application discussions. An extension of these freedoms should play a role in reinvigorating local politics, including freedom from the increasingly prescriptive national hand-over of almost every aspect of the planning process.

The other side of the coin might be greater day-to-day freedom for planning professionals to deliver on the agenda defined by their political leaders. Thus, local politicians should also concentrate on establishing broad policy objectives and monitoring delivery, and less on taking everyday decisions on planning issues. In this regard, planning has often been criticised for its failure to focus on the fundamental planning concerns, and for the undue attention it gives to matters of detail, as well as on the inconsistency of political decision-making. The emphasis in the 2002/2003 national performance indicators for planning on raising the rate of delegated decision-making may encourage a switch in emphasis. The case can also be made (particularly in the light of ongoing recruitment problems into the profession) for planners to delegate more of the routine development control work to planning technicians and administrators, to allow professional planners themselves to concentrate on the more creative and positive policy and implementation activities, including negotiation tasks. Planners need to reinvent themselves as the professional experts in the management of urban and environmental change, rather than – as is too often the case – as simply the administrators of the statutory planning process.

The final element of increased freedom should be increased responsibility, not least to ensure that an up-to-date policy framework is in place, as a robust basis on which to determine planning applications. Indeed, most of the key recommendations in this book flow from this basic requirement. In the light of slimmer, district-wide core strategies, supplemented by proposal statements and action plans for specific areas or sites constituting the LDF, the duty should be placed on local authorities to have up-to-date action plans for all developments over a certain specified size, within a specified period of the legislation and thereafter (perhaps three years). The sanction for failure should be removal of plan-led status, and a local reversion to a presumption in favour of development, with draft or out-of-date policy frameworks treated simply as another material consideration. Such an approach would in effect remove significant powers from authorities if they did not meet their responsibility to determine applications on the basis of an adequate, preconceived policy framework. The tendency for authorities to divert resources from plan-making to other functions, and for plans to take up to ten years to adopt has brought the planning system in to disrepute. On this front, stern and decisive action is required.

More or less planning?

So is more planning or less planning the answer to delivering more homes? Pennington (2002) has argued that planning can never hope to provide an effective remedy for the perceived failures of a free market, because it is impossible for planners to gather and interpret the vastly complex information that would be required to operate an efficient land-use planning system, hence interventions are simplistic and often misguided. Furthermore, planners are rarely motivated by a desire to serve the true public interest, but are inevitably subject to pressure from special interest groups resistant to new development. The result, he argues, has been an artificial scarcity of land, over-centralisation of planning, a lack of experimentation, and inappropriate incentive structures for those affected by development. Instead of nationalisation of development rights through comprehensive planning, he argues for local entrepreneurial action in the market through local proprietary communities. These would hold development rights to sell, and protect valued amenities through private covenants and deed restrictions.

Although not going nearly so far, other commentators have agreed that a less restrictive mode of planning could help to free market potential to meet housing need. Boyfield and Mather (2001, p. 80), for example, have argued that 'the outmoded planning system is at the root of the housing problem', and that 'the key flaw in the government's reform programme for housing is its reluctance to adopt a more market oriented approach'. They suggest that although a genuine market in housing should be allowed to develop with demand matched by supply in both owner-occupier and rental (including private rental) markets, planning should still have a role in guaranteeing national heritage and landscapes and in maintaining design standards – including architectural excellence. The new emphasis for planning, he argues (somewhat contradicting the argument for less planning) should be on the quality as opposed to the quantity of provision.

Rudlin and Falk (1999, pp. 238–45) make a similar argument, arguing that in some circumstances it might be appropriate to lift many planning controls and encourage providers to deliver housing as they see fit in an incremental manner. The proviso is that a clear physical framework should be first established and then supplemented – in the case of low demand urban areas – by a comprehensive package of urban regeneration measures, including appropriate development incentives and public sector investment in the public realm.

Most commentators on the state of British planning would accept that the cumulative impact of planning over time has led to inflated land and house prices, and that this has resulted in a shortage of new homes (particularly where demand is at its greatest). The solution for others (for example, the CPRE – Dewar, 2002c), is more planning in the form of a stronger regional growth strategy to direct demand to where land and the potential for supply (if matched by demand) are more plentiful. However, perhaps because of the resource implications involved, a serious regional growth strategy has not been a feature of British planning since the 1970s (Hall, P. in Cullingworth, 1999, pp. 80–2). Such a strategy also seems unlikely to feature strongly in government policy in the near future, despite plans to strengthen regional planning contained in the 2003 Planning Act, or to introduce directly elected regional assemblies in England (ODPM, 2002f).

Some have argued for greater powers for planners in the form of more proactive land assembly powers. The Joseph Rowntree Land Inquiry, for example, called for a mechanism based on land pooling principles, by which owners are given fiscal or financial incentives to participate, so making the value of their collective pool of land greater than the sum of its parts (Barlow *et al.*, 2002). The authors of the report argued that England lacks effective mechanisms and institutions for land assembly (including redeveloping poor quality housing areas), and that such mechanisms represent an essential pre-requisite for proactive planning. More effective land assembly mechanisms were also a major theme of the Urban Task Force report. Other commentators have neither argued for more or less planning, but simply for a different sort of planning (see pp. 310–11) – more efficient (in the case of the housebuilders), more effective (in the case of RSLs), or more positive (in the case of planners).

Restricting the supply of land has not been without its benefits, not least for some housebuilders in the profits made on their sometimes extensive land holdings. Most importantly, however, the (often substantial) dividend that the granting of planning permission effectively confers on the price of land is increasingly being used to pay for the planning gains – including affordable homes – that the public sector has largely opted out of providing itself. In this regard planning remains the goose that lays the golden eggs, and also retains the potential (often not realised – Carmona, 2001b, p. 280) to aid the delivery of better quality and more sustainable patterns of development that all but the most anti-planning commentators recognise are important.

As expectations increase on what planning can deliver – for example, the Draft London Plan (GLA, 2002b) envisages that 50 per cent of new homes in the capital will be affordable (35 per cent social rented and 15 per cent intermediate) – it is difficult to conceive of this scale of planning gain, unless delivered out of the increasingly valuable dividend conferred on residential land by the granting of planning permission. In the final analysis, planning gain – of whatever form – will only be delivered as long as it is economically possible to do so, whilst still delivering an adequate profit on the development opportunity. As soon as the demand for public gain outstrips the capacity of development to deliver (something that will vary from place to place), the result will be no planning gain, and no new housing at all. A careful and informed case-by-case assessment needs to be made. In this regard the rejection of across-the-board tariffs by central government (see Chapter 9) may retain local flexibility, although their existence as a starting point for negotiation (either up or down) would have offered a welcome certainty and transparency in the process.

An agenda for change – a new culture

Discussion in this book has not necessarily supported the case for either more or less planning, but has argued for better planning, and that approaches to policy prescription and subsequent intervention should be determined at the local level and according to local circumstances. In this regard, beleaguered planning authorities need to find a new confidence in what they are doing, and a new belief in the value of planning. Sometimes this will also need to be matched by a renewed competence in areas of professional practice that have been undermined in recent years by the excessively narrow technocratic conceptualisation of planning which has been adopted by necessity.

In Chapter 2 a number of agendas for planning were discussed. This research has revealed its own set of challenges aimed at giving planning back its purpose and confidence, and at addressing the complexities of contemporary society in a more sustainable manner. The essential features of such a planning process offer eight challenges.

A planning system that is:

1. Efficient in decision-making – which is the hallmark of a professional approach to planning, recognising that planning in the public sector is a public service with far-reaching economic, social and environmental consequences. As such, an appropriately resourced planning service is fundamental for streamlined decision-making.
2. Equitable in processes and outcomes – the argument has been made for more inclusive approaches to planning, but equity goes to the heart of planning's mission, to reconcile often conflicting interests, and to ensure that decisions are made in the wider public interest. This implies that planning processes are operated in an equitable fashion, and also that outcomes deliver the widest possible range of benefits to the full range of stakeholders.
3. Providing coordinated policy responses to complex problems – reflecting the complexity of the contemporary development climate, and the need for more integrated responses from across public agencies and private interests. In this regard the wide remit of planning has too often been fragmented for short-term administrative reasons, but requires more coordination on policy, action and process fronts.
4. Sensitive to change, not least to market and social contexts – because uninformed planning decisions are likely to be poor planning decisions, and yet an ignorance (or at least a convenient dismissal of the facts) too often clouds decision-making. In this regard a new realism is required, which recognises local, regional and national needs, and the responsibility to provide for them, as well as different stakeholder aspirations and objectives.
5. Capable of delivering predictable high quality outcomes – which is a prerequisite for the delivery of new homes. In this regard, most new housing (including much affordable housing) will be supplied by the market without subsidy, although the market requires the right conditions to flourish, which includes greater certainty. In particular, it requires clarity in design requirements and other social and environmental requirements as early as possible in the process if these objectives are to be met.
6. Ethical and accountable – in mediating often very diverse interests, local planning authorities should also be transparent in articulating their own priorities and interests. In this regard their responsibility extends equally to the powerless and less articulate as it does to the powerful and articulate. It also extends to future generations and therefore to the delivery of more sustainable patterns of development.
7. Visionary – the argument has been made for a more positive approach to planning. This implies the need to clearly articulate a local vision that is more than woolly aspirations and policies, but instead offers a clear short-, medium- and long-term spatial strategy (at the level of the site in three dimensions). It also implies a willingness to communicate and, where appropriate, to promote the vision in order to encourage its shared acceptance, but should not imply a dogmatic inflexibility, as markets and opportunities invariably change.
8. Effective at delivering change – because planning is about delivering change for the better, through proactive, action-oriented processes that aim to harness the skills and resources of the range of stakeholders (public and private) to deliver the preconceived vision. In this endeavour the full range of tools available to planners should be harnessed, including negotiation, persuasion, coordination, direct investment, regulation and enforcement.

These overarching qualities are reflected in the recommendations outlined in Chapters 11 to 15 of this book. Collectively they provide the means to dismiss a range of common critiques of planning; that planning is negative, reactive, technocratic and bureaucratic, divorced from market realities, uncreative, simplistic, and marginalised and insignificant. They also confirm that planning is not risk-free, but requires decisive political will and vision (both local and national). Finally, they confirm that by itself, planning is just one contribution to solving an increasingly complex range of housing and urban problems, and that the right housing in the right place will never be delivered without the inputs, expertise and resources of the housing providers. In this regard, making the system work is as much the responsibility of the housing providers as of the planners themselves. But for planners, this suggests a change in culture, away from one of planning as development control to one of planning as a vehicle for enabling positive change.

Provision of enough decent quality housing also remains a national responsibility. As regards private housing, this means delivery of a planning process that in turn delivers enough land (either through the market or by direct land assembly), and is appropriately resourced and enabled to demand rigorous quality standards. It might also imply a more proactive regional growth strategy (emphasising urban renaissance in the north and the Midlands) and fiscal incentives (carrots and sticks) to encourage development on brownfield sites or in areas of low demand, for example, reductions in stamp duty or levying VAT on greenfield development. It should also include removal of the current thresholds in Circular 6/98 under which the provision of affordable housing can no longer be required, in other words the assumption should be that all market housing should make a contribution to the provision of affordable housing, either on or off-site, unless market realities or other planning gain requirements make a contribution demonstrably uneconomic. A recent report from Cambridge University (2002) has even suggested extending planning obligations for affordable housing to non-residential land, but predicts considerable opposition to such a move from landowners and developers. It also advocates the introduction of an urban version of the rural exceptions policy, to allow housing to be built on land that would otherwise not obtain permission, as long as it is affordable. The case study at Hammersmith and Fulham demonstrated the potential of such an approach (see Chapter 15).

Finally, the case should be made for a greater re-engagement of the state in the direct provision of social housing. Although this has not been the focus of this book, it is clear that great housing need continues to exist, and in large parts of the country this need is unlikely ever to be met by the market or planning mechanisms or by current levels of direct funding for social housing allocated through the Housing Corporation. Although it is unlikely that local authorities will retrieve their role as providers in the near future, funding allocated through RSLs will need to greatly increase if rising need is to be met. The Joseph Rowntree Land Inquiry, for example, identified that under two-thirds of the household projections in England between 2006 and 2016 could be met by the market sector, whilst the rest will require varying degrees of government assistance if homes are to be affordable. They comment, however, that to date government has only shown itself ready to increase funding available for new affordable housing to about 50 per cent of what is required, and that the planning system will be expected to deliver the rest. They argue that so far the evidence suggests that the planning system can only deliver a small proportion of what is required, and that government needs to support affordable housing in a more proactive manner (Barlow *et al.*, 2002).

In this respect the announcement in the 2002 Comprehensive Spending review (HM Government, 2002) that spending in the housing sector would rise by 4.2 per cent above inflation for the next three years is welcome, amounting to some £1.1 billion of additional funds per annum by 2005. The funds were tied by the Deputy Prime Minister in his subsequent speech to a major expansion in the supply of new affordable housing in the south east, and to tackling the problems of low demand and abandonment in parts of the north and the Midlands (Prescott, 2002a, p. 4). It is yet to be seen how the additional funds work themselves out in terms of extra houses on the ground, and as regards the contribution they make to rectifying the increasingly obvious national housing shortfall. A subsequent discussion paper even raised the possibility of local authorities once again taking on a responsibility for funding social housing provision by funding RSLs directly rather than through the Housing Corporation (ODPM, 2002g). Clearly a move away from local authorities as strictly enablers is on the cards.

The 2002 Comprehensive Spending review also brought with it some relief for the chronic resource problems in planning, with an extra £350 million allocated for planning authorities in the form of an 'incentive grant' over the three-year period of the review, tied to improved performance. The Deputy Prime Minister argued 'It is crucial this new money goes hand in hand with reform. We need a culture of change in planning to deliver major improvements to our communities' (Prescott, 2002b, p. 1). The 'Sustainable Communities' Planning Policy Statement clarified that the extra resources would only go to authorities that demonstrated their commitment to a high-quality planning service, measured against Best Value Performance Indicators (including a promised new indicator to measure the quality of planning outcomes – see Chapter 6), and that they would sit alongside extra resources from a 14 per cent rise in planning application fees (ODPM, 2002a, pp. 8–9). None of the incentive money would be ring-fenced for planning, but the incentive grant would only be allocated to authorities that improved their planning performance.

16.5 *Rubbish services! (Cowan, 2002).*

Commentators on the announcement variously cautioned that tying the resources to performance could entrench the 'tick-box and bean counting culture' and leave poor performing authorities without the resources to improve (Dewar, 2002d), whilst the lack of ring fencing might ensure that the extra funds are siphoned off to other local authority priorities (see Fig 16.5). It is hoped, however, that the extra resources for planning, alongside those for housing, represents the start of a longer-term recognition that as public interest services, planning and housing will only ever be as effective as the resources invested in them, and that to deliver anything other than the most basic of statutory responsibilities, more resources are required. The 2002 Comprehensive Spending review represented a step in the right direction. The research revealed that a superior service is demanded by all stakeholders.

The next fifty years

So will planning in England play its part in meeting the housing challenges over the next fifty years? If the 2003 legislative changes are to be as long-lasting in their influence as those in the 1947 Act, then the ideas contained in the 2001 Planning Green Paper will have been truly far-reaching in their impact. A comparison of the key provisions in the Planning Green Paper against the five fundamental principles outlined in Chapters 11 to 15 indicates that in principle (if not yet in detail) much of the new agenda espoused by government will take forward the key recommendations emanating from this book (see Table 16.3). To conclude, however, it is instructive to briefly examine four key responses to the consultation exercise held on the Planning Green Paper, representing the views of planners, private housebuilders, RSLs and amenity interests.

The first three of these constituents (the main subjects of this book) were largely positive about the changes, although each with their own reservations (see Fig. 16.6). The RTPI (2002, paras 12–14), for example, argued that:

> Government has wrestled with the shortcomings of the development plan system since the 1991 Planning and Compensation Act introduced the 'plan-led' system. Over this period, the Institute has argued consistently that the changes that can be achieved on the margin, without resort to new primary legislation, are insufficient to make any real impact. . . . The radical changes proposed in the Green Paper clearly recognise this. . . . In contrast, the Green Paper's proposals for the reform of development control, and the processing of planning applications, are less than radical, and represent a missed opportunity.

For the RTPI the restatement of the importance of planning and renewed faith in a plan-led system were important, although for them and the HBF, the constant review proposed for the new forms of plans and three year anticipated life spans would not offer the certainty required for development. Perhaps responding to the criticisms, these latter proposals were dropped in the subsequent Planning Policy Statement in favour of a flexible system of review and updating as necessary (ODPM, 2002a, para. 35).

The HBF (2002d, para. 1) commented 'The recognition by Government of the need for reform of the planning system is welcome, as is the shared commitment to bring greater simplicity, speed, predictability and customer focus to the system.' They, in common with the RTPI and CPRE supported the maintenance of some form of subregional planning, in their case to ensure that adequate allocations were made at the district scale, and argued strongly in favour of measures to streamline development

Table 16.3 Routes to better practice and the Planning Green Paper compared

	Identified problems (including page numbers)	Government's Planning Green Paper Response (2001) (including page numbers)
Strive to streamline implementation processes	▶ Planning delays make businesses uncompetitive (3) ▶ The preparation of plans is slow and expensive (12) ▶ High proportion of authorities failing to turn around applications in required time (3) ▶ Speed of decision-making varies greatly between planning authorities, making the time required to determine decisions unclear (4) ▶ There is a lack of speed in dealing with appeals and call-ins (4)	▶ **Delegation** of 90 per cent of decisions to planning officers (58) ▶ **Handling targets** for authorities, making distinction between business and householder applications (29) ▶ **Delivery contracts** between authorities and business for biggest applications (30); business waiving right of appeal against non-determination in return for contract date (36) ▶ LDFs to be prepared in 'months rather than years' (16) ▶ Move away from Local **Public Inquiries** towards wider public participation, or examination before independent chair or public informal hearings ▶ Introduce **planning checklist** for applications (29) and tighter targets handled under Best Value (33) ▶ Support **pre-application discussions** and allow LPAs to charge for this 'service' (32) ▶ **Review Fee regime** as a means of funding planning authorities (56) and look at resourcing in 2002 Spending Review ▶ Applications missing determination target to be moved to immediate fast-track (36) ▶ **Master planning** viewed as a mechanism to speed up development (39) ▶ Reduce number of **statutory consultees** and set time limit for response (37) ▶ Allow consultations prior to application (37) ▶ Establish statutory time targets for call-ins (54) ▶ Contract out **applications** to private sector planners (59) ▶ 'Intervene decisively' in failing LPAs and transfer planning powers elsewhere (60)
Adopt inclusive planning and decision-making processes	▶ 'Planning is remote, hard to understand and difficult to access' (3) ▶ Communities feel detached from the planning process (3). It fails to engage communities, and others, because of protracted processes that people 'give up' on, because decisions are sometimes made without 'the applicant or significant objectors having the opportunity to present their case', and because legalistic procedures are socially exclusive.	▶ LDFs to have stronger element of community participation, including **Statement of Community Participation** (14/17); compliance to statement will be a material consideration on larger developments (17) ▶ Greater input into **Action Plans**, around which involvement will be focused (17) ▶ LPAs to work with **Local Strategic Partnerships** to establish mechanisms for involvement (17) ▶ Offer community groups advice on planning issues (30) and further support for the **Planning Aid Network** (45) ▶ Create opportunities for communities to engage prior to applications in line with Statements of Community Involvement (43) ▶ Keep communities informed using e-planning (43) ▶ Planning Committees discussing applications to be held in public (45) and Best Value Inspectors to view closed meetings of this type as contrary to principles of Best Value.

Table 16.3 continued

Adopt integrated and realistic working practices	▲ Different levels of planning (regional, county and local) are inconsistent with one another (3) ▲ Inconsistencies in national guidance	▲ **LDFs** to contain statement on how they take account of other policy areas (14) ▲ Possibility of authorities **preparing joint LDFs** (16) ▲ Continuous updating of LDFs to ensure that they are consistent with national policy and regional policy (16/18) ▲ **Abolition of Structure Plans** (16/20) ▲ Integrated appraisal of LDFs covering economic, environmental and social impacts (17) ▲ New **Regional Spatial Strategies** (21) with statutory status: LDFs to be consistent with RSSs – a requirement to be set out in PPG11 ▲ **Refocus national guidance**, but make it less prescriptive and more aware of local circumstances (25)
Strive for certainty and transparency	▲ National guidance is unfocused (3) ▲ Planning guidance applying to different types of development is unclear (3) ▲ The appeal system is obscure, difficult to understand and unclear (3) ▲ Criteria against which applications are judged are uncertain (4) ▲ Time to deliver decisions is uncertain (4) ▲ The plan adoption process is complex and obscure (12)	▲ Move to clear **criteria-based policies** in LDFs (14) ▲ Clarify national policy and distinguish from advice (27) ▲ Tougher enforcement against those flouting regulations (30) ▲ **Planning advice for community groups** (to clarify processes/policies) (30) ▲ Increase transparency by allowing applicants to 'track' applications, possibly with the use of e-planning (32) ▲ **'One-stop-shop'** for applications and standardised application procedures (33) ▲ GPDO and Use Classes thought to add complexity to system: to be subject to simplification (42) ▲ Reasons to be given as to why applications are approved (42) ▲ LPAs to provide open access to planning papers (plans, committee reports and planning applications) but allowed to charge for hard-copies (45) ▲ Proposed changes to planning obligations and movement to system of tariffs (46) ▲ **Reject Third Party Rights of Appeal** (55) on the grounds that it would heighten uncertainty: instead strengthen community involvement ▲ LPAs to keep closer accounting on planning expenditure (58)
Adopt a positive and proactive approach to planning and development	▲ Planning is under-skilled ▲ Planning lacks a strategic focus (5) ▲ Local plans, in their current form, are too inflexible (12)	▲ Continuous review of core LDF policies (18) and annual review of Action Plans (19) ▲ LDF to 'steer development and use growth to define the vision for their areas' (5/12) ▲ Action Plans for town centres, neighbourhoods and villages: could take the form of **Area Master Plans or Design Statements** (15) ▲ Clear strategy for defining LDF objectives (14) ▲ **Promotion of master planning** to improve quality of development (30): master plans also to be used to ensure that concepts are translated into reality (39) ▲ **Simplify CPO powers** for land assembly (41) ▲ **Re-skill planning** to create a 'confident and dynamic profession' (59)

Royal Town Planning Institute

➤ The purpose and duty of planning should be defined, with a statutory duty on local authorities for its delivery
➤ Exactly what constitutes the statutory plan should be clarified
➤ LDFs should have a geographic basis on an OS map base
➤ Continuous review of policies needs to be squared with rigorous testing and certainty
➤ Greater community involvement and speed of decision-making conflict
➤ The radical changes to plan making are supported, but the changes to development control are regarded as a missed opportunity
➤ The time taken to plan is the price paid for democratic accountability and inclusivity
➤ Lack of skills and resources is the fundamental problem facing planning
➤ A clear relationship between the Community Strategy and LDF is fundamental and will enhance planning
➤ Speed does not necessarily follow from brevity
➤ The LDF should not be restricted to the narrow confines of land use planning
➤ Abandoning supplementary planning guidance in favour of action plans is supported
➤ Action plans dealing with new housing allocations are likely to be subject to considerable public opposition, and thus delay
➤ Three-yearly review of LDFs is too short
➤ Subregional planning is still required, to balance housing numbers across districts, and to integrate planning and transport policy
➤ Pre-applications discussions should not be mandatory
➤ Decision-making targets relate poorly to the actual quality of the service
➤ Delivery contracts are unlikely to be robust and suggest a two-tier system of development control
➤ Certificates do not add value over outline planning permissions
➤ Third party rights of appeal are not supported

House Builders Federation

➤ A plan-led system is still required, with the statutory planning consisting of the Regional Spatial Strategy and LDF
➤ Plans should be map-based
➤ Action plans should be produced concurrently with the LDF within enforceable timescales
➤ Greater public involvement would be valuable, but may lead to delays
➤ Regular review of policy may undermine certainty
➤ Subregional planning is required to bridge the gap between the LDF and regional strategy
➤ Clear arrangements need to be made for distributing housing provision to the districts
➤ Guidance notes on implementation must be issued at the same time as new national guidance to avoid delay
➤ Planning needs to be adequately resourced and skilled and made more efficient
➤ Planning should be viewed in authorities as a positive force for change
➤ The use of project champions and timetables for decision-making on large projects with appropriate sanctions is supported
➤ Delivery contracts should not be required but could be used if locally supported
➤ Statements agreed between applicant and authority should record pre-application discussions
➤ Developers should seek to personally brief councillors
➤ Masterplanning for large development is supported, involving authority and developers
➤ Outline permissions should be retained as they give the confidence to proceed
➤ Limiting consents to three years is opposed
➤ Increased use of mediation is the best way to resolve disputes
➤ Development tariffs are opposed

National Housing Federation

➤ Simpler statements of core policies supplemented by action plans are supported
➤ The LDF should be supported by a district-wide map base
➤ LDFs will need to move beyond community strategies, including providing for unpopular developments
➤ Affordable housing action plans may be useful
➤ Greater consultation is desirable, but takes time and is essential
➤ Attempts to speed up the system should not be at the expense of the time taken to negotiate on-site affordable housing
➤ Masterplanning is supported
➤ Limiting consents to three years is opposed
➤ Planning is under-resourced and under-skilled
➤ The system of tariffs is supported as effectively a reintroduction of a betterment tax. Identifying such liabilities early will ensure they are paid for by landowners rather than developers
➤ Tariffs will require planning staff to understand the financial aspects of development proposals
➤ Too much discretion to authorities in setting tariffs may undermine the provision of social housing
➤ The delivery of affordable homes should be the primary aim of the tariff system
➤ Sites for affordable housing should be identified

Council for the Protection of Rural England

➤ Reforms should develop the existing system, not reinvent the wheel
➤ The purpose of planning should be clearly recognised, incorporating community involvement, 'plan, monitor and manage' and environmental sustainability
➤ Business caricatures of a slow and inefficient system should be rejected
➤ More resources are required for good planning
➤ Abolition of the county tier would leave strategic gaps in policy that regional policy could not fill
➤ It would also undermine integration with transport and waste planning
➤ LDFs need to be statutory, geographically comprehensive, map-based, and detailed enough to deliver a plan-led approach
➤ Third parties should have the right to appeal in cases that breach planning policy
➤ Planning gain should be transparent and accountable
➤ Tariffs for development might undermine sustainable development by giving an incentive for greenfield development

16.6 2001 Planning Green Paper responses – key issues for housing.

control. However, in contrast to the NHF, they strongly rejected the notion of a tariff-based system of planning obligations. The widespread support for subregional planning was accepted by government through proposals that subregional issues should be more fully integrated into the regional strategy-making process, with provision for county councils to act as agents to regional planning bodies in this regard (ODPM, 2002a, para. 31).

For their part, the NHF (2002a, p. 3) in their capacity representing RSLs, argued strongly in favour of an explicit tariff-based system to planning obligations:

The National Housing Federation welcomes the continued emphasis on provision of affordable housing through the planning system. The basis for our

support for the proposals is that affordable housing is provided within the standard tariff, and furthermore that the anticipated 'large proportion' of tariff levied
(para. 4.19) will be used for additional provision of affordable housing where
there is a need for it.

They also expressed a concern that a greater emphasis on speed might undermine
the delivery of affordable housing, which inevitably takes time to negotiate (NHF, 2002b,
p. 5).

Significantly, the NHF, alongside the HBF and RTPI, strongly endorsed the proposed
changes to plan making, including the new hierarchy of policy and removal of the county
tier. The final respondent examined here – the CPRE, representing the amenity lobby –
argued equally strongly in favour of retaining the established system of development
plans, for two tiers of plan making under the regional level, and – in stark contrast to the
other respondents – in favour of third party rights of appeal against planning decisions.
The CPRE (2002, pp. 2–4) argued that: 'Planning is the unsung hero of environmental
protection, economic prosperity and quality of life. . . . Reforms should develop and
improve the existing system, and resist the temptation to reinvent the wheel. . . . We urge
the Government to reconsider its proposals.' For the CPRE, the proposals seemed to
reflect business interests much more than amenity and community interests, whilst the
proposals threatened rather than reinforced the position of third parties by attempting
to streamline the policy and development control processes, effectively cutting out
opportunities to influence proposals. The CPRE and other amenity interests were less
successful in making their case and third party right of appeal in particular remains a
distant prospect.

Nevertheless, all parties agreed on:

- the very obvious conflict that existed at the heart of the proposals between a desire
  for greater community involvement in planning, and the objective to streamline the
  system;
- that there was a clear need for a district-wide spatial expression of policy in
  geographic terms, in order that housing allocations at the regional level could be
  interpreted on the ground;
- the need for more resources for planning (whatever shape the new system took), if
  planning was to deliver on its potential;
- the value of the plan-led system, to increase certainty and to provide a basis to
  reconcile their often conflicting objectives.

Clearly, planning in England, and in different ways in the rest of the UK has reached
a crossroads. It appears that the changes, arguably the most radical for over fifty years,
have the broad support of many key planning and housing interests, even if, as yet, many
amenity interests remain sceptical. The next few years will represent a nationwide
experiment, but will also build upon a solid basis of what the planning system has been
able to achieve over the preceding fifty years, often on shoestring resources.

The principles and processes outlined in this book apply equally to the system as
constituted prior to legislation in 2003, as to the changes that are now being implemented. Nowhere is it more important that such processes are adopted than in the
delivery of new homes in order to meet society's most basic need, the need for shelter.
Coming back to the three fundamentals that structured discussion in Chapter 1 – quality,
quantity and location – that means enough well-designed housing, in the right places to

support our complex social, economic and environmental needs. This represents the everyday, yet incredibly and increasingly complex domain of planning. The research discussed in this book reveals that on all fronts those engaged in the process of delivering new homes still have a long way to go. It also revealed considerable scope for optimism that, given the resources, shared understanding and determination, planners and housing providers will increasingly rise to meet the challenge.

References

Adam R. (1997) 'The Consumer, the Developer, the Architect and the Planner: Whose Design is Good?' paper given to the Good Design in Speculative Housing Seminar, Royal Fine Art Commission, London.

Adams D. (1994) *Urban Planning and the Development Process*, London, UCL Press.

Adams D., Disberry B., Hutchison N. and Munjoma, T. (2002) 'Brownfield Land: Owner Characteristics, Attitudes and Networks', in Rydin Y. and Thornley A. (Eds) *Planning in the UK: Agendas for the New Millennium*, Aldershot, Ashgate.

Adler M. and Asquith S. (Eds) (1981) *Discretion and Welfare*, London, Heinemann.

Alexander C. (1965) 'A City is Not a Tree', *Architectural Forum*, **122**, 1, 58–62 and 2, 58–61.

Allen C., Gallent N. and Wong C. (2002) 'Late Modernity and the Sustainability of Local Housing Strategies: Evidence from the North West of England' (unpublished paper).

Ambrose P. (1986) *Whatever Happened to Planning?* London, Methuen.

Andrews L., Townsend M. and Reardon-Smith W. (2002) *But Will We Want to Live There? Planning for People and Neighbourhoods in 2020*, www.women2020.com.

Anon. (1996) 'HBF to Draw Up Hit-List of Tardy Councils', *Planning Week*, **4**, 30, 6.

Anon. (1998a) 'Britain's Best Selling Homes', *Building Housing Supplement*, 18 March, 12–14.

Anon. (1998b) 'Planning and Affordable Housing', *Housing and Planning Review*, **53**, 2, 3.

Anon. (2001a) 'Democracy Takes Longer', *Building Design*, 1510, 16 November, 7.

Anon. (2001b) 'The DTLR Has Confirmed', *Planning*, 1447, 30 November, 3.

Anon. (2001c) 'Haslam Says New Housing Can Fall Victim to Dissent', *Planning*, 1427, 13 July, 1.

Arnstein S. (1969) 'A Ladder of Citizen Participation', *American Institute of Planners Journal*, July, 216–24.

Arup Economics and Planning (2000) *Survey of Urban Design Skills in Local Government*, London, DETR.

Audit Commission (1992) *Building in Quality: A Study of Development Control*, London, HMSO.

Audit Commission (1998) *Building in Quality: A Review of Progress on Development Control*, London, Audit Commission Publications.

Audit Commission (1999) *A Life's Work*, London, Audit Commission Publications.

Baeten G. (2001) 'Urban Regeneration, Social Exclusion and Shifting Power Geometries on the South Bank, London', *Geographische Zeitschrift*, **89**, 2–3, 104–13.

Balchin, P. and Rhoden M. (2001) *Housing Policy: An Introduction*, London, Routledge.

Ball M. (1999) 'Chasing the Snail: Innovation and Housebuilding Firms' Strategies', *Housing Studies*, **14**, 1, 9–22.

Banham R., Barker P., Hall P. and Price C. (1969) 'Non-Plan: An Experiment in Freedom', *New Society*, 20 March, 435–43.

Barlow J. (1997) *Towards Positive Partnering*, Bristol, The Policy Press.

Barlow J., Bartlett K., Hooper A. and Whitehead C. (2002) *Land for Housing: Current Practice and Future Options*, York, York Publishing.

Barlow J. and Chambers D. (1992) *Planning Agreements and Affordable Housing*, Brighton, University of Sussex, Centre for Urban and Regional Research.

Barlow J., Cocks R. and Parker M. (1994) *Planning for Affordable Housing*, London, DoE.

Baron T. (1983) 'The Challenge for the UK Housing Industry in the 1980s and the Planning System', *Construction Management and Economics*, **1**, 1, 17–29.

Barrett H. and Phillips J. (1993) *Suburban Style: The British Home 1840–1960*, London, Little, Brown and Company.

Barrett S., Stewart M. and Underwood J. (1978) *The Land Market and the Development Process: A Review of Research and Policy*, Occasional Paper No. 2, School for Advanced Urban Studies, Bristol, University of Bristol.

Bateman A. (1995) 'Planning in the 1990's – A Developer's Perspective', Report for the Natural and Built Environment No.1 (Ambit Publications), February, 26–9.

Bauman Z. (1991) *Modernity and Ambivalence*, Cambridge, Polity.

Beer A. and Booth P. (1981) *Development Control and Design Quality*, Five Reports, Sheffield, Sheffield Centre for Environmental Research.

Berry F. (1974) *Housing: The Great British Failure*, London, C. Knight.

Birchall J. (Ed.) (1992) *Housing Policy in the 1990s*, London, Routledge.

Birkbeck D. (1999) 'Top 50 Housebuilders', *Building Homes*, 65, May, 20–2.

Birmingham City Council (2000) *Building a Better Birmingham: A Charter for Development*, Birmingham, Birmingham City Council.

Bishop Associates (2001) *Delivering Affordable Housing Through the Planning System*, London, RICS and the Housing Corporation.

Bishop J. and Davison I. (1989) *Good Product; Could the Service be Better?* London, The Housing Research Foundation.

Bishop K. and Hooper A. (1991) *Planning for Social Housing*, London, National Housing Forum.

Black J. (1997) 'Quality in Development, by Design or Process?', *TCPSS Proceedings*, 1997, London, RTPI, 80–2.

Boddy M. (1981) 'The Property Sector in Late Capitalism: The Case of Britain', in Dear M. and Scott A., *Urbanization and Urban Planning in Capitalist Society*, London, Methuen, 267–86.

Booth P. (1982) 'Housing as a Product: Design Guidance and Residential Satisfaction in the Private Sector', *Built Environment*, **8**, 1, 20–4.

Booth P. (1995) 'Zoning or Discretionary Action – Certainty and Responsiveness in Implementing Planning Policy', *Journal of Planning Education and Research*, **14**, 2, 103–12.

Booth P. (1996) *Controlling Development: Certainty and Discretion in Europe, the USA and Hong Kong*, London, UCL Press.

Boyfield K. (2001) 'The Housing Morass: A Public Policy Response', in Boyfield K. and Mather G. (Eds), *Britain's Unsolved Housing Dilemma*, London, European Policy Forum, pp. 74–92.

Boyfield K. and Mather G. (Eds) (2001) *Britain's Unsolved Housing Dilemma*, London, European Policy Forum.

Bramley G., Bartlett W. and Lambert C. (1995) *Planning, the Market and Private Housebuilding*, London, UCL Press.

Bramley G. and Watkins C. (1996) *Steering the Housing Market: New House Building and the Changing Planning System*, Bristol, The Policy Press.

Breheny M. (Ed.) (1999) *The People: Where Will They Work?*, London, Town and Country Planning Association.

Breheny M. and Hall P. (Eds) (1996) *The People: Where Will They Go?*, London, Town and Country Planning Association.

Breheny M. and Ross A. (1998a) *Urban Housing Capacity: What Can Be Done?*, London, Town and Country Planning Association.

Breheny M. and Ross A. (1998b) 'Providing More Housing in Urban Areas – What Can Be Done?', *Town and Country Planning*, **67**, 4, 138–40.

Brindley T., Rydin Y. and Stoker G. (1996) *Remaking Planning: The Politics of Urban Change*, 2nd edn, London, Routledge.

Brown C. and Dühr S. (2002) 'Understanding Sustainability and Planning in England: An Exploration of the Sustainability Content of Planning Policy at the National, Regional and Local Levels', in Rydin Y. and Thornley A. (Eds) *Planning in the UK: Agendas for the New Millennium*, Aldershot, Ashgate.

Cadell C., Falk N., Carmona M. and Hall P. (2000) *Living Places: Urban Renaissance in the South East*, London, Government Office for the South East/DETR.

Cadman D. and Topping R. (1998) *Property Development*, 4th edn, London, E. and FN Spon.

Cambridge Econometrics (1995) *Housing Market Report*, London, HBF.

Cambridge University Centre for Planning and Research (2002) *Fiscal Policy Instruments to Promote Affordable Housing*, Cambridge, Cambridge University.

Campbell H., Ellis H., Gladwell C. and Henneberry J. (1999a) *Planning Obligations: The Views of Planning, Development and Third Party Organisations*, Working Paper 1, Planning Gain Series, University of Sheffield, Department of Town and Regional Planning.

Campbell H., Ellis H., Gladwell C. and Henneberry J. (1999b) *Planning Obligations: A Survey of Local Authority Policy and Practice*, Working Paper 2, Planning Gain Series, University of Sheffield, Department of Town and Regional Planning.

Campbell H., Ellis H., Gladwell C. and Henneberry J. (1999c) *Planning Obligations: A Local Authority Perspective*, Working Paper 3, Planning Gain Series, University of Sheffield, Department of Town and Regional Planning.

Campbell H., Ellis H., Henneberry J., Poxon J., Rowley S., and Gladwell C. (2001) *Planning Obligations and the Mediation of Development*, RICS Foundation Research Papers, London, RICS Foundation.

Carmona M. (2001a) 'Implementing Urban Renaissance – Problems, Possibilities and Plans in South East England', *Progress in Planning*, 56, 4, 169–250.

Carmona M. (2001b) *Housing Design Quality, through Policy, Guidance and Review*, London, Spon Press.

Carmona M., Carmona S. and Gallent N. (2001) *Working Together: A Guide for Planners and Housing Providers*, London, Thomas Telford Publishers.

Carmona M., Heath T., Oc T. and Teisdell S. (2003) *Public Places – Urban Spaces*, Oxford, The Architectural Press.

Carmona M., Punter J. and Chapman D. (2002) *From Design Policy to Design Quality: The Treatment of Design in Community Strategies, Local Development Frameworks and Action Plans*, (RTPI), London, Thomas Telford Publishing.

Carter H. and Lewis C. R. (1990) *An Urban Geography of England and Wales in the Nineteenth Century*, London, Edward Arnold.

Case Scheer B. and Preiser W. (Eds) (1994) *Design Review: Challenging Urban Aesthetic Control*, New York, Chapman and Hall.

Centre for Economic and Business Research (2002) *Housing Futures 2012*, London, CEBR.

Chadwick Edwin, Sir (1842) *Report to Her Majesty's Principal Secretary of State for the Home Department, from the Poor Law Commissioners: On an Inquiry into the Sanitary Condition of the Labouring Population of Great Britain*, London, W. Clowes and Sons.

Cherry G. (1974) *The Evolution of British Town Planning*, Leighton Buzzard, Leonard Hill Books.

Chestertons (2001) *Urban Capacity Study for Stevenage*, May 2001, London, Chestertons.

Christie I., Walker P. and Warburton D. (2002) *Putting the Community at the Heart of Development*, Reading, Green Issues Communications.

Citizen's Charter (1992) *First Report*, London, HMSO.

Civic Trust Regeneration Unit (1999) *Brownfield Housing – 12 Years On*, London, Civic Trust.

Cloke P. J. (1979) *Key Settlements in Rural Areas*, London, Methuen.

Cohen Committee (1971) *Housing Associations*, London, HMSO.

Cole I. and Furbey R. (1994) *The Eclipse of Council Housing*, London, Routledge.

Commission for Architecture and the Built Environment (2001) *Design and Planning: CABE States the Case for Reform*, London, CABE.

Commission for Architecture and the Built Environment (2002) 'Bungalows are Still People's Choice According to MORI Poll', CABE Press Release, 25 June, London, CABE.

Committee on Public Participation in Planning (1969) *People and Plans: Report of the Committee on Public Participation in Planning*, London, HMSO.

Committee on Standards in Public Life (The Nolan Committee) (1997) *Third Report of the Committee on Standards in Public Life: Standards of Conduct in Local Government*, London, The Stationery Office.

Confederation of British Industry (2001) *Planning for Productivity: A Ten-Point Action Plan*, London, CBI.

Cope H. (1999) *Housing Associations: Policy and Practice*, Basingstoke, Macmillan.

Couch C. (1986) *MSc Report: What's Happening to the Local Housebuilder*, Bartlett School of Architecture and Planning, London, University College London.

Council for the Protection of Rural England (2000) *PPG3 – Housing: A CPRE Briefing*, London, CPRE.

Council for the Protection of Rural England (2001a) *Breaking the Inertia*, London, CPRE.

Council for the Protection of Rural England (2001b) *Sprawl Control – First Year Report*, London, CPRE.

Council for the Protection of Rural England (2001c) *Greenfield Housing*, London, CPRE.

Council for the Protection of Rural England (2002) *Planning to Improve*, London, CPRE.

Countryside Commission (1996a) *Village Design – Making Local Character Count in New Development – Part 1*, Cheltenham, Countryside Agency.

Countryside Commission (1996b) *Village Design – Making Local Character Count in New Development – Part 2*, Cheltenham, Countryside Agency.

Cowan R. (1999) 'The Role of Planning in Local Government', *Planning*, 1313, 9 April, 20.

Cowan R. (2002) 'Planning Matters', *Planning*, 1480, 2 August, 11.

Cronin A. (1993) 'The Elusive Quality of Certainty', *Planning Week*, 1, 4, 16–17.

Crook A., Jackson A., Rowley S., Whitehead C., Monk S., Curry J. and Smith K. (2001) *The Provision of Affordable Housing through the Planning System*, Cambridge, Universities of Sheffield and Cambridge.

Crow S., Harris N., Thomas H. and Yewlett C. (2000) *Fitness for Purpose: Quality on Development Plans*, London, RTPI.

Cullingworth B. (1996) 'A Vision Lost', *Town and Country Planning*, **65**, 6, 172–4.

Cullingworth B. (1997a) 'Fifty Years of the 1947 Act', *Town and Country Planning*, **66**, 5, 130.

Cullingworth B. (1997b) 'British Land-use Planning: A Failure to Cope with Change?', *Urban Studies*, **34**, 5–6, 945–60.

Cullingworth B. (1999) *British Planning: 50 Years of Urban and Regional Policy*, London, The Athlone Press.

Cullingworth B. and Nadin V. (1997) *Town and Country Planning in the UK*, 11th edn, London, Routledge.

Cullingworth B. and Nadin V. (2002) *Town and Country Planning in the UK*, 13th edn, London, Routledge.

Daly G. P. (1996) *Homeless: Policies, Strategies, and Lives on the Street*, London, Routledge.

Davison I. (1987a) 'Volume Housing, 1: Rules of the Game', *Architects' Journal*, 2 September, 63–7.

Davison I. (1987b) 'Volume Housing, 2: Urban Designs', *Architects' Journal*, 9 September, 59–65.

Davison I. (1989) 'Designs on Customers', *House Builder*, February, 38–44.

Davison I. (1991) 'Land Values, Part of the Design Equation', *Housebuilder*, March, 38–44.

Day J. (1996) 'Measuring Quality in Development Control', unpublished MA dissertation, University of Nottingham, Nottingham.

Delafons J. (2000) 'The Great Housing Crisis', *Town and Country Planning*, **69**, 1, 35.

DEMOS (1999) *Living Together: Community Life on Mixed Tenure Estates*, London, DEMOS.

Department of the Environment (1975) *Review of the Development Control System*, Final Report, London, HMSO.

Department of the Environment (1980) *Circular 22/80: Development Control – Policy and Practice*, London, HMSO.

Department of the Environment (1983) *Circular 22/83: Town and Country Planning Act 1971: Planning Gain*, London, DoE.

Department of the Environment (1984) *Circular 15/84: Land for Housing*, London, DoE.

Department of the Environment (1985) *Circular 1/85: The Use of Conditions in Planning Permissions*, London, DoE.

Department of the Environment (1987) *Housing: The Government's Proposals*, London, DoE.

Department of the Environment (1988) *Planning Policy Guidance Note 3: Land for Housing*, London, DoE.

Department of the Environment (1989) *Planning Policy Guidance Note 3 (Redraft): Housing*, London, DoE.

Department of the Environment (1991) *Circular 7/91: Planning and Affordable Housing*, London, DoE.

Department of the Environment (1992a) *Planning Policy Guidance (PPG3): Housing*, London, HMSO.

Department of the Environment (1992b) *Development Plans: A Good Practice Guide*, London, HMSO.

Department of the Environment (1994) *Quality in Town and Country*, London, DoE.

Department of the Environment (1995a) *Our Future Homes: Opportunity, Choice, Responsibility*, London, DoE.

Department of the Environment (1995b) *Circular 11/95: The Use of Conditions in Planning Permissions*, London, DoE.

Department of the Environment (1996a) *Circular 13/96: Planning and Affordable Housing*, London, DoE.

Department of the Environment (1996b) *Analysis of Responses to the Discussion Document 'Quality in Town and Country'*, London, HMSO.

Department of the Environment (1997a) *Planning Policy Guidance (PPG1): General Policy and Principles*, London, The Stationery Office.

Department of the Environment (1997b) *Circular 1/97: Planning Obligations*, London, The Stationery Office.

Department of the Environment (n.d.) *Development Plans: What You Need to Know*, London, DoE.

Department of the Environment and Department of Transport (1992) *Design Bulletin 32: Residential Roads and Footpaths: Layout Considerations*, 2nd edn, London, HMSO.

Department of the Environment and Housing Research Foundation (HRF) (1976) *Design Guidance Survey*, London, DoE.

Department of the Environment, Transport and the Regions (1997) *Circular 13/96 (Re-draft) Planning and Affordable Housing*, London, DETR.

Department of the Environment, Transport and the Regions (1998a) *Planning for the Communities of the Future*, London, The Stationery Office.

Department of the Environment, Transport and the Regions (1998b) *English House Conditions Survey 1996*, London, The Stationery Office.

Department of the Environment, Transport and the Regions (1998c) *Circular 6/98: Planning and Affordable Housing*, London, DETR.

Department of the Environment, Transport and the Regions (1998d) *Places, Streets and Movement: A Companion Guide to Design Bulletin 32 Residential Roads and Footpaths*, London, DETR.

Department of the Environment, Transport and the Regions (1998e) *Planning for Sustainable Development: Towards Better Practice*, London, The Stationery Office.

Department of the Environment, Transport and the Regions (1998f) *The Use of Density in Urban Planning*, London, DETR.

Department of the Environment, Transport and the Regions (1998g) *Modern Local Government, in Touch with the People*, London, DETR.

Department of the Environment, Transport and the Regions (1998h) *Rethinking Construction*, London, The Stationery Office.

Department of the Environment, Transport and the Regions (1998i) *Planning and Development Briefs: A Guide to Better Practice*, London, DETR.

Department of the Environment, Transport and the Regions (1999) *Projections of Households in England to 2021*, London, DETR.

Department of the Environment, Transport and the Regions (2000a) *Planning Policy Guidance Note 3: Housing*, London, DETR.

Department of the Environment, Transport and the Regions (2000b) *North West Housing Need and Demand Research*, London, DETR.

Department of the Environment, Transport and the Regions (2000c) *Quality and Choice: Decent Homes for All*, London, DETR.

Department of the Environment, Transport and the Regions (2000d) *Our Town and Cities: The Future, Delivering an Urban Renaissance*, London, DETR.

Department of the Environment, Transport and the Regions (2000e) *Best Value Performance Indicators 2001/2002*, London, DETR.

Department of the Environment, Transport and the Regions (2000f) *Development Control Statistics, 1999–2000*, London, DETR.

Department of the Environment, Transport and the Regions (2000g) *Millennium Villages and Sustainable Communities*, London, DETR.

Department of the Environment, Transport and the Regions (2000h) *Preparing Community Strategies: Government Guidance to Local Authorities*, London, DETR.

Department of the Environment, Transport and the Regions (2000i) *Mediation in the Planning System*, London, DETR.

Department of the Environment, Transport and the Regions (2000j) *Tapping the Potential, Assessing Urban Housing Capacity: Towards Better Practice*, London, DETR.

Department of the Environment, Transport and the Regions (2000k) *Planning Policy Guidance 12: Development Plans*, London, DETR.

Department of the Environment, Transport and the Regions (2001) *Design for Living – Falconer*, News Release 385, 11 September, London, DTLR.

Department of the Environment, Transport and the Regions and CABE (2000) *By Design. Urban Design in the Planning System: Towards Better Practice*, London, Thomas Telford Publishing.

Department of the Environment, Transport and the Regions and Housing Corporation (1999) *Housing Quality Indicators*, London, DETR.

Department for Transport, Local Government and the Regions (2001a) *Planning: Delivering a Fundamental Change*, London, DTLR.

Department for Transport, Local Government and the Regions (2001b) *Housing in England 1999–2000*, London, National Centre for Social Research (for DTLR).

Department for Transport, Local Government and the Regions (2001c) *Housing Statistics 2001*, London, DTLR.

Department for Transport, Local Government and the Regions (2001d) *Planning to Deliver: The Managed Release of Housing Sites: Towards Better Practice*, London, DTLR.

Department for Transport, Local Government and the Regions (2001e) *Strong Local Leadership – Quality Public Services*, London, DTLR.

Department for Transport, Local Government and the Regions (2001f) *Planning Obligations – Delivering a Fundamental Change*, London, DTLR.

Department for Transport, Local Government and the Regions (2002a) *Delivering Affordable Housing through Planning Policy*, London, DTLR.

Department for Transport, Local Government and the Regions (2002b) *Land Use Change in England: Residential Development to 2001*, London, DTLR.

Department for Transport, Local Government and the Regions (2002c) *Best Value Performance Indicators 2002/2003*, London, DTLR.

Department for Transport, Local Government and the Regions (2002d) *Resourcing of Local Planning Authorities*, London, DTLR.

Department for Transport, Local Government and the Regions and Commission for Architecture and the Built Environment (2001) *Better Places to Live, By Design: A Companion Guide to PPG3*, London, DETR.

Dewar D. (2001a) 'Show Me the Money', *Planning*, 1440, 12 October, 12.

Dewar D. (2001b) 'Targets are Missing the Point', *Planning*, 1439, 5 October, 14–15.

Dewar D. (2002a) 'Prescott's New Empire to Look after Planning', *Planning*, 14 June, 1473, 9.

Dewar D. (2002b) 'Figures Reveal a Nation Unable to House Itself', *Planning*, 13 May, 1467, 2.

Dewar D. (2002c) 'Planning Blamed for Housing Crisis', *Planning*, 1466, 26 April, 1.

Dewar D. (2002d) 'Increased Funding at a Price', *Planning*, 1479, 26 July, 8.

Drury A. (2000) *First Steps in Partnering: An Introductory Guide for Registered Social Landlords*, London, National Housing Federation.

Egan J. (1998) *Rethinking Construction: The Report of the Construction Task Force to the Deputy Prime Minister, John Prescott*, London, DETR.

Elcock H. (1994) *Local Government, Policy and Management in Local Authorities*, 3rd edn, London, Routledge.

English Heritage (2001) *Planning for the Historic Environment: A Study of Resources*, London, English Heritage.

Eppi M. and Tu C. (1999) *Valuing the New Urbanism: The Impact of New Urbanism on Prices of Single-Family Homes*, Washington, DC, Urban Land Institute.

European Commission (1998) *Housing Statistics in the European Union*, Brussels, European Commission.

Evans G., Lercher P., Meis M., Ising H. and Kofler W. (2001) 'Community Noise Exposure and Stress in Children', *Journal of the Accoustical Society of America*, **109**, 3, 1023–7.

Falconer C. (2001) *Design for Living* – Falconer, News Release 386, 11 September, London, DTLR.

Faludi A. and Waterhout B. (2002) *The Making of the European Spatial Development Perspective: No Masterplan*, London, Routledge.

Farthing S. and Ashley K. (2002) 'Negotiations and the Delivery of Affordable Housing through the Planning System', *Planning Practice and Research*, **17**, 1, 45–58.

Farthing S. and Winter J. (1988) *Residential Density and Levels of Satisfaction with the External Residential Environment, A Research Report on New Private Sector Housing Schemes in West Totton, Hampshire*, Bristol, Bristol Polytechnic.

Fisk M. (1997) *Home Truths: Issues for Housing in Wales*, Llandysul, Gomer Press.

Forrest R., Kennett T. and Leather P. (1997) *Home Owners on New Estates in the 1990s*, Bristol, The Policy Press.

Fraser R. (1991) *Working Together in the 1990s*, Coventry, Institute of Housing.

Freudenberg W. and Pastor S. (1992) 'NIMBYs and LULUs: Stalking the Syndromes', *Journal of Social Issues* **48**, 4, 39–61.

Friends of the Earth (1997) 'Friends of the Earth Slams Prescott's Decision to Sacrifice West Sussex Countryside to New Houses', Press Release, 8 December 1997.

Gallent N. (2000) 'Planning and Affordable Housing: From Old Values to New Labour', *Town Planning Review*, **71**, 2, 123–47.

Gallent N. (2002) *Memoranda to the Transport, Local Government and the Regions Select Committee on Affordable Housing*, London, Bartlett School of Planning.

Gallent N. and Bell P. (2000) 'Planning Exceptions in Rural England – Past, Present and Future', *Planning Practice and Research*, **15**, 4, 375–84.

Gallent N. and Kim K. S. (2001) 'Land Zoning and Local Discretion in the Korean Planning System', *Land Use Policy*, **18**, 3, 233–43.

Gallent N., Mace A. and Tewdwr-Jones M. (2002) *Policy Advice on Second Homes in Rural Areas*, London, Countryside Agency.

Geddes P. (1915) *Cities in Evolution: An Introduction to the Town Planning Movement and to the Study of Civics*, London, Williams and Norgate.

Giddens A. (1998) *The Third Way*, London, Polity.

Goodlad R. (1993) *The Housing Authority as Enabler*, Coventry, Chartered Institute of Housing.

Gore T. and Nicholson D. (1991) 'Models of the Land-Development Process: A Critical Review', *Environment and Planning A*, **3**, 705–30.

Goss S. and Blackaby B. (1998) *Designing Local Housing Strategies: A Good Practice Guide*, Coventry, Chartered Institute of Housing and the Local Government Association.

Greater London Authority (2001) *Spatial Development Strategy for London*, London, GLA.

Greater London Authority (2002a) *Future Housing Provision: Speeding Up Delivery (SDS Technical Report 2)*, London, GLA.

Greater London Authority (2002b) *The Draft London Plan*, London, GLA.

Green Balance (2002) *Third Party Rights of Appeal in Planning*, London, CPRE.

Guinness Trust Group (n.d.) *Planning and Architecture Guide*, High Wycombe, Guinness Trust Group.

Gummer J. (1995) DoE Press Release 162: 'The Way to Achieve "Quality" in Urban Design', 30 March, London, DoE.

Gummer J. (2002) 'Concreting Over the Countryside', *Planning*, 1469, 17 May, 9.

Gurney C. and Hines F. (1999) 'Rattle and Hum – Gendered Accounts of Noise as a Pollutant: An Aural Sociology of Work and Home', paper prepared for British Sociological Association 1999 Conference: For Sociology, University of Glasgow, 6–9 April.

Hall A. (1990) *Generation of Objectives for Design Control*, Chelmsford, Anglia Polytechnic Enterprises Ltd.

Hall P. (1992) *Urban and Regional Planning*, 3rd edn, London, Routledge.

Hall P. (1995) 'Planning and Urban Design in the 1990s', *Urban Design Quarterly*, **56**, 14–21.

Hall P. (2002) *Cities of Tomorrow: An Intellectual History of Urban Planning and Design in the Twentieth Century*, 3rd edn, Oxford, Blackwell.

Halton Borough Council (1999a) *Halton UDP Key Issues Report*, Halton Borough Council, Halton Lea, Runcorn.

Halton Borough Council (1999b) *Residential Land Availability Register*, Halton Borough Council, Halton Lea, Runcorn.

Halton Borough Council (1999c) *Site Appraisal Methodology Report*, Halton Borough Council, Halton Lea, Runcorn.

Hambleton R., Essex S., Mills L. and Razzaque K. (1996a) *Findings 44: Inter-Agency Working in Practice*, York, Joseph Rowntree Foundation.

Hambleton R., Essex S., Mills L. and Razzaque K. (1996b) *The Collaborative Council: A Study of Inter-Agency Working Practice*, York, LGC Communications.

Hambleton R., Essex S., Mills L. and Razzaque K. (1996c) *Findings Local and Central Government Relations Research 44: Inter-Agency Working in Practice*, York, Joseph Rowntree Foundation.

Hambleton R. and Sweeting D. (1999) 'Restructuring Our Decision Making', *Planning*, 11 November, 1344, 16–17.

Hamilton J. (1976) 'Alan Reason's Rationale for the Essex Design Guide', *House Builder*, **35**, September.

Hamnett C. (2001) 'London's Housing', *Area*, **33**, 1, 80–4.

Hanson J. (1999) *Decoding Homes and Houses*, Cambridge, Cambridge University Press.

Harris D. (1995) 'Council of Europe Seminar on Public Participation in Planning', *Planning Inspectorate Journal*, 1, Autumn.

Harvey D. (1985) *The Urbanization of Capital*, Oxford, Blackwell.

Harvey J. (1996) *Urban Land Economics*, London, Macmillan.

Healey P. (1991) 'Models of the Development Process: A Review', *Journal of Property Research*, **8**, 219–38.

Healey P. (1992) 'An Institutional Model of the Development Process', *Journal of Property Research*, **9**, 33–44.

Healey P., Purdue M. and Ennis F. (1993) *Gains from Planning? Dealing with the Impacts of Development*, York, Joseph Rowntree Foundation.

Hedges B. and Clemens S. (1994) *Housing Attitudes Survey*, London, HMSO.

Hellman L. (1995) 'Democratic Planning Process', *Building Design*, 1224, 9 June, 9.

Hellman L. (1996) 'Theory . . . Practice . . .', *Built Environment*, **22**, 4, 252.

Hertfordshire County Council (1998) *Examination in Public: Structure Plan – Pane Report*, Hertford, HCC.

Heseltine M. (1979) *Secretary of State's Address, Report of Proceedings of the Town and Country Planning Summer School 1979*, London, Royal Town Planning Institute, 25–9.

HM Government (2002) *Opportunity and Security for All: Investing in an Enterprising, Fairer Britain, New Public Spending Plans 2003–2006*, London, HM Treasury.

Hogg A. (1996) 'I'm Having Trouble Finding My Way Through this Housing Provision Debate', *Planning*, 6 December, 1198, 4.

Holmans A. E. (1970) 'A Forecast of Effective Demand for Housing in Great Britain in the 1970s', *Social Trends*, 42, 1.

Holmans A. E. (1987) *Housing Policy in Britain: A History*, London, Croom Helm.

Holmans A. E. (1995) *Housing Demand and Need in England 1996–2011*, York, Joseph Rowntree Foundation.

Holmans A. E. (1996) 'Housing Demand and Need in England to 2011: The National Picture', in Breheny M. and Hall P. (Eds) *The People: Where Will They Go?* London, Town and Country Planning Association.

Holmans A. E. (2001) 'Households and their Houses – New Estimates for England and the Regions', *Town and Country Planning*, **70**, 3, 85–7.

Holmans A. E., Morrison N. and Whitehead C. (1998) *How Many Homes Will We Need? The Need for Affordable Housing in England*, London, Shelter.

Hooper A. (1996) 'Housing Requirements and Housing Provision: The Strategic Issues', in Breheny M. and Hall P. (Eds) *The People: Where Will They Go?* London, Town and Country Planning Association.

Hooper A. (1999) *Design for Living: Constructing the Residential Built Environment in the 21st Century*, London, Town and Country Planning Association.

Hooper A. and Nicol C. (1999) 'The Design and Planning of Residential Development: Standard House Types in the Speculative Housebuilding Industry', *Environment and Planning B: Planning and Design*, **26**, 6, 793–805.

House Builders Federation (1999) *Urban Life: Breaking Down the Barriers to Brownfield Development*, London, HBF.

House Builders Federation (2002a) *Employment Survey*, London, HBF.

House Builders Federation (2002b) *Detailed Proposals for Planning Reform*, London, HBF.

House Builders Federation (2002c) Press Release: 'Building a Crisis – Britain's Housing Shortage', 1 May, London, HBF.

House Builders Federation (2002d) *Response of the House Builders Federation to the Planning Green Paper*, London, HBF.

House of Commons (2002) *Planning and Compulsory Purchase Bill*, *Explanatory Notes*, London, The Stationery Office.

Housing Corporation (1998) *F2–42/98 Planning Issues Relating to the Provision of Affordable Housing and Section 106 Contributions by Registered Social Landlords*, London, Housing Corporation.

Housing Corporation (1999) *Registered Social Landlords and Development Plans*, London, National Housing Federation.

Housing Corporation (2000) *Scheme Development Standards*, London, The Housing Corporation.

Housing Corporation (2002) *Capital Funding Guide 2002–2003*, London, Housing Corporation.

Housing Corporation and London Research Centre (2000) *Taking Stock for What we Know – a Statistical Assessment of Black and Minority Ethnic Housing Needs*, London, Housing Corporation.

Housing Forum (2000) *How to Survive Partnering – It Won't Bite!* London, The Housing Forum.

Hutton R. H. (1991) 'Local Needs Policy Initiatives in Rural Areas: Missing the Target?', *Journal of Environmental and Planning Law*, April, 303–11.

Jackson A., Monk S., Royce C. and Dunn J. (1994) *The Relationship Between Land Supply and Housing Production*, York, Joseph Rowntree Foundation.

Jenks M., Burton E. and Williams K. (1996) *The Compact City, A Sustainable Urban Form?* London, E. and FN Spon.

Johnson W. C. (1984) *Citizen Participation in Local Planning in the UK and USA: A Comparative Study*, Oxford, Pergamon.

Jones C. (2000) 'House Proud Winners', *Building Design*, 1450, 21 July, 2.

Joseph Rowntree Foundation (2001) *Findings N41: The Effectiveness of Planning Policies for Affordable Housing*, York, JRF.

Jowell J. (1977) 'Bargaining and Development Control', *Journal of Planning and Environmental Law*, 414–33.

Karn V. and Sheridan L. (1994) *New Homes in the 1990s: A Study of Design, Space and Amenities in Housing Association and Private Sector Housing*, York, Joseph Rowntree Foundation.

Karn V., Wong C., Gallent N. and Allen C. (1998) *Housing Needs in Bolton Borough*, Bolton, Bolton Metropolitan Borough Council.

Kemeny J. (1992) *Housing and Social Theory*, London, Routledge.

Kitchen T. (1997) *People, Politics, Policies and Plans: The City Planning Process in Contemporary Britain*, London, Paul Chapman Publishing.

Lang J. (1994) *Urban Design: The American Experience*, New York, Van Nostrand Reinhold.

Lees A. (1993) *Enquiry into the Planning System in North Cornwall District*, London, DoE.

Leopold E. and Bishop D. (1983) 'Design Philosophy and Practice in Speculative Housebuilding: Part 1', *Construction Management and Economics*, **1**, 2, Autumn, 119–44.

Levin P. H. and Donnison D. V. (1969) 'People and Planning', *Public Administration*, 13, 473–9.

Likierman A (1993) 'Performance Indicators: 20 Early Lessons from Managerial Use', *Public Money and Management*, **13**, 4, 15–21.

Linden Homes (n.d.) Caterham Barracks Planning Weekend, Linden Homes, Godstone, Surrey.

Littler S., Tewdwr-Jones M., Fisk M. and Essex S. (1994) 'Corporate Working for the Provision of Affordable Housing in Welsh District Authorities', Department of City and Regional Planning, Cardiff University (unpublished).

Llewelyn-Davies (1996) *Review of Urban Capacity Studies*, London, UK Round Table on Sustainable Development.

Llewelyn-Davies (1998a) *Sustainable Residential Quality: New Approaches to Urban Living*, London, LPAC, GOL and DETR.

Llewelyn-Davies (1998b) *Sustainable Residential Quality in the South East*, Guildford, GOSE.

Llewelyn-Davies (2000) *Sustainable Residential Quality: Exploring the Housing Potential of Large Sites*, London, London Planning Advisory Committee.

Local Government Association (2000) *The Planning User's Concordat*, London, LGA.

Local Government Association (2001) *Follow the Leaders: A Survey of Local Authority Approaches to Community Leadership*, London, LGA.

Local Government Association and Department of the Environment, Transport and the Regions (1999) *Planning Concordat*, London, LGA.

Local Government Association, National Housing Federation and Housing Corporation (2001) *A Framework for Partnership*, London, LGA.

London Housing Federation (2002) *Capital Gains: Making High Density Housing Work in London*, London, LHF.

Lowndes V., Stoker G., Pratchett L., Wilson D., Leach S. and Wingfield M. (1998) *Guidance on Enhancing Public Participation in Local Government*, London, Department of the Environment, Transport and the Regions.

Lyall S. (1985) 'From Rags to Riches', *A Building Supplement*, 22 March, 28–31.

Madden L. (1982) 'The Volume House-Builders', *Building*, 16 April, 26–33.

Malpass P. and Murie A. (1999) *Housing Policy and Practice*, Basingstoke, Macmillan.

Manns S. (2000) 'Deciding Who Decides', *Planning*, 1398, 8 December, 13.

Meen G. (1996) 'Ten Propositions in UK Housing Macroeconomics: An Overview of the 1980s and Early 1990s', *Urban Studies*, **33**, 3, 425–44.

Meen G., Gibb K., MacKay D. and White M. (2001) *The Economic Role of New Housing*, London, Housing Research Foundation.

Monk S. (1991) *Discussion Paper 31: The Speculative Housebuilder, A Review of Empirical Research*, Department of Land Economy, Cambridge, University of Cambridge.

Monk S. and Whitehead C. (1999) 'Land Supply and Housing: A Case-Study', *Housing Studies*, **11**, 3, 407–23.

Morris H. (2002a) 'Property Shortage Worsens', *Planning*, 1476, 5 July, 8.

Morris H. (2002b) 'Underpaid and Overworked', *Planning*, 1470, 24 May, 13.

Morrison N. and Pearce B. (2000) 'Developing Indicators for Evaluating the Effectiveness of the UK Land use Planning System', *Town Planning Review*, **71**, 2, 191–211.

Mulholland and Associates (2000), *PPG3: The Consumer Response*, London, HBF.

Mulholland Research Associates Ltd (1995) *Towns of Leafier Environments? A Survey of Family Home Buying Choices*, London, HBF.

Nadin V., Brown C. and Dühr S. (2002) *Sustainability, Development and Spatial Planning in Europe*, London, Routledge.

National Housing Federation (1998) *Standards and Quality in Development: A Good Practice Guide*, London, NHF.

National Housing Federation (2000) *First Steps in Partnering: An Introductory Guide for Registered Social Landlords*, London, NHF.

National Housing Federation (2001a) *Agenda for Change: Reform of Planning*, London, NHF.

National Housing Federation (2001b) *Mind the Gaps: Housing London's Workers*, London, NHF.

National Housing Federation (2002a) *NHF Response on Reforming Planning Obligations*, London, NHF.

National Housing Federation (2002b) *NHF Response on Planning: Green Paper*, London, NHF.

Newchurch and Co. (1999) *A Working Definition of Local Authority Partnerships*, London, DETR.

Newchurch and Co. (2000) *Mapping Partnerships in Eleven Local Authorities*, London, DETR.

New Economics Foundation (1998) *Participation Works! 21 Techniques of Community Participation for the 21st Century*, London, New Economics Foundation.

Office of the Deputy Prime Minister (2002a) *Sustainable Communities – Delivering Through Planning*, London, ODPM.

Office of the Deputy Prime Minister (2002b) *Planning Applications January–March 2002*, London, ODPM.

Office of the Deputy Prime Minister (2002c) *Making the System Work Better: Planning at Regional and Local Levels*, London, ODPM.

Office of the Deputy Prime Minister (2002d) *Making Plans: Good Practice in Plan Preparation and Management of the Development Plan Process*, London, ODPM.

Office of the Deputy Prime Minister (2002e) *Compulsory Purchase Powers, Procedures and Compensation: The Way Forward*, London, ODPM.

Office of the Deputy Prime Minister (2002f) *Your Region, Your Choice: Revitalising the English Regions*, London, ODPM.

Office of the Deputy Prime Minister (2002g) *The Way Forward for Housing Capital Finance (Consultation Paper)*, London, ODPM.

Office of the Deputy Prime Minister (2002h) *Circular 01/02: The Town and Country Planning (Residential Density) (London and South East England) Direction*, London, ODPM.

Osborne T. (1991) 'The Developer's Role in Design and the Environment', *The Planner* TCPSS Proceedings, 13 December, 26–30.

Osmond J. (1994) 'When Dignity Can Grow from Despair: Developments at Penrhys in the Rhondda', *Planet*, 102, 55–9.

Pacione M. (1989) 'The Site Selection Process of Speculative Residential Developers in an Urban Area', *Housing Studies*, **5**, 4, 219–28.

Page D. (1993) *Building for Communities*, York, Joseph Rowntree Foundation.

Parfect M. and Power G. (1997) *Planning for Urban Quality: Urban Design in Towns and Cities*, London, Routledge.

Parker Morris Report (1961) *Homes for Today and Tomorrow*, London, HMSO.

Pattie C. and Johnston R. (2001) 'A Low Turnout Landslide: Abstention at the British General Election of 1997', *Political Studies*, **49**, 2, 286–305.

Pennington M. (2002) *Liberating the Land: The Case for Private Land-use Planning*, London, IEA.

Planning Officers Society (1998) *Public Involvement in the Development Control Process: A Good Practice Guide*, London, Local Government Association.

Planning Officers Society (2000) *A Guide to Best Value and Planning*, contact at http://www.planningofficers.org.uk.

Planning Officers Society (2001) *Moving Towards Excellence in Development Control*, London, Improvement and Development Agency for Local Government.

Planning Officers Society (2002a) *Moving Towards Excellence in Urban Design and Conservation*, contact at http://www.planningofficers.org.uk.

Planning Officers Society (2002b) *Moving Towards Excellence in Planning Policy*, contact at http://www. planningofficers.org.uk.

Planning Officers Society, Housebuilders Federation and DETR (1998) *Housing Layouts – Lifting the Quality*, London, HBF.

Pollitt C. (1994) 'The Citizen's Charter: A Preliminary Analysis', *Public Money and Management*, **14**, 2, 9.

Popular Housing Forum (1998) *Kerb Appeal: The External Appearance and Site Layout of New Houses*, Winchester, Popular Housing Forum.

Power A. (1999) *Estates on the Edge: The Social Consequences of Mass Housing in Northern Europe*, London, Macmillan.

Prescott J. (2002a) *Sustainable Communities, Housing and Planning*, London, Office of the Deputy Prime Minister.

Prescott J. (2002b) *News Release 039: Planning to Drive Communities' Future*, London, Office of the Deputy Prime Minister.

Prince's Foundation (2000) *Sustainable Urban Extensions: Planned Through Design*, London, The Prince's Foundation.

Public Services Productivity Panel (2001) *Public Service Productivity: Meeting the Challenge*, London, HM Treasury.

Punter J. and Carmona M. (1997) *The Design Dimension of Planning: Theory, Content and Best Practice for Design Policies*, London, E & FN Spon.

Purbeck District Council (1999) *District Local Plan, Revised Deposit Draft*, Wareham, Purbeck District Council.

Purdue M. (1994) 'The Impact of Section 54A', *Journal of Planning and Environmental Law*, 399–407.

Quality Assurance Agency for Higher Education (2002) *Town and Country Planning Subject Benchmark Statement*, Gloucester, QAAHE.

Raggett B. (1999) 'New Investment in Positive Planning for the New Millennium', paper given at the National Planning Conference.

Ravetz A. (2001) *Council Housing and Culture: The History of a Social Experiment*, London, Routledge.

Raynsford N. (1998) Press Release 755, 'Pedestrians' Needs Must Come First', London, DETR, 16 September.

Read L. and Wood M. (1994) 'Policy, Law and Practice', in Wood M. (Ed.) *Planning Icons: Myth and Practice* (Planning Law Conference, *Journal of Environmental Planning Law*), London, Sweet and Maxwell.

Reade E. (1987) *British Town and Country Planning*, Milton Keynes, Open University Press.

Reynolds O. M. Jr, (1999) 'The "Unique Circumstances" Rule in Zoning Variances – An Aid in Achieving Greater Prudence and Less Leniency', *Urban Lawyer*, **31**, 1, 127–48.

Roger Tym and Partners (1989) *The Incidence and Effects of Planning Delays*, London, Roger Tym and Partners.

Roger Tym and Partners (1999) *Housing in the South East: The Inter-relationship Between Supply, Demand and Land Use Policy*, London, DETR.

Roger Tym and Partners (2002) *Planning, Competitiveness and Productivity*, London, ODPM: Housing, Planning, Local Government and the Regions Committee.

Rogers R. and Power A. (2000) *Cities for a Small Country*, London, Faber and Faber Ltd.

Room (2000) *Defining Positive Planning, Briefing Paper*, London, Room.

Room (2002) *Positive Planning in Action: Delivering the Urban and Rural White Papers, Briefing Paper*, London, Room.

Rose P. (1998) 'Putting the Finger on Quality Control', *Planning*, 23 October, 1291, 12.

Roskrow B. (1997) 'The Great Subjective Subject', *Housebuilder*, October, 30–2.

Roskrow B. (1998) 'Housing Snobs are Out of Touch', *Housebuilder* October, 3.

Royal Commission on Environmental Pollution (2002) *Environmental Planning, Summary of the Royal Commission on Environmental Pollution Report*, London, RCEP.

Royal Institution of Chartered Surveyors (2000) *Transport Development Areas: A Study into Achieving Higher Density Development around Public Transport Nodes*, London, RICS.

Royal Institution of Chartered Surveyors (2001) 'Unclear Planning Policy Limits Supply of Low Cost Housing', Press Release (pr145), 8 November 2001, London, RICS.

Royal Institution of Chartered Surveyors Policy Unit (2001) *Delivering Affordable Housing Through the Planning System*, London, RICS.

Royal Society for the Protection of Birds (2002) *Living Spaces: A Vision for the Future of Planning*, Sandy, Bedfordshire, RSPB.

Royal Town Planning Institute (1995a) 'Performance Indicators Should Give "Flavour" of Whole Planning Process', *Planning Week*, 5 October, **3**, 40, 21.

Royal Town Planning Institute (1995b) *Planners as Managers: Shifting the Gaze*, London, RTP.

Royal Town Planning Institute (1997) *The Role of Elected Members in Plan Making and Development Control*, London, RTPI.

Royal Town Planning Institute (1999) *The Role of Planning in Local Government*, London, RTPI.

Royal Town Planning Institute (2000) *Fitness for Purpose: Quality in Development Plans*, London, RTPI.

Royal Town Planning Institute (2001a) *Planning to Deliver: A Submission to the Minister for Housing, Planning and Regeneration*, London, RTPI.

Royal Town Planning Institute (2001b) *A New Vision for Planning: Delivering Sustainable Communities, Settlements and Places*, London, RTPI.

Royal Town Planning Institute (2001c) *Towards a Spatial Development Framework*, London, RTPI.

Royal Town Planning Institute (2002) *Planning: Delivering a Fundamental Change, Memorandum of Observations to the DTLR on the Planning Green Paper*, London, RTPI.

Royal Town Planning Institute Think Tank on Modernising Local Government (2001) *We Can Do Better: Opportunities for the Planning Profession*, London, RTPI.

Rudlin D. and Falk N. (1995) *21st Century Homes, Building to Last*, London, URBED.

Rudlin D. and Falk N. (1999) *Building the 21st Century Home: The Sustainable Urban Neighbourhood*, Oxford, Architectural Press.

Russell H. (2001) *Local Strategic Partnerships: Lessons from New Commitment to Regeneration*, York, The Policy Press.

Rydin Y. (1998) *Urban and Environmental Planning in the UK*, London, Macmillan.

Salter M. and Bird, R. (2002) *Building the Public Voice into the Design and Development of Towns and Cities*, London, CABE.

Savage R. (2001) 'Planning for Acceptable Housing Development', unpublished MPhil Thesis, University College London, London.

Schopen F. and Lindsay N. (2002) 'DTLR Misses High-Density Targets', *Regeneration and Renewal*, 31 May, 1.

Select Committee on Environment, Transport and Regional Affairs (1998) *Memorandum by the Town and Country Planning Association (H110) (Minutes of Evidence)*, London, The Stationery Office.

Select Committee on Transport, Local Government and the Regions (2002) *Thirteenth Report: Planning Green Paper*, London, HM Government.

Shenton D. (2001) 'Town Planning Red Tape Cupboard', *Building Design*, 6 July, 11.

Short J., Fleming S. and Witt S. (1986) *Housebuilding, Planning and Community Action*, London, Routledge.

Smith K. (2002) 'Delivering Affordable Housing through the Planning System – Tracking the Efficiency of Current Practice', *Town and Country Planning*, **71**, 4, 108–10.

Social Exclusion Unit (2000) *National Strategy for Neighbourhood Renewal: A Framework for Consultation*, London, Cabinet Office.

Somerville P. and Sprigings N. (Eds) (2003) *Housing and Social Policy*, London, Spon Press.

Spawforth P. (1995) 'Vox Pop', *Planning Week*, **3**, 27, 16–17.

Stephens M. (2001) 'Housing Policy in England: A Review of Literature and Recent Research', in Boyfield K. and Mather G. (Eds), *Britain's Unsolved Housing Dilemma*, London, European Policy Forum, 5–19.

Stevenage Borough Council (2001) *Unitary Development Plan: Second Deposit Draft*, Stevenage, SBC.

Stewart J. (1997) *Housing and the Economy*, London, Council of Mortgage Lenders.

Stewart J. (2002) *Building a Crisis: Housing Under-Supply in England*, London, HBF.

Stewart J. and Kieron W. (1994) 'Performance Measurement: When Performance Can Never be Finally Defined', *Public Money and Management*, **14**, 2, 45.

Strutt and Parker (2001) *Changing Perceptions: A Survey of People's Attitudes to High Density Housing*, London, Strutt and Parker.

Syms P. and Knight P. (2000) *Building Homes on Used Land*, Coventry, RICS Books.

Taussik J. and McHugh T. (1997) *Pre-Application Enquiries: A Review of Good Practice*, Occasional Paper, Department of Land and Construction Management, Portsmouth, University of Portsmouth.

Taylor M. (1997a) *The Best of Both Worlds: The Voluntary Sector and Local Government*, York, York Publishing Services.

Taylor M. (1997b) *Foundation 5: Partnership Between Government and Voluntary Organisations*, York, Joseph Rowntree Foundation.

Tewdwr-Jones M. (1999) 'Discretion, Flexibility and Certainty in British Planning: Emerging Ideological Conflicts and Inherent Political Tensions', *Journal of Planning Education and Research*, 18, 244–56.

Tewdwr-Jones M. (2002) *The Planning Polity: Planning, Government and the Policy Process*, London, Routledge.

Tewdwr-Jones M., Gallent N., Fisk M., and Essex S. (1998) 'Developing Corporate Working Approaches for the Provision of Affordable Housing in Wales', *Regional Studies*, **32**, 1, 85–91.

Thatcher M. (1993) *The Downing Street Years*, London, HarperCollins.

Thomas K. (1997) *Development Control: Principles and Practice*, London, UCL Press.

Thomas T. and Ansbro S. (2000) 'Housing Guidance Set to Redefine the Local Plan Process', *Planning*, 28 July, 12–13.

Town and Country Planning Association (1999) *Your Place or Mine – The Report of the TCPA Inquiry into the Future of Planning*, London, TCPA.

Town and Country Planning Association (2000) *Housing Policy Statement*, London, TCPA.

Urban Design Group (1998) 'Involving Local Communities in Urban Design: Promoting Good Practice', *Urban Design Quarterly*, 67, July, 15–38.

Urban Design Skills Working Group (2001) *Report to the Minister for Housing, Planning and Regeneration*, London, CABE.

Urban and Economic Development Group (1998) *Tomorrow: A Peaceful Path to Urban Reform*, London, Friends of the Earth.

Urban and Economic Development Group, MORI and University of Bristol (1999) *But Would You Live There? Shaping Attitudes to Urban Living*, London, Urban Task Force.

Urban Task Force (1999) *Towards an Urban Renaissance*, London, Spon Press.

Urban Task Force (2000) *Paying for an Urban Renaissance*, London, Urban Task Force.

Ward S. (1994) *Planning and Urban Change*, London, Paul Chapman Publishing.

Ware A. and Goodin R. (1990) *Needs and Welfare*, London, Sage.

Weaver M. (2002) 'Home Start', *The Guardian*, Wednesday 3 April.

Welsh J. (1994) 'Tick for Tat', *RIBA Journal*, **101**, 11, 5.

Welsh Office (1991) *Circular 31/91: Planning and Affordable Housing*, Cardiff, WO.

Whitehead, C. (2002) 'The Provision of Affordable Housing through the Planning System', paper presented at ERES conference, Glasgow, June.

Wilcox S. (2000) *Housing Finance Review 2000–2001*, York, Joseph Rowntree Foundation.

Wilson D. and Game C. (1994) *Local Government in the United Kingdom*, Basingstoke, Macmillan Press.

Winkley R. (2002a) 'Will Density Plans Add to the North-South Divide?', *Planning*, 26 July, 1479, 9.

Winkley R. (2002b) 'Coalition Calls for Third Party Rights', *Planning*, 1451, 11 January, 1.

Wong C. and Gallent N. (1999) *Halton Housing Requirement Study*, Halton Borough Council, Runcorn.

Wright C. (1999) *Commissioning Quality*, London, RIBA Publications.

Wycombe District Council (1999) *Wycombe 21 Resource Pack*, High Wycombe, Wycombe District Council.

Index

Note: figures and tables are indicated by *italic page numbers*